EMERGING CAPITAL MARKETS

EMERGING CAPITAL MARKETS

Financial and Investment Issues

Edited by
J. Jay Choi
John A. Doukas

QUORUM BOOKS
Westport, Connecticut • London

332.673
E53

Library of Congress Cataloging-in-Publication Data

Emerging capital markets : financial and investment issues / edited by
   J. Jay Choi, John A. Doukas.
      p.   cm.
   Includes bibliographical references and index.
   ISBN 1–56720–177–6 (alk. paper)
      1. Capital market.   2. Corporations—Finance.   3. Stock exchanges.
   I. Choi, Jongmoo Jay, 1945–   II. Doukas, John.
   HG4523.E455   1998
   332.67′3—dc21   98–6842

British Library Cataloguing in Publication Data is available.

Library of Congress Catalog Card Number: 98–6842
ISBN: 1–56720–177–6

First published in 1998

Quorum Books, 88 Post Road West, Westport, CT 06881
An imprint of Greenwood Publishing Group, Inc.

Printed in the United States of America

The paper used in this book complies with the
Permanent Paper Standard issued by the National
Information Standards Organization (Z39.48–1984).

10 9 8 7 6 5 4 3 2 1

JK

Contents

PART I

An Overview of Emerging Market Finance

Financial and Investment Issues in Emerging Capital Markets

J. Jay Choi
and John A. Doukas

Emerging markets have gained the growing attention of academics and practitioners over the recent past, despite the turbulent times they have experienced. Practitioners' main interests in emerging markets stem from corporations, investors, and financial institutions that foresee substantial benefits by investing and/or operating in these markets in the long run. The recent Asian financial crisis, however, underscored the risks inherent in investing in emerging market countries, and led policymakers, as well as and private institutions, to reassess their strategy.

A primary characteristic of emerging markets is domestic rigidity and international segmentation. While these countries are still subject to institutional regulations, main factors that keep them partially segmented from the international capital markets are political and exchange-rate uncertainty. These market imperfections, however, preserve potentially superior risk-return trade-offs that will continue to attract international capital in the emerging markets, as the growth opportunities of these countries will play a key role in foreign investors' decisions to invest.

At the same time, the institutional and market characteristics of the emerging markets provide an interesting area of research from an academic standpoint as well. The emerging market setting is provided to test the robustness of certain empirical regularities documented in the finance literature. Moreover, the unique experience in emerging markets, as in the case of the Asian financial crisis, provides an opportunity for new insight. The outcome of this research will either lead us to accept the traditional finance paradigms or to develop new ones that need to internalize the idiosyncracies of the emerging market economies.

Despite the growing importance of emerging market economies, the academic literature on the emerging market finance area is still in infancy and fragmented. While several articles have been published in academic journals and other publication outlets dealing with financial issues as they relate to specific countries, no unified attempt has been made to address some of the main issues that confront the emerging market economies in their march to the next century.

The traditional paradigm in finance literature is that of perfect, efficient, and integrated capital markets. However, this body of the literature has been questioned lately by several empirical studies that uncovered numerous "anomalies" that did not fit the traditional paradigm. Others have shown that these anomalies are related to data and methodological limitations associated with these studies. The international finance literature, despite the general belief that markets have converged more over the recent years, still envisions a world of partially segmented international capital markets mainly due to divergent government policies, regulations, political risk, and exchange-rate uncertainty. The emerging market finance, although not yet a well-defined area of research, is often viewed as a subfield of the international finance literature. It should be pointed out, however, that the emerging market finance field addresses financial and investment issues based on elements of market imperfections both across and within countries. Therefore, emerging market finance is a holistic research area. However, a prerequisite for its acceptance as a distinct finance field, say, in the order of development economics field, is the development of a general paradigm for emerging capital markets.

This edited volume brings together a set of original research studies on emerging market finance issues that enhance the existing body of knowledge in this area. The chapters were selected on the basis of three criteria:

1. Presents a conceptual basis for broadening the traditional finance and international finance literature to emerging market countries where markets may be imperfect, inefficient, or segmented;

2. Analyzes the potential risk and returns of investing and/or operating in emerging markets;

3. Examines the functions and characteristics of financial markets and practices of emerging market countries in a coherent framework.

A salient feature of this book is its breadth of coverage. While individual chapters may be deep and narrow in scope, the book as a whole includes diverse subjects and areas. The book cuts across all subfields of finance—corporate finance, investments, financial markets and institutions, and international finance, as well as development finance. While many chapters are technically written for academic audiences, others are more general and suitable for policy and practitioner communities.

The research subject of this volume is quite diverse in the sense that it covers emerging markets at various levels. Of the 23 chapters, 6 deal with emerging market countries as a whole, while another 6 papers cover specific areas as a region—three for Asia, two for Latin America, and one for transitional economies. In addition, 11 chapters examine separate individual emerging market or transitional economies including China and Russia. All in all, virtually all the major emerging market countries are covered in one way or another.

The volume is also extremely diverse in author representation: 43 authors have contributed to the volume and are affiliated with governments, central banks, stock exchanges, research institutes, private banks and firms, international institutions, as well as universities. By country of affiliation, 14 are from the United States, 3 are affiliated with international institutions, and 26 are from outside the United States. Countries of author affiliation include Australia, Hong Kong, the Philippines, Malaysia, Singapore, Indonesia, Taiwan, Korea, Israel, Canada, Mexico, Turkey, Greece, the United Kingdom, and the United States. This book is truly an international venture.

In sum, this edited volume offers a collection of studies on various aspects of emerging market finance, for various areas of the world, and by a broad author representation. By including chapters that have a general theme for emerging capital markets or geographical areas, as well as those that focus on a single country, it attempts to establish a benchmark of reference for researchers, practitioners, and policymakers interested in emerging market finance, and thereby help develop emerging market finance as a distinct subarea of finance.

Choices of Financial Development for Transition Economies

Qaizar Hussain

INTRODUCTION

As transition economies are establishing and reforming their financial systems, it is critical that they learn from the experiences, and avoid the pitfalls, of the systems of developed nations. Transition economies are dramatically different from developed economies in terms of the "stages of financial development" (see Figures 2.1 and 2.2). The typical stages for developed economies are characterized by relatively strong emphasis on retained earnings, debt finance, and equity finance. However, in transition economies all forms of financing are equally undeveloped and have to be developed in accordance.

Numerous issues need to be considered when selecting the choice of financial reforms. Some of the issues relate to the nature of the initial conditions prevailing in the country in question and include the nature of corporate ownership structure, speed of privatization, shareholder concentration, property rights, bankruptcy laws, disclosure requirements, bank deposit insurance, state credit guarantees, wealth allocation, expected profits of firms, degree of openness of the country, degree of reputation established by firms through monitoring, and the nature of regulations. However, in the case of newly formed financial sectors of transforming economies, some factors such as shareholder concentration, property rights, and the degree of reputation established by firms are expected to attain greater significance once the economies have been completely liberalized and the legal systems are firmly in place.

In this chapter I shall highlight some of these issues in order to motivate the discussion on the sequence of financial development in transition economies with a particular relevance to Poland and the Baltic states, especially Estonia (see Tables 2.1, 2.2, and 2.3). The focus will be on the *earliest* stages of the financial system. The topic is important because a carefully designed efficient

Figure 2.1. Stages of Financial Development

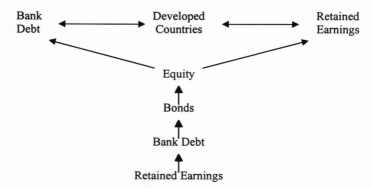

Note: These are typically observed stages of financial development in most economies. There is some evidence that developed financial sectors are now increasingly dominated by bank debt and retained earnings (see Singh and Hamid, 1992; Hussain, 1995).

Figure 2.2. Financial Development in a Transition Economy

Bank Debt ⟷ Retained Earnings ⟷ Bonds ⟷ Equity

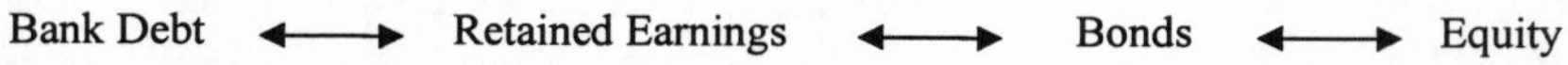

Note: This is a pattern of financial development in a transition economy where all the forms of financing are equally (un)available at the time of transition.

financial sector helps reduce asymmetric information problems and other market imperfections. The discussion pertaining to the nature of financial systems has been divided into three subsections: Stock Market-Oriented System; Bank-Dominated System; and Corporate Structure, Governance, and Rules. The next section specifically deals with the set of opportunities that are available for transition economies in choosing their financial systems and is divided into three subsections: Narrow Bank System, Domestic Versus Foreign Sector, and Gradualist Versus Simultaneous Approach.

NATURE OF FINANCIAL SYSTEMS

Potential Benefits of the Stock Market-Oriented System

In their proposals for financial reforms, most authors mistakenly associate stock market development with capitalism. Stock trading can be initially handled by a small exchange or banks. The large exchanges dealing in sophisticated instruments would endogenously evolve over time.[1] As a matter of fact, most capitalist countries such as Japan, Germany, and Sweden have small stock markets and concentrated ownership. Dispersed ownership of stock makes it difficult for firms to be monitored effectively, especially in the early stages of

Table 2.1. Key Indicators—Poland

Year	88	89	90	91	92	93	94	95
Lending Rate (average)	16.7	64.0	504.2	54.6	39.0	35.3	32.8	33.5
Refinancing Rate (end per.)	6.0	140.0	55.0	40.0	38.0	35.0	33.0	29.0
Consumer Prices (1990=100)	4.4	15.3	100.0	176.7	256.8	351.5	468.4	593.9
Industrial Prod. (index)	138.1	134.1	100.0	84.0	87.3	—	—	—
GDP (m zlotys)	2,963	11,832	56,027	80,883	114,944	155,780	210,377	292,600*
GDP at const. prices (%)		0.2	-11.6	-7.0	2.6	3.8	6.0	7.0*
Foreign Direct Inv. (m $)	15	11	89	291	678	1,715	1,875	136**
Portfolio Equity Flows (m $)	0	0	0	0	0	0		

*Estimated.   **2nd Quarter.
Sources: International Monetary Fund, *International Financial Statistics* (August 1996) and *World Economic Outlook* (1994).

Table 2.2. Equity Market—Poland

Year	91	92	93	94	95
Number of Listed Comp.	9	16	21	36	53
Avg. Market Cap (US$ Mil)	75	225	1,084	3,933	3,731
Avg. Market Cap./GDP (%)	0.098	0.266	1.259	4.244	3.086
Avg. P/E Ratio	4.1	3.4	13.3	16.4	7.8
Div. Yield at Year End (%)	0.0	5.5	0.4	0.4	2.3
Turnover Ratio (%)	18.5	49.1	194.6	128.7	67.5
Avg. Exch. Rate (PLN/US$)	1.06	1.36	1.81	2.27	2.42

Source: Warsaw Stock Exchange, Annual Statistics (1995).

Table 2.3. Key Indicators—Estonia

Year	92	93	94	95	96 (March)
Exchange Rate (kroons/$)	12.600	13.223	12.991	11.465	11.822
Lending Rate (average)	30.5	27.3	23.1	16.0	16.0
Consumer Prices (1992=100)	100.0	189.8	280.3	361.3	435.3
GDP, 1992 Prices (m kroons)	16,279	14,255	13,145	—	—
Foreign Direct Inv. (m kroons)	1,036.9	2,144.8	2,789.4	2,321.9	—
Portfolio Equity Flows (m kroons)	0	-3.0	-183.4	-189.2	

Sources: International Monetary Fund, *International Financial Statistics* (August 1996); *World Economic Outlook* (1994); and *Statistical Datasheets*, Bank of Estonia.
Note: The Tallinn Stock Exchange was established in 1996; therefore the figures for the stock market are not available.

financial development. The costs associated with the establishment of the stock market would outweigh the benefits. Meyer (1988) makes an interesting empirical observation for the case of developed financial systems that firms in countries with the most developed and most competitive stock exchanges (the United States and the United Kingdom) rely least on stock issues for their investment funding in relation to those countries (Germany and Japan) which have less competitive exchanges. This observation, therefore, has dramatically different policy implications from the industrial organization point of view. The policy implication of this observation for a transition economy is that at the earlier stage, less emphasis needs to be placed on the development and competitiveness of the stock market. The sale of vouchers for privatization can be handled by banks at the earlier stage until the regulatory structure of the stock exchange is firmly in place.

On the other hand, some new studies conducted at the World Bank in 1996[2] find a positive link between stock market development and economic growth for a sample of 49 emerging markets covering the period 1976 to 1993. The authors create several measures as proxies for market development that include size, volatility, and liquidity. They do not obtain a clear relationship between size or volatility and economic growth. However, interestingly, the most important result is the strong positive link between market liquidity and growth. This finding points to the negative role of large shareholders in the market that results in the nondilution of shares. One policy implication is to grant incentives to small shareholders in owning equity. It will thereby add to a well-functioning secondary market through an increase in liquidity. One criticism of these studies is that the correlations found between variables may not necessarily imply causation. It is likely that countries enjoying rapid economic growth, such as Malaysia, may have developed highly liquid stock markets. The studies, however, have attempted to take account of this simultaneous-equations bias.

Though these studies have some validity for emerging markets, transition economies ought to be treated differently for three related reasons. First, massive privatization in these economies at the initial stages makes effective control and monitoring of firms critical, which can best be handled by established institutions such as banks or investment companies. Second, large stock exchanges can be very expensive to set up and operate. Third, lack of liquidity and high volatility at the early stage can lead to a large outflow of funds and an erosion of confidence in the financial system that may be irreversible for a long time.

Potential Benefits of the Bank-Dominated System

Since banks act as monitors, they are vital at the earlier stages of financial development until firms have attained a favorable reputation (Diamond, 1991). Furthermore, authors such as Nuti (1992) recommend a German or Japanese type of financial system where financial markets are dominated by banks. In this system banks act as insiders by controlling and monitoring firms. Bank managers sit on boards of corporations and sometimes even act as chairperson of the board. The argument is further supported by the fact that there have been only three hostile takeovers in Germany since the Second World War and none in Japan. In the case of Poland, privatized banks would act as joint stock companies which would be responsible for selling shares in the form of vouchers that will be auctioned.

The author proposes a competition in product markets but not in ownership, since competition in ownership may lead to hostile takeovers and a free rider problem that may not be first-best from the financial stability standpoint. Nuti admits that the bank-dominated system is open to controversy. According to him, the main criticisms are short-termism[3] and monopolistic practices of banks. Another argument against the establishment of the bank-dominated system at an early stage is that the development of the stock exchange may lag behind for an extended period, partly because banks enjoy formidable political power and are reluctant to dilute their strong influence over the financial sector. This bank bias can be observed in a majority of financial systems around the world. It is correct to conclude that this bank bias is due to a combination of economic and political reasons.

As indicated in the previous subsection, the importance of a highly developed and a *liquid* stock market existing concurrently with banks has gained credibility even for emerging markets in a series of recent studies at the World Bank.[4] The studies conclude that a liquid stock market encourages banks to lend more since greater information becomes available on companies. Thus, in highly liquid markets we are likely to find ratios of bank loans to gross domestic product (GDP) high. Moreover, Diamond (1996), in his World Bank paper, provides an additional case for liquid financial markets. He suggests that banks offer more short-term instruments when financial markets are liquid than otherwise. In liquid financial markets, banks can more easily substitute and exchange certain types of liquid assets (short-term loans) with other types of liquid assets (Treasury bills). Furthermore, the gap between short-term finance and long-term finance diminishes with liquidity, since short-term instruments of varying maturities can be traded for long-term instruments.

As Nuti argues, the German system also works well partly because of the presence of a relatively well-developed and liquid stock exchange. Using various measures to estimate liquidity, such as the turnover ratio,[5] Levine (1996) classifies Germany to be a "liquid" market where categories range from "very liquid" to "very illiquid." More interestingly, the International Finance Corporation (1993) estimates the German market's turnover ratio for 1992 to be almost 241%—the highest in the world. Therefore, even though Germany is regarded as a bank-dominated system, it also enjoys a highly developed and liquid stock market. One drawback of the German system is that it fails to provide a proper and clear link between production and finance through an efficient allocation of resources, since often the same institutions have control over both production and finance. Therefore, even though it is a second-best option for the transition economies, it is recommended by the author.

Phelps et al. (1993) suggest an eventual phaseout of state banks and the establishment of *new* private banks. This is for two main reasons. First, old banks are wrought with bad loans (assets) that could be easily transferred to new banks along with a substantial portion of the deposits (liabilities). Second, a preferred corporate governance structure would constitute an outside enterprise control by new banks for effective monitoring of management rather than an insider or employee control. Moreover, most insiders are too small to conduct monitoring (employees or cooperatives) in relation to potential outsiders. With outside control, managers will have an incentive to behave in a proper manner. This will further increase the availability of outside finance and help lower the cost of capital to firms. The proposal of the authors appears persuasive, to some extent, since debt of old banks has been eroded because of inflation.[6] This proposal seems to be already instituted in Poland where permission has been granted to open almost 80 new banks.[7] Poland, for example, has numerous small firms with employee and cooperative ownership. To summarize, in the opinion of this author, their argument does not appear to be economically feasible, since it would be outrageously costly to establish and supervise so many new banks to resolve the problem of control. Moreover, the benefits of a liquid stock market in a transition economy can be realized once the monitors (such as banks) are firmly established.

Table 2.4. Types of Ownership of 100 Largest Companies

Ownership	U.S.A.	Europe	Japan
Dispersed ownership	90	36	40
Dominant ownership	7	33	57
Family owned	3	13	2
Government owned	0	18	1
Total	100	100	100

Sources: *Japan Company Handbook*, 1995; Stoford, 1992; *Who Owns Whom*, 1994.

Table 2.5. Ownership of 100 Largest Companies in 12 European Nations

	Dispersed	Dominant	Family	Foreign	Coop	State
Austria	0	7	25	38	10	20
Belgium	4	20	6	61	3	6
Denmark	10	9	30	23	17	11
Finland	12	25	23	11	10	19
France	16	28	15	16	3	22
Germany	9	30	26	22	3	10
Great Britain	61	11	6	18	1	3
Italy	0	22	20	29	0	29
Netherlands	23	16	7	34	13	7
Norway	6	14	29	19	19	13
Spain	6	22	8	45	5	14
Sweden	4	31	18	14	12	21

Source: European Ownership Database in Thomsen and Pedersen (1995).

Corporate Structure, Governance, and Rules

The structure of firm ownership has an important effect on corporate governance and performance. In turn, the nature of corporate governance has an influence on economic growth (Wihlborg, 1995). In their recent paper, Thomsen and Pedersen (1995) examine a set of 100 largest companies in 12 European countries. They find significant international differences in the nature of ownership structure between countries. Moreover, though the United States and the United Kingdom enjoy widely dispersed ownership, most countries in Europe have dominant, family-owned, or state ownership (see Tables 2.4 and 2.5). Perhaps the proximity of Poland and Estonia to Europe would justify a dominant ownership structure (German model) at the early transition stage, since banks perform multiple functions, including monitoring, in relation to cooperatives. The cooperatives do not alleviate the agency costs problems as effectively as dominant shareholders. They have many objectives in addition to profit maximization.

In this regard, the state can play a vital role in improving the monitoring role of banks and, at the same time, supervising the allocation of shares of privatized enterprises. In both countries the family ownership is almost nonexistent, and these countries are eager to do away with state ownership. Thomsen and Pedersen (1995) expect that economic, institutional, and cultural factors may be contributing to the differences in ownership structure and corporate governance, and ultimately on corporate performance. We can relate the conclusions and lessons learned from Europe to the case of Poland and the Baltic states. The type of corporate ownership structure that emerges will have an important bearing on the performance and level of international competitiveness of these economies through changes in the cost of capital. More important, institutional and cultural factors of each country should be taken into account while designing the structure of firm ownership as state enterprises are privatized.

Corbett and Meyer (1991) propose that industrial policy such as privatization is moving at a far more rapid pace than financial sector reform. In their view it is critical that the financial sector should be liberalized *hand in hand* with the industrial sector. One possible strategy is the formation and promotion of control groups along the lines of the German or Japanese financial systems, where banks often provide an effective monitoring function of firms. These monitors are useful at the early stage of financial development when company risk categories have not been clearly established. Moreover, the large shareholders in the equity market provide a monitoring role in addition to banks in most financial systems.

In transition economies, due to the obvious absence of significant control groups such as large families, banks would naturally provide the most effective monitoring of firms. The authors, however, caution on the likelihood of monopolies and collusive behavior of banks. But they point out that clear-cut policies and rules could be implemented that would discourage the anticompetitive behavior of these groups. In sum, the more popular German-type model will prove to be of greater usefulness to transition economies such as Poland in their early attempts toward financial reform. Moreover, given the rudimentary nature of monitoring technology in these financial systems, the *duplication* and repetition of monitoring by both banks and large shareholders will prove to be fruitful in the identification of risk characteristics of firms in the long run. Some duplication of monitoring may be optimal in cases where firms do not enjoy high reputation. Moreover, since banks are permitted to hold equity in Poland (up to 50% of total capital and reserves),[8] it is likely that the same set of the largest firms which are listed also borrow from banks. Therefore, benefits from increasing returns to scale in monitoring through *information sharing*[9] can be realized.

A combination of duplication and increasing returns to scale in monitoring
would result in a superior solution in effective monitoring than if banks were not
permitted to hold shares of stock (for example, the United States and Indonesia).
Bank holdings of stock (*only by financial service companies*)[10] would, therefore,
contribute to a more rapid growth of the stock market because more information
would be available regarding reputation of firms leading to an increased participation by small shareholders in the market. However, one obvious disadvantage
is the likelihood of moral hazard[11] by banks and bank runs and failures due to
the accumulation of excessive debt resulting in high debt-equity ratios.

Meanwhile, Corbett and Meyer (1991) argue that Japanese and German
systems are quite competitive as compared to the U.S. or the U.K. systems of
dispersed ownership. The groups comprising mainly of banks often hold corporate equity, maintain seats on boards of firms, and also have cross-holdings of
shares between companies. Unlike the U.S. and U.K. systems, another benefit of
these systems is that they also prevent hostile takeovers. As the authors admit,
there is a trade-off between efficiency and stability. Although these takeovers
may be highly efficient in principle, they may also tend to short-termism and
instability in the financial sector. What is particularly important at the earlier
stages is credibility, which can only be achieved through a stable and forward-
looking financial system.

OPPORTUNITIES FOR TRANSITION ECONOMIES

Most transition economies are unique in the sense that they are not
following the typical stages of financial development (see Figure 2.1). In fact,
they are also establishing new banks from the very start (see Figure 2.2). These
economies are also facing tight budgets and spending limits. In this process, it is
critical that they do not follow the similar route as the Western financial system;
more specifically, the U.S. banking and savings and loans systems. In these
systems, there exist tremendous opportunities for moral hazard on the part of
lending institutions mainly due to the prevalence of deposit insurance.

Given the rudimentary state of the financial sector in transition economies
characterized by the lack of effective supervision and regulations, the problems
caused by moral hazard and adverse selection[12] are expected to be even more
severe. For example, in Lithuania, the state has openly *declared* that it would
rescue all banks facing bankruptcy. In fact, it has supplemented its declaration
with deeds. During 1995, it helped two medium-sized banks with a rescue
package amounting to U.S.$15 million. It is obvious that banks would engage in
risky activities if the state pledges to bail them out. This system is a state credit
guarantee,[13] which is even more dangerous than a simple deposit insurance.

On the other hand, the recent experience of Estonia suggests that the
country has quite successfully combined regulation with competition, where the
number of banks fell from 42 in 1992 to 16 in 1995. This can be attributed to
regulatory changes (increase in minimum capital requirements), small bank

failures, and bank mergers, resulting in the share of overdue loans that declined to an insignificant 2-3% of assets.

All these issues provide justification for an implementation of the Narrow Bank Proposal in transition economies. Therefore, the pitfalls found in the U.S. banking model, and other state credit guarantee systems, can be avoided by the prudent implementation of financial reforms in the transforming economies. Other issues which need to be addressed for these economies include the promotion of domestic or foreign participation, and the need for gradual or rapid financial liberalization.

Narrow Bank System

The Narrow Bank Proposal for the United States outlined by Pierce (1991), partly aimed at reducing the likelihood of moral hazard in the banking sector, deserves careful review. In his proposal for the U.S. banking sector, Pierce emphasizes that the intermediaries should be viewed in terms of financial functions and not financial institutions, given the recent advances in technology. In fact, bank regulations, which have remained almost unchanged since the New Deal, have failed to adapt to changes in the technological environment, world market integration, and a relaxed regulatory framework faced by investment and brokerage houses. He proposes the establishment of two types of financial institutions: monetary service companies (MSCs) and financial service companies (FSCs). The MSCs would strictly deal in short-term safe assets and liabilities, while the FSCs would be permitted to issue relatively risky liabilities backed by risky assets in their portfolios. Only the liabilities of the MSCs would be eligible for federal deposit insurance. Moreover, the formation of bank holding companies to bypass these rules would be prohibited. There would be no overlap of the functions of the MSCs and the FSCs.

We can apply the insights from this proposal to the countries of Central and Eastern Europe. The MSCs can be formed that will be state-owned or dominated at the early stage, thereby enjoying deposit insurance. These institutions would earn their profits through fees and commissions on deposits. The FSCs, however, can be privately owned and will not benefit from any state insurance.[14] It is therefore important for these countries that only the FSC-type institutions, which do not enjoy federal deposit insurance, play the role of investment banks or mutual fund companies when the shares of state enterprises are available for sale to the public. This will also make it possible for these domestic institutions to compete effectively with foreign investment banks. On the other hand, according to Pierce, the authorities should only regulate and protect the *monetary* activities of banks (MSCs), which has traditionally been true. Obviously, private insurers would emerge in this economy who would insure FSCs' liabilities, but the premiums would be risk-based as determined by default risk since in general bank run is a one-time event.[15]

This proposal critically depends on the availability of a well-functioning "payments system,"[16] which provides an efficient means of transmitting information and settling accounts between parties. A good system also reduces risk and uncertainty experienced in the settlement of transfers. One precondition for the MSCs to operate smoothly is the prevalence of a well-regulated and closely monitored system of money transfers in the form of either cash or bank deposits. Otherwise, there is a potential for MSCs to become more risky, which may impose an additional burden on deposit insurance.

Recently, system reforms have been introduced in several transition economies, including Poland. These reforms have been preceded by the formation of the two-tier banking arrangements which followed the mono-banking institutions that existed during the communist era. In sum, these economies have become more suited to the adoption of the Narrow Bank Proposal than numerous industrialized economies, partly because they are reforming their systems, such as their payments systems, at a later stage and can take advantage of the lessons learned from other countries.

Clearly the Narrow Bank Proposal is subject to a number of important questions and criticisms. First, what if MSCs are owned by foreign companies that can easily bypass the domestic laws? Second, what prevents the MSCs from becoming too big and the insurance fund cannot keep up? Third, can too many MSCs fail? and what if an MSC is not sufficiently profitable for firms and the proportion of FSCs increases to such a degree that the overall default risk rises? Then will the government have enough reserves to prevent runs by the public? Fourth, especially in case of transition economies, since there is a dearth of very safe assets and liabilities of banks, how will the balance sheets of MSCs differ from those of FSCs?

Despite its limitations, this proposal is being seriously reviewed for the reformation of the U.S. banking sector and deserves careful attention, especially for those economies with newly emerging financial sectors. The key advantages of the Narrow Bank Proposal are the potential alleviation of asymmetric information problems in the financial system and the separation of the institutions by their respective functions, such as monetary and financial functions.

Domestic Versus Foreign Sector

Some authors (Corbett and Meyer, 1991; Hussain, 1995) contend that less emphasis ought to be placed on foreign ownership of capital as a necessary condition for financial development. According to these authors, foreign ownership signifies a loss of control rather than a solution to a control problem. They maintain that very few countries have enjoyed economic development as a result of foreign participation, especially in foreign direct investment. Large inflows and outflows of capital also make exchange rate management rather difficult.

Hussain (1995) also finds for the case of Indonesia that domestic shareholder participation is more important than foreign shareholder participation, for the long-term development of the stock market. In Indonesia, foreign portfolio investment was highly volatile during the 1990s. In many emerging markets, the objectives of foreign shareholders have been somewhat temporary, resulting in a reduced domestic demand for financial instruments once the conditions in their home countries improved for investment. These conditions included the rise in interest rates and economic recovery in their home countries. These arguments can easily be extended to other entities in the financial system such as domestically incorporated banks with domestic depositors. To recapitulate, the authorities in transition economies should provide incentives (such as tax breaks and subsidies) that are specially targeted toward the domestic sector.

Gradualist Versus Simultaneous Approach

McKinnon (1994) conducts an insightful examination of the order of economic liberalization. He argues for a gradualist approach to economic liberalization, as in China, in contrast to a cold-turkey approach as applied in Chile, Russia, and Eastern Europe. In his stages of economic liberalization, domestic liberalization should precede international liberalization. His preferred order is: (1) fiscal controls, (2) price-level stability combined with exchange rate unification, (3) trade liberalization, and finally (4) capital account liberalization.

Clearly, this approach is subject to a number of criticisms. First, this preferred order may take a long time and the transition economies such as Estonia and other Baltic republics cannot afford to wait for an extended period since they are eager to join the European Union in the near future. Second, Indonesia appears to be a successful example of a country where international liberalization preceded domestic liberalization. This serves as a counterexample to McKinnon's order of liberalization. Third, there is no explicit discussion of the evolution of the financial markets and intermediaries as part of economic liberalization. Estonia and other transition economies differ from China (and possibly Poland) because China could *afford*[17] to reform its economy gradually, which may not be the case with Estonia, since Estonia is entering the world market at a later stage in political and economic transformation. It may lose considerably if it is too slow to integrate into the world economy.

The size of the economy also plays an important role in determining the effectiveness of policy. China enjoyed an immense internal market for goods and services and therefore was able to absorb large exogenous shocks, but

Figure 2.3. Financial System for Transition Economies

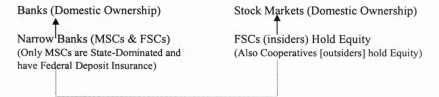

Banks (Domestic Ownership)   Stock Markets (Domestic Ownership)

Narrow Banks (MSCs & FSCs)   FSCs (insiders) Hold Equity
(Only MSCs are State-Dominated and   (Also Cooperatives [outsiders] hold Equity)
have Federal Deposit Insurance)

Note: This structure of the financial system is believed to be first best for transition economies.

Estonia is a small economy that largely relies on external trade for growth. Therefore, a rapid transformation and integration of the Estonian economy, particularly in the European Union (EU), may be warranted. It should be noted that Estonia is designing policies that will hasten its chances for membership in the EU. One such example is the formation of the currency board that will maintain monetary discipline. Given the reasons outlined above, the gradualist approach proposed by McKinnon may not be the best option for small Baltic republics in relation to a simultaneous approach to economic and financial liberalization.

CONCLUSION

As transforming economies such as Poland and the Baltic states develop their financial sectors, they should take into account the lessons learned in the West. The Baltic states, however, are even more fortunate than Poland. They can combine the lessons learned from the West with those of other transition economies.

This conceptual study has outlined some important issues for transition economies in the midst of reforms. The discussion in the preceding sections can also be summarized in Figure 2.3. After discussing the various types of financial systems, we contend that the Narrow Bank-dominated domestically owned financial sector,[18] illustrated in Figure 2.3, appears to be the most appropriate system for these economies. This financial framework would result in the duplication and information-sharing of monitoring by the FSCs, which would lead to an improvement of reputation of firms, and hence access to low-cost external finance. It would also be most suitable from the corporate governance (control) standpoint. Clearly, some of the disadvantages of this system include risks of moral hazard by FSCs, leading to their failures due to an accumulation of excessive debt. However, these disadvantages can be alleviated through good rating agencies, effective supervision of banks, and enabling regulation of the financial sector.

In this paradigm only the MSCs would enjoy government deposit insurance in order to minimize the problems of moral hazard. The MSCs should be state-dominated at the early stage of financial development, being permitted to earn fees and commissions but to be privatized gradually. With the establishment of effective payments systems, the MSCs are expected to function smoothly. As long as clear rules pertaining to bank functions and supervision are not in place, the state-dominated safety net for MSCs is crucial. Otherwise, the banking system will experience capital flight or a transfer of funds into the foreign-denominated accounts. Moreover, universal banking would be permitted where domestic commercial banks (FSCs) could effectively compete with domestic and foreign investment companies.

Finally, although a gradualist approach may have worked reasonably well for countries such as Poland and China, a simultaneous approach to financial liberalization is recommended for the Baltic republics.

NOTES

The author is highly indebted to Clas Wihlborg and Victor Murinde for helpful comments.

1. See Sweeney (1996) for historical evidence on the endogenous evolution of U.S. and Swedish stock markets.

2. Cited in *The Economist*, July 27, 1996, p. 68. Also see Levine and Zervos (1996).

3. But short-termism should qualify as a disadvantage of a stock market-dominated and not a bank-dominated system.

4. See Levine and Zervos (1996).

5. Turnover ratio can be defined as the value of shares traded as a proportion of market capitalization.

6. This phenomenon applies especially for Estonia, where small insolvent banks merged with larger banks. Thus the problem of bad debt has been largely resolved.

7. It is even more true in the former Soviet republics.

8. In addition, a single individual or firm may own up to a maximum of 50% of a bank.

9. Here the input would be the degree of monitoring and output would be the reduction in moral hazard.

10. If the Narrow Bank Proposal is adopted and financial service companies do not enjoy government deposit insurance (see next section).

11. Moral hazard occurs after the transaction when borrowers may engage in risky or undesirable activities (Mishkin, 1995).

12. Adverse selection in the intermediation sector occurs before the transaction when risky borrowers are more likely to be selected for loans (Mishkin, 1995).

13. Though Mullineux (1996) argues for the provision of state-backed loan guarantees to small and medium-sized enterprises for some time period, this author disagrees and proposes a distinct separation of safe and risky assets in the form of the Narrow Bank Proposal, right from the very beginning.

14. Deposit insurance can be treated as a put option that is exercised only when the value of assets falls due to risky activities, thereby causing the bank's capital base to also decline in value significantly.

15. Deposit insurance differs from other types of insurance, such as automobile insurance, where an individual can have several accidents and premiums rise with claims. In deposit insurance, claims are not realized unless there is a bank run.

16. It could afford since the economy is larger and the transformation process could easily be reversed under the communist state. Therefore, it could afford in terms of time and money.

17. See Balino, Johnson, and Sundararajan (1996).

18. See Pierce (1991).

REFERENCES

Balino, T.J.T., O.E.G. Johnson, and V. Sundararajan, 1996. Payment system reforms and monetary policy, *Finance and Development* 33(1), 2-5.

Bennett, A.G.G, 1993. The operation of the Estonian currency board, International Monetary Fund Staff Papers, 40 (2), June.

Bank of Estonia, 1996. *Statistical Datasheets*.

Corbett, J. and C.P. Meyer, 1991. Financial reform in Eastern Europe: progress with the wrong model, CEPR Discussion Paper, No. 603.

Diamond, D.W., 1991. Monitoring and reputation: the choice between bank loans and directly placed debt, *Journal of Political Economy* 99 (4).

Diamond, D.W., 1996, Liquidity, banks, and markets: effects of financial development on banks and the maturity of financial claims, World Bank Policy Working Paper, No. 1566.

The Economist, July 27, 1996, p. 68.

Eesti Pank (Bank of Estonia), 1995 Bulletin. No. 6 and 7.

ESA Statistical Yearbook 1995. Statistical Office of Estonia.

FT Extel Database 1996. London.

Hussain, Q., 1992. Country reports: Poland, International Monetary Fund.

Hussain, Q., 1995. Banking and equity markets in middle-income countries, Ph.D. Dissertation, University of California, Berkeley.

International Finance Corporation, 1993. *Emerging Stock Markets Factbook*.

International Monetary Fund, 1995, 1996. *International Financial Statistics*, November, August.

International Monetary Fund, 1994. *World Economic Outlook*.

Japan Company Handbook, 2nd ed., 1995. Tokyo: Tokyo Keizai, Spring.

Levine, R., 1996. Stock Markets: A spur to economic growth, *Finance and Development*, March.

Levine, R. and S. Zervos, 1996. Capital control liberalization and stock market development, World Bank Policy Working Paper, No. 1622.

Levine, R. and S. Zervos, 1996. Stock markets, banks and economic growth, World Bank Policy Working Paper, forthcoming.

Mart, S. and M. Miljan, 1996. Banking risks in transition countries, Presented at the Conference on Economic Performance and Financial Sector Reform in Central and Eastern Europe, Tallinn, Estonia.

McKinnon, R.I., 1994. *The Order of Economic Liberalization: Financial Control in the Transition to a Market Economy*, 2nd ed. Baltimore: The Johns Hopkins University Press.

Meyer, C., 1988. New issues in corporate finance, *European Economic Review*, 32 1167-1189.

Mishkin, F.S., 1995. *The Economics of Money, Banking, and Financial Markets*. New York: HarperCollins College Publishers.

Mullineux, A., 1996. Banking sector restructuring, debt consolidation and small and medium-sized enterprise financing in transition economies, University of Birmingham Working Paper.

Nuti, D.M., 1992. Remonetization and capital markets in the reform of centrally-planned economies. In *Banking and Finance in Eastern Europe*, Andreas R. Prindl, ed. Cambridge: Woodhead-Faulkner (Publishers) Ltd.

Phelps, E.S., R. Frydman, A. Rapaczynski, and A. Shleifer, 1993. Needed mechanisms of corporate governance and finance in Eastern Europe, European Bank for Reconstruction and Development, Working Paper No. 1, March.

Pierce, J., 1991. *The Future of Banking: A Twentieth Century Fund Report*. New Haven, CT: Yale University Press.

Singh, A. and J. Hamid, 1992. Corporate financial structures in developing countries, International Finance Corporation Technical Paper 1, World Bank.

Stoford, John M., 1992. *Directory of Multinationals*, 4th ed. New York: Baskingstoke, MacMillan, Stockton Press.

Sweeney, R.J., 1996. Emerging stock markets: lessons from industrialized country history, Göteborg School of Economics Working Paper.

Thomsen, S. and T. Pedersen, 1995. European models of corporate governance, WP 4-95, Institute of International Economics and Management, Copenhagen Business School.

Vensel, V., 1995. The political economy of macroeconomic developments, central bank and tax system reform in Estonia, CERT Working Paper, June.

Warsaw Stock Exchange, 1995. Annual Statistics.

Who Owns Whom: North America, Continental Europe, 1994. London: Dun & Bradstreet.

Wihlborg, C., 1995. Financial sector reforms in emerging market economies, Göteborg School of Economics Working Paper.

3

Reexamination of Sovereign Debt Service Capacity Volatility by Using Standardized Sovereign Debt Volatility Coefficient

Weiping Liu

INTRODUCTION

Both corporate debt service capacity (DSC) and sovereign DSC have been extensively studied. However, very few studies are devoted to the comparison of the differences of the behaviors between these two types of DSC. The aim of this chapter is to make some exploration in this field by examining the different behaviors when sovereigns and corporations have high DSC indicator volatilities.

Compared with sovereign DSC, corporate DSC is much more extensively studied. Methodologies used in these studies are better established and the scale of documentation is much bigger. Therefore, our attention will be directed more toward the study of sovereign debt.

International lending is an important business for many banks. Almost half the total earnings of the 12 largest U.S. banks, according to the *World Development Report* of the World Bank (1985), is derived from international lending, especially to the developing countries. Since the sovereign debt crisis of the early 1980s, lenders have become more cautious when dealing with international sovereign borrowers. The assessment of country risk has been a big concern for both the lending institutions and the borrowing countries in the international credit market. Several models were built to measure country risk—for example, Frank and Cline (1971), Feder et al. (1981), Kutty (1990), Balkan (1992), and Sommerville and Taffler (1994). All these models are built by using DSC indicators (which are usually economic ratios of the borrowing countries) as the measurement of country risk. When any of these indicators exceed the benchmarks that were set previously, we will take that as a warning of a possible DSC problem in that country.

Several recent studies try to examine the possible effect of the volatility of these indicators on sovereign DSC. For example, Pettis (1994) examines the volatility by using debt to export ratio, Liu (1998) uses a relative variability index—that is, the coefficient of variance of debt service ratio—to study the effect of the volatility of debt service ratios on the DSC.

One of the possible problems in these studies is that their attention focuses only on the volatility of export revenue, and the effects of import costs are basically neglected. However, the fluctuation of the import costs could play a very important role in predicting a country's DSC. When a country encounters financial shocks, for example, the export revenue is sharply lower, if the country can adopt an austerity policy to cut down its imports and reduce the trade deficit, the likelihood of that country's debt rescheduling or default can be reduced. On the other hand, if a country is unable to reduce its imports when its export revenues plummet, the probability of a DSC problem will be greatly increased. Consequently, the effect of import costs, or more precisely the simultaneous effects of import costs and export revenue, should be incorporated in the study of volatility effects.

A similar problem exists in the study of corporate DSC and this problem has been adequately addressed. We will use some of the techniques in studying corporate DSC to study the effects of sovereign DSC indicators volatility on sovereigns' DSC.

The rest of the chapter is organized as follows: standardized sovereign debt volatility coefficients are developed, based on the principle of developing standardized debt coverage ratio which is a commonly used DSC indicator in corporate finance; several hypotheses on DSC indicator volatility are reviewed; sources of data and methodologies used in this study are discussed; and results of the empirical tests are reported.

STANDARDIZED SOVEREIGN DEBT VOLATILITY COEFFICIENT

In estimating a company's debt service capacity, a commonly used accounting indicator is debt coverage ratio. It is computed by dividing interest expenses into earnings before interest and taxes. One of the weaknesses of the method is that these ratios do not reflect the possible differences in the volatility of the earnings stream between firms. Donaldson (1962) suggests that DSC analysis should focus on the ability of the firm to meet cash flow obligations with various amounts of debt. DSC can be defined in terms of the probability of default.

To serve this purpose and to remedy the shortcoming of debt coverage ratio, Wyman (1977) proposes a Standardized Debt Coverage Ratio (SDCR), which is defined as:

$$SDCR = EBIT - FC / \sigma\{EBIT\} \tag{1}$$

where $EBIT$ = earnings before interest and taxes, FC = fixed cost, $\sigma\{EBIT\}$ = standard deviation of EBIT. One of the advantages of this ratio is that it reflects volatility of earnings in the standard deviation and this ratio can be applied to all kinds of industries and all types of firms because it is standardized.

As pointed out by Shapiro (1996), in the situation of sovereign DSC, what matters is not just the coverage ratio but also the variability of the difference between export revenues and import costs. This shows that in sovereign DSC analysis, we need an indicator which is similar to SDCR, hence the Standardized Sovereign Debt Volatility Coefficient (SSDVC) is developed. This coefficient is based on the same principle as SDCR so that the ratio obtained can reflect the volatility of DSC indicators and can be used to compare the risks between countries. This coefficient is obtained as follows:

1. Compute the difference of Import Cost (denoted by MGS in the World Debt Table [World Bank, 1994]) and Export Revenue (denoted by XGS in the World Debt Table) and the mean of the difference for country i over the period examined.
2. Compute the standard deviation of these differences for country i over the period examined, the result is $\sigma_i\{XGS - MGS\}$.
3. Compute the mean of country i's total debt service (TDS) and the result is denoted by $\mu_i\{TDS\}$.
4. Divide $\sigma_i\{XGS - MGS\}$ by $\mu_i\{TDS\}$, we obtain the SSDVC.[1]

Thus, SSDVC can be defined as:

$$SSDVC = \frac{\sigma_i\{XGS - MGS\}}{\mu_i\{TDS\}} \tag{2}$$

This coefficient has several advantages: First, it reflects the simultaneous effects of export and import. Second, it incorporates the volatility of the differences of export and import. Therefore, it should be a better indicator of a country's DSC. Third, it is standardized so it can be applied to compare the risks between countries.

THEORIES ABOUT DSC INDICATOR VOLATILITY

In the past few years, several hypotheses were advanced by financial researchers about the effects of DSC indicator volatility on DSC.

1. *Sovereign Debt Option Hypothesis*: Proponents of this hypothesis (e.g., Pettis, 1994) suggest that sovereign debt lending can be visualized as creditors "write" the sovereign debtors' put options on the debt service ratio. If debt service ratio exceeds a certain level, the borrower would exercise the put and default or rescheduling will take place.

One of the flaws of this theory is that it does not distinguish the difference between private debt and sovereign debt. Private debts are subject to laws. Taking corporate bond as an example, the stockholders have limited liabilities. When the value of a leveraged firm is below the face value of the debt, stockholders will exercise the right of limited liability and give up the firm to the bondholders. In this sense, lending to a firm is just like writing a put option to stockholders.

However, in a sovereign debt situation, sovereign borrowers are not subject to the jurisdiction of the lenders. In very rare situations, sovereign creditors can seize the assets of the borrowing country or otherwise impose judicial sanctions on defaulting nations when debt default occurs. In this sense, sovereign nations always have the incentive to repudiate their debt voluntarily.

Thus the key issue in sovereign lending is how to ensure the enforceability of debt contracts—that is, how to keep borrowers from incurring debts and then defaulting voluntarily. This question has been studied by several authors, such as Froot et al. (1989), Schwartz and Zurita (1992).

Because of this enforceability problem, sovereign debt borrowers' behavior is different from option investors. Option investors are contingent claimers of underlying assets. When the price of the underlying assets is volatile, the option investors would have more chances to exercise their options. Therefore, they prefer high volatility of underlying assets. Sovereign debt borrowers' behavior does not seem to fit in this pattern.

2. *Sovereign Reputation Hypothesis*: This hypothesis posits that the major concern of a sovereign is its reputation in the international credit market. Models built by Cole et al. (1995), Chowdhry (1991), and Grossman and Van Huyck (1988) all point out that a trustworthy reputation is valuable because it provides continued access to loans. International loans are one of the most important financial resources for many developing countries. The default or rescheduling of debt will prevent the country from obtaining future loans. This is detrimental to the development of the country's economy.

Obviously, if a sovereign's major concern is its reputation, when DSC indicators are volatile, the sovereign would try its best to prevent debt default from taking place. Thus, high volatility of DSC indicators will not affect a country's DSC.

3. *Minimum Consumption Level Hypothesis*: Lee and Powell (1995) suggest that minimum consumption requirements are very important in sovereign debt rescheduling decision. According to this theory, there are two possibilities that debt rescheduling will take place: (1) The consumption levels of some countries (e.g., sub-Sahara African countries) were at the lowest level of survival. Additional income losses will result in debt rescheduling. In this case, the important factor which affects DSC should be the mean of the indicator rather than the variance of the DSC indicators. (2) The living standards in some countries (e.g., most Latin American countries) are well above the poverty line in the world. In the situation when high volatility of DSC occurs, these countries can reduce demand for imports and free up capacity for exports. This austerity policy will slow down the growth of the economy and decrease per capita consumption. However, some of the governments are too weak politically to carry out the austerity policy. When the country encounters high volatility of DSC indicators, attempting to lower the people's consumption will most likely result in discontent. The discontented people will not reelect those officials who

were responsible for the austerity policy. In this case, the administration would rather sacrifice the national reputation to maintain the consumption level. In this case, high volatility does affect the DSC and results in debt rescheduling.

DATA AND METHODOLOGY

Some empirical tests on these three hypotheses were conducted in the past. Variables used in those tests are coefficient of variation, which only considers the effects of export revenue of a country. When the effects of import cost fluctuation are considered, the difference between export revenue and import cost of a country could be either positive or negative. This makes coefficient of variation not an appropriate measurement of relative variability (see Neter et al., 1993). To address this problem, the SSDVC is a good indicator of the sovereign DSC volatility.

Data used in this study are collected from World Debt Tables published by World Bank (1994). All countries whose data on export, import, total debt service, and debt service problems are available are included in the data set. Altogether 90 countries are included in this data sample.

To study the possible effect of per capita income level on the DSC problem, data on per capita income of each country are collected from the *Information Please Almanac* (1994). Countries whose per capita income is greater than $2,500 are classified as medium-income countries and others are low-income countries.

To facilitate the study of regional effects, the countries studied are divided into four groups: Asia, Latin America, Sub-Sahara Africa, and North Africa and the Middle East. The following methods are employed:

1. *Logistic Analysis.* The experience of the country's debt service capacity is used as a dependent variable. When a country experienced a debt service problem (either a debt default or rescheduling), a value of 1 is assigned to the country, otherwise 0 is assigned.

Because the dependent variable is binary, the ordinary regression analysis is not suitable in this case. Therefore, logistic regression analysis is employed here. Logistic regression analysis, like other regression analysis, is used for describing the nature of the relationship between a dependent variable and one (or more) independent variable(s).

Both theoretical and empirical considerations suggest that when the dependent variable is binary, the shape of the response function will frequently be sigmoid. The logistic response functions are of the form:

$$E\{Y\} = \frac{Exp(b'x)}{[1 + Exp(b'x)]} \tag{3}$$

where $E\{Y\}$ is the mean response (i.e., the probability when the dependent variable is 1); b is the vector of regression parameters; and x is the vector of explanatory variables.

An interesting property of logistic response functions is that they can easily be linearized. If we denote $E\{Y\}$ by π and let $\pi'=log_e[\pi/(1-\pi)]$, then $\pi'=b'x$ is easily obtained. This transformation is called the logistic transformations of the probability π. The ratio $\pi/(1-\pi)$ in the logistic transformation is the odds. The transformed response function is referred to as the logistic response function, and π' is called the logistic mean response.

At the empirical level, for both description and prediction of DSC, the parameters of the logistic response function need to be estimated first. The logistic regression analysis assumes the general form of:

$$\pi = \frac{Exp(b'x)}{1 + Exp(b'x)} \tag{4}$$

or

$$\pi = [1 + Exp(-b'x)]^{-1} \tag{5}$$

where x is a vector of measures or indices perceived to be relevant in determining DSC, and b is the vector of parameters to be estimated. More information about logistic regression can be found in Neter et al. (1996).

To test whether SSDVC of countries of different per capita income and in different regions will have different effects on the sovereign's DSC, the following forward stepwise logistic regression analyses with dummy variables are conducted in this study (details of this method can be found in Hardy, 1993).

Test 1. The dependent variable is regressed against SSDVCs of all countries.

Test 2. The dependent variable is regressed against SSDVCs of countries (1) whose per capita income is above or equal to $2,500; (2) whose per capita income is less than $2,500. These two groups of countries are indicated by dummy regressors.

Test 3. The dependent variable is regressed against SSDVCs of four regional groups of countries   (Asia, Latin America, North Africa and the Middle East, and Sub-Sahara Africa). The regions are also represented by dummy regressors.

The null hypotheses tested in these analyses are:
H_0: SSDVCs are not related to the high probability of DSC problems.

If b obtained in these analyses are significant at a certain significance level, H_0 will be rejected. Otherwise, it will be supported.

2. *Chi-square Test.* First, countries which never have DSC problems are categorized into N Group and otherwise into Y Group. Second, countries with high debt service ratio volatility (whose SSDVC <1.00) are classified into H group and others in L Group. Thus, a 2x2 contingency table is formed (see Table 3.1).

In the second Chi-square test, countries whose per capita income is greater than $2,500 are categorized into the medium-income group. The other countries in the data set are categorized into the low-income group. Thus Table 3.1 becomes a 2x2x2 contingency table (see Table 3.2).

Table 3.1. Contingency Table for Chi-square Test

	High Volatility	Low Volatility	Row Total
No Default	Observed: 22 Expected: 24.6	Observed: 19 Expected: 16.4	41 45.6%
Default	Observed: 32 Expected: 29.4	Observed: 17 Expected: 19.6	49 54.5%
Column Total	54 60%	36 40%	90 100%

Table 3.2. Contingency Table When Data are Split Into Medium-Income and Low-Income Countries

DSC Problem	Medium Income			Low Income		
	Low Volatility	High Volatility	Row Total	Low Volatility	High Volatility	Row Total
No	Obs.: 11 Exp.: 14.05	Obs.: 9 Exp.: 5.94	20 54.1%	Obs.: 11 Exp.: 11.09	Obs.: 10 Exp.: 9.9	21 39.6%
Yes	Obs.: 15 Exp.: 11.94	Obs.: 2 Exp.: 5.05	17 45.9%	Obs.: 17 Exp.: 16.91	Obs.: 15 Exp.: 9.06	32 60.4%
Column Total	26 70.3%	11 29.7%	37 100%	28 52.8%	25 47.2%	53 100%

EMPIRICAL RESULTS

The results of logistic regression analysis are reported in Table 3.3. From this table, we can see that when SSDVC of medium-income countries and of Latin American countries are used as independent variables, βs obtained are significant at 90% confidence level. In other cases, βs are not significant. These results indicate that generally speaking the Sovereign Reputation Hypothesis is supported while the Sovereign Debt Option Hypothesis should be rejected. These results also demonstrate that, under some circumstances, the volatility of DSC indicators does affect DSC of a country. This is consistent with the Minimum Consumption Level Hypothesis.

The result of Chi-square tests are reported in Table 3.4. From this table, we can find that only in medium-income countries is the probability of debt rescheduling and default linked with the volatility of DSC indicators. This seems to be another supporting evidence to the Minimum Consumption Level Hypothesis. Thus we can conclude that when the effects of import cost are incorporated into our analysis, the results are consistent with the findings in Liu (1998).

**Table 3.3. Results of Logistic Regression Analyses When SSDVC
and Dummy Variables Are Used as Regressors**

Independent Dummy Variables	β	P-value	Exp (β)
All countries	-.1485	.2866	.8620
Medium-income countries	-1.0036	.0846	.3666
Low-income countries	-.0857	.5824	.9179
Asia	.2121	.5404	1.2363
Latin America	-1.2377	.0941	.2901
North Africa & Middle East	-3.6963	.1991	.0248
Sub-Sahara Africa	-.1326	.4904	.8758

Table 3.4. Results of Chi-square Tests

Group	Pearson's Statistics	P-value
All countries	1.26182	.26131
Low-income countries	.00282	.95767
Medium-income countries	4.85863	.02751

CONCLUDING REMARKS

In this study, we use SSDVC as a measurement of sovereign DSC volatility. SSDVC is developed on the same principle of SDCR in corporate finance. By using SSDVC as the independent variable to study the effects of DSC volatility on a sovereign's DSC, we found that the DSC indicators' volatility usually does not affect a sovereign's DSC. Many researchers (e.g., Mauer and Lewellen, 1987) have reported that firms with stable earnings have a high debt service capacity. Thus we find that sovereign DSC behavior is somewhat different from the corporate DSC behavior.

However, among medium-income countries, DSC indicators' volatility does affect a sovereign's DSC. This is most probably because governments in those countries are politically vulnerable and worry about losing voters at home if they cannot maintain the consumption level of their people. In the case of high volatility of DSC indicators, they do not want to lose the support of voters. Therefore, they would rather lose the sovereign reputation abroad than lose the internal reputation among voters. This finding shows that the behavior of sovereign DSC behavior is much more complicated than corporate DSC behavior and needs to be handled with discretion. The primary technique of estimating the volatility is to develop pro forma financial statements of the borrowing countries under different scenarios.

NOTE

1. This coefficient is reversely related to DSC volatility—that is, when the coefficient decreases, the risk increases. The reason why the reciprocal is not used is because sometimes the standard deviation can be very small or even zero. In those cases, the coefficient obtained could be either very difficult to interpret or, even worse, undefined.

REFERENCES

Balkan, E.M., 1992. Political instability, country risk and probability of default, *Applied Economics* 24(9), 999-1008.

Chowdhry, B., 1991. What is different about international lending? *Review of Financial Studies* 4(1), 121-148.

Cole, H.L., J. Dow, and W.B. English, 1995. Default, settlement, and signaling: lending resumption in a reputational model of sovereign debt, *International Economic Review* 36, 365-385.

Donaldson, G., 1962. New framework for corporate debt capacity, *Harvard Business Review* 40 (March-April), 117-131.

Feder, G., R. Just, and K. Ross, 1981. Projecting debt servicing capacity of developing countries, *Journal of Financial and Quantitative Analysis* 16(5), 651-669.

Frank, C.R. Jr. and W.R. Cline, 1971. Measurement of debt servicing capacity: an application of discrimination analysis, *Journal of International Economics* 1(3), 327-344.

Froot, K.A., D.S. Scharfstein, and J.C. Stein, 1989. LDC debt: forgiveness, indexation, and investment incentives, *Journal of Finance* 64(5), 1335-1350.

Grossman, H. and J.B.Van Huyck, 1988. Sovereign debt as a contingent claim: excusable default, repudiation, and reputation. *American Economic Review* 78, 1088-1097.

Hardy, M.A., 1993. *Regression with Dummy Variables.* Beverly Hills, CA: Sage Publications.

Information Please Almanac, 1994. 44th ed. Boston: Houghton Mifflin.

Kutty, G., 1990. Logistic regression and probability of default of developing countries debt, *Applied Economics* 21, 1649-1660.

Lee, B.C. and J.G. Powell, 1995. A behavioral approach to sovereign debt rescheduling, *Applied Economics Letter* 2, 64-66.

Liu, Weiping, 1998, An empirical study of the impact of debt service ratio volatility on debt service capacity, *Global Business and Finance Review,* forthcoming.

Mauer, D.C. and W.G. Lewellen, 1987. Debt management under corporate and personal taxes, *Journal of Finance* 42, 1275-1291.

Neter, J., W. Wasserman, and G.A.Whitmore, 1993. *Applied Statistics*, 4th ed. Englewood Cliffs, NJ: Prentice Hall.

Neter, J., M. Kutner, C.J. Nachtsheim, and W. Wasserman, 1996. *Applied Linear Statistical Model.* Homewood, IL: Irwin.

Pettis, M., 1994. Debt export ratios and default probabilities, *Columbia Journal of World Business* 24(2), 78-83.

Schartz, E.S. and S. Zurita, 1992. Sovereign debt: optimal contract, underinvestment, and forgiveness, *Journal of Finance* 67(3), 981-1004.

Shapiro, A.C., 1996. *Multinational Finance Management*, 5th ed. Englewood Cliffs, NJ: Prentice Hall.

Sommerville, R.A. and R.J. Taffler, 1994. The predictability of debt-servicing difficulties among less developed countries, *Review of Quantitative Finance and Accounting,* 4 339-356.

World Bank, 1994. World Debt Table. Washington, D.C.

World Bank, 1985. *World Development Report.* New York: Oxford University Press.

Wyman, H.E., 1977. Standardized debt coverage ratios, *The Accounting Review* 52(2), 503-507.

PART II
International Market Linkages

4

Volatility and Openness of Emerging Markets: Some Empirical Evidence

Vince J. Hooper

INTRODUCTION

The purpose of this chapter is to examine the relationship between the volatility of emerging stock markets (ESMs) and their degree of openness. The findings of this research may have policy-relevant implications for governments of developing countries who may be interested in the association between market volatility and openness. It is not the aim of this chapter to determine whether greater volatility brought about by increased openness is desirable or not, but to establish whether such a relationship exists.

The emergence of stock markets in developing countries has its origins with the change in global political dynamics that occurred during the 1980 (Hale 1994). Throughout the 1980s there was a lessening of tensions between East and West and emerging markets in Eastern Europe were set up. China's progressive moves toward a social market oriented economy unleashed a newfound confidence in the merits of capital markets. The Shanghai Stock Market even reopened in December 1990. The governments of many South American countries have transformed their economies from a high dependence upon state-run industries to the more open ones.

There is now a great demand for the international portfolio of capital necessary to finance firms in both developing and developed countries. The World Bank (1993) recorded that total portfolio flows around the globe to developing countries increased to a level of $55.8 billion in 1993 (a sevenfold increase from 1989). Countries now find that they are competing more fiercely with other nations for equity capital.

The potential of emerging markets to enhance the mean-variance efficiency of international stock market portfolio investment strategies has been focused upon from the perspective of the international investors, who are seeking to improve the risk-return trade-off of their portfolios by investing across markets. Statistical evidence on the correlation matrix of returns between emerging markets demonstrates that this may be achieved (International Finance Corporation [IFC], 1995). The correlation matrix between the market indices of emerging markets is nearly an identity matrix, implying that investors who invest a proportion of their wealth in emerging stocks are able to improve their risk-return trade-off, as emerging stocks are added to the world portfolio of risky assets (Harvey, 1993; Divecha, Drach, and Stefak, 1992). There is research by Harvey (1995) which implies that this correlation matrix is becoming less of an identity matrix over time as emerging markets become more integrated with world markets.

The internationalization of capital and its flow from developed countries to developing countries has raised an important policy issue, from the perspective of developing countries' governments. This question is whether portfolio flows of capital to developing countries increase market volatility and destabilize their economies (Reisen, 1993). Some research has been undertaken by Claessens, Dooley, and Warner (1995) on this issue. They found inconclusive evidence of any relationship between volatility and flows of capital to ESMs. Rogers (1994) discovered that emerging markets that were relatively isolated at the time of the stock market crash in October 1987 did not experience price spillovers from developed markets. Tesar and Werner (1995) supported these findings and discovered that there was no relationship between U.S. portfolio capital flows to developing markets and volatility. Kim and Singal (1993) conducted event studies to measure the behavior of emerging stock prices following the opening of a market to foreign investors. They found that there was no effect of liberalization upon stock market volatility. Using cointegration analysis, Cornelius (1992) discovered that repatriation of capital constraints was effective in insulating ESMs from industrialized countries' stock markets and predicted that their removal would lead to higher volatility. There seems to be conflicting evidence in the research literature on the relationship between emerging stock market volatility and their openness. This chapter seeks to investigate whether a relationship exists between volatility and degree of openness, but not to judge whether volatility is good or bad.

HYPOTHESIS

It is assumed in this chapter that as the openness of ESMs increases, funds will flow from developed countries to developing countries in order to maintain the equilibrium relationship between risk and return, through arbitrage opportunities taken by the international investor. Attention has been focused by academics upon an extended version of the capital asset pricing model (Sharpe, 1964), known as the international capital asset pricing model (ICAPM) (Stulz, 1981), as the best model of the risk-return trade-off within an international context.

Buckberg (1995) tested whether ESMs are now an integral component of the global financial market by testing a conditional version of the international capital asset pricing model. She found that the large capital inflows from industrial countries, commencing at the end of the 1980s, caused stock prices in emerging markets to reflect more strongly the covariance risk with the world market portfolio between December 1984 and December 1991 (i.e., conforms more with the ICAPM). Buckberg found that between 1977 and 1984, emerging markets were virtually completely isolated. It is unclear in the research literature whether integration of emerging stocks with the world market portfolio induces an increase in volatility or a decrease, or whether their volatility remains the same. In addition, there is also an inconsistency between what Buckberg discovered in relation to emerging stocks conforming with ICAPM, and what Kim and Singal (1993) found regarding volatility and openness. One would expect the volatility of the emerging stock market to be altered when its degree of openness changes and arbitrage opportunities on offer to the international investor begin to modify the variance-covariance matrix of emerging stocks, with relation to the world market portfolio. Hence, a primary null hypothesis of this research is:

H_1: The volatility of ESMs is not related to the degree of openness.

CHOICE OF VARIABLES

This section develops how the variables were chosen for the factor model developed in this study, based on the available research literature, in order to measure openness of the market. The research literature focuses around the barriers that inhibit emerging markets from integrating with the world market portfolio which, essentially, can be considered to be a proxy for openness, since emerging markets that are completely insulated would attract zero capital (Demirguc-Kunt and Huizinga, 1992).

Bekaert (1995) cited the barriers to integration or openness as being either macroeconomy specific or stock market specific. Macroeconomic specific instability is due to poor credit ratings, high and variable inflation, exchange controls, economic policy risk, liquidity risk (as distinguished from liquidity of the market), and currency risk. Since these risks are diversifiable by the investor they are not considered in the factor model, except for exchange controls in the form of repatriation because this would restrict capital outflows.

Stock exchange specific barriers are influenced by the degree to which the stock market is developed in terms of the presence of domestic and international brokers as well as market size. Other factors like the propensity for insider trading will imply that the market is stacked against outsiders. Bekaert also suggested that the de facto openness of the stock market is an important consideration such as a lack of country funds. Bekaert suggested that restrictions on foreign ownership are not relevant since these may be circumvented or are usually nonbinding for most emerging stock markets. Further, Bekaert said that the functioning of the stock market is important such as the quality of the accounting and legal system, degree of deregulation, level of automation, and length of settlement periods. Demirguc-Kunt and Huizinga (1992) argued that harmonization of capital gains taxes are also an important consideration.

Therefore based around Bekaert's "barriers to integration" as a proxy for openness, variables listed in Table 4.1 are collected from the IFC Emerging Stock Market Factbook (1994, 1995) and the 1995 reports supplied by Equitor Group (U.K.) Ltd. in order to measure the degree of openness of emerging stock markets. The effect of increases in the variables on openness is also given because of different calibrations. Thus in defining openness of emerging markets, for the purpose of this chapter, it is considered to be a combination of factors such as market maturity, liquidity, degree of financial deregulation, market concentration, commercial and securities law framework, openness, and taxes (Baekert, 1995).

Table 4.1. Data Sources

Variable	Source	The effect of increases in the variable upon the openness of the emerging market
Automation	IFC	Increases Openness
Availability of Derivatives	Equitor	Increases Openness
Capital Gains Tax	IFC	Decreases Openness
Transaction Costs	IFC	Decreases Openness
Openness of Market	Equitor	Increases Openness
Domestic Brokers	Equitor	Increases Openness
International Brokers	Equitor	Increases Openness
Liquidity	IFC	Increases Openness
Market of the 10 Largest Stocks	IFC	Decreases Openness
Market Size	IFC	Increases Openness
Number of Stocks	IFC	Increases Openness
Insider Trading	Equitor	Increases Openness
Quality of Accounting and Legal System	Equitor	Increases Openness
Quality of Research	Equitor	Increases Openness
Ratio of Traded/Total Market Capitalization in 12 Months (i.e., Turnover)	IFC	Increases Openness
Reliability of Settlement	Equitor	Increases Openness
Repatriation Controls	IFC	Decreases Openness
Settlement Period	Equitor	Increases Openness
Trading Hours	Equitor	Increases Openness
Value Traded of the Top 10 Shares	IFC	Increases Openness
Value Traded in a Year	IFC	Increases Openness
Withholding Taxes	IFC	Decreases Openness

SAMPLE

Fifty emerging markets were analyzed according to the variables collected in Table 4.1. These emerging markets were located in the following main geographic areas: North Asia, Latin America and Caribbean, Central and Southern Europe, Eastern Europe, Africa, and the Middle East.

METHOD

There are two stages to the method employed in this study. The first stage involved a factor analysis of the variables that were used to measure the openness of emerging stock markets. These factors are interpreted and factor scores created for each factor. In the second stage of the research, a regression equation was formed between a proxy for volatility and the factors extracted from the first stage of the research.

First Stage

A factor analysis was conducted on the 22 variables listed in Table 4.1. The rationale behind using factor analysis was to reduce the number of variables to a smaller number of interpretable dimensions or "common threads," called factors. The factors can be thought of as new variables.

The SPSS (Statistics Package for the Social Sciences, 1990) Varimax rotation procedure, using a principal components extraction method for the factors, was applied to the data set for the variables listed in Table 4.1. Principal component analysis seeks to determine the number and characteristics of the factors or "variable groups" that affected the emerging markets. The importance of each factor can be identified by comparing each factor's eigenvalue (see Table 4.2). The larger the eigenvalue, the more important the factor is in contributing to the total variance in the data. Factors with an eigenvalue of less than 1 are considered to have negligible impact and can be ignored. Seven factors were identified which explained 76% of the variation in the responses. Table 4.3 shows the resultant factor loading matrix after rotation. The robustness of the factor solution was tested using a Kaiser-Meyer-Olkin statistic (0.69) and the model was found to be a very good fit. The appropriateness of using factor analysis was supported by the Bartlett's test of sphericity statistic which demonstrated that the correlation matrix of input variables was a nonidentity matrix (Table 4.4), which is an important consideration when factor analysis is being employed. The factors can be interpreted as:

Factor 1: Market Maturity

Factor links the number of domestic and international brokers, liquidity, market size, the quality of research, and the reliability of settlement. All of these attributes are associated with a relatively developed market. Therefore factor 1 can be interpreted as *market maturity*.

Table 4.2. Eigenvalues and Percentage Variances for Each Factor

Factor	Eigenvalue	Percentage of Variance	Cumulative Percentage
1	6.86	31.2	31.2
2	2.26	10.3	41.5
3	2.11	9.6	51.1
4	1.57	7.2	58.3
5	1.50	6.8	65.1
6	1.36	6.2	71.3
7	1.00	4.6	75.9

Table 4.3. Rotated Factor Matrix–Factor Loadings

Variable	Factor						
	1	2	3	4	5	6	7
Automation	0.24	0.19	0.39	-0.15	**-0.42**	-0.09	-0.19
Availability of Derivatives	0.05	-0.01	**0.81**	0.01	-0.01	-0.23	-0.09
Capital Gains Tax	0.22	-0.01	0.06	0.16	-0.15	**0.48**	**0.42**
Transaction Costs	0.13	-0.19	-0.11	-0.10	-0.06	**0.70**	0.03
Openness of Market	0.23	-0.24	0.13	-0.35	-0.17	**-0.57**	0.14
Domestic Brokers	**0.92**	0.12	0.16	0.07	0.07	-0.02	0.08
International Brokers	**0.91**	0.09	0.14	0.04	0.01	0.09	-0.01
Liquidity	**0.81**	0.26	0.04	0.20	0.03	-0.09	-0.06
Market of the 10 Largest Stocks (% age)	-0.33	-0.36	-0.15	**-0.66**	0.26	-0.08	-0.15
Market Size	**0.50**	**0.55**	0.36	0.35	0.15	-0.09	0.15
Number of Stocks	0.24	0.02	0.04	**0.81**	-0.13	-0.09	-0.09
Insider Trading	0.08	-0.03	0.09	-0.28	**0.78**	0.06	-0.11
Quality of Accounting and Legal System	0.22	0.18	-0.08	0.01	**0.79**	-0.10	0.01
Quality of Research	**0.89**	0.15	0.14	0.18	-0.09	0.05	0.12
Ratio of Traded/Total Market Capitalization in 12 Months (i.e., Turnover)	0.27	**0.87**	-0.02	-0.05	-0.02	-0.10	0.03
Reliability of Settlement	**0.79**	0.29	0.01	-0.03	0.27	0.12	-0.10
Repatriation Controls	0.03	0.17	**0.55**	-0.22	0.07	**0.46**	-0.27
Settlement Period	-0.26	-0.22	-0.13	0.01	**0.42**	0.10	0.39
Trading Hours	0.37	0.22	**0.59**	0.18	-0.02	-0.16	0.26
Value Traded of the Top 10 Shares	-0.34	**-0.55**	0.02	**-0.46**	0.04	-0.19	-0.25
Value Traded in a Year	0.21	**0.91**	0.08	0.09	0.07	-0.01	0.08
Withholding Taxes	0.05	0.20	0.01	-0.01	-0.04	-0.05	**0.90**

Strong correlations with factors (i.e., factor loadings) are highlighted in bold.

Table 4.4. Robustness of the Factor Solution Statistics

Kaiser Meyer Olkin Measure of Sampling Adequacy	= 0.6951 [1 is best, 0 is worse]
Bartlett's Test of Sphericity Statistic	= 693.91 (Significance = 0.000)
Varimax converged in 14 Iterations	

Factor 2: Liquidity

There is an association between market size, ratio of the value of traded shares/market capitalization (i.e., turnover), and value traded in a year. The value traded of the top 10 shares, a measure of market concentration, loaded negatively on this factor (which is due to the inverse relationship with market size). Liquidity also had a relatively high loading of 0.26, although not greater than 0.4. Clearly this factor can be interpreted as *liquidity*.

Factor 3: Financial Deregulation

A connection can be made for the attributes with high loadings on factor 3 between the availability of derivatives, automation, repatriation controls, and number of trading hours. This factor is interpreted as *financial deregulation*, since all the attributes can be associated with a relaxation of rules by the authorities.

Factor 4: Market Concentration

For the interpretation of this factor, an association can be made between the number of stocks, market of the 10 largest stocks, and value traded of the top 10 shares (which has a high negative factor loading). This factor can be interpreted as *market concentration*. Intuitively, the higher the concentration of the emerging market, the worse the factor score for this factor.

Factor 5: Commercial and Securities Law Framework

Factor 5 links insider trading, the quality of the accounting and legal system, and settlement period. This factor is thus interpreted as a *commercial and securities law framework*.

Factor 6: Openness of Economy

A relationship can clearly be seen between capital gains taxes, transaction costs, repatriation controls, and openness of market (loading negatively). The direction of this factor is reversed in order to calculate the factor score for consistency of comparison with the other factor scores. Thus, higher factor scores on this factor are associated with a higher degree of openness of the economy. This factor was thus interpreted as *openness of economy*.

Factor 7: Taxes

Factor 7 associates capital gains taxes with withholding taxes. This is obviously a *tax* factor.

Factor scores were then calculated for each emerging market in order to quantify the newly created factors. Each of these factors can be considered to be a subset of a proxy measure for openness. Factor 1 to Factor 7 can thus be considered to be a decomposition of openness according to Bekaert's (1995) openness criteria.

Second Stage

In the second stage of the research, a multiple regression equation was estimated for the relationship between volatility and the factor scores calculated in the first stage. The annualized standard deviation, calculated over an ex-post five-year horizon (IFC *Emerging Stock Markets Factbook*) was regressed against the factors extracted from the first stage, as a proxy for volatility:

$$\sigma_j = \alpha + B_1F_1 + B_2F_2 + B_3F_3 + B_4F_4 + B_5F_5 + B_6F_6 + B_7F_7$$

where σ_j is the mean annualised standard deviation of returns on the index of emerging market j, α is a constant, $B_1 ... B_7$ are the regression slope coefficients and $F_1 ... F_7$ are the extracted factor scores for each factor for each emerging market j.

The adjusted R^2 for the regression equation was discovered to be .36743 (see Table 4.5). However there are no similar studies with which to compare this value of R^2. A histogram and normal probability plot of the standardized residuals revealed that the distribution of residuals did not differ markedly from a normal distribution. There were no influential outliers in the regression model. There is also no multicollinearity problem with this regression equation because the principal component extraction of factors in the first stage, with varimax rotation results in the production of orthogonal factors (i.e., vectors at 90 degrees to one another defined in hyperspace). The correlation matrix of orthogonal factors is thus an identity matrix reflecting zero correlation between each pair of factors, representing no multicollinearity.

The sign of the standardized Beta coefficients shows the influence of the openness factors upon volatility (see Table 4.6). The magnitude of the standardized Beta coefficient shows the relative strength of variables in the regression equation. From Table 4.6, it can be seen that there is a positive association between volatility and market maturity. The standardized regression coefficient indicates that market maturity has the greatest influence in the regression model on volatility. Thus more mature markets are riskier than less developed emerging markets. This supports the rejection of the null hypothesis, H_1. That is, a

Table 4.5. Goodness of Fit of the Regression Equation

Multiple R	.67661
R^2	.45780
Adjusted R^2	.36743
F = 5.06605	Significance of F = .0003

Table 4.6. Regression Coefficients

Factor	Beta Unstandard. Regression Coefficient	Standard Error of Beta	Beta Standardized	T Statistic	Sig. T
Market Maturity	3.713	0.958	0.440	3.874	0.000
Liquidity	1.691	0.958	0.200	1.764	0.085
Financial Deregulation	3.025	0.958	0.359	3.156	0.003
Market Concentration	0.888	0.958	0.105	0.927	0.359
Commercial and Securities Law Framework	-1.778	0.958	-0.211	-1.855	0.071
Openness of Economy	1.549	0.958	0.184	1.617	0.113
Taxes	-0.654	0.958	-0.077	-0.683	0.498
(Constant)	6.862	0.949		7.232	0.000

greater degree of openness of emerging markets heightens volatility. A higher degree of financial deregulation and liquidity were associated with higher volatility. Again, this points to a rejection of H_1. Higher levels of deregulation and liquidity are both connected with a greater degree of market openness, according to Baekert.

Financial deregulation was the second most important factor influencing volatility. Market concentration (although the coefficient was not significant) had a positive relationship with volatility. Earlier, in the paper (under the first stage) it was highlighted that high factor scores on this factor meant a lower market concentration. Therefore, lower market concentration is associated with higher volatility. Lower market concentration is usually representative of a more mature and open market (Divecha, Drach, and Stefek, 1992). Volatility was negatively correlated with the quality of the commercial and securities law framework (significant at the 10% level). This implies that the better the rules or legal system in the developing country relating to commercial transactions, the lower the volatility. This is an area where a developing country could perhaps take positive action in order to damp down unnecessary excess volatility. Many developing countries have enhanced their accounting and regulatory frameworks by implementing international accounting standards (Wallace, 1993). The greater the openness of the economy, the higher the volatility. This finding is consistent with the rejection of hypothesis H_1. Finally, lower taxes (associated with a higher degree of openness) has the effect of increasing volatility. This is also consistent with the rejection of H_1.

Overall, the interpretation of the regression model produced in the second stage of the research rejects convincingly the null hypothesis H_1, which stated that there was no relationship between the volatility and openness of emerging markets. It has been discovered that there is a positive relationship between volatility and openness. Emerging markets with a higher degree of openness have higher volatilities than emerging markets that are less open.

CONCLUSION

There is inconclusive evidence in the literature of a relationship between volatility and the degree of openness of emerging markets. There is also a dichotomy between the findings of some researchers that emerging markets are becoming increasingly integrated with the world market portfolio (i.e., beginning to conform to the international asset pricing model), and yet there has been the discovery of no detectable modification in emerging stock market volatility by other researchers. This chapter finds a significant positive relationship between volatility and openness. Awareness of this relationship is important from the perspective of both the international investor and the governments of developing countries. Developing country governments should implement policies which best represent their view on stock market volatility.

However, it was not an aim of this study to argue whether volatility is good or bad. Implicit in the findings of this study is the assertion that volatility of ESMs may be damped down through fiscal policy and by fortifying the securities and commercial law framework. Also, the findings of the research have implications for the international investor who should be aware of the varying nature of volatility of ESMs with respect to their degree of openness. Ironically, international investors are lured to investing a proportion of their wealth in ESMs because of the low correlations ESMs have with other markets, which gives rise to an improvement in the risk-return trade-off of the investor's overall portfolio. However, the findings of this research suggest that the volatility of ESMs is modified as they are opened up, thereby altering their correlation matrix with respect to other stock markets, in the long-run and changing their diversification benefits.

REFERENCES

Bekaert, G., 1995. Market integration and investment barriers in emerging equity markets, *The World Bank Economic Review* 9, 75-107.

Buckberg, E., 1995. Emerging stock markets and international asset pricing, *The World Bank Economic Review* 9, 51-74.

Claessens, S., M. Dooley, and A. Warner, 1995. Portfolio flows: hot or cold, *The World Bank Economic Review* 9, 153-174.

Cornelius, P.K., 1992. Capital controls and market segmentation of emerging stock markets, *Seoul Journal of Economics* 5, 289-299.

Demirguc-Kunt, A. and H. Huizinga, 1992. Barriers to portfolio investments in emerging stock markets, World Bank Policy Research working paper 984. Washington, DC.

Divecha, A., J. Drach, and D. Stefak, 1992. Emerging markets: a quantitative perspective, *Journal of Portfolio Management* 19, 41-50.

Equitor Group (UK) Ltd., 1995. Reports on emerging markets.

Hale, D., 1994. Stock markets in a new world order, *Columbia Journal of World Business* 29, 14-28.

Harvey, C., 1993. Portfolio enhancement using emerging markets and conditioning information, in: Stijin Claessens and Sudarshan Gooptu, eds., *Portfolio Investment in Developing Dountries*, World Bank discussion paper 228. Washington, DC.

Harvey, C., 1995. The risk exposure of equity markets, *The World Bank Economic Review* 9, 19-50.

International Finance Corporation, various years, *Emerging Stock Markets Factbook*. Washington, DC.

Kim, E.H. and V. Singal, 1993. Opening up of stock markets by emerging economies: effect on portfolio flows and volatility of stock prices. In Stijin Claessens and Sudarshan Gooptu, eds., *Portfolio Investment in Developing Countries*, World Bank discussion paper 228. Washington, DC.

Reisen, H., 1993. The case for sterilised intervention in Latin-America. Proceedings of the 6th annual inter-American seminar on economics, May 28-29, Caracas.

Rogers, J.H., 1994. Entry barriers and price movements between major and emerging stock markets, *Journal of Macroeconomics* 16, 221-241.

Sharpe, W.F., 1964. Capital asset prices: a theory of market equilibrium under risk, *Journal of Finance*, September, 425-442.

SPSS, 1990. *Statistics for the Social Sciences: Reference Guide*.

Stulz, R.M., 1981. A model of international asset pricing, *Journal of Financial Economics* 9, 383-406.

Tesar, L. and L. Werner, 1995. U.S. equity investment in emerging stock markets, *The World Bank Economic Review* 9, 109-130.

Wallace, R.S.O. 1993. Development of accounting standards for developing and newly industrialized countries, *Research in Third World Accounting* 2, 121-165.

World Bank, 1993. World Debt Tables. Washington, DC.

5

Intertemporal Stability of Stock Returns and Relationship with Stock Index Futures

Gordon Y.N. Tang

INTRODUCTION

Stock index futures contracts were first introduced in the United States in February 1982 by the Kansas City Board of Trade. The underlying stock index is the Value Line Composite Index. Since then, many different stock index futures contracts were introduced and traded on stock exchanges around the world: for example, S&P 500 (U.S.) in 1982, All Ordinaries Index (Australia) in 1983, FTSE 100 Index (U.K.) in 1984, Maxi Major Market Futures Index (U.S.) in 1985, Hang Seng Index (Hong Kong) in 1986, SIMEX Stock Average Index (Singapore) in 1986, Topix Index (Japan) in 1988, and others. The growth in the number of stock index futures traded on stock exchanges proves themselves as valuable financial instruments to investors.

One of the main functions of stock index futures contracts is to provide investors an instrument for hedging against their investments in cash position in the stock market. The common objective of hedging with index futures is risk minimization. Because of the high correlation between the stock index futures and the underlying stock index, a portfolio with a long (short) position in cash stock market and a short (long) position in futures contract has very low risk. However, as index futures and the underlying stock index are not perfectly correlated due to basis risk, a perfect hedge is very difficult to find.

Stein (1961) argued that the usual method of estimating the risk-minimizing hedge ratio is to use ordinary least squares (OLS) regression. The optimal minimum hedge ratio is estimated by the b coefficient in the following regression model:

$$S_t - S_{t-k} = a + b * (F_t - F_{t-k}) + e_t \qquad (1)$$

where S_t and F_t are the spot index and index futures prices, respectively, at time t; k is the holding period for the hedge; and e_t is the error term. The minimum variance hedge ratio, b depends on the correlation between cash index and index futures prices.

Many studies have been carried out on the empirical analysis of hedging share portfolios using stock index futures. Figlewski (1984) examined the use of S&P 500 futures to hedge the risk of five portfolios of shares by regressing returns of stock portfolios on that of index futures to obtain the risk-minimizing hedge ratios. He found that the hedging strategy works well for portfolios of large stocks but is less effective for portfolios that contain smaller companies. Junkus and Lee (1985), using daily closing prices, found that the minimum-risk hedge ratios outperform the one-to-one hedge ratios. Similar studies using other markets' stock index futures also exist—for example, Yau, Hill, and Schneeweis (1990) on the Nikkei Stock Average; Lam and Yu (1992) on the Hang Seng Index Futures.

Most of the previous studies used index futures to hedge the cash index and examined the hedging effectiveness. However, a stock index is actually a hypothetical stock portfolio. Replicating the index portfolio is subject to two problems. First, transaction costs are very high, particularly if the stock index is an all-shares index. Second, there is the execution problem because not all stocks are traded at the same time. It would be more realistic to use only a small number of frequently traded stocks and hedge them with index futures. However, the ex-ante hedging effectiveness would depend on the intertemporal stability in the relationship among returns of individual stocks.

A considerable amount of work has been done on the intertemporal stability of correlation among international stock markets (e.g., Maldonado and Saunders, 1981; Meric and Meric, 1989). However, to the best of our knowledge, no similar study has been done on the intertemporal stability in returns of individual stocks and in relationships between these stocks and stock index futures. This study helps fill the gap by examining the intertemporal stability of (1) correlation among returns of 16 individual stocks, which are all constituent stocks of the Hang Seng Index, and (2) relationship between returns of these 16 stocks and that of the Hang Seng Index Futures across different time periods. The empirical results show that while correlations of stock returns are rather stable across adjacent index futures contract months, relationships between individual stocks and the Hang Seng Index Futures are less stable, particularly in the even-months contract period.

DATA AND METHODOLOGY

Data

Daily closing prices of 16 stocks, which are most heavily traded on the Stock Exchange of Hong Kong, were collected from DATASTREAM. All are constituent stocks of the Hang Seng Index during our sample period. The Hang

Seng Index consists of 33 blue-chips. Hence, our data are around 50% of this sample. Daily settlement prices of the Hang Seng Index Futures (HSIF) were collected from the Hong Kong Futures Exchange. HSIF contracts were first introduced on May 6, 1986. Our sample period covers June 1986 to August 1990. The whole sample period is then divided into three subperiods: pre-crash period (June 1986 to September 1987); postcrash period (November 1987 to January 1989); and even-month-contract period (January 1989 to August 1990). Daily index futures returns and stock returns were calculated as $ln(P_t/P_{t-1})*100\%$, where P_t and P_{t-1} are the closing/settlement prices at time t and $t-1$ respectively.

Test of Equal Correlation

To test the equality of correlation between the HSIF returns and any individual stock returns, the Normal Distribution Test is used. Each correlation coefficient is first converted into Z, the Fisher transformation, which is defined as:

$$Z_{ij} = 1/2 * ln \left[(1 + r_{ij})/(1 - r_{ij}) \right] \qquad (2)$$

where r_{ij} is the sample correlation coefficient between returns of stock i and the HSIF, j. Then the hypothesis that the correlation coefficients in two time periods are equal is tested by the following statistic, D:

$$D = \frac{Z_{ij}^{\,1} - Z_{ij}^{\,2}}{\sqrt{[1/(n_1 - 3)] + [1/(n_2 - 3)]}} \qquad (3)$$

where $Z_{ij}^{\,k}$ is the Fisher transformation of correlation coefficient between returns of stock i and HSIF, j in the first period ($k=1$) and the second period ($k=2$). N_k is the number of observations in the first and second periods, respectively. Given that the original variables are distributed normally, the statistic D also follows a normal distribution, and hence, the level of significance can be inferred by the critical values of a normal distribution.

Test of Stability in Covariance Matrices

Box (1949) proposed a joint test on the equality of two or more variance-covariance matrices across different time periods. Box's M statistic is calculated as follows:

$$M = n \ln |\mathbf{C}| - \sum_{i=1}^{T} n_i * \ln |\mathbf{C}_i| \qquad (4)$$

$$\mathbf{C} = 1/n \sum_{i=1}^{T} n_i * \mathbf{C}_i$$

where C_i is the variance-covariance matrix calculated from sample time period i,

T is the number of total sub-periods where the equality of matrices is tested, $n = n_1 + n_2 + ... + n_T$, and n_i = sample size in time period *i* minus 1.

Box derived that *M/b* is distributed approximately as an *F* distribution with f_1 and f_2 degrees of freedom.

$$D_1 = \frac{2 p^2 + 3p - 1}{6(p + 1)(T - 1)} \left[\sum_{i=1}^{T} \frac{1}{n_i} - \frac{1}{n} \right] \tag{5}$$

$$D_2 = \frac{(p - 1)(p + 2)}{6(T - 1)} \left[\sum_{i=1}^{T} \frac{1}{n_i^2} - \frac{1}{n^2} \right]$$

where $b = f_1 / (1 - D_1 - f_1 / f_2)$, $f_1 = p (p + 1) (T - 1) / 2$, p = number of variables (stocks) in the matrix, and $f_2 = (f_1 + 2) / (D_2 - D_1^2)$.

Test of Stability in Correlation Matrices

In testing the hypothesis of equal correlation matrices of stock returns, we employed an extension of Box's M test (Tang, 1995). The test procedures are described as follows: we directly apply Box's M test on the equality of correlation matrices by first transforming the raw data into standard scores for each time period before applying Box's M testing procedures. According to Tang, testing the hypothesis of equal variance-covariance matrices of these standardized returns by transforming raw returns into standard scores is equivalent to testing the hypothesis of equal correlation matrices of raw returns.

EMPIRICAL RESULTS

In our analysis, we test the stability of using HSIF contracts to hedge individual stocks with the following procedures. For any two adjacent time periods (in our sample, these periods refer to two adjacent index futures contract months), the hypothesis of equal correlation between returns of individual stocks and HSIF is tested for all 16 stocks. Those stocks that reject the hypothesis at least at the 10% level are excluded from further analysis. Our second stage of analysis is interested in whether those stocks that cannot reject the hypothesis have a stable variance/covariance or correlation matrix across the same time periods. Box's M tests are used in this stage for all pairs of adjacent index futures contract months. Because the whole sample period is divided into three subperiods, our empirical results are also presented in three parts.

Pre-crash Period

Table 5.1 presents the results in testing the hypothesis of equal correlation between HSIF and 16 stocks for all pairs of adjacent contract months from June 1986 to September 1987. Out of the possible 15 pairs of months, two pairs (9-10/86 and 7-8/87) show that all 16 stocks cannot reject the hypothesis of

Table 5.1. Test of Equal Correlation with Stock Index Futures
Between Two Adjacent Months for the Period 6/86-9/87

Stock			Adjacent Months		
	6-7/86	7-8/86	8-9/86	9-10/86	10-11/86
S1	-0.4487	1.2644	-0.4692	0.3577	-0.0353
S2	-0.5876	-0.8293	1.2725	-0.8246	-0.2526
S3	-0.6084	-0.1234	1.2586	-1.3649	0.6861
S4	-0.3689	-1.4235	1.2216	-0.2160	0.1074
S5	0.4929	-0.4025	-0.6762	-1.0257	-0.4255
S6	-2.3871*	-0.3842	1.2612	-1.1433	0.2901
S7	-0.9459	0.6972	-1.0218	-0.4222	-0.6320
S8	-1.1240	0.6198	-0.1154	-0.6524	0.9802
S9	-1.0438	0.0759	0.3195	0.0345	1.6323
S10	-2.0633*	1.8668+	-0.3466	-0.9338	-0.3460
S11	-1.9526+	0.5851	0.7419	0.5767	-3.1479#
S12	-0.5054	-1.7021+	1.0961	-1.0132	-0.4852
S13	0.9384	-2.5616*	2.1382*	-1.1780	-0.4615
S14	0.8705	0.5804	-1.7712+	-0.4661	-0.3372
S15	-0.4380	0.0932	-0.5713	0.6332	-1.7714+
S16	-0.4270	-0.6479	1.0434	-1.3958	0.5151

Stock			Adjacent Months		
	11-12/86	12/86-1/87	1-2/87	2-3/87	3-4/87
S1	0.6820	-1.1590	1.1006	-1.0012	0.3376
S2	0.0001	0.5260	-0.0058	0.6664	0.1022
S3	0.7775	-1.3984	1.8605+	-1.9592+	1.2865
S4	0.7708	-1.8307+	1.3895	-1.2228	0.7773
S5	1.9551+	-0.2607	-0.1671	-0.8364	2.0220*
S6	0.8955	0.6787	-0.9457	0.0900	1.3447
S7	1.4713	-0.0336	0.2876	-0.5725	0.7866
S8	0.2444	-0.3411	-0.2159	-0.5947	1.8575+
S9	-0.5215	-0.6556	1.5342	-1.2292	0.4117
S10	2.0094*	-1.5526	3.0467#	-2.2839*	1.0320
S11	4.5643#	-3.0509#	2.0667*	-1.9459+	1.1141
S12	2.0186*	-1.9306+	1.9353+	-0.4564	-0.2933
S13	0.8971	-1.0002	0.2325	-0.9677	1.8593+
S14	0.7738	-0.1922	0.9523	-0.3921	0.8829
S15	1.4324	-0.3303	1.2487	-1.7238+	0.3880
S16	-0.4546	0.7533	0.3701	-2.1326*	1.9566+

table continues . . .

Table 5.1. Continued

			Adjacent Months		
Stock	4-5/87	5-6/87	6-7/87	7-8/87	8-9/87
S1	1.2817	-1.7242	1.5239	-0.9424	-0.0385
S2	0.4017	-0.5763	0.7778	0.0287	0.5795
S3	1.1536	-0.7173	-0.9866	-0.2923	1.8314
S4	0.7385	-0.2750	-0.2868	0.4010	-0.5110
S5	0.7277	-0.0867	-2.1924*	1.2388	-0.7909
S6	-1.0379	-0.8304	0.5675	-0.1468	1.1254
S7	0.0201	-1.9554+	1.2775	0.2838	0.2835
S8	-0.0799	-1.5145	0.2182	0.4501	0.0554
S9	-0.4849	0.6251	-0.5286	0.4231	1.1271
S10	-0.8869	0.7984	-0.6557	0.0219	-0.0144
S11	0.5500	-1.3996	0.1254	0.4599	-1.0231
S12	2.2507*	-3.4555#	2.1390*	0.3647	-1.4540
S13	-0.5632	0.3704	-1.4166	1.3992	0.3351
S14	0.3989	-0.5659	-0.0497	0.2071	-0.3845
S15	0.9291	-1.2434	0.3358	1.6460+	-0.1989
S16	0.3342	0.8163	-0.8133	0.3390	-1.1775

Notes: All values are z values
          #significant at the 1% level
          *significant at the 5% level
          +significant at the 10% level

Code of stocks:

S1 = Cathay Pacific Airways Ltd.	S2 = Cheung Kong (Holdings) Ltd.
S3 = China Light & Power Co., Ltd.	S4 = Hong Kong Land Holdings Ltd.
S5 = Hong Kong Bank Ltd.	S6 = Hutchison Whampoa Ltd.
S7 = Jardine Matheson Holdings Ltd.	S8 = Wharf (Holdings) Ltd.
S9 = Sun Hung Kai Properties Ltd.	S10 = Swire Pacific Ltd. 'A'
S11 = New World Development Co., Ltd.	S12 = Henderson Land Development Co., Ltd.
S13 = Hong Kong Electric Holdings Ltd.	S14 = Hong Kong and Shanghai Hotels Ltd.
S15 = Hang Lung Development Co., Ltd.	S16 = Hang Seng Bank Ltd.

equal correlation with HSIF. For all the other pairs of months, there are usually three or four stocks which can reject the hypothesis at the 10% level. However, these stocks are not the same across the whole subperiod, suggesting that those stocks having unstable correlation with HSIF vary over time.

Table 5.2 presents the test results of the hypothesis of equal variance-covariance/correlation matrix between two adjacent index futures contract months for stocks with stable correlation with HSIF. The first conclusion drawn is that the correlation matrix is more stable than the variance-covariance matrix. Two-thirds of the 15 pairs of contract months reject the hypothesis of equal variance-covariance matrix at the 5% level. However, only one-fifth of the pairs

**Table 5.2. Test of Equal Covariance Matrices and Correlation Matrices
Across Adjacent Months for the Period 6/86-9/87**

Months	Covariance Matrix			Correlation Matrix		
	M	F	Prob>F	M	F	Prob>F
6/86-7/86	162.50	1.1302	0.1891	134.62	0.9363	0.6504
7/86-8/86	174.40	1.2130	0.0841	154.00	1.0711	0.3045
8/86-9/86	223.50	1.2447	0.0478*	200.89	1.1188	0.1944
9/86-10/86	346.34	1.3671	0.0034*	317.63	1.2538	0.0261*
10/86-11/86	239.66	1.3347	0.0136*	167.50	0.9328	0.6728
11/86-12/86	201.07	1.6647	0.0002*	135.99	1.1259	0.2120
12/86-1/87	234.27	1.5510	0.0007*	208.09	1.3777	0.0108*
1/87-2/87	128.51	1.0287	0.4102	124.78	0.9988	0.4822
2/87-3/87	137.85	1.4282	0.0135*	106.83	1.1069	0.2595
3/87-4/87	155.18	1.2778	0.0516	143.46	1.1813	0.1335
4/87-5/87	365.04	1.6390	0.0000*	340.46	1.5287	0.0002*
5/87-6/87	151.90	1.0272	0.4100	144.31	0.9759	0.5454
6/87-7/87	246.93	1.4199	0.0035*	203.20	1.1684	0.1176
7/87-8/87	281.90	1.3492	0.0073*	231.84	1.1096	0.1978
8/87-9/87	369.56	1.4526	0.0006*	302.11	1.1875	0.0706

Notes: M = Box's M statistic
F = F value (approx. for M)
*significant at the 5% level
Test of equality in covariance/correlation matrices is across all stocks that cannot reject the hypothesis of equal correlation with stock index futures.

can reject the hypothesis of equal correlation matrix at the 5% level. For those contract months that reject the hypothesis of equal variance-covariance matrix, the hypothesis of equal correlation is also rejected. Our results indicate that using historical correlation information in approximating the ex-ante correlation structure of stock returns is quite satisfactory in the precrash period. The results are much better than using historical information of variance-covariance matrix of stocks.

Postcrash Period

Table 5.3 presents the results in testing the hypothesis of equal correlation for pairs of index futures contract months from November 1987 to January 1989 and 14 pairs of contract months are possible. The results show that more stocks can reject the hypothesis of equal correlation in the first seven pairs of contract months than in the last seven pairs of months. For the period November 1987 to June 1988, there are usually three stocks which reject the hypothesis of equal correlation. However, from June 1988 to January 1989, only one stock in most pairs of contract months can reject the hypothesis. In fact, two pairs (6-7/88 and

Table 5.3. **Test of Equal Correlation with Stock Index Futures Between Two Adjacent Months for the Period 11/87-1/89**

Stock	11-12/87	12/87-1/88	Adjacent Months 1-2/88	2-3/88	3-4/88
S1	0.0706	-0.1608	-0.5388	1.1409	-2.2545*
S2	-0.5463	-1.6082	1.2942	0.2869	-1.7217+
S3	0.7542	-2.1478*	1.1273	-0.1059	0.1645
S4	-0.2874	-1.2584	0.2036	0.6531	-0.3665
S5	-0.6089	-1.0707	1.7350+	0.2658	-1.3024
S6	-0.9303	-1.4436	1.6774+	0.5315	-0.9219
S7	0.2092	-2.2756*	1.1107	0.2419	0.1540
S8	-1.8805+	0.0710	1.0143	0.5453	-1.5993
S9	-1.0490	-2.5592*	1.9062+	1.3505	-1.4511
S10	-0.4456	-0.6082	0.4232	0.2976	0.2011
S11	-0.6600	-1.2840	0.5632	0.9826	-0.9022
S12	0.4509	-1.5177	0.7460	0.8810	-1.5370
S13	-0.7747	0.2310	-0.2475	0.0410	1.4209
S14	0.0235	-0.2948	-0.7632	1.5958	-0.4589
S15	-0.9780	-1.0314	0.4542	1.0663	-0.5267
S16	-0.8570	0.2127	-0.7390	2.4614*	-2.0177*

Stock	4-5/88	5-6/88	Adjacent Months 6-7/88	7-8/88	8-9/88
S1	2.3786*	1.0325	-1.2238	0.7296	-1.9108+
S2	1.7734+	0.4161	-0.2203	-0.4287	0.0833
S3	0.5030	0.4500	-0.2793	-0.0628	-0.7332
S4	2.2973*	-2.1964*	0.7506	-1.0031	0.3909
S5	2.5086*	-0.7518	0.6407	-0.4560	-0.1102
S6	0.4060	0.5911	-0.0376	0.5179	-1.4776
S7	1.8015+	0.3134	-1.1243	-1.3275	0.9922
S8	0.2256	2.4138*	-1.4067	1.0947	-0.5239
S9	0.4960	1.1207	-0.0964	2.1143*	-3.0637#
S10	0.1117	0.7985	-0.7491	0.6155	-0.0833
S11	0.4223	0.8960	-0.3504	-0.0327	-0.3841
S12	0.0924	0.8648	0.5788	0.3594	-1.3469
S13	-0.6324	0.1915	-0.8562	0.5186	0.1859
S14	0.1816	0.1740	0.6710	-1.0349	1.1520
S15	-0.2475	1.7584+	-1.1116	1.1291	-0.6511
S16	1.8297+	-1.3369	0.0544	-0.2226	0.8923

table continues . . .

Table 5.3. Continued

Stock	Adjacent Months			
	9-10/88	10-11/88	11-12/88	12/88-1/89
S1	0.2479	0.8460	0.4947	-1.4378
S2	-1.7682+	1.8307+	0.7090	-0.3270
S3	0.5191	1.0610	-0.1550	0.3177
S4	-0.8602	1.2776	1.0767	-0.3530
S5	-1.6022	1.3921	-0.0511	-0.2715
S6	-0.3544	1.4713	-0.3709	-0.4624
S7	-0.3447	1.3393	0.0059	-0.7787
S8	-0.7512	0.4306	1.1525	-0.0696
S9	0.3587	0.5438	0.6948	-0.6439
S10	-0.1124	0.7649	0.0041	-0.6898
S11	-0.7012	0.1378	2.0591*	-1.1922
S12	-0.4875	1.3068	-0.0896	-0.4924
S13	-0.5735	1.3685	-0.7733	-0.8886
S14	0.8974	0.8709	-0.7714	-0.9483
S15	-0.6972	0.7933	0.4027	-0.1676
S16	-0.9275	1.5480	-0.1510	0.1987

Notes: All values are z values. For code of stocks, see notes to Table 5.1.
#significant at the 1% level
*significant at the 5% level
+significant at the 10% level

12/88-1/89) show that all 16 stocks cannot reject the hypothesis of equal correlation with HSIF. Although those stocks having unstable correlation with HSIF are not the same across the whole subperiod, as in the case of the precrash period, they are quite consistent across two groups of contract months for a few stocks. The results suggest that these 16 stocks have a more stable relationship with HSIF in this subperiod.

Table 5.4 presents the test results of the hypothesis of equal variance-covariance/correlation matrix between two adjacent index futures contract months for stocks having a stable correlation with HSIF. Again, the correlation matrix is more stable than the variance-covariance matrix. Three-sevenths and one-seventh of the 14 pairs of contract months reject the hypothesis of equal variance-covariance matrix and of equal correlation, respectively, at the 5% level.

Using historical correlation information in approximating the ex-ante correlation structure of stock returns is more fruitful in the postcrash period than in the precrash period. This is particularly true for the period June 1988 to January 1989, as both the correlation between the 16 stocks and HSIF and the correlation matrix among individual stocks are very stable over time, indicating the ex-ante hedging performance would be very effective. The result may be

**Table 5.4. Test of Equal Covariance Matrices and Correlation Matrices
Across Adjacent Months for the Period 11/87-1/89**

Months	Covariance Matrix			Correlation Matrix		
	M	F	Prob>F	M	F	Prob>F
11/87-12/87	302.29	1.4566	0.0010*	262.13	1.2631	0.0290*
12/87-1/88	199.22	1.3677	0.0123*	154.78	1.0626	0.3238
1/88-2/88	185.59	1.1776	0.1222	167.82	1.0648	0.3193
2/88-3/88	303.74	1.3665	0.0055*	284.53	1.2801	0.0229*
3/88-4/88	172.84	1.1465	0.1639	148.88	0.9876	0.5141
4/88-5/88	92.38	1.1616	0.1947	63.00	0.7921	0.8656
5/88-6/88	166.53	1.1642	0.1381	167.57	1.1715	0.1288
6/88-7/88	235.47	0.9295	0.7083	202.92	0.8010	0.9557
7/88-8/88	221.95	1.0695	0.2875	199.30	0.9603	0.6049
8/88-9/88	245.27	1.4187	0.0035*	212.73	1.2304	0.0570
9/88-10/88	237.83	1.0978	0.2223	194.07	0.8958	0.7835
10/88-11/88	269.82	1.2701	0.0263*	199.02	0.9368	0.6745
11/88-12/88	279.89	1.3174	0.0125*	249.56	1.1747	0.0963
12/88-1/89	308.50	1.1860	0.0721	266.63	1.0250	0.4052

Notes: M = Box's M statistic
         F = F value (approx. for M)
         *significant at the 5% level
         Test of equality in covariance/correlation matrices is across all stocks that cannot reject the
         hypothesis of equal correlation with stock index futures.

because the period was in recovery after the stock crash in October 1987. Small investors were out of the market, leaving institutional and/or knowledgeable investors. These investors utilized all available information, including information of both market and individual companies, in stock valuation and effectively used the index futures contracts as hedging tools. Hence, stock relationships with HSIF and among themselves are relatively more stable during this period.

Even-Months Contracts Period

Starting from February 1989, the index futures contracts traded on the Hong Kong Futures Exchange changed from spot-month to even-months contracts. Hence, unlike in the precrash and postcrash periods, test of stability in relationships between stocks and HSIF is carried out on a bimonthly (i.e., even-months index futures contract) basis.

Table 5.5 presents the results in testing the hypothesis of equal correlation between HSIF and individual stocks for pairs of bimonths from January 1989 to August 1990. In this subperiod, only nine pairs of bimonths of index futures contract are possible. The results show that correlation between HSIF and the 16 stocks are very unstable across two adjacent bimonths' periods. In fact, all 16

Table 5.5. Test of Equal Correlation with Stock Index Futures Between Two Adjacent Bimonths for the Period 1/89-8/90

Stock	2-4/89	4-6/89	6-8/89	8-10/89	10-12/89
			Adjacent Bimonths		
S1	1.1399	-4.1735#	4.1135#	-1.0431	2.6087*
S2	0.1255	-4.5002#	4.4852#	-0.4542	2.4619*
S3	1.8356+	-3.7780#	3.8966#	-2.4968*	4.2451#
S4	0.1780	-2.6580*	2.9228#	-0.3236	2.3149*
S5	1.2588	-4.6011#	5.3497#	-1.0867	1.1363
S6	-0.6110	-4.9409#	4.1618#	-1.0547	2.2969*
S7	0.7088	-4.4194#	3.4124#	-0.3636	1.8446+
S8	-0.0066	-5.6357#	5.4159#	-1.5396	2.1703*
S9	-0.2047	-4.1536#	4.3809#	-0.0406	2.5988*
S10	2.3688*	-5.1401#	3.2771#	-1.2511	3.2460#
S11	1.5511	-4.4747#	2.5686*	-1.1875	3.6492#
S12	0.1693	-4.7764#	3.8683#	-1.3554	3.0262#
S13	2.5660*	-3.7999#	4.1839#	-1.9944*	2.3899*
S14	1.5331	-5.6220#	5.0050#	-2.4879*	4.0275#
S15	1.6743	-5.4607#	3.8900#	-0.9078	4.1040#
S16	2.7206#	-4.7686#	4.0577#	-1.5805	2.3488*

Stock	12/89-2/90	2-4/90	4-6/90	6-8/90
		Adjacent Months		
S1	-2.7598#	2.2333*	-1.3135	-0.7801
S2	-1.8478+	1.4586	-0.0772	-1.5780
S3	-1.5255	1.0600	1.1691	-4.4147#
S4	-1.4211	1.4192	0.7839	-3.1739#
S5	-2.1938*	4.3531#	-0.7597	-3.4380#
S6	-0.4032	1.2204	0.3741	-0.9744
S7	-0.8518	1.7749	0.7064	-2.7924#
S8	-0.8086	0.4859	2.3107*	-2.3056*
S9	-1.5487	1.6832+	-0.0721	-2.5602*
S10	-0.0590	0.0553	1.2768	-3.8023#
S11	-3.2683#	3.1191#	1.3048	-3.3014#
S12	-0.9464	1.5712	0.2057	-1.7271+
S13	-1.1911	1.0061	0.7214	-3.8992#
S14	-3.2481#	3.9014#	-1.6385	-1.4799
S15	-4.1309#	3.5437#	1.2267	-3.9494#
S16	-1.3757	3.2228#	-1.2864	-3.3929#

Notes: All values are z values. For code of stocks, see notes to Table 5.1.
#significant at the 1% level
*significant at the 5% level
+significant at the 10% level

stocks in three pairs of bimonths (4-6/89, 6-8/89, and 10-12/89) reject the hypothesis of equal correlation with HSIF at the 5% level. In the remaining six pairs of bimonths, only three pairs (2-4/89, 8-10/89, and 4-6/90) show a high degree of stability in correlation between most of the stocks and HSIF. The results suggest that it is very difficult to have stocks that are intertemporally stable with HSIF during this subperiod. Hence, using past information on correlation between stocks and HSIF in hedging stock portfolios may be very ineffective in this even-months' contracts period.

Table 5.6 presents the test results of the hypothesis of equal variance-covariance/correlation matrix between two adjacent bimonths for stocks with stable correlation with HSIF. However, for the three pairs of bimonths with all stocks having unstable relationships with HSIF, the tests of equality in variance-covariance and in correlation matrices are carried out across all 16 stocks. The results show that the correlation matrix is more stable than the variance-covariance matrix. Two-thirds and one-third of the nine pairs of bimonths reject the hypothesis of equal variance-covariance matrix and of equal correlation, respectively, at the 5% level. However, the three pairs of bi-months which reject the hypothesis of equal correlation matrix are those in which all 16 stocks are unstably related to HSIF. Hence, in these 3 pairs of bi-months periods, both the stock market and the index futures market are intertemporally unstable. The reason is quite obvious. China's June 4 event happened in June 1989. Because the Hong Kong financial market is closely related to the political situation in China, the June 4 Tiananmen Square event had a great impact on Hong Kong

Table 5.6. Test of Equal Covariance Matrices and Correlation Matrices Across Adjacent Months for the Period 1/89-8/90

Months	Covariance Matrix			Correlation Matrix		
	M	F	Prob>F	M	F	Prob>F
2/89-4/89	119.47	1.2673	0.0561	101.41	1.0757	0.3039
4/89-6/89	351.44	2.0268	0.0000*	723.61	4.1732	0.0000*
6/89-8/89	340.92	1.9878	0.0000*	627.54	3.6589	0.0000*
8/89-10/89	118.96	1.0817	0.2796	97.67	0.8881	0.7685
10/89-12/89	240.14	1.3808	0.0023*	289.98	1.6673	0.0000*
12/89-2/90	96.36	1.5101	0.0087*	62.52	0.9797	0.5174
2/90-4/90	56.93	1.4038	0.0549	45.88	1.1314	0.2703
4/90-6/90	210.63	1.3963	0.0028*	179.81	1.1920	0.0751
6/90-8/90	30.64	2.8938	0.0013*	9.48	0.8957	0.5361

Notes: M = Box's M statistic
F = F value (approx. for M)
*significant at the 5% level
Test of equality in covariance/correlation matrices is across all stocks that cannot reject the hypothesis of equal correlation with stock index futures.
For the three periods 4/89-6/89, 6/89-8/89, and 10/89-12/89, the test of equality is across all 16 stocks.

stock and index futures markets. The markets not only become more volatile, but also became intertemporally unstable in the correlation structure among stocks and between stocks with HSIF.

Using historical correlation information in approximating the ex-ante correlation structure of stock returns is useless in these three pairs of bimonths' periods. However, in the remaining six pairs of bimonths, all of them cannot reject the hypothesis of equal correlation structure. Hence, using ex-post correlation information in estimating the ex-ante correlation structure is still acceptable in these periods, although the choice of stocks that have a stable relationship with HSIF in the same periods is limited. The Gulf War crisis, which happened in 1990-91, is believed to be the cause of most stocks (see Table 5.5) having an unstable relationship intertemporally with HSIF during the latter part of our even-months' contracts sample period.

CONCLUSIONS

This study provides a first attempt to examine the intertemporal stability in (1) relationships between returns of individual stocks and that of the Hang Seng Index Futures, and (2) variance-covariance and correlation matrices among individual stocks, across adjacent index futures contract months. The study is important and interesting because the ex-ante hedging performance and effectiveness with index futures contracts would depend on the stability in the relationships among stocks and with index futures across different time periods. Our findings show that the variance-covariance structure of stock returns is less stable than the correlation structure, suggesting that ex-post correlation rather than variance-covariance information should be used to approximate the ex-ante comovement structure of stock returns in forming stock portfolios.

Our empirical results show that most stocks in our sample have a stable relationship with HSIF across two adjacent index futures contract months in the precrash and postcrash periods. During the even-months' contracts period, very few stocks show a stable relationship with HSIF intertemporally due to the China's June 4 event in 1989 and the Gulf War crisis in 1990-91. However, the correlation structure among those stocks with stable relationship with HSIF is intertemporally stable across most pairs of index futures contract months, particularly in the postcrash period. Our results suggest that using ex-post correlation structure to form ex-ante stock portfolios and hedge them with HSIF is acceptable except in some periods with political crises.

REFERENCES

Box, G.E.P., 1949. A general distribution theory for a class of likelihood criteria, *Biometrika* 36, 317-346.

Datastream online data service. Dun & Bradstreet.

Figlewski, S., 1984. Hedging performance and basis risk in stock index futures, *Journal of Finance* 39, 657-669.

Junkus, J.C. and C.F. Lee, 1985. Use of three stock index futures in hedging decisions, *Journal of Futures Markets* 5, 201-222.

Lam, K. and P.L.H. Yu, 1992. Hedging performance of the Hang Seng Index Futures Contract, *Review of Futures Markets* 11, 447-465.

Maldonado, R. and A. Saunders, 1981. International portfolio diversification and the intertemporal stability of international stock market relationships, 1957-78, *Financial Management* 10, 54-63.

Meric, I. and G. Meric, 1989. Potential gains from international portfolio diversification and intertemporal stability and seasonality in international stock market relationships, *Journal of Banking and Finance* 13, 627-640.

Stein, J.L., 1961. The simultaneous determination of spot and futures prices, *American Economic Review* 51, 1012-1025.

Tang, Gordon Y.N., 1995. Intertemporal stability in international stock market relationships: a revisit, *Quarterly Review of Economics and Finance* 35, 579-593.

Yau, J., J. Hill, and T. Schneeweis, 1990. An analysis of the effectiveness of the Nikkei 225 futures contracts in risk-return management, *Global Finance Journal* 1, 255-276.

6

International Diversification of U.S. Portfolios with Segmented Markets

Philip Fanara, Jr., Sandip Mukherji, and Yong H. Kim

INTRODUCTION

In a recent paper, Sinquefield (1996) questions whether U.S. portfolios can benefit from diversification with international equities. He presents empirical evidence that the Europe, Australia, Far East (EAFE) Index of Morgan Stanley Capital International does not have higher returns or lower risk than the S&P 500 Index during 1970-94. Further, returns on the EAFE and S&P 500 Indexes are strongly positively correlated. The author concludes that U.S. portfolios do not gain from geographical diversification with foreign equity portfolios. He also shows that international value stocks and small stocks provide more efficient diversification for U.S. portfolios than the EAFE Index.

The EAFE Index comprises 22 of the largest and most developed stock markets outside the United States. As Sinquefield acknowledges, the EAFE Index represents integrated markets; segmented markets may yield different results. Further, U.S. stock returns may be more integrated with returns on a broad international index of several markets, such as the EAFE, than with narrower indexes of individual countries. In addition, both the EAFE and S&P 500 are value-weighted indexes that give more weight to larger capitalization stocks. Larger companies are more likely to have international business, be listed in foreign markets, and have foreign shareholders. Returns on their stocks should therefore be more closely integrated internationally than returns on average stocks. Diversification benefits may be more apparent with equally weighted individual-country indexes than with broad value-weighted indexes dominated by large companies from developed markets.

We investigate whether equally weighted equity portfolios from relatively segmented foreign markets offer diversification benefits for U.S. portfolios.[1] Our study involves two large Pacific-Basin markets, Japan and Korea, which are not well integrated with the U.S. market and have data on stock returns and exchange rates available for a reasonably long period.[2] We find that combining U.S. port-folios with Japanese and Korean portfolios increases returns and reduces risk, resulting in substantial decreases in the coefficient of variation during 1978-89.

EVIDENCE AND IMPLICATIONS OF MARKET SEGMENTATION

Stock markets in different countries may be segmented because of the follow-ing factors:

1. investment barriers, such as taxes, transaction costs, and restrictions on foreign owner-ship of stocks;

2. heterogeneous expectations of investors regarding inflation and exchange rate risks in different countries; and

3. different degrees of risk aversion, based on social factors.

Harvey (1991) tests whether conditional versions of the Capital Asset Pricing Model (CAPM) are consistent with the behavior of returns in 17 countries. He finds that there are wide variations in reward-to-risk ratios across countries and time-varying covariances do not capture all of the dynamic behavior of the country returns, suggesting that either financial markets are not perfectly integrated or the asset pricing model is misspecified.

Harvey's results also show that for risk-averse investors, the U.S. stock portfolio is unconditionally dominated by the world market portfolio, which has a lower standard deviation and higher expected return. This indicates that U.S. inves-tors should benefit from international diversification. In addition, Harvey presents evidence that the price of risk may be higher in Japan, suggesting that U.S. inves-tors, being relatively less risk-averse, may gain from investing in Japan.

Arbitrage Pricing Theory (APT) may be more suitable for international asset pricing than the CAPM, because it can incorporate the additional risk factors related to international investing. An empirical study by Cho, Eun, and Senbet (1986), however, rejects the joint hypotheses that the international capital market is integrated and the APT is internationally valid.

In segmented markets, countries with more risk-averse investors may have higher risk premiums than countries with less risk-averse investors. U.S. investors may therefore boost portfolio performance by investing in segmented markets where investors are relatively more risk-averse. The results of Harvey (1991) indi-cate that the Japanese stock market was largely segmented from the U.S. market during 1970-89. Cheung and Lee (1993) provide evidence that the Korean stock market was completely segmented, by showing that Korean investors were re-warded for bearing only domestic risk during the 1982-89 period.

The evidence of segmentation of the Japanese and Korean markets may reflect restrictions on foreign ownership of equity and limited participation by foreigners in these markets. Japan restricts equity purchases by foreigners in certain selected industries and firms considered to be in the national interest. Before 1992, foreigners could invest in Korean stocks only through mutual funds and closed-end investment companies. During our study period, foreign ownership of listed stocks ranged between 2.3% and 6.3% in Japan (Tokyo Stock Exchange, 1995: 109) and from 1.3% to 3.3% in Korea (Korea Stock Exchange, 1992: 80).

RESEARCH DESIGN

We obtained the data for Japan and Korea from the Pacific-Basin Capital Markets (PACAP) Databases compiled by the PACAP Research Center at the University of Rhode Island. The U.S. data are from the University of Chicago's Center for Research in Security Prices (CRSP) tapes. Our study covers a 12-year period, from January 1978 through December 1989, because data for Japan and Korea were available for this period.

We used the monthly returns, with dividends reinvested, on the equally weighted indexes of the Korea Stock Exchange (KSE), Tokyo Stock Exchange (TSE), and New York and American Stock Exchanges (NYSE/AMEX). From the won/dollar and yen/dollar exchange rates at the end of each month, we also computed the monthly percentage changes in dollar/won and dollar/yen exchange rates. For the foreign markets, the monthly returns in foreign currencies are converted to dollar returns by using the formula:

$$r_d = (1 + r_f)(1 + e_d) - 1$$

where r_d is the percentage return in dollars, r_f is the percentage return in the foreign currency, and e_d is the percentage change in the spot exchange rate of the dollar per unit of the foreign currency.

We investigate international diversification benefits from the perspective of an investor holding a portfolio of U.S. equities. In calculating the returns of U.S. investors in dollars, we assume that they do not hedge exchange rate risk. We examine unconditional returns and risk because tests using asset pricing models have several problems:

1. the practical problems of measuring such variables as the return on the market portfolio and the risk-free rate are more severe in an international context;

2. the results cannot be interpreted unambiguously because the tests involve joint hypotheses that the model is valid and it is correctly specified; and

3. the models are not valid across segmented markets.

First, we report correlations between the returns in terms of the foreign currencies as well as dollars. Next, we conduct regressions with the foreign markets' returns as dependent variables and U.S. returns as the independent variable. Finally, we examine the means, standard deviations, and coefficients of variation of returns in the three markets and equally weighted portfolios of these markets.

EMPIRICAL RESULTS

Table 6.1 shows that there are weak correlations between U.S. stock returns in dollars and Korean stock returns in terms of both won (0.17) and dollars (0.18). U.S. stock returns have a moderate correlation with Japanese stock returns in yen (0.38), but a weak correlation with Japanese stock returns in dollars (0.19). These results are in sharp contrast to the findings of Sinquefield (1996) that returns on the S&P 500 Index have correlations of 0.70 and 0.57 with returns on the EAFE Index in foreign currencies and dollars, respectively. Clearly, the U.S. stock market is less integrated with the Korean and Japanese markets than with the combined EAFE markets.

Stock returns in local currencies and dollars are more strongly positively correlated in Korea (0.92) than in Japan (0.72), indicating that the won was relatively more stable in terms of the dollar, compared to the yen. Our data show that, during the test period, the dollar/won rate rose by an average of 0.25% per month, while the dollar/yen rate fell by 0.43% per month. The Korean and Japanese stock returns in local currencies have a moderate positive correlation (0.31). Changes in the dollar/won and dollar/yen rates, however, have a negative correlation (-0.42). As a result, the correlation between Korean and Japanese stock returns in dollars (0.13) is not significant at the 5% level. Overall, these results indicate that the United States, Korean, and Japanese stock markets were not well integrated with each other during the study period, particularly in terms of dollar returns.

In Table 6.2, regressions using returns in local currencies show that the betas of U.S. returns for Korea (0.20) and Japan (0.24) are significant at the 5% and 1% levels, respectively. This one-factor model explains 13.69% of the variations in Japanese stock returns, but only 2.10% of variations in Korean stock returns. In relation to the United States, the Korean stock market is therefore more segmented than the Japanese market. The alphas for Korea (1.69%) and Japan (1.65%) are both significant at the 1% level.

Table 6.1.   Correlations Between Monthly Returns on Equally Weighted Indexes of U.S., Japanese, and Korean Stocks, in Local Currencies and U.S. Dollars During 1978-89

	U.S. ($)	Korea (Won)	Japan (Yen)	Korea ($)
Korean (Won)	0.17*			
Japan (Yen)	0.38**	0.31**		
Korea ($)	0.18*	0.92**	0.30**	
Japan ($)	0.19*	0.25**	0.72**	0.13

*Significant at 5% level.
**Significant at 1% level.

Table 6.2. Regressions of Monthly Returns on Equally Weighted Indexes of Japanese and Korean Stocks Against Monthly Returns on Equally Weighted Index of U.S. Stocks During 1978-89

Country	Alpha	Beta	Adjusted R^2
	Returns in Local Currencies		
Korea	0.0169**	0.2003*	0.0210
	(2.99)	(2.02)	(0.0458)
Japan	0.0165**	0.2438**	0.1369
	(5.81)	(4.87)	(0.0000)
	Returns in U.S. Dollars		
Korea	0.0138*	0.2426*	0.0258
	(2.20)	(2.19)	(0.0302)
Japan	0.0218**	0.1910*	0.0305
	(4.72)	(2.35)	(0.0204)

t-statistics are shown in parentheses below the alpha and beta estimates. Significance levels for the regressions are given in parentheses below the adjusted R^2 values.
*Significant at 5% level.
**Significant at 1% level.

When stock returns in dollars are used as the dependent variable, the beta and adjusted R^2 increase slightly, while the alpha decreases, for Korea. In the regression for Japan, the beta decreases, adjusted R^2 falls dramatically, and alpha increases. For both Korea and Japan, the betas are significant at the 5% level. The adjusted R^2s, however, are only 2.58% for Korea and 3.05% for Japan. The alpha is significant at the 5% level for Korea and 1% level for Japan.

These regression results show that U.S. stock returns had statistically significant, but weak, explanatory power for Korean and Japanese stock returns. The significant alphas indicate that both Korean and Japanese stocks earned positive returns after controlling for the influence of U.S. returns.

In Table 6.3, the returns in local currencies are highest for Japan (2.03%), followed by Korea (2.00%) and the United States (1.55%). The standard deviation of returns is highest for Korea (6.58%), followed by the United States (5.48%), and Japan (3.53%). The combination of high returns and low risk results in a very low coefficient of variation (CV) of 1.74 for Japan. The CV for Korea (3.29) is slightly lower than that of the United States (3.54). Portfolios combining U.S. stocks with foreign stocks have higher returns and lower risk, resulting in substantially lower CV, compared to U.S. stocks alone. The CV of equally weighted portfolios of U.S. and Korean stocks (2.61), U.S. and Japanese stocks (2.11), and U.S., Korean, and Japanese stocks (2.02) are all considerably lower than that of U.S. stocks (3.54).

Compared to the stock returns in local currencies, the stock returns in dollars are higher for Japan and lower for Korea. Appreciation of the yen increases Japanese stock returns, whereas depreciation of the won reduces Korean stock

66 *Emerging Capital Markets*

Table 6.3. Comparison of Percentage Monthly Returns on Equally Weighted Indexes of U.S., Japanese and Korean Stocks, and Equally Weighted Portfolios of These Indexes During 1978-89

Country/ Portfolio	Mean (%)	Standard Deviation (%)	Coefficient of Variation
Returns in Local Currencies			
U.S.	1.55	5.48	3.54
Korea	2.00	6.58	3.29
Japan	2.03	3.53	1.74
U.S. and Korea	1.77	4.62	2.61
U.S. and Japan	1.79	3.78	2.11
U.S., Korea, and Japan	1.86	3.75	2.02
Returns in U.S. Dollars			
U.S.	1.55	5.48	3.54
Korea	1.76	7.35	4.18
Japan	2.48	5.42	2.19
U.S. and Korea	1.65	4.97	3.01
U.S. and Japan	2.01	4.21	2.09
U.S., Korea, and Japan	1.93	4.08	2.11

returns. The performance ranks of the three markets, however, remain the same, with Japan earning the highest dollar return (2.48%), followed by Korea (1.76%) and the United States (1.55%).

Owing to the additional risk of exchange-rate fluctuations, the standard deviation of returns is higher for dollar returns, compared to returns in local currencies. The increase in risk is more marked for Japan than Korea, reflecting the fact that the dollar rate was more volatile for the yen than the won. Our data indicate that the variance of Japanese stock returns in yen accounts for only 42% of the variance in Japanese stock returns in dollars. The remaining 58% is due to the variance of exchange rate changes and the covariance of exchange rate changes with stock returns in yen. By contrast, the variance of Korean stock returns in won comprises 80% of the variance in Korean stock returns in dollars and only 20% is due to the variance of exchange rate changes and the covariance of exchange rate changes with stock returns in won.

The additional exchange rate risk makes the standard deviation of dollar returns in Japan almost as high as those of the United States. The increased return in terms of dollars, however, keeps the CV for Japan well below that for the United States. In the case of Korea, conversion into dollars reduces returns and increases risk, raising its CV above that for the United States. Combining U.S. stocks separately into equally weighted portfolios with Korean and Japanese stocks, however, reduces the CV by 15% and 41%, respectively. The CV of the equally weighted portfolio combining all three markets is 40% lower than that of the United States.

Our results show that Japanese stocks dominated U.S. stocks, with a lower standard deviation and higher return. Between U.S. and Korean stocks, neither dominated. The portfolio combining U.S. and Korean stocks, however, dominated the portfolio of U.S. stocks.

As Sinquefield (1996) observes, dividend withholding taxes in foreign countries reduce returns for U.S. investors, particularly those who are tax-exempt and do not have taxable income against which to offset foreign taxes. Both Korea and Japan have bilateral tax treaties with the United States, under which dividends paid to U.S. investors are subjected to a 15% withholding tax, compared to rates of 20% (Japan) and 25% (Korea) for investors from other countries. However, Japanese and Korean stocks carry fairly low dividend yields. The average dividend yield declined steadily from 1.60% in 1978 to 0.47% in 1989 for Japanese stocks (Tokyo Stock Exchange, 1995: 108). Data available for Korean stocks show that the average dividend yield declined from 8.6% in 1982 to 2.0% in 1989 (Korea Stock Exchange, 1992: 78). Most of the returns on stocks in these countries are therefore in the form of capital gains. The tax treaty exempts U.S. investors from capital gains tax in Korea. In Japan, only those capital gains obtained from frequent and large transactions were taxed during the study period. Most U.S. investors who were not tax-exempt would therefore have paid lower taxes overall on equity investments in Korea and Japan.

SUMMARY AND CONCLUSIONS

Sinquefield (1996) has shown that U.S. stock portfolios cannot be efficiently diversified with the EAFE Index, a stock portfolio representing markets that are well integrated the United States. However, he observes that country-specific portfolios from segmented markets may yield different results. We empirically investigate whether U.S. stock portfolios could have benefited from diversification with the Korean and Japanese stock markets, which were largely segmented from the U.S. market.

Our results show that, during 1978-89, Korean and Japanese stock returns had weak correlations with U.S. stock returns. Further, U.S. stock returns had very low explanatory power for stock returns in Korea and Japan; and in both these countries, stocks earned significant positive returns after controlling for the influence of U.S. stock returns. Finally, the coefficient of variation is lower for portfolios combining U.S. stocks with Korean and Japanese stocks, both separately and together, compared to a portfolio of U.S. stocks alone.

These findings indicate that U.S. stock portfolios can benefit from diversification with stocks from markets that are not well integrated with the U.S. market. Our results do not imply that U.S. portfolios will gain from diversification specifically with the Japanese and Korean markets in the future. However, they illustrate that potential diversification benefits are likely to be found in segmented markets, especially if investors in those markets are more risk-averse than domestic investors.

NOTES

1. The fact that a market is segmented does not necessarily imply that it offers diversification benefits. Whether such benefits actually exist is an empirical issue influenced by several factors, such as degrees of risk aversion, exchange rate changes, and standard deviations and correlations of returns as well as exchange rate changes.

2. Japan has the largest stock market outside the United States and Korea had the tenth-largest stock market in the world at the end of 1989 (see Caires and Fletter, 1990). As discussed in the next section, however, both these markets were segmented from the United States during our study period owing to low participation by foreign investors.

ACKNOWLEDGMENTS

The authors thank Manjeet S. Dhatt for his help and useful comments. Fanara received support from a summer research grant from Howard University's School of Business. Kim received partial funding from the George Scull Fund through the University of Cincinnati Foundation.

REFERENCES

Caires, B. de and D. Fletter, 1990. *Guide to World Equity Markets*. London: Euromoney Publications.

Cheung, C. Sherman and Jason Lee, 1993. Integration vs. segmentation in the Korean stock market, *Journal of Business Finance and Accounting* 20, 267-273.

Cho, D. Chinhyung, Cheol S. Eun, and Lemma W. Senbet, 1986. International arbitrage pricing theory: an empirical investigation, *Journal of Finance* 41, 313-330.

Harvey, Campbell R., 1991. The world price of covariance risk, *Journal of Finance* 46, 111-158.

Korea Stock Exchange, 1992. Fact Book.

Sinquefield, Rex A., 1996. Where are the gains from international diversification? *Financial Analysts Journal* 52, 8-14.

Tokyo Stock Exchange, 1995. Fact Book.

PART III

Foreign Exchange and International Investments

7

Parity Relationships and Investment Risks in Emerging Markets

Arvind K. Jain

Foreign investments, direct as well as portfolio, have played an important role in the rapid growth of emerging economies over the past two decades. In turn, these economies have become important areas of growth for international firms. Firms invest in these economies to serve domestic markets as well as to source products for global markets. Of the many risks associated with these investments, especially for investments in assets whose production is destined for international markets, none would appear to be as volatile as the risk arising from changes in exchange rates. The volatility of exchange rates has increased steadily since the advent of the floating-rates system in 1973, which brought about large fluctuations in the values of investments in various currencies. Exchange-rate changes influence the values of investments by changing the relative prices between various markets and by changing the relative costs of inputs, real as well as financial, used by firms. In spite of its importance, there has been no systematic study of how changes in exchange rates have influenced investments in the past. This chapter attempts to fill this gap.

Exchange-rate changes create risks for firms when these changes do not conform to known relationships between economic variables. Changes in real exchange rates—that is, nominal rates corrected for inflation differentials between countries—may, for example, change a country's competitiveness against other countries. If the real exchange rate of a country rises, its goods become more expensive in international markets, making it more difficult for firms that produce in that country to sell their output abroad. Similarly unexpected changes in exchange rates will cause the relative costs of debt denominated in the two currencies to become unequal. Such unexpected changes in the exchange rates imply deviations from the relationship stipulated by the interest rate parity theorem. The seriousness of these effects on the costs of traded goods or of debt will depend upon whether these changes are random and unpredictable or systematic and predictable.

Firms that make international investments are affected by the frequency and extent of deviations of exchange rates from their equilibrium relationships. When the changes are infrequent and small, firms may be able to ignore or "ride out" these changes. It is, however, difficult for firms to ignore large and frequent fluctuations. Theory provides little guidance as to the nature of these deviations. Which currencies will go through large deviations and which through small ones is largely an empirical question. This chapter is an attempt to quantify the behavior of changes in the exchange rates of selected emerging economies since the advent of the floating-rates period in order to better understand the currency risks associated with direct investment in these markets. The research is based on the premise that only certain types of exchange-rate changes are sources of risk for investors and on the assumption that the past behavior of exchange rates can serve as a guide to their future behavior.

We begin by looking at the patterns of actual changes in the exchange rates. These changes are then broken down into expected and unexpected changes on the basis of the purchasing power parity (PPP) relationship. We test the extent to which the exchange rates have followed the PPP theory for these currencies. The interest rate parity theorem provides the basis for examining the nature of unexpected changes. We test whether movements in exchange rates have allowed unexploited opportunities for interest arbitrage to exist.

This research focuses on the behavior of the exchange rates of 14 emerging countries which can be broken down into four groups. These countries include two Latin American countries: Chile and Mexico; three South Asian countries: Bangladesh, India, and Pakistan; five far-eastern Asian countries: Indonesia, South Korea, Malaysia, the Philippines, and Thailand; and four other countries: Greece, Portugal, South Africa, and Turkey. Although we analyzed data for Argentina and Brazil as well, results for those two countries are not included here since the periods of hyperinflation in those countries make comparisons with other emerging countries meaningless. To avoid making conclusions based on changes in the value of emerging countries' currency against only one currency, say the US dollar, this analysis was carried out for the values of emerging market currencies against four currencies in the Organization for Economic Cooperation and Development (OECD): the U.S. dollar, the Japanese yen, the German mark, and the British pound.

PAST PATTERNS OF CHANGES IN THE EXCHANGE RATES

It is well known that exchange rates have become more volatile since generalized floating was introduced in 1973. Currencies of emerging countries have not been immune to this increased volatility. The volatility of a currency's value can be measured by its coefficient of variation, which is the ratio of the standard deviation to the mean value of the currency over the measurement period. Table 7.1 summarizes the coefficients of variation for quarterly changes in the values of exchange rates for the floating and the fixed exchange-rate periods as well as the ratio of these coefficients for the two periods. Under each OECD

Table 7.1. Volatility of Exchange Rates: Comparison of Coefficients of Variation

Against →	US$			Yen			DM			UK £		
Currency of ↓	Coefficients of Variation During fixed and floating rates periods and their ratio											
Greece	–	2.5	–	–	1.6	–	4.1	1.4	0.3	7.3	1.8	0.2
Portugal	–	5.2	–	–	2.4	–	4.3	1.8	0.4	7.6	3.9	0.5
South Africa	–	2.7	–	–	2.2	–	4.3	2.3	0.5	6.2	0.8	0.1
Turkey	5.8	0.7	0.1	5.8	0.8	0.1	5.5	0.7	0.1	6.2	0.8	0.1
Chile	3.1	1.5	0.5	3.1	1.7	0.6	3.0	2.0	0.7	3.2	2.2	0.7
Mexico	–	1.4	–	–	1.6	–	4.1	1.7	0.4	7.3	1.7	0.2
Bangladesh	–	1.6	–	–	2.6	–	–	3.4	–	–	5.6	–
India	7.4	1.8	0.2	7.3	1.8	0.2	6.0	2.1	0.3	10.2	2.6	0.3
Pakistan	–	1.2	–	–	1.7	–	4.2	2.0	0.5	7.5	2.5	0.3
Korea	4.2	8.4	2.0	4.2	3.8	0.9	4.1	5.6	1.4	4.5	12.6	2.8
Malaysia	–	13.5	–	–	3.6	–	4.4	5.4	1.2	7.7	23.6	3.1
Philippines	4.9	3.1	0.6	4.8	2.6	0.5	4.5	2.9	0.6	5.5	3.6	0.7
Thailand	13.4	12.7	0.9	13.8	3.3	0.2	3.8	5.1	1.3	7.8	21.8	2.8
US				–	5.8	–	4.1	11.5	2.8	7.3	72.0	9.9

Indonesia is not included because the data for the fixed rate period is available only from 1967.
For Bangladesh, fixed period exchange rates are the same as for Pakistan.

currency column in the table, the coefficient of variation for the fixed-rates period is shown in the first column, that for the floating-rates period in the second, and the ratio of the floating-rates period value to the fixed-rates period value in the third. For comparison, the data for changes in the value of the three OECD currencies against the dollar is also included in the table. For comparisons of volatility, these values were calculated for two periods of equal lengths: the last 14 years of the fixed-rates period from 1957 to 1970, and the most recent 14 years of the floating-rates period from 1983 to 1996. All exchange-rate values are period averages from the International Monetary Fund's *International Financial Statistics*.

Three of the four countries in the geographically diverse group—Greece, Portugal, and South Africa—had stable currencies during the fixed-rates period. The patterns of changes in the values of the currencies of these three are quite similar. First, very large changes can now take place in the values of these currencies against the dollar (and the yen). The coefficients of variation—that is, the ratios of standard deviations to means—are smaller during the fixed-rates period than during the floating-rates period. This, however, is due to very small values of average changes during the fixed-rates period. The coefficients of variation against the mark and the pound, however, are smaller during the fixed-rates period. Second, the par values of these three currencies against the dollar were never changed during the fixed-rates period; hence, any volatility of these currencies against the yen, mark, or pound was due to changes in the par values of these industrialized countries' currencies. During the floating-rates period, however, these emerging market currencies could change by very large amounts during a quarter. The maximum quarterly changes for these currencies approached 50% in some cases.

These patterns of changes imply that investors in these economies face large risks during turbulent periods in the currency markets. There are two reasons to believe that these three emerging economies themselves, rather than the OECD currencies against which their rates have been analyzed, are sources of increased volatility. As shown in the bottom row of Table 7.1, the fluctuations for the mark, the yen, and the pound also increased during the floating-rates period. The maximum fluctuations in the values of the emerging market currencies, however, are much larger than those in the values of the OECD currencies. Moreover, the values of maximum changes during a quarter follow similar patterns for the three currencies against all four OECD currencies. The risk associated with these three currencies would appear to originate much more in these economies than in the OECD economies against which we measure the currency values.

Turkey, the fourth country in this group, had increased the par value of the dollar by 200% in 1958 and then by 67% in 1970. During the floating-rates period, its currency exhibits even larger fluctuations than those of the other three countries in this group. Its currency changed by more than 50% during some of the quarters. The coefficients of variation, on the other hand, indicate that, given the average changes in the values of the currency, the dispersion of the changes in lira is smaller than the dispersion of the changes in the currencies of the other countries in this group as well as other emerging countries in our sample. The risk of large absolute changes in this currency, however, would appear to be larger than for those in the other three economies in this group of emerging countries.

The remaining ten emerging countries can be divided into two groups according to the patterns of changes in their exchange rates. One group consists of countries whose currencies' par values against the dollar were not changed during the fixed-rates period. This group includes Mexico, Pakistan (and hence Bangladesh), Malaysia, and Thailand. The par values of the currencies of the second group were changed by large amounts during the fixed-rates period. In general, this second group of currencies also continued to exhibit large fluctua-tions during the floating-rates period. Often, the fluctuations of these currencies were larger than those of the currencies which had not changed at all during the fixed-rates period. There were, however, some notable exceptions. Fluctuations in the Mexican peso were the largest in the entire group of 14 emerging countries, although its value had remained pegged to the dollar at the same rate of 12.5 pesos/dollar during the entire fixed-rates period. At the opposite end was the Thai baht. Its par value was not changed at all during the fixed-rates period and the fluctuations in its value during the floating-rates period were among the lowest of all the countries in our sample.

A few observations can be made about the fluctuations in the values of these ten currencies. The volatility of four of these currencies—the Pakistani (and Bangladeshi) rupee, Korean won, Malaysian ringgit, and Thai baht—is comparable to those of the OECD currencies. The maximum possible quarterly changes are of the same order as those for the mark, yen, and pound. Moreover, the coefficients of variation for these emerging countries' currencies are always lower than those for the three OECD currencies. The remaining five currencies exhibit higher volatility that the OECD currencies during the floating-rates period.

The next section decomposes these fluctuations in the exchange rates into expected and unexpected components.

EXCHANGE-RATE CHANGES AND INFLATION

To understand what kinds of risks are created for investors by the fluctuations in exchange rates identified in the previous section, we examine the relationship of the exchange rates with two macroeconomic variables: inflation rates and interest rates.

Inflation is, at least theoretically, one of the most important determinants of changes in exchange rates. According to the theory of exchange rates that has probably endured the longest, the exchange rate between two currencies should change to compensate for the differences in the inflation rates in the two economies. Known as the purchasing power parity theory, this relationship is based on the argument that deviations of exchange rates from their parity values will cause prices of real goods and services in two countries to become unequal, thus giving rise to opportunities for arbitrage. If the markets of the real goods are relatively open, such arbitrage would tend to equalize prices between the two countries, thus restoring the PPP relationship. The PPP theory has endured extensive testing since it was first formalized by Gustav Cassel in 1921. Most of the studies test the relative version of this theory for bilateral or effective exchange rates. Tests over short as well as long periods lead consistently to the conclusion that, at least in the short term, exchange rates deviate from their PPP values significantly, and often unpredictably. The only exception to this rule would appear to be hyperinflationary periods (Frenkel, 1978). Over the long term, however, purchasing power parity seems to determine the exchange rates (Oh, 1996; Rogoff, 1996).

From the point of view of investors concerned with the risks associated with fluctuations in exchange rates, the relationship between exchange rates and inflation provides an indication of the extent to which the competitiveness of two markets can change. Exchange rate changes that do not conform to inflation differences—that is, when real exchange rates change, competitiveness of goods produced in one country changes in relation to the goods produced in the other country. Such deviations, if they persist for any length of time, make planning of exports of output from investments in the country very difficult. The Mexican peso provides a very good example of such a situation just before the peso crisis of December 1994. From 1990 to just before the crisis, the peso changed from 2.9454 pesos/dollar to 3.4498 pesos/dollar. The consumer price index in Mexico changed from 100 to 170.3 during that period. The U.S. inflation index during the same period, however, increased from 100 to only 114.6. Thus the 17.1% increase in the value of the dollar in terms of the peso was far below Mexico's excess inflation of 48.6%. As a result of this overvaluation of the peso, Mexican exporters lost their competitiveness to the extent that the Mexican current account deficit reached 8% of the GDP in 1994. Within a few months of the devaluation of the peso in December, when the purchasing power of the peso was restored, the Mexican trade balance was able to show a surplus.

Our analysis of the relationship between exchange rates and inflation tries to determine the extent to which the volatility of the exchange rates identified in the previous section was caused by the volatility of the inflation differentials between the countries. We raise two questions concerning this relationship. First, we examine if the exchange rates for the emerging economies followed the (relative) PPP relationship. Second, since the exchange rates are likely to have deviated from their PPP values, we investigate if the deviations of the exchange rates persist from one period to another. We carry out two tests to answer these questions.

The first test consists of measuring the range of cumulative deviations between an actual exchange rate and the real or PPP exchange rate. The PPP exchange rate is calculated as the value that the exchange rate should have if it were to follow the relative PPP from a base period. We test for PPP deviations over the entire floating-rates period from the second quarter of 1973 to the end of 1996, as well as over the most recent ten years. The test over the entire floating-rates period is based on the assumption that the exchange rates had been set at their equilibrium values when the floating-rates period commenced. The test for the most recent ten years is based on the belief that the future behavior of the exchange rates is more likely to replicate their recent performance, rather than that of the entire quarter-century of the floating-rates period. The tests for the most recent ten years implicitly assume that the exchange rates were at their equilibrium values ten years ago.

The second test examines the serial correlation in quarterly deviations of the actual exchange rate from its PPP value. The quarterly deviation is defined as the amount by which an exchange rate has deviated from its PPP value during the previous quarter. The test attempts to ascertain if investors who observe a deviation of an exchange rate from its real value during one quarter can expect a similar deviations in the subsequent quarters or not.

Table 7.2 summarizes the analysis of the average cumulative deviation and the range of deviations for the entire floating-rates period as well as the most recent decade. Table 7.3 summarizes the autocorrelations of quarterly deviations with one, two, and three lags. We interpret the information in the two tables jointly. Our aim is to discern broad patterns in the behavior of a currency against the four OECD currencies. Some of the conclusions we draw may only apply to two currencies—with the data for the other two being ambiguous, or only to three currencies—with the data for the fourth currency contradicting the conclusion for the first three. A few patterns can be identified for the relationship between exchange rates and inflation for this group of 14 emerging countries.

Table 7.2. Purchasing Power Parity Deviations: Floating-Rates Period and the Last Decade

Against → Currency of ↓	US$		Yen		DM		UK £	
	\multicolumn{8}{Purchasing Power Parity Deviations Average deviation and range during the period}							
Greece	18.4	34.5	6.4	12.1	35.2	22.6	-17.1	16.0
	89.6	55.9	61.4	45.5	72.1	41.4	66.1	43.7
Portugal	10.5	34.6	-1.3	12.0	25.9	22.6	-23.6	16.2
	107	67.8	69.1	47.1	85.5	46.3	53.2	56.1
South Africa	-16.5	24.0	-24.2	3.3	-3.7	13.5	-39.5	7.4
	64.7	38.8	62.8	26.6	69.1	27.4	69.5	41.4
Turkey	30.5	72.0	16.4	43.5	48.5	55.4	-11.0	47.5
	221	207	191	184	232	178	116	185
Chile	2434	23.8	2124	3.5	288	12.8	1647	6.3
	5047	66.4	4460	63.73	7128	55.0	4583	59.5
Mexico	78.3	312	55.2	243	103	279	15.5	257
	394	524	348	476	449	513	194	429
Bangladesh	-35.7	3.0	-46.6	-14.0	-32.5	-5.0	-55.0	-10.0
	106	18.9	107	31.7	96.1	43.9	120	56.7
India	-25.9	-22.1	-30.7	-34.9	-12.9	-27.9	-43.6	-31.5
	79.5	49.0	92.8	49.4	87.1	51.1	95.1	55.4
Pakistan	11.5	-12.1	2.9	-26.5	30.1	-19.1	-16.7	-23.3
	85.6	22.5	123	32.2	129	32.5	108	39.5
Indonesia	17.6	4.1	9.6	-13.0	37.0	-4.4	-10.9	-9.6
	142	13.2	172.2	26.2	150	30.4	144	42.6
Korea	15.8	26.0	4.8	5.2	35.0	15.6	-17.8	9.4
	50.1	37.7	59.9	38.9	105	52.9	64.1	52.0
Malaysia	-16.8	-6.0	-23.2	-21.4	-2.9	-13.8	-38.3	-18.5
	53.5	19.1	76.3	33.1	89.7	24.0	81.6	32.3
Philippines	22.8	11.3	11.4	-6.8	42.1	1.5	-12.3	-4.2
	85.9	55.0	76.4	59.8	106	48.9	75.6	46.1
Thailand	8.4	4.6	-0.6	-12.7	26.9	-3.9	-20.7	-9.3
	33.4	13.7	71.3	25.2	105	21.8	78.0	36.9

There are two columns under each OECD currency. The first column contains information for the entire floating-rate period and the second column for the last decade. The top number in each box is the mean deviation for the period. The bottom number is the range (= maximum - minimum) over which the deviations are distributed over the period.

Table 7.3. Persistence of Deviations from Real Exchange Rates

Against →	US$			Yen			DM			UK £		
Currency of ↓	Autocorrelation Values of Quarterly Deviations One, two, or three lags											
Greece	0.8	-.14	.14	.09	.07	-.06	-.12	0.2	.18	.27	.18	.01
Portugal	.15	-.10	.15	.08	0	-.07	.15	.14	.21	.28	.21	.01
South Africa	.06	-.14	.21	.02	-.01	.17	-.13	-.19	.35	.10	-.19	.23
Turkey	.12	-.13	.11	.19	-.15	.11	.18	-.12	.12	.17	-.11	.24
Chile	.35	.38	.30	.30	.32	.31	.33	.26	.25	.32	.30	.23
Mexico	.37	.19	.24	.36	.13	.19	.35	.14	.20	.33	.13	.22
Bangladesh	-.24	-.12	.16	-.16	-.12	.06	-.22	-.07	.16	-.13	-.07	.16
India	.33	.19	.21	.17	-.03	.36	-.04	0	.28	.24	.02	.11
Pakistan	.53	.37	.36	.30	.01	.19	.02	-.01	.26	.16	.03	.19
Indonesia	.12	.11	.07	.16	.04	.13	.10	.04	.20	.11	.15	.10
Korea	.30	.30	.31	.25	-.09	.14	.06	-.11	.10	.13	-.04	.07
Malaysia	.17	-.08	.08	.18	-.05	.18	.09	-.07	.26	.27	.07	.13
Philippines	.19	.44	-.15	.08	-.02	-.02	.02	-.02	.04	.16	.07	-.05
Thailand	.26	.06	-.04	.19	-.17	.22	.05	-.13	.25	.18	-.04	.20

The three numbers in each grouping are the correlation values of quarterly deviations with those in the first, the second, or the third previous quarter.

The conclusions are once again similar for the three countries among the first group, Greece, Portugal, and South Africa. Relative to the other countries included in our study, the average cumulative deviations for these countries were neither very large nor very small. These deviations fluctuated within a range that was about three times as wide as the average cumulative deviation for each currency. A comparison of the performance of these currencies over the most recent decade against that of the entire floating-rates period shows that some of these currencies have smaller deviations against the OECD currencies in the recent decade, whereas some others have larger deviations. This conclusion does not depend upon the choice of the emerging economy currency or the choice of the OECD currency to which it is compared. This could point to the absence of any structural change during the most recent decade in the determinants of exchange rates for these countries. There does not seem to be any indication that deviations persist from one quarter to another: there are only isolated incidences of significant autocorrelations between the values of the quarterly deviations (Table 7.3).

As in the case of the volatility of the exchange rates, the nominal value of Turkish lira deviated from its real value by large amounts. The range of deviations, measured in terms of the average deviation, was larger than for the other three currencies in this group of emerging economies. There was no discernible difference in the extent of changes in the lira's value during the last decade to those during the entire floating-rates period. Quarterly deviations do not seem to follow any patterns at all. The autocorrelation values for the lira were among the lowest of the countries examined in this study—indicating that the direction of fluctuations in the lira's values are among the least predictable in this group of countries.

The currencies of two of the South Asian countries, India and Pakistan, seemed to follow similar patterns. The values of the average deviations between the nominal and the real rates are in the middle of the range for the emerging countries, but the range over which these deviations can move is quite small. The deviations have become larger in the most recent ten years than they used to be. The deviations also persist in some cases, especially for the Pakistani rupee against the dollar.

Mexican and Chilean pesos also have some patterns in common. Nominal values of both of these currencies deviated by large amounts from their real values. Quarterly deviations also tend to persist—that is, a deviation in one direction in one quarter is likely to be followed by a further deviation in the same direction in the subsequent quarter. In the case of Chile, such behavior may persist for three quarters. The two currencies, however, differ in one respect. The Chilean peso has become more stable in the most recent decade, whereas the Mexican peso has become less so.

The five currencies of the far-eastern economies, and that of Bangladesh, seem to follow a different pattern from all the other currencies. The nominal rates of all of these currencies deviate very little, on the average, from their real values. The range of these deviations appears to be high when compared to their average values. In absolute terms, however, these ranges are not higher than those for other emerging economies. In most cases, the averages and the ranges of deviations have become smaller in the last ten years. This observation appears to be true for the exchange rates of these emerging economies against all OECD currencies, not only against the dollar to which some of these currencies had been effectively pegged. Of the 72 autocorrelations examined for these currencies, only two turn out to be significant. Thus, although these currencies can deviate from their real values by fair amounts, these deviations seem not to persist from one period to another. In most cases, a deviation in one direction in one quarter provides no information about the direction of the deviation in the subsequent quarter. It would also appear that, in the long run, nominal rates tend to follow their real values quite closely. These six currencies appear to have created the lowest risks of potential changes in competitiveness over long periods of time—at least up to the end of 1996.

UNEXPECTED EXCHANGE RATE CHANGES AND INTEREST RATES

The nature of unexpected changes in exchange rates can be further understood with the help of interest-rate parity relationship. According to this relationship, expected changes in an exchange rate should equal the difference in the interest rates in the two currencies. Covered interest parity defines the relationship between the spot and the forward exchange rates, and uncovered interest parity postulates the relationship between the current spot rate and the expected future spot rate. According to the covered interest-rate parity relationship, the forward exchange rate between two countries should differ from the spot exchange rate by the difference in the interest rates in the two currencies. The uncovered interest parity predicts the value of the future spot rate based on the present spot rate and the difference between the interest rates in the two currencies. If investors' expected future exchange rate does not differ from the current spot rate by the difference between the two interest rates, they would have opportunities for earning excess returns by undertaking arbitrage between the two financial markets. Unexpected changes in exchange rates can, and most often do, cause the future spot rate to deviate from its uncovered interest parity predicted rate. If investors can predict the nature of these unexpected changes, arbitrage profits become possible. If, however, these unexpected changes are unpredictable, investors may make money only if they are willing to take risks. When these unexpected changes are distributed with a mean of zero, profits from the arbitrage activities will have an expected value of zero.

Investors who employ real assets in emerging economies have to be concerned about the validity of the interest-rate parity relationship. Given that all direct investments are partially funded through borrowed funds, the currency of denomination of these borrowed funds becomes important. The currency of denomination of debt would be irrelevant only if the exchange rate always changed according to the interest-rate parity relationship. In that case, the real cost of funds will be the same regardless of the currency in which the debt is denominated. If, however, exchange rates deviate systematically from those predicted by the interest parity relationship, investors may have incentives to denominate their debt in a currency in which the costs are expected to be lower. Our examination of the unexpected changes in the currencies of the emerging economies attempts to determine if the unexpected changes in the exchange rates have followed some patterns.

We examine the patterns of unexpected changes in the exchange rates by calculating what may be called a break-even or an uncovered parity interest rate for the emerging country. This rate is defined as the interest rate in the OECD currency adjusted for the actual change in the exchange rate between that OECD country and the emerging country. This break-even rate would have eliminated any profit in an uncovered interest arbitrage operation if it had been the interest rate in the emerging country. This break-even interest rate is then compared to the actual interest rate in the emerging economy with the following regression equation:

$$(\text{Break-even interest rate}) = a + b * (\text{Actual interest rate})$$

An insignificant regression implies that investors in emerging economies who have to make decisions on currency of denomination of their debt cannot expect systematic profits from their currency denomination decisions. A significant regression, on the other hand, implies that investors would have been better off if they had always denominated their debt in one or the other of the two currencies.

For the test of uncovered interest-rate parity, we have made the assumption that during periods of very high probability of large changes in the values of the exchange rate, managers will not rely upon interest rate parity. Periods of high volatility are frequently accompanied by rumors in the marketplace. Most investors would recognize such periods as unsuitable for negotiating loans in the currency that is rumored to appreciate. Moreover, such periods may be accompanied by restrictions in the financial markets, making it difficult to exploit differences in interest rates to earn arbitrage profits. We have, therefore, removed up to a maximum of two observations per country that appear to be outliers from the perspective of interest arbitrage.

To allow for any structural changes in the money and the foreign currency markets, these regressions were carried out for data only over the most recent ten years. Of the 56 comparisons reported in that figure, only 12 turn out to be significant at a 10% (or better) level of confidence. Six of these 12 cases are against the dollar, four against the mark, but none against the pound. Details of these 12 regressions are summarized in Table 7.4.

Interest rates of some countries always appear to follow interest-rate parity. These countries are South Africa, India, Pakistan, Malaysia, and the Philippines. The absence of a significant regression does not, however, imply that the interest rates in these countries followed interest-rate parity in all periods. It merely implies that, although there may have been frequent and even large violations of the parity relationship, the violations would not have permitted excess profits from a strategy of always denominating debt in one currency or the other. Investors would not have made profits systematically if they had made decisions to select

Table 7.4. Deviance of Uncovered Interest Parity

Currency of	Against US			Against Germany			Against Japan		
Greece				2.74	1%	.27	6.60	1%	.30
Portugal				1.002	10%	.05	2.75	5%	.10
Turkey	0.63	11%	.06						
Chile	0.46	5%	.07						
Mexico	0.57	1%	.26						
Bangladesh	0.78	5%	.09						
Indonesia				-3.2	10%	.06			
Korea	0.48	5%	.10	3.68	5%	.08			
Thailand	0.70	5%	.11						

Each box shows the estimated coefficient of the regression, the level of significance of the estimated coefficient, and the value of the adjusted R^2 for the regression.

one of the two currencies to denominate their debt. The six cases in which the uncovered parity is systematically violated against the dollar, the domestic interest rate in the emerging economy was higher than it should have been to maintain the interest parity. Thus, the regression coefficient of 0.63 for Turkish lira against the dollar means that, on the average, the Turkish interest rates should have been 63% of what they were if interest rate parity had to be maintained between the dollar and the lira over the last decade. Similarly, regression results show that the interest rates in Greece, Portugal, Indonesia, and Korea should have been higher if they had to maintain the parity against the mark and the yen. Together, these results mean that the exchange rates of these economies should have declined more against the dollar and less against the mark and the yen. It is not possible, however, *ceteris paribus*, for one currency to simultaneously depreciate against one currency, say the dollar, while appreciating against another, say the mark. We therefore must conclude that violations of interest rate parity by the emerging economies' currencies were caused by violations of this relationship between the dollar on the one hand and the mark and the yen on the other. Research on OECD exchange rates confirms that conclusion (Jain, 1997).

These results indicate that borrowers in Turkey, Chile, Mexico, Bangladesh, Korea, and Thailand would have been better off if they had denominated their debts in dollars instead of in the local currencies during the past decade. Similarly, borrowers in Greece, Portugal, Indonesia, and Korea that denominated their debt in marks or yen would have been better off if they had chosen domestic currency instead. For all the other combinations of currencies, the currency of debt did not affect the ex-post cost of debt in any systematic manner.

EXCHANGE-RATE CHANGES AND RISK FOR FOREIGN INVESTORS

In this chapter, we examined the volatility of exchange rates of 14 emerging economies over the past 25 years in order to understand whether this volatility was explained either by inflation differentials or by interest rate differentials. Table 7.5 provides a brief summary of the results by dividing these 14 into six groups. It is hard to draw an overarching conclusion from these results. Each group or country has to be looked at by itself.

It appears that exchange rates of these currencies follow very different patterns. The range of fluctuations between these currencies is quite wide. Some currencies follow their real values quite closely, other deviate from their real values by large amounts—sometimes for short periods of time and sometimes for long duration. Investors in these economies cannot assume that, over the long run, fluctuations in exchange rates will cancel each other out and thus ignore their potential effects on their investments. Exchange risks of each country must be assessed along with other risks of investment in that economy. It is hoped that research will help that process.

Table 7.5. Summary of the Conclusions

Volatility …	… explained by inflation, or …	… by interest rates.	Conclusions about risks created by changes in exchange rates.
Greece, Portugal, and South Africa			
Larger fluctuations than OECD currencies; in the middle of the range of emerging economies …	… deviations from real exchange rate are also in the middle of the range of emerging economies, but they do not seem to continue from one quarter to another.	Currencies should have devalued (more) against the mark and the yen.	Currency fluctuations can sometimes change the competitive strength of investments; borrowing in mark or yen is not recommended.
Turkey			
Larger fluctuations …	… cause large deviations from real exchange rates …	… but only minor disparity between interest rates.	Competitive position of investments is subject to large swings
India and Pakistan			
Fluctuations are comparable to those of OECD currencies …	… and nominal rates often remain undervalued for long periods …	… but interest rates were comparable to those in OECD countries.	Investments remain competitive except for occasional large swings in currency values.
Chile			
After large volatility, the exchange rate seems to have become more stable …	… but it has large deviations from its real value with large swings …	… and borrowing in dollars has been costly.	Competitive position can be change, but currency seems to be stabilizing.
Mexico			
With large volatility, the exchange rate seems to have becomes less stable …	… and it has large deviations from its real value with large swings …	… and borrowing in dollars has been costly.	Risks of this currency seem to have increased over the past decade.
Bangladesh, Indonesia, Korea, Malaysia, Philippines, Thailand			
Except for Bangladesh, seem to have become very stable …	… and currencies seem to follow their real values better than other emerging economies …	… and provide some incentives for interest arbitrage with a choice for currencies for debt denomination.	Among the least risky emerging economies, except for denominations of debt.

ACKNOWLEDGMENTS

The author is grateful to Social Sciences and Humanities Research Council, Ottawa, for funds that made this research possible. Ms. Katrin Kopvillem provided very valuable research assistance for this project.

REFERENCES

Frenkel, Jacob A., 1978. Purchasing power parity: doctrinal perspective and evidence from the 1920s, *Journal of International Economics* 8, 169-191.

Jain, Arvind K., 1997. Exchange rate changes and strategic risks. Paper presented at Global Finance Conference, Montreal, May.

Oh, Keun-Yeob, 1996. Purchasing power parity and unit root tests using panel data, *Journal of International Money and Finance* 15, 405-418.

Rogoff, Kenneth, 1996. The purchasing power parity puzzle, *Journal of Economic Literature* 34, 647-668.

8

Cointegration Analysis of Official and Free Market Exchange Rates in an Emerging Market: The Turkish Case

Ayce Yuce
and Can Simga-Mugan

INTRODUCTION

Relationships among spot and forward exchange rates have been investigated by many researchers such as Baillie and Bollerslev (1989, 1994), Hakkio and Rush (1989), and Diebold, Gardeazabal, and Yilmaz (1994) in different developed markets.

Baillie and Bollerslev (1989) conclude that seven spot rates are cointegrated. On the other hand, Sephton and Larsen (1991) find a very weak evidence of cointegration by using the same data as Baillie and Bollerslev (1989). Diebold, Gardeazabal, and Yilmaz (1994) include a constant term in the cointegration equation and check the existence of long-run dynamics among the seven spot rates to conclude that a cointegration relation does not exist. In their recent study, Baillie and Bollerslev (1994) find that the exchange rates are tied through a long memory and the process may be described as a fractionally integrated one.

In recent years we have observed that many small investors in Turkey view foreign currencies as investment alternatives. Since 1987, foreign exchange offices serve investors who continuously trade foreign currencies. The observed behavior of small investors in choosing between investing in dollar and deutschemark exchange markets motivated us to examine the long-run relationship between the official and free market prices of these currencies. We expect that official and free market rates will be cointegrated, and hence error correction models could be estimated by using the past values of the other.

In light of recent research, we want to examine the long run dynamics of the spot exchange rates in the emerging market of Turkey. This study contributes to the existing literature by providing evidence on the dynamics of spot exchange rates in an emerging market, and informing the Turkish and international investors about different opportunities of earning returns in Turkey.

In this chapter we will introduce the reader to the history and the character-istics of the Turkish financial markets and instruments; mention the relevant work in unit root and cointegration studies; examine the long-run relationship between the series as we present data and methodologies utilized; and, finally, explain the result and offer recommendations for future studies.

BACKGROUND OF TURKISH FOREIGN EXCHANGE MARKETS

The available instruments for investments in Turkey include securities such as stocks, private-sector bonds, mutual funds, Treasury Bills, profit sharing certifi-cates on one hand, and gold and foreign currencies on the other.

Until the mid 1980s, a black market and an official market for foreign currencies coexisted in Turkey. In 1984 Turkish citizens were given the right to keep foreign currency deposits in Turkish banks. However, there were restrictions on freely trading foreign currencies. On October 21, 1986, the Turkish govern-ment allowed free trade of foreign currencies. As a result, private exchange offices, which are officially called authorized agencies, were established July 1987. Such bureaus were first founded in Istanbul, the trade center of Turkey, and later were opened in other parts of the country. The liberalization that started in 1981 was a gradual process and it ended in 1989. An important result of this process was that investors started to use foreign currencies as a short-term invest-ment alternative.

A governmental decree amending a previous one regarding the protection of the value of Turkish lira (TL) was issued on June 20, 1991. Some of the changes that affect the investors follow:

• nonresidents were allowed to transfer TL and foreign currency funds abroad through banks, special finance institutions, and authorized agencies;

• third parties were allowed to trade in the international securities market; and

• trade of precious metals (except gold) can be carried out by individuals.

These measures taken by the government are aimed to make the Turkish markets more attractive to foreign investors, and thus to integrate the Turkish market with the world markets.

As of the end of March 1995, there were 715 authorized agencies in the country. They can deal either within or outside the interbank market. Some 58 agencies deal in the interbank market. The criteria to be eligible for the interbank market are set by the Central Bank.

Table 8.1 discloses the purchases and sales of the foreign currencies by the authorized exchange dealers. Purchases reflect the amount of foreign currency purchased from the Central Bank and from other sources; and sales reflect the amounts sold to the public and to the banks. These agencies are required to issue receipts for their purchases and sales. However, they fail to give receipts to general public in most cases. Thus, these legal figures should be examined with skepticism

Table 8.1. Purchase and Sale of Foreign Exchange by Authorized Agencies

Years	Foreign Exchange Purchased (million U.S.$)	Foreign Exchange Sold (million U.S.$)
1990	1,905	778
1991	2,770	1,488
1992	4,086	2,425
1993	834	
1994	9,000	

Note: 1993 and 1994 figures are not finalized.

Source: *Main Indicators of the Turkish Financial System*, March 1994 and September 1994. Prime Ministry of the Republic of Turkey, Undersecreteriat of the Treasury and Foreign Trade-General Directoriate of Banking and Exchange.

because one cannot be sure about the real turnover. We believe that the real turnover is at least twice as much. Nonetheless, the increase in the amounts is striking.

As with other hyperinflationary countries, investors continuously buy and sell foreign currencies to hedge against inflation and to realize real gains. Selcuk (1994) shows that investors prefer to substitute foreign currencies for domestic currency (Turkish lira) because of real exchange rate depreciation. He shows that the currency substitution (approximated as the ratio of foreign currency deposits by residents to the sum of M2 and foreign currency deposits in the same period) in Turkey started at around 5% in 1984 and reached 21% by the end of 1987. At the end of 1988, currency substitution reached 24%. Although the exchange rates increased sharply in 1989 and 1990, currency substitution stayed around 20%, and reached 37% in August 1992. One could easily observe the interest of small investors in foreign currencies on paydays. People form long queues in front of the exchange bureaus and change their payments to foreign currencies with the purpose of investing in those currencies. Turkish investors usually trade U.S. dollars and deutschemarks (DM). Table 8.2 shows the annual inflation rates (CPI), and changes in the price of dollars and DMs during the period under study. Examination of Table 8.2 reveals that before 1991, percentage increases in the price of dollars and DMs were considerably lower than the general price increase in the same period.

UNIT ROOTS AND COINTEGRATION

Starting at the beginning of the 1980s, researchers have exploited unit root and cointegration methods in modeling financial time series. Meese and Singleton (1982) pointed out that exchange rates and other financial time series are nonstationary and therefore it is not appropriate to use economic theories like rational expectations which require stationarity in modeling exchange rates.

Table 8.2. Annual Increase in CPI, Deutschmarks, and U.S. Dollars

Year	CPI %	DM %	U.S.$ %
1988	75.4	45.9	62.4
1989	69.6	31.1	26.3
1990	60.3	30.0	23.0
1991	66.0	68.5	71.4
1992	70.0	58.0	69.4
1993	66.0	57.7	67.4
1994	125.5	187.9	158.3

Source: CPI: State Statistics Institute Year Books; DM and U.S.$ figures are calculated from the data used in this study.

Baillie and Bollerslev (1989) examined the relationship among daily spot and 30-day forward exchange-rate data from the New York Foreign Exchange Market for the price of British, German, French, Italian, Swiss, Japanese, and Canadian currencies. They concluded that there is strong evidence for the presence of a unit root for all seven spot and forward rates. All series appear to be integrated of order 1.

Copeland's (1991) findings indicated the lack of cointegration of major currencies in spot markets. Although cointegration was apparent in forward markets, no patterns were established. Diebold, Gardeazabal, and Yilmaz (1994) used the same data set as Baillie and Bollerslev (1989). They, however, included an intercept term to the cointegration equation and rejected the cointegration relationship among nominal exchange rates. In their last paper Baillie and Bollerslev (1994) concluded that the deviations from the cointegrating relationship suggest that it possesses long memory and may possibly be described as a fractionally integrated process.

LONG RUN DYNAMICS OF THE SPOT RATES IN TURKEY

In recent studies (Yuce and Simga-Mugan, 1996) cointegration analysis was used in the Turkish financial markets to determine the relationship between the stock prices and foreign exchange rates in Turkey. The findings of the studies show that stock market and free market rates are both integrated of order 1, but not cointegrated.

Before the complete legalization of the foreign currency markets and opening of the foreign exchange bureaus in 1987, Booth and Mustafa (1991) found that the official and black market rates of the same currencies were cointegrated using 512 observations during the transition period from September 1985 through August 1987.

The opening of the exchange offices marks the end of the black market in Turkey. Since then Turkish citizens have been free to trade foreign currencies, and as a result they use foreign currencies as another investment alternative. This fact is reflected in the increase in foreign currency deposits from $0.4 billion in 1984 (Selcuk, 1994) to $13 billion in 1993 and staying almost at that level ($12 billion) despite the high appreciation of foreign currencies against Turkish lira by the end of September 1994 (*Main Indicators*, 1994). Increases in currency substitution, discussed earlier in the chapter, and the striking increase in the purchase and sale of foreign currencies (Table 8.1) also support this fact.

In this study we exploit the daily prices of the dollar and the DM from January 1, 1988, through December 31, 1994. The free and official rates used in this study are obtained from Merkez Bankasi (Central Bank). The official rates are calculated as the average of the bid and ask prices; and the free rates are the dealing prices among the foreign exchange dealers in the market.

The foreign exchange offices were opened in the second half of 1987, therefore the data used in this study include observations starting from January 1, 1988, and consist of 1,744 matched observations of both official and free market dollar and DM prices. The matched observations used in this study reflect the weekday prices.

In this chapter we will examine not only the existence of cointegration relationships between different series, but we will also try to find error correction models for the cointegrated series.

In the analysis, the prices are expressed as logarithms:

FUSD = ln (closing price of the free market U.S. dollar)
FDM = ln (closing price of the free market DM)
OUSD = ln (closing price of the official market U.S. dollar)
ODM = ln (closing price of the official market DM)

First, we perform the Augmented Dickey-Fuller and Phillips-Perron tests to determine whether or not the series are stationary. The Augmented Dickey-Fuller test is as follows:

$$\Delta X_t = \alpha + \beta X_{t-1} + \sum_{i=1}^{m} \gamma_i \Delta X_{t-i} + e_t \tag{1}$$

H_0: a unit root exists

If a unit root exists, then the coefficient b is not significantly different from zero. The Phillips-Perron test corrects the test statistic for possible time dependencies in the series by using nonparametric techniques.

Existence of unit roots indicates that the series are nonstationary, and differencing may be required to make the series stationary. If unit roots do not exist in the difference series, then this shows that the series are integrated of order 1, that is, I(1).

Although individual series that contain stochastic trends are nonstationary, if the stochastic trends are common across series, there will be stationary linear combinations of the series. If these linear combinations exist, then the series are said to be cointegrated. If X_t and Y_t are series of $I(d)$, then their linear combination

$Z_t = X_t - aY_t$ will also be $I(d)$. However, if there exists a constant a such that $Z_t = X_t - aY_t$ is I(d-b) b>0, then X_t and Y_t are said to be cointegrated—that is, $(X_t, Y_t) \sim CI(d,b)$. In the special case of $d = b = 1$, there exist an a? such that Z_t becomes stationary although both X_t and Y_t are nonstationary.

The existence of a cointegrating vector in the two series is investigated with three methods: Augmented Dickey-Fuller, Phillips-Perron, and finally the vector error correction method suggested by Engle and Granger (1987). For the first two methods, we run the following regressions and obtain error terms u_t and e_t:

$$X_t = a + g \, Y_t + u_t \tag{2}$$

$$Y_t = c + h \, X_t + \varepsilon_t \tag{3}$$

If two series X_t and Y_t are cointegrated, then the stochastic error terms u_t and e_t should be stationary. Therefore, we check the existence of unit roots in u_t and e_t.

Finally we use the methodology suggested by Engle and Granger (1987) to search for long-term linkages between each pair of series. First we estimate the values of k and l from the following regressions:

$$X_t = a + \kappa \, Y_t + \varepsilon_t \tag{4}$$

$$Y_t = b + \lambda \, X_t + v_t \tag{5}$$

Then using k and l we estimate values Y_t and P_t such that:

$$\Psi_t = X_t - \kappa \, Y_t \tag{6}$$

$$\Pi_t = Y_t - \lambda \, X_t \tag{7}$$

If two series are cointegrated, then there exist error correction models as follows:

$$\Delta X_t = \xi + \zeta \Psi_{t-1} + \sum_{i=1}^{m} \gamma_i \Delta X_{t-i} + \sum_{j=1}^{m} \beta_j \Delta Y_{t-j} + \phi_t \tag{8}$$

$$\Delta Y_t = \iota + \eta \Pi_{t-1} + \sum_{i=1}^{m} \delta_i \Delta Y_{t-i} + \sum_{j=1}^{m} \beta_j \Delta X_{t-j} + \omega_t \tag{9}$$

We can use the above error correction formulae to test for long-term relationships between each pair of the series. The long-run components are represented by P and Y, and short-run components are given by the coefficients of DX and DY terms. The series X_t and Y_t are cointegrated when at least one of the coefficients z and h is significantly different from zero.

If any two series are cointegrated, causality has to exist at least in one direction. If Y series cause X series—that is, if information on Y series help to predict future X series—then the b coefficients of DY at different lags should be significantly different from zero. If, on the other hand, past values of X series help to predict the future values of Y series, then the b coefficients of DX at different lags should be significantly different from zero. If X series cause Y series and Y series cause X series, then there is feedback between the two series. After checking for short-run dependency in the individual lags, we proceed to test the null hypotheses of causality between different series:

H_1: Y does not cause X
H_2: X does not cause Y

with the F-statistics that are calculated after running the above regression models for both unconstrained (full) and constrained (reduced) models as:

$$F = [(SSE_r - SSE_f) / m] / (SSE_f / T - 2m - 1) \qquad (10)$$

where SSE_r and SSE_f are the sum of squares of the residuals of the reduced model, and full model respectively, m the number of lags, and T the number of observations.

RESULTS AND INTERPRETATION

We start our investigation of the short- and long-term relationship between different series by checking the stationarity of the series. The autocorrelations in all series do not die out gradually, indicating the possibility of a unit root and non-stationarity. Difference transformations lead to stationary series.

Our null hypothesis is that a unit root exists in all series. To check for the presence of a unit root in the series we use both Phillips-Perron and the Augmented Dickey-Fuller methods (see Table 8.3). The models used in the unit root analysis for both methods include a constant and a trend term because all rates are increasing during the study period. Initially we started our analysis by determination of the optimal lag length using the Akaike and Schwarz information criteria. We checked different lag lengths (from 1 to 100 day lags) and found that lag 5 performed better than the others. Therefore, in our analyses we used a five-day lag. Based on the critical values at 5%, we fail to reject the presence of unit root in all series. Next, we check the presence of unit root in the difference series. The results are reported in Table 8.4.

Table 8.4 rejects the presence of unit roots in all of the series based on the critical values at the 5% level, which indicates that all rates are integrated of order 1, I(1). Then we proceed to check whether the series are cointegrated. To check the cointegration relation, we again use Phillips-Perron and Augmented Dickey-Fuller tests on the residuals of cointegrating regressions. No trend in the residuals is expected; therefore, the models used in all cases include a constant, but not a trend. If any two series are found to be cointegrated, then this indicates a long-run equilibrium relation between these two rates.

Table 8.3. Unit Root Tests for the Original Series

		Phillips-Perron	Augmented Dickey-Fuller
U.S.$	: OFF.	-0.699	-0.935
	: FREE	-0.625	-1.135
DM	: OFF.	-0.844	-1.052
	: FREE	-0.872	-1.254
Critical Values at 5%:		-3.34	-3.34

Table 8.4. Unit Root Tests for Difference Series

		Phillips-Perron	Augmented Dickey-Fuller
U.S.$	: OFF:	-515.17*	-516.37*
	: FREE:	-569.58*	-557.69*
DM	: OFF:	-489.86*	-476.05*
	: FREE:	-546.79*	-515.55*
*Critical Values at 5%:		-3.34	-3.34

Findings of the cointegration tests at the 5% significance level are presented in Table 8.5. Results of both of the cointegration tests show that official dollar and official DM series are not cointegrated. Similarly, free market dollar rates and free market DM rates are not cointegrated according to both of the tests. However, official and free market dollar rates; and official and free market DM rates, are cointegrated according to both of the tests.

Next we formulate the error correction models for the cointegrated series and report the results in Table 8.6. We expect negative signs on the error correction terms in the official rate equations, and positive signs in the free-rate equations. These signs are expected because in Turkey generally first free rates adjust by appreciating, and official rates follow.

Free and official rates of both dollar and DM exhibit long-term relation. These results conform to the cointegration findings reported earlier. The signs of error correction terms are significant and in the expected direction.

Then we proceed to check the null hypotheses of no causality with F-statistics in the short run (see Table 8.6). Feedback relationship in the Granger sense is observed between all the series involved. However, stronger results are obtained from regressing the official rates on the free market rates. The F-statistics obtained from regressions of official dollar on free dollar, and official DM on free DM are 118.97 and 119.48, respectively. Furthermore, one-day lag t-statistics of the above regressions are 23.56 and 23.83, respectively. These findings demon-

Table 8.5. Cointegration Tests, 5-Days Lag

Dependent Variable	Independent Variable	Phillips-Perron	Augmented Dickey-Fuller
OFF : U.S.$:	OFF.DM	-2.576	-2.762
: U.S.$:	FREE.U.S.$	-9.248*	-5.607*
FREE : U.S.$:	OFF.U.S.$	-9.242*	-5.529*
: U.S.$:	FREE.DM	-2.623	-2.433
OFF : DM:	OFF.U.S.$	-2.540	-2.747
: DM:	FREE.DM	-9.639*	-5.730*
FREE : DM:	OFF.DM	-9.633*	-5.656*
: DM:	FREE.U.S.$	-2.588	-2.399
*Critical Values at 5%:		-3.34	-3.34

Table 8.6. Error Correction Estimations

Dependent Variable	Independent Variable	z,h	b_1	b_2	b_3	b_4	b_5	F
OFF:U.S.$:	FREE.U.S.$	-.071 (-7.41)*	.568 (23.56)*	.195 (7.00)*	.115 (4.11)*	.070 (2.49)*	-.062 (-2.32)*	118.970*
FREE:U.S.$:	OFF.U.S.$	.054 (4.68)*	-.216 (-6.85)*	-.128 (-4.07)*	.073 (2.28)*	.055 (1.75)	.072 (2.99)*	18.621*
OFF:DM:	FREE.DM	-.071 (-7.38)*	.565 (23.83)*	.187 (6.77)*	.073 (2.62)*	.064 (2.33)*	-.067 (-2.54)*	119.478*
FREE:DM:	OFF.DM	.046 (3.93)*	-.161 (-5.12)*	-.069 (-2.21)*	.055 (1.73)	.042 (1.37)	.677 (3.23)*	10.439*

*Critical values of F-statistic at 5%: 2.21

strate that free exchange rates influence the official rates significantly. In Turkey, the Central Bank continuously observes the changes of free rates in the domestic market and developments in the international currency market, and then announces the official rates; our results reflect this phenomenon.

CONCLUSION AND RECOMMENDATIONS

In light of the recent research, we examined the long-run and short-run dynamics of the official and free market exchange rates in an emerging market, Turkey, through cointegration analysis and Granger causality tests.

All markets are found to be nonstationary and integrated of order 1, I(1). The results of the cointegration tests indicate that the official series are not cointegrated with each other. Similarly, free market series are not cointegrated with each other either. Therefore long-run equilibrium relationships do not exist between these series. On the other hand, free and official rates of the same currency are cointegrated indicating to long-run equilibrium.

We also estimated the error correction models for the cointegrated series. Granger causality tests show that all series establish a feedback relation in the Granger sense. These results conform to the previous findings of recent research, which examined the characteristics of foreign exchange markets. Thus, we believe that the present study contributes to the literature by informing the international investors about the characteristics of foreign exchange markets, and by providing evidence on short-term and long-term dynamics of spot exchange rates in an emerging market, Turkey.

In the future, we plan to examine the relationships among other currencies, cross rates in the Turkish market, and other emerging markets.

REFERENCES

Baillie, R.T. and T. Bollerslev, 1989. Common stochastic trends in a system of exchange rates, *The Journal of Finance* 44, 167-181.

Baillie, R.T. and T. Bollerslev, 1994. Cointegration, fractional cointegration, and exchange rate dynamics, *The Journal of Finance* 49, 737-745.

Booth, G.G. and M. Chowdhury, 1991. Long run dynamics of black and official exchange rates, *Journal of International Money and Finance* 10, 392-405.

Copeland, L.S., 1991. Cointegration tests with daily exchange rate data, *Oxford Bulletin of Economics and Statistics* 53, 185-198.

Dickey, D.A. and W. Fuller, 1979. Distribution of the estimators for autoregression time series with a unit root, *Journal of American Statistical Association* 74, 427-431.

Diebold, F.X., J. Gardeazabal, and K. Yilmaz, 1994. On Cointegration and Exchange Rate Dynamics, *The Journal of Finance* 49, 727-735.

Engle, R.F. and C. Granger, 1987. Cointegration and error correction: Representation, estimation and testing, *Econometrica* 55, 251-276.

Granger, C., 1980. Testing for causality: a personal viewpoint, *Journal of Economic Dynamics and Control* 2, 329-352.

Granger, C., 1988. Some developments in a concept of causality, *Journal of Econometrics* 39, 199-211.

Hakkio, C.S. and M. Rush, 1989. Market efficiency and cointegration: An application to the sterling and deutschemark exchange markets, *Journal of International Money and Finance* 8, 75-88.

Harvey, A., 1990. *The Econometric Analysis of Time Series*, 2nd ed. Cambridge, MA: The MIT Press.

Main Indicators of the Turkish Financial System, 1994. Prime Ministry of the Republic of Turkey, September. Undersecreteriat of the Treasury and Foreign Trade-General Directoriate of Banking and Exchange.

Meese, R.A. and K.J. Singleton, 1982. On unit roots and the empirical modelling of exchange rates, *The Journal of Finance* 37,1029-1035.

Selcuk, F., 1994. Currency substitution in Turkey, *Applied Economics* 26, 509-518.

Sephton, P.S. and H.K. Larsen, 1991. Tests of exchange market efficiency: fragile evidence from cointegration tests, *Journal of International Money and Finance* 10, 561-570.

Yuce, A. and C. Simga-Mugan, 1996. An investigation of the short and long term relationships between Turkish financial markets, *European Journal of Finance* 2, 305-317.

9

Foreign Direct Investment in the Asia-Pacific Region: The Gravity-Model Approach

Bang Nam Jeon
and Susan F. Stone

INTRODUCTION

The purpose of this chapter is to investigate the determinants of foreign direct investment (FDI) flows in the Asia-Pacific region by examining bilateral flows of FDI in a cross-sectional study using the gravity-type model. The chapter will examine empirically, first, whether FDI is determined by home-country factors or host-country factors; second, whether FDI is a trade-induced activity or not; and third, whether geographical distance plays a role in determining FDI flows or not. We also will look at the effect of the regional economic integration, if any, by investigating if a common membership in a specific regional trading bloc, such as the Association of South East Asian Nations (ASEAN) or the Asia Pacific Economic Cooperation (APEC), impacts the nature of FDI flows in the Asia-Pacific region. The economic impact of geographical location has been addressed so far in various forms in the trade literature, but has not been applied empirically in explaining the nature of FDI flows.

The importance of investment flows in the world economy has increased drastically in recent years. FDI flows have grown at a compound annual rate of over 16% between 1986 and 1995. FDI inflows reached $315 billion in 1995 alone, with an unprecedented increase by more than 40% from the preceding year. Outward FDI stock in the world totaled $2.7 trillion in 1995. The growth in FDI has outstripped growth in trade and world output. World trade and GDP increased at an annual rate of 8% and just over 2%, respectively, between 1986 and 1995. The increased liberalization of the investment regime at the bilateral as well as multilateral levels, aided by regional economic integration and the formation of the World Trade Organization (WTO), is an important factor in the explanation of the tremendous recent growth in FDI flows around the globe. Developing countries have been liberalizing their FDI regimes in the hope of obtaining access to developed countries' capital and technology. While, for the most part, the process of FDI liberalization has lagged that of trade liberalization, annual growth in FDI flows has still exceeded that in trade during at least the last two decades.

The Asia-Pacific region is a particularly important area of the world given its impressive growth. Foreign investment and trade have been critical parts of this growth in the region. The Asian economies have been liberalizing their FDI regimes since the mid-1980s in an effort to sustain their economic growths, which have been the envy of the world. The role of FDI as an engine of economic growth is expected to increase greatly in the region. The rules of games and principles are, however, still vague in the FDI area, and it has not been easy to reach consensus among policymakers, especially at the international level. This chapter attempts to fill the gap by providing some empirical evidence on the determination of bilateral FDI flows, with emphasis on the Asia-Pacific region, including the role of the home-country (supply) factors and the host-country (demand) factors, the relevance of the geographical distance between the centers of two economies, and the implications of regional economic integration on FDI flows.

We will discuss the increasing trend of the FDI activity in the Asia-Pacific region in the recent years; develop the gravity model-type FDI equation and examine the data series; present the results of the empirical estimation of the gravity equation on bilateral FDI flows; and, finally, reach conclusions and discuss various policy implications.

FDI IN THE ASIA-PACIFIC REGION

The Asia-Pacific countries have engaged actively in FDI activity as both FDI recipients and FDI donors. The estimated inflows to the region in 1995 reached $62 billion, an increase of more than 20% over the preceding year, and accounted for 19.7% of total world FDI inflows. Table 9.1 shows the changing patterns of FDI inflows, and outflows (Panel 1) and FDI inward stock and outward stock (Panel 2) for selected Asia-Pacific countries and regions during the 1980s and the 1990s.

In recent years, China became a dominant recipient of FDI, while newly industrialized economies (NIEs) increased their importance as FDI donors. In 1995 China attracted an unprecedented total of $37.5 billion, which was 11.9% of world total FDI inflows. An increasing role of NIEs as FDI providers was equally impressive by supplying $34.6 billion of FDI resources to the world. As an investor, the importance of Japan, on the flow basis, dropped significantly from a share of 20% of world total in 1991 to less than a 7% share in 1995. NIEs have surpassed Japan as more important FDI donors since 1993. ASEAN nations hosted FDI consistently with a world share of 6-8%, totaling $19.4 billion in 1995. The sustained increase in FDI inflows to ASEAN every year during the last two decades has accumulated FDI inward stock in the region to a total of $168.6 billion as of 1995, accounting for 6.3% of world total. ASEAN countries have also witnessed their new role as FDI resource countries, providing still only 2% of world total FDI outflows in 1995, notwithstanding.

Increasing engagement in the outward FDI activities by the NIEs and ASEAN nations, which is particularly noteworthy, reflects their economic prosperity and liberalization of the investment regime, and their efforts for pursuing economies of scale by expanding markets overseas. A sharp increase in wages due to shortage of labor and labor strikes, and trade frictions with developed countries, also encouraged producers in NIEs to move their production facilities to overseas, especially to ASEAN countries. By contrast, Hong Kong is the second largest FDI donor after Japan.

The Asia-Pacific countries as a group have increased importance as FDI recipients from an annual average of $9.5 billion, or 8.2% of world total, during the period of 1984 through 1989, to $62 billion, or almost 20% of world total, in 1995, which is attributable to China and ASEAN. FDI outflows from the Asia-Pacific countries have increased steadily from $25.9 billion, or 21.3% of world total, during the second half of the 1980s, to $62.9 billion in 1995, which is almost 20% of world total.

The Asia-Pacific countries, firms, and governments alike have been realizing FDI as a key vehicle to obtain foreign technology, and management skills, among others, to enhance their international competitiveness. Governments and monetary authorities in the region have liberalized FDI policies and regulations and reduced restrictive measures on market accessibility and business operations. Nongovernmental sectors have also participated actively, at the bilateral, regional, and multilateral levels, in facilitating international arrangement for FDI.[1]

The pattern of FDI inflows and outflows, as described above, will be determined by the interaction of supply-side factors in the home country, such as economic prosperity and economies of scale motivation, and demand-side factors, such as market size, income, and investment host policies. Other institutional or physical factors will also affect FDI flows as resisting forces or enhancing forces. The former may include the government restrictions on inward and outward FDI flows, cultural differences, or geographic distance between the home country and the host country, while the examples for the latter may be liberalization of the investment regime, FDI promotion policies, and common membership in a specific regional economic integration. The following sections will empirically investigate the impact of these factors on the bilateral FDI flows, with emphasis on the Asia-Pacific region.

THE MODEL AND THE DATA

The Model

We adopt the gravity equation model, developed and used in the recent literature of trade and geography, to investigate the major determinants of bilateral FDI flows in the Asia-Pacific region. The gravity model specifies that

Table 9.1. Foreign Direct Investment in the Asia-Pacific Region (Flow and Stock)

Panel 1:

FDI inflows, by host region, and FDI outflows, by home region, 1984-1995

	1984 - 1989 (Annual Average)				1991			
	In		Out		In		Out	
	$bil.	%	$bil.	%	$bil.	%	$bil.	%
Japan	0.08	0.1	20.8	17.1	1.7	1.1	42.6	20.2
China	2.3	2.0	0.6	0.5	4.4	2.8	0.9	0.4
ASEAN	4.4	3.8	0.6	0.5	12.9	8.2	1.6	0.8
NIEs	4.9	4.2	4.2	3.5	7.9	5.0	7.2	3.4
Asia-Pacific	9.5	8.2	25.9	21.3	22.0	13.9	51.3	24.3
World	115.4	100.0	121.6	100.0	157.8	100.0	210.8	100.0

Panel 2:

FDI inward stock, by host region, and outward stock, by home region, 1980-1995

	1980				1985			
	In		Out		In		Out	
	$bil.	%	$bil.	%	$bil.	%	$bil.	%
Japan	3.3	0.7	18.8	3.7	4.7	0.6	44.3	6.5
China	–	–	–	–	3.4	0.5	0.1	0.0
ASEAN	24.8	5.2	1.3	0.3	49.8	6.8	2.3	0.3
NIEs	11.4	2.4	0.9	0.2	21.2	2.9	4.3	0.6
Asia-Pacific	33.3	6.9	20.3	4.0	66.1	9.0	49.6	7.2
World	481.9	100.0	513.7	100.0	734.9	100.0	685.5	100.0

Notes: % denotes the share of the world total. The ASEAN includes Malaysia, Thailand, Indonesia, Philippines, Singapore, and Brunei Darussalam. The NIEs include Korea, Taiwan, Hong Kong, and Singapore. Asia-Pacific is the total of Japan, China, ASEAN, and NIEs, with the amount for Singapore subtracted to take into account its double counting.

| | 1993 | | | | 1995 | | | |
| | In | | Out | | In | | Out | |
	$bil.	%	$bil.	%	$bil.	%	$bil.	%
Japan	0.2	0.1	15.5	6.9	0.04	0.0	21.3	6.7
China	27.5	13.2	4.4	2.0	37.5	11.9	3.5	1.1
ASEAN	14.7	7.1	3.3	1.4	19.4	6.2	6.3	2.0
NIEs	8.2	3.9	23.4	10.4	10.4	3.3	34.6	10.9
Asia-Pacific	45.6	21.9	44.8	19.9	62.0	19.7	62.9	19.8
World	207.9	100.0	225.5	100.0	314.9	100.0	317.8	100.0

| | 1990 | | | | 1995 | | | |
| | In | | Out | | In | | Out | |
	$bil.	%	$bil.	%	$bil.	%	$bil.	%
Japan	9.9	0.6	204.7	12.2	17.8	0.7	305.5	11.2
China	14.1	0.8	2.5	0.1	129.0	4.9	17.3	0.6
ASEAN	95.5	5.6	7.6	0.5	168.6	6.3	25.3	0.9
NIEs	63.9	3.7	32.9	2.0	106.9	4.0	134.4	4.9
Asia-Pacific	151.0	8.8	243.0	14.4	366.8	13.8	468.7	17.2
World	1,716.9	100.0	1,684.1	100.0	2,657.9	100.0	2,730.1	100.0

Source: World Investment Report 1995 and 1996, United Nations.

flows of trade or FDI from the home country i to host country j can be explained by supply conditions at the home country (usually income and population), by demand conditions at the host country (usually income and population), and by economic forces either assisting or resisting the flow's movement.

The distinctive feature of the model is to specify explicitly the resistance forces such as distance, trade barriers, or cultural differences, and the assistance forces such as regional membership, common language, openness, or economic similarity. The model, in the past, has been criticized for its lack of theoretical foundation. However, works by Anderson (1979), Thursby and Thursby (1987), and Bergstrand (1989) have made great strides toward addressing this criticism. The model's empirical success, however, is widely known.[2]

The general form of the gravity equation is specified as follows:[3]

$$X_{ij} = \beta_0 (Y_i)^{\beta_1} (Y_j)^{\beta_2} (N_i)^{\beta_3} (N_j)^{\beta_4} (R_{ij})^{\beta_5} (A_{ij})^{\beta_6} U_{ij} \qquad (1)$$

where X_{ij} is the bilateral flow of good or investment from country or region i to country or region j, Y_i and Y_j are incomes in country i and country j, N_i and N_j are population in country i and country j, and R_{ij} and A_{ij} are the resistance factor including distance and the assistance factor such as the grouping effect, respectively, from the economic center of country (region) i to that of country (region) j. The U_{ij} is a log-normally distributed error term with $E(U_{ij}) = 0$.

There are three general explanations for the gravity model. The first is grounded in physics. It draws on the laws of gravitation and electrical forces for arriving at the conclusion that the flow of goods from country i to country j equals the product of the potential trade capacities (i.e., income) of the two countries, divided by the resistance factor (i.e., geographical distance between the two economies). The second explanation is based on a Walrasian general equilibrium model with each country having its own supply and demand functions for all goods. Aggregate income proxies the level of demand in the importing country and the level of supply in the exporting country. The gravity model is viewed as a reduced-form equation for trade volume (proxied by value) in which prices do not enter because they are endogenous. Distance proxies transportation costs, which drive a wedge between supply and demand.

The third explanation is based on probability theory. Let Z_i be country i's total imports, which is an unidentified reduced-form function of income, population, and other possibly unobservable variables. The set $[Z_i/T]$, where $T = \Sigma_i Z_i$ and world trade, has the form of a probability distribution. Alternatively, Z_i/T represents trade potential for country i. The probability of the occurrence of flows between country i and country j is taken to be $Z_i Z_j / T^2$. Alternatively, trade potential between country i and country j is the product of country i's and country j's potentials. The expected size of the flow, given T, is then $M_{ij} = Z_i Z_j / T$. The term T is a constant in the cross-sectional study and can be neglected.

Resistance to trade, proxied by distance, can be inserted into the equation. When transformed to the log-linear form, we have the traditional gravity equation. The third explanation forms the basis for the model applied here. The magnitude of bilateral trade flows between two countries may be determined by supply conditions at the origin, by demand conditions at the destination, and by stimulating or restraining forces relating to the specific flows between the two countries.

The role of geography in determining trade patterns has received renewed interest of late. This economic geography theory states that historical geographic conditions often factor heavily in the development of certain industries in certain locations. These industries tend to become focused in one geographic region, due to many reasons. The development of a regional block of industries could be due to the proximity of a needed resource to the available pool of specialized (or nonspecialized as the case may be) labor or end-market locations. In any event, this argument provides further justification for the consideration of a distance or geographic factor in explaining trade/FDI patterns, as well as the inclusion of regional dummy variables.

After specifying the resistance and assistance variables and taking logarithms with equation (1), the gravity-type equation for our purpose takes the following form:

$$FDI_{ij} = \beta_0 + \beta_1 GDP_i + \beta_2 Pop_i + \beta_3 GDP_j + \beta_4 Pop_j + \beta_5 Distance_{ij}$$
$$+ \beta_6 Trade_{ij} + \beta_7 APEC + \beta_8 ASEAN + \beta_9 DEA + \varepsilon_{ij} \quad\quad (2)$$

In equation (2), FDI_{ij} and $Trade_{ij}$ represent total bilateral FDI/trade flows between two countries, where subscripts i and j identify the home country and the host country, respectively. *GDP* is the gross domestic product, *Pop* is the population, and *Distance* is the geographical distance between the two countries i and j. All economic variables are in their natural logarithm form.

We include bilateral trade, T_{ij}, as an independent variable to examine whether trade complements FDI activity (when β_6 is significantly positive) or supplements FDI activity (when β_6 is significantly negative). As stated above, we are also looking for regional effects as they relate to the Asia-Pacific region. We believe that the region's dynamics provide stimulus to trade and foreign direct investment over and above what can be explained by simple geographic proximity. We have included APEC, ASEAN, and DAE (Dynamic Asian Economics) dummy variables in the estimation equations.[4] These represent dummies which take on a value of "1" when both country i and country j are members of a specific regional grouping. Thus, the equation states that FDI flows between two countries depend on each country's GDP, population, regional membership, distance, and FDI (trade) flows.

The expected signs for GDP in the estimation equation are not straightforward. It is well documented that most FDI flows take place among developed countries. Assuming that these FDI flows are not taken in search of cost-saving but rather market-penetration, one would expect a positive relationship between FDI flows and GDP in the host country as well as in the home country. Large and developed countries also tend to breed large companies that are capable of overseas FDI activities, leading to a positive coefficient of the home GDP.

However, when FDI activities are motivated for the cost-saving purpose, utilizing abundant skilled and nonskilled labor and natural resources in the local markets of developing countries, a negative sign on the coefficient of the host GDP in the FDI equation is expected.

While GDP proxies the economy's wealth and production capacity, population proxies market size and potential for purchasing power.[5] A larger population may indicate a large domestic market and lead to a decreased need for overseas investment. To the contrary, an economy with a smaller population, indicating a limited domestic market, would seek for overseas market opportunities to exploit economies of scale. Thus, the home-country population is expected to have a negative sign for FDI flows. A large host-country population, however, would entice foreign investment to meet domestic demand for foreign capital. Firms also tend to have a physical presence in markets that they deem key. Thus, the host population is expected to have a positive sign for FDI flows.

Overpopulation, as in many populous developing countries in the Asia-Pacific region, however, may deter an effective hosting of foreign investment, especially at their early stages of economic development and emerging markets. This implies a possibility of a negative sign of the host population in the FDI equation. Therefore, the sign for the host country population variable is an empirical question.

Further distances may encourage firms to invest directly in the remote host market for the purpose of reducing transportation costs and serving their customers better, implying a positive sign of the distance variable in the FDI equation. However, greater distances usually mean unfamiliar language, culture, and higher transaction costs, and, accordingly, may detract from the FDI activities. Thus, the expected sign of the distance variable in the FDI gravity equation is not clear. When both country i and country j are members of a regional economic grouping, this regional effect is captured by the membership dummy. If the regional dummies are significant, it would indicate that such groupings affect FDI flows over and above distance factors. That is, the regional grouping enhances, if positive, FDI flows beyond what can be explained simply by the fact that they are located close to each other. A positive sign on a membership dummy would indicate that common membership in a regional economic organization increases FDI flows between the two countries.

What is unknown is the sign of the trade variable in the FDI equation. Resource extraction and outsourcing FDI tend to lead to increased trade on a complementary basis, and would indicate a positive sign. However, FDI motivated by barriers to trade or market penetration would tend to be a substitute for trade and indicate a negative sign. The signs of the trade variable in the FDI gravity equation, therefore, will be determined empirically.

The Data

We have applied a cross-sectional study to a number of countries involved in the FDI activity and trade around the world. Our data set was limited by the amount of information available for each country involved. The gravity equation investigates bilateral flows of trade and FDI between two different economies. Therefore, it was necessary to obtain pertinent data not only for each individual country but also for flows between countries as well.

We collected data for bilateral FDI flows, inflows and outflows, along with bilateral trade, exports and imports, for the selected group of countries, during the years 1987 through 1993. Given our focus on the Asia-Pacific region, we centered our country selection around the nine major economies of East Asia, as already defined by the DAE dummy variable, as well as China, India, Australia, and other major trading partners. We attempted to keep the data sets consistent across time periods for better comparisons.

The data for bilateral FDI flows were obtained from the UN's *World Investment Directory* for various years, OECD's *Foreign Direct Investment Statistics Yearbook,* and individual country source data.[6] Bilateral trade data were obtained from the International Monetary Fund's (IMF) *Direction of Trade Statistics Yearbook* for various years. Other data were collected from the IMF's *International Financial Statistics* for various years.

EMPIRICAL EVIDENCE

We report the cross-sectional estimation results of the gravity equation for FDI flows during the years 1987, 1989, 1991, and 1993 in Table 9.2. The overall performance of fit of the FDI gravity equation to the data seems good, with around 50 to 60 % of R^2.

First of all, the coefficients of the home GDP and population variables are highly significant every year. The sizes of the coefficients of the home GDP variable, which are the home-country income elasticities of FDI flows, have been in the range of 0.5 to 0.8, while those of the home population variable, which are the home country population elasticities of FDI flows, have been varying in the range of -0.4 to -0.8. For example, in 1993, every 1% increases in the GDP and population in the home country were responsible for increasing FDI flows by 0.53% and decreasing FDI flows by 0.49%, respectively.

The positive sign of the home GDP variable and the negative sign of the home population variable together imply that high-income countries with the smaller size of domestic markets have been more active in investing directly in overseas markets in the pursuit of the economies of scale effect than the countries with large populations. The smaller the market size in the home country, the more need to expand into foreign markets to exploit economies of scale.

As Table 9.2 indicates, however, the coefficients of the host GDP and population variables are not significant and vary in signs and magnitudes. This seems to imply that FDI flows in the region are driven more by market size and income in the home country than by those in the host country, in general. It is suggested that the FDI activity undertaken in the Asia-Pacific countries during the sample period were supply-side driven, complementary to trade, and not overwhelmingly based on serving host markets in the region.

Table 9.2. Estimation Results for the FDI Gravity Equation

	1987	1989	1991	1993
Constant	-12.70***	-11.70***	-8.40***	-7.10***
	(2.301)	(2.292)	(2.710)	(2.277)
Home GDP	0.650***	0.756***	0.795***	0.529***
	(0.164)	(0.154)	(0.212)	(0.156)
Host GDP	-0.089	0.150	-0.247	-0.183
	(0.149)	(0.155)	(0.173)	(0.120)
Home Pop.	-0.380***	-0.690***	-0.810***	-0.490***
	(1.148)	(0.128)	(0.215)	(0.165)
Host Pop.	-0.044	-0.087	0.086	-0.045
	(0.115)	(0.117)	(0.141)	(0.093)
Distance	0.157	-0.065	0.033	-0.048
	(0.161)	(0.159)	(0.205)	(0.143)
Trade	1.132***	0.931***	0.917***	1.113***
	(0.160)	(0.168)	(0.207)	(0.146)
APEC	-0.396	-0.020	-0.161	-0.403
	(0.349)	(0.324)	(0.355)	(0.311)
ASEAN	0.519	-0.752	0.366	-0.556
	(0.674)	(0.687)	(0.644)	(0.709)
DAE	-0.068	0.616	-0.212	-0.427
	(0.422)	(0.414)	(0.459)	(0.468)
R^2	58.3%	56.6%	49.6%	54.7%
SSE	1.793	1.658	1.655	1.559
DW	1.61	1.75	1.88	1.87
White Test	0.553	0.382	0.299	0.512
Number of Observations	225	215	155	195

Note: Coefficients are reported with their standard errors in parentheses. *, **, and *** represent significance at the 10%, 5%, and 1% levels, respectively. The White test was conducted to detect heteroskedacity in the error term. DW refers to the Durbin-Watson test for autocorrelation in the error term.

One of the most interesting results comes from the trade variable. The coefficient of the trade variable is highly significant across the entire period and has a positive sign. The size of the coefficient has fluctuated somewhat but remained at around 1.0. In 1993, for example, a 1% increase in bilateral trade led to a 1.11% increase in FDI flows between the two countries. Throughout the sample period, a 1% increase in trade was associated with an increase in FDI flows by somewhere between 0.92% and 1.13%. It is suggested that bilateral FDI flows were greatly enhanced by bilateral trade flows, and trade-driven FDI flows were more prevalent than other types of FDI, at least during the sample period in the Asia-Pacific economies. These results also suggest the dominance of the complementary relationship, rather than the supplementary relationship, between trade and FDI flows.

Table 9.2 also shows that distance is not a significant factor in determining FDI. It is evident that geographical distance between the home country and the host country may be a significant resistance factor for trade, but not for FDI flows. The coefficients on regional dummies are not statistically significant either. Overall, it seems to indicate that regional arrangements have only rarely been influential in determining bilateral FDI flows during the sample period in the Asia-Pacific region.

The empirical findings discussed above can lead to some policy implications. First, the complementary nature of trade and FDI should be considered importantly in the process of negotiating greater liberalization of FDI and establishing a comprehensive multilateral framework for FDI. Second, the overall insignificance of distance and the regional grouping effect in determining bilateral FDI flows is a drastic contrast with the results reported in the trade literature. This evidence is suggestive of the need for drastically different approaches to negotiating for the changes in the FDI regime in the region, especially at the multilateral level under the auspices of the newly launched WTO system.

CONCLUSIONS

This chapter investigated the main determinants of bilateral FDI flows, with emphasis on the Asia-Pacific economies, applying the cross-sectional, gravity-model approach. The estimation results suggest that the FDI activity undertaken in the Asia-Pacific countries were, in general, supply-side driven, complementary to trade, and irrelevant to both the geographical distance and the regional grouping effect.

First, the home-country variables of GDP and population were significant in explaining bilateral FDI flows, while the host-country variables were not. It is suggested that less populous high-income countries with smaller size of domestic markets in the region tend to engage in the FDI activity more actively than others in the pursuit of economies of scale. Second, the estimation results also provide evidence of a significant and positive relationship between bilateral flows of trade and FDI. The FDI activity was shown to have been greatly enhanced by trade with a unit trade elasticity of FDI flows, suggesting that a certain percent increase in trade between two countries tends to generate the same percent increase in bilateral FDI flows in the region. Finally, the geographical distance between two economies on FDI flows were found to be insignificant. It is evident that distance between the home country and the host country may be a significant resistance factor for trade, but not for FDI flows.

The regional dummy variables, representing the grouping effects of APEC, ASEAN, and DAE, showed little explanatory power in the FDI gravity equation. It could be said that these groupings might be more instrumental in promoting bilateral and intragroup trade than FDI flows. The formation of APEC in 1989 seems to have had little impact on FDI in the Asia-Pacific region. This could be explained by still early stages of the liberalization of foreign investment and capital flows in the region. The recent decision by the annual APEC Summits to liberalize trade and investment and the on-going process of establishing multi-lateral rules and guidelines for international investment are expected to create a more favorable climate for FDI flows into the APEC nations and for intragroup investment in the region.

NOTES

1. For detailed examples, see Tables V.2-V.4, "Main international instruments dealing with FDI, 1948-1996," and "Examples of bilateral investment treaties," pp. 135-146, in *World Investment Report* (United Nations, 1996).

2. Gravity models have been applied successfully to different types of flows, such as commuting, migration, and interregional and international trade. See Deardorff (1984) for a review of the application of the gravity equation to model bilateral trade flows.

3. For discussion on theoretical foundations of the gravity equation, see Anderson (1979).

4. We have formulated our own grouping for the DAE, composed of the nine most dynamic members in the region: Hong Kong, Indonesia, Japan, Korea, Malaysia, Philippines, Singapore, Taiwan, and Thailand. China would have been included if more complete data were available.

5. The model was also run using per capita income (PCI) as a proxy for market size or potential. However, the model using population performed better. A possible explanation is that the GDP variable already captured the country's wealth, and thus market size or potential for purchasing power is more purely captured through the population variable. Of course, China and India immediately come to mind when considering countries with large populations and limited current market performances. However, the large FDI flows into China in recent years indicates that population may be in some instances a better explanatory variable when income is already captured through GDP.

6. The individual country sources for the data include Bank of Japan's Quarterly Bulletin, Bank of Korea's Quarterly Review, Bank of Indonesia's Quarterly Review, Bank Negara Malaysia's Quarterly Bulletin, Bank of Thailand's Quarterly Bulletin, Singapore Economic Development Board's Annual Yearbook, and Taiwan's Statistical Data Book.

REFERENCES

Anderson, James E., 1979. A theoretical foundation for the gravity equation, *The American Economic Review* 69(1), pp. 106-116.

Bank of Japan, 1994. Economic growth in East Asia and the role of foreign direct investment, *Quarterly Bulletin*, February, pp. 40-67.

Bergstrand, Jeffrey H., 1989. The generalized gravity equation, monopolistic competition and the factor-proportions theory in international trade, *The Review of Economics and Statistics* February, pp. 143-153.

Deardorff, A., 1984. Testing trade theories and predicting trade flows. In R.W. Jones and P.K. Kenen, eds., *Handbook of International Economics*, Vol. 1. Amsterdam: North-Holland.

Frankel, Jeffrey A., 1998. Is Japan establishing a trade bloc in East Asia and the pacific? In *Japan's Economy After the Miracle*, Mitsuaki Okabe, ed. New York: Macmillan Press.

Frankel, Jeffrey A., David Romer, and Teresa Cyrus, 1995. Trade and growth in East Asian countries: cause and effect? Presented at the AEA meetings, Washington, DC, January.

Lall, Sanjaya, 1991. Direct investment in South-East Asia by the NIEs: trends and prospects, *Banca Nazionale del Lavoro* No. 179, pp. 463-480.

Lucas, Robert E., 1991. On the determinants of direct foreign investment: evidence from East and Southeast Asia, *World Development*, 21(3), 391-406.

Maehara, Yasuhiro, 1995. The role of foreign direct investment in the economies of East Asia, *Economic Cooperation and Challenges in the Pacific*, U.S.-Korea Academic Symposium.

OECD, 1995. *Foreign Direct Investment: OECD Countries and Dynamic Economies of Asia and Latin America*. Paris.

OECD, 1993. *Foreign Direct Investment Relations Between the OECD and the Dynamic Asian Economies*. Paris.

Ramstetter, Eric D., 1991. *Direct Foreign Investment in Asia: Developing Economies and Structural Change in the Asia-Pacific Region*. Boulder, CO: Westview Press.

Riedel, James, 1992. Intra-Asian trade and foreign direct investment, *Asian Development Review* 9(1).

Stone, Susan F. and Bang Nam Jeon, 1997. The cointegration relationship between foreign direct investment and trade in the Asia-Pacific region, mimeo, Drexel University.

Thursby, Jerry G. and Marie C. Thursby, 1987. Bilateral trade flows, the Linder Hypothesis and exchange risk, *The Review of Economics and Statistics,* August, pp. 488-495.

United Nations, Transnational Corporations and Management Division, 1993. *Foreign Investment and Trade Linkages in Developing Countries*. New York.

United Nations Conference on Trade and Development (UNCTAD), *World Investment Report,* 1995 and 1996.

PART IV
Corporate Finance and Banking

10

Executive Views on Dividends and Capital Structure Policy in the Asia-Pacific Region

George W. Kester, Rosita P. Chang, Erlinda S. Echanis, Mansor Md. Isa, Michael T. Skully, Susatio Soedigno, and Kai-Chong Tsui

This chapter reports the survey results of executives that have been conducted over the past five years in six countries in the Asia-Pacific region—Australia, Hong Kong, Indonesia, Malaysia, the Philippines, and Singapore—regarding their views on two major areas of corporate financial policy: dividends and capital structure. These surveys are part of a continuing research effort to assess the views of executives in the region regarding issues related to corporate financial policy. The views of these executives are compared to the views of executives in the United States based upon the results of previously reported surveys.[1]

SURVEY DESIGN

To assess the perceptions of executives in the six Asia-Pacific Countries, we surveyed a sample of firms listed on the Australian Stock Exchange, Stock Exchange of Hong Kong, Kuala Lumpur Stock Exchange, Jakarta Stock Exchange, Philippine Stock Exchange, and Stock Exchange of Singapore.

Mail questionnaires were used to obtain information regarding dividends and capital structure policy. In the cases of Australia, Malaysia, and Singapore, the surveys on dividends and capital structure were conducted separately. In the other countries, the questionnaires were combined. The first mailings were followed by complete second mailings to improve the response rates.

The questionnaires, which were mailed either to the sample firms' chief executive officers (CEOs) or chief financial officers (CFOs), consisted of several closed-ended and open-ended questions about various issues concerning dividend policy and capital structure policy. They did not require the firms to identify themselves. The questionnaires used in Hong Kong, Malaysia, the Philippines, and Singapore were written in English. The questionnaires used in

Indonesia were written in both English and Bahasa Indonesia, the national language. The dividend policy portion of the questionnaires was adapted by permission from the questionnaire used by Baker, Farrelly, and Edelman (1985). The capital structure policy portion was adapted by permission from the questionnaire used by Pinegar and Wilbricht (1989).

Table 10.1 contains comparative data on the surveys including, for each survey, month and year of the survey, executives surveyed, number of listed companies at the time of the survey, number of companies in the survey sample, and response rate. Table 10.2 contains a breakdown of the industries (self-reported) represented in the responses.

DIVIDEND POLICY: BACKGROUND

The focal point of financial management is the goal of shareholder wealth maximization, which is operationalized by the net present value (NPV) criterion for accepting or rejecting investments. According to the NPV criterion, a firm should accept all investment opportunities promising returns in excess of their required rates of return. From this follows the residual dividend policy: dividends should be paid from earnings leftover after financing the equity portion of all positive NPV projects. Any leftover earnings should be distributed to the firm's shareholders who can in turn earn higher returns in other investments with the same level of risk. However, depending upon the timing and magnitude of earnings and the investment opportunities available to the firm, strict adherence to the residual policy on a year-to-year basis results in an erratic pattern of dividends. Much of the debate surrounding dividend policy deals with the effects that changes in dividends have on share value.

Traditionalists believe that shareholders prefer dividends to the capital gains that would be expected to result from the reinvestment of earnings by the firm. All else remaining constant, any cuts in dividends resulting from the residual policy would likely result in a decrease in share price. Early proponents of this so-called bird-in-the-hand theory, Gordon (1959) and Lintner (1962), argued that dividends are less risky than capital gains. Capital gains depend upon not only the profitable reinvestment of earnings by the firm, but also upon movements in the overall stock market. Because dividends are less risky than capital gains, shareholders will value the shares of firms with high dividend payout ratios than firms with low payout ratios, all else remaining constant.

An alternate view is that dividend policy is irrelevant. In a seminal theoretical paper, Nobel laureates Miller and Modigliani (1961) demonstrated that dividend policy is irrelevant in a world of perfect and efficient capital markets. This position, which has been extended by Black and Scholes (1974), Miller and Scholes (1978), and others, argues that shareholders are concerned only with the firm's earnings, not the proportions retained in the firm and paid out as dividends. Shareholders are indifferent to whether or not dividends are paid and consequently would be indifferent to the erratic dividends that would result from adherence to the residual policy.

Table 10.1. Comparative Data on Surveys

Country	Month/Year of Survey	Executives Surveyed	Number of Listed Companies[a]	Number in Sample	Number of Responses	Response Rate	Language of Questionnaire
Australia							
Dividend Policy	7/94	CFOs	1,163	119	65	54.6%	English
Capital Structure	10/96	CFOs	1,230	159	55	34.6%	English
Hong Kong	4/92	CEOs	357	246	37	15.0%	English
Indonesia	11/94	CEOs	210	210	53	25.2%	English[b] Bahasa Indonesia
Malaysia							
Capital Structure	8/93	CEOs	370	361	104	28.8%	English
Dividend Policy	4/96	CFOs	543	543	104	19.2%	English
Philippines	10/95	CEOs	205	185	41	22.2%	English
Singapore							
Dividend Policy	4/90	CEOs	151	123	85	69.1%	English
Capital Structure	11/92	CEOs	215	140	65	46.4%	English

[a]The number of firms shown are the number of listed firms that existed at the times of the surveys.

[b]Two survey questionnaires were mailed to each sample firm in Indonesia, one written in English and the other in Bahasa Indonesia. The returned questionnaires consisted of 34% written in English and 66% in Bahasa Indonesia.

116

Table 10.2. Industry Sectors Represented in Responses

Country	Finance	Hotel	Industrial	Wholesale or Retail	Properties	Multiple or Other
Australia						
Dividend Policy	16.9%	0.0%	50.8%	6.1%	0.0%	26.2%
Capital Structure	9.1%	0.0%	45.5%	3.6%	0.0%	41.8%
Hong Kong	10.8%	8.1%	32.5%	0.0%	13.5%	35.1%
Indonesia	24.5%	1.9%	41.5%	3.8%	11.3%	17.0%
Malaysia						
Dividend Policy	6.7%	0.0%	35.6%	6.7%	11.5%	39.5%
Capital Structure	6.7%	0.0%	28.9%	4.8%	7.7%	51.9%
Philippines	9.8%	2.4%	12.2%	0.0%	4.9%	70.7%
Singapore						
Dividend Policy	9.4%	7.1%	30.6%	9.4%	9.4%	34.1%
Capital Structure	13.8%	4.6%	21.6%	12.3%	10.8%	36.9%

Notwithstanding the debate that continues among academicians, practitioners behave as though dividend policy does matter; behavior may or may not be rational and theoretically justified. In a classic study based upon interviews with U.S. corporate executives in the mid-1950s, Lintner (1956) reported that although many firms do have long-run payout ratios based upon earnings, year-to-year dividends respond slowly to earnings. Temporary increases or decreases in earnings have little effect on dividends in the short run. In short, he found that firms are reluctant to increase dividends to levels that cannot be sustained for fear of later having to cut dividends.[2]

As a result of these interviews, Lintner hypothesized a lagged partial adjustment model that relates changes in dividends to both past dividends and current earnings. Lintner's behavioral model, or variations of it, has been empirically tested over the years by a number of researchers. For example, it has been applied to developed financial market data in the United States by Fama and Babiak (1968), Watts (1973), and Roy and Cheung (1985); in Canada by Chateau (1979); in the United Kingdom by Ryan (1974); in Australia by Shevlin (1982); and in Singapore by Ariff and Johnson (1989). In general, the results of these studies are consistent with Lintner's hypothesized partial adjustment toward a target payout ratio.

Lintner's findings have been updated and supported by more recent surveys of policy makers. For example, Baker, Farrelly, and Edelman (1985) surveyed the CFOs of U.S. firms in and found that executives continue to place importance on maintaining dividend continuity. Most respondents agreed that firms should avoid making changes in dividends that might soon be reversed and should strive for an uninterrupted record of dividend payments. In another survey of U.S. firms, Pinegar and Wilbricht (1989) found additional evidence of strong managerial preference for dividend continuity.

One explanation offered to justify stable dividend policies is the "clientele effect," which describes the tendency of each firm to attract its own clientele of investors who are in part attracted to the firm because of its dividend policy.[3] Some investors prefer high payout stocks, whereas others prefer capital gains. If the firm strictly adheres to the residual policy on a year-to-year basis, the result-ing volatile dividends would cause shifts in the composition of its shareholders (its clientele) which may, at least temporarily, disrupt its share price as the old shareholder group sells its shares.[4]

Another reason offered for this practice is the "signaling effect" (or "infor-mation content of dividends"), which focuses upon the information that changes in dividends convey to investors.[5] According to the signaling effect, changes in the level of dividends may convey new information to investors regarding future earnings or cash flows. This is due to information asymmetries between man-agers and investors. Therefore, reductions in dividends that may periodically result from year-to-year adherence to the residual policy would send out negative signals to shareholders regarding the prospects of the firm, thereby adversely affecting its share price.

In short, actual corporate practice, which may be somewhat explained on the basis of the clientele and signaling effects, suggests that shareholders may not be indifferent to significant changes in a firm's dividend policy.

DIVIDEND POLICY: SURVEY RESULTS

To assess executive views on issues concerning dividend policy, the respondents were asked to indicate their level of agreement with each of the 14 closed-end statements (identified later by "S") based upon a 7-point scale: -3 = strongly disagree, -2 = moderately disagree, -1 = slightly disagree, 0 = no opinion, +1 = slightly agree, +2 = moderately agree, and +3 = strongly agree. Table 10.3 contains summary statistics on the responses to the closed-end statements from all six countries in the study, and, for comparative purposes, the United States. The statements are not listed in the order in which they appeared in the questionnaires.

The summary statistics on the responses of U.S. executives included in Table 10.3 were derived from Baker, Farrelly, and Edelman (1985, p. 81), and include manufacturing and wholesale/retail firms. Utilities are excluded.[6]

It should be noted that 11 statements were common to the questionnaires in all seven countries. Two statements (S12 and S13) did not appear on the ques-tionnaire used in Singapore, which instead contained S14, a slightly different version of S13.

Table 10.3. Comparative Survey Results

| | Level of Agreement | | | | |
| | Disagreement | Agreement | | | |
	(-3 -2)	(-1 0 +1)	(+2 +3)	Mean	Country
Attitudes on Dividends and Share Value					
1. Dividend payout affects	3.1%	28.1%	68.8%	1.63	Australia
the share price.	2.7%	21.6%	75.7%	1.92	Hong Kong
	3.8%	35.8%	60.4%	1.43	Indonesia
	10.7%	45.6%	43.7%	1.02	Malaysia
	2.4%	46.3%	51.2%	1.59	Philippines
	7.1%	42.4%	50.6%	1.24	Singapore
	6.9%	40.2%	52.9%	1.42	U.S.
2. Capital gains expected	7.9%	69.8%	22.2%	0.49	Australia
to result from earnings	10.8%	70.3%	18.9%	0.19	Hong Kong
retention are riskier than	11.3%	56.6%	32.1%	0.64	Indonesia
dividend expectations.	13.7%	55.9%	30.4%	0.56	Malaysia
	20.5%	61.5%	17.9%	-0.13	Philippines
	18.8%	37.6%	43.5%	0.53	Singapore
	9.0%	56.5%	34.5%	0.69	U.S.
Attitudes on Lintner's Findings					
3. A firm should strive to main-	1.6%	35.9%	62.5%	1.83	Australia
tain uninterrupted dividend	0.0%	13.5%	86.5%	2.16	Hong Kong
payments.	3.8%	13.2%	83.0%	2.25	Indonesia
	2.9%	16.3%	80.8%	2.12	Malaysia
	4.9%	29.3%	65.9%	1.56	Philippines
	1.2%	14.1%	84.7%	2.39	Singapore
	1.9%	21.6%	76.5%	2.06	U.S.
4. A firm should avoid making	7.8%	31.3%	60.9%	1.39	Australia
changes in dividends that	5.4%	16.2%	78.4%	1.78	Hong Kong
might have to be reversed	9.4%	39.6%	50.9%	1.04	Indonesia
in a year or so.	7.7%	18.3%	74.0%	1.71	Malaysia
	4.9%	26.8%	68.3%	1.76	Philippines
	4.7%	23.5%	71.8%	1.85	Singapore
	3.0%	9.8%	87.2%	2.38	U.S.
5. A firm should have a target	9.4%	43.8%	46.9%	0.95	Australia
payout ratio and periodically	0.0%	27.0%	73.0%	1.84	Hong Kong
adjust its payout toward	1.9%	15.0%	83.0%	2.06	Indonesia
that target.	6.7%	26.0%	67.3%	1.55	Malaysia
	4.9%	34.1%	61.0%	1.54	Philippines
	8.2%	30.6%	61.2%	1.47	Singapore
	6.4%	26.1%	67.5%	1.64	U.S.

| | Level of Agreement | | | | |
| | Disagreement | Agreement | | | |
	(-3 -2)	(-1 0 +1)	(+2 +3)	Mean	Country
6. A change in the existing	30.2%	55.6%	14.3%	-0.43	Australia
dividend payout is more	8.1%	64.9%	27.0%	0.70	Hong Kong
important than the actual	17.0%	52.8%	30.2%	0.28	Indonesia
amount of dividends.	12.6%	58.3%	29.1%	0.46	Malaysia
	29.3%	61.0%	9.8%	-0.29	Philippines
	21.4%	48.8%	29.8%	0.20	Singapore
	13.3%	49.7%	37.0%	0.73	U.S.

Attitudes on Signaling Effects

7. Reasons for dividend policy	0.0%	31.3%	68.8%	1.83	Australia
changes should be adequately	2.7%	45.9%	51.4%	1.32	Hong Kong
disclosed to investors.	0.0%	9.4%	90.6%	2.42	Indonesia
	6.7%	26.9%	66.3%	1.59	Malaysia
	0.0%	9.8%	90.2%	2.49	Philippines
	2.4%	28.2%	69.4%	1.81	Singapore
	1.5%	20.2%	78.3%	2.11	U.S.

8. Dividend payments provide	10.9%	42.2%	46.9%	1.05	Australia
a "signaling" device of	2.7%	51.4%	45.9%	1.32	Hong Kong
future company prospects.	17.0%	35.8%	47.2%	0.68	Indonesia
	9.6%	39.4%	51.0%	1.18	Malaysia
	9.8%	31.7%	58.5%	1.37	Philippines
	15.3%	43.5%	41.2%	0.80	Singapore
	6.9%	41.2%	51.9%	1.32	U.S.

9. The market uses dividend	9.4%	40.6%	50.0%	1.00	Australia
announcements as informa-	2.7%	54.1%	43.2%	1.08	Hong Kong
tion for assessing security	5.7%	41.5%	52.8%	1.40	Indonesia
values.	18.3%	52.9%	28.8%	0.56	Malaysia
	4.9%	46.3%	48.8%	1.29	Philippines
	20.0%	52.9%	27.1%	0.35	Singapore
	6.4%	55.0%	38.6%	1.03	U.S.

Attitudes on the Clientele Effect

10. Management should be	1.6%	48.4%	50.0%	1.47	Australia
responsive to its share-	5.4%	67.6%	27.0%	0.70	Hong Kong
holders' preferences	0.0%	20.8%	79.2%	1.87	Indonesia
regarding dividends.	8.7%	46.6%	44.7%	1.15	Malaysia
	2.4%	19.5%	78.0%	1.83	Philippines
	14.3%	51.2%	34.5%	0.71	Singapore
	11.3%	54.7%	34.0%	0.74	U.S.

table continues . . .

Table 10.3. Continued

| | Level of Agreement | | | | |
| | Disagreement | Agreement | | | |
	(-3 -2)	(-1 0 +1)	(+2 +3)	Mean	Country
11. Investors are basically	45.3%	46.9%	7.8%	-1.05	Australia
indifferent between returns	51.4%	40.5%	8.1%	-0.86	Hong Kong
from dividends versus those	39.6%	37.7%	22.6%	-0.45	Indonesia
from capital gains.	49.0%	29.8%	21.2%	-0.79	Malaysia
	32.5%	40.0%	27.5%	-0.25	Philippines
	51.8%	25.9%	22.3%	-0.73	Singapore
	57.0%	37.1%	5.9%	-1.37	U.S.
Attitudes on the Residual Policy					
12. New capital investment	7.8%	43.8%	48.4%	0.97	Australia
requirements of the firm	16.2%	54.1%	29.7%	0.41	Hong Kong
generally have little effect	20.8%	28.3%	50.9%	0.75	Indonesia
on modifying the pattern	38.5%	40.4%	21.2%	-0.37	Malaysia
of dividend behavior.	43.9%	34.1%	22.0%	-0.58	Philippines
	24.6%	36.5%	38.9%	0.30	U.S.
13. Dividend distributions	34.4%	50.0%	15.6%	-0.47	Australia
should be viewed as a	13.5%	43.2%	43.2%	0.73	Hong Kong
residual after financing	17.0%	45.3%	37.7%	0.51	Indonesia
desired investments from	21.2%	37.5%	41.3%	0.63	Malaysia
available earnings.	14.6%	29.3%	56.1%	1.15	Philippines
	31.0%	33.5%	35.5%	0.07	U.S.
14. Dividends should be viewed					
as a residual after financing					
financing desirable investments					
from available earnings:					
(a) in the short run.	22.0%	41.4%	36.6%	0.32	Singapore
(b) in the long run.	23.8%	38.1%	38.1%	0.42	Singapore

Attitudes on Dividends and Share Value

As previously noted, much of the controversy in the literature deals with the relationship between dividends and share value. Executives in all seven countries agreed that dividend payout affects share prices (S1) and therefore is not irrelevant. There was no strong consensus regarding whether returns from capital gains are more risky than returns from dividends (S2), the basic justification offered by traditionalists in support of the belief that shareholders prefer dividends to capital gains.

Attitudes on Lintner's Findings

Another issue was the level of agreement with statements supporting Lintner's findings, specifically S3, S4, S5, and S6. Executives in all seven countries agreed that a firm should strive to maintain uninterrupted dividend payments (S3) and should avoid making changes in dividends that might have to be reversed in a year or so (S4). They also agree that firms should have a target payout ratio and periodically adjust its payout toward that target (S5), although the level of agreement among Australian executives was not as high as the other countries.

Lintner's findings also suggest that a change in existing dividend payout is more important than the actual amount of dividends (S6). There was no strong consensus regarding this statement.

Attitudes on Signaling Effects

Three statements involved signaling effects: S7, S8, and S9. The highest ranking statement in Australia, Indonesia, and the Philippines, as well as in the United States, was that reasons for dividend policy changes should be adequately disclosed to investors (S7). Executives in the other countries also agreed. Executives in all seven countries agreed that dividend payments provide a "signaling of the firm's prospects" (S8), although executives in Indonesia and Singapore expressed only slight agreement. There was no strong consensus among executives in Malaysia and Singapore regarding whether the market uses dividend announcements as information for assessing security values (S9). Executives in the other countries expressed only slight agreement.

Attitudes on the Clientele Effect

Three statements dealt with clientele effects: S2, S10, and S11. Executives in Australia as well as Indonesia, Malaysia, and the Philippines agreed that management should be responsive to its shareholders' preferences regarding dividends (S10). Executives in Hong Kong, Singapore, and the United States expressed slight agreement with this statement. Executives in all seven countries expressed slight disagreement with the statement that investors are indifferent between returns from dividends versus those from capital gains (S11). As previously mentioned, there was no strong consensus regarding whether shareholders have different perceptions regarding the riskiness of dividends and capital gains (S2).

Attitudes on the Residual Policy

An implication of the signaling and clientele effects is that the residual policy should not be adhered to in the short run (i.e., year-to-year) due to the erratic pattern of dividends that may result. If applied, it should be done over a longer period in order to smooth the firm's dividend payments. Statements S12, S13 and S14 address application of the residual policy. Whereas executives in Australia and Indonesia expressed slight agreement with the statement that new capital investment requirements have little effect on modifying the pattern of dividend behavior (S12), there was no strong consensus among executives in the other countries. On the other hand, executives in the Philippines slightly agreed with the statement that dividend distributions should be viewed as a residual after financing desired investments from earnings (S13). There was no strong consensus among executives in Australia, Hong Kong, Indonesia, Malaysia, and the United States. Executives in Singapore expressed no strong opinion with the statement that dividends should be viewed as a residual, either in the short run (S14a) or long run (S14b).

Determinants of Dividends

The closed-ended statements included in the dividend policy portion of the questionnaire are based upon theories derived from Western models of financial markets and institutions. And, as indicated in the previous section, the response patterns among executives in the Asia-Pacific region were similar to those in the United States. However, there may be other issues related to dividend policy in countries of the region that were not included. In an attempt to identify determinants of dividend policy that may be unique to these countries, the questionnaires used in Hong Kong, Malaysia, and Indonesia also included open-ended questions asking executives to identify the major factors in determining the dividend policies of their firms.

The responses to this question were varied. However, they were generally consistent with the perceptions of U.S. executives.[7] The two most frequently identified determinants included the firm's investment opportunities/requirements and the profitability of the firm. Respondents also cited the need to maintain stable dividends. The availability of cash, the firm's cash flows, and the firm's share price were also cited. Most of the determinants listed did not appear to be country-specific.[8]

The questionnaire used in the Philippines specifically listed three possible determinants of dividend policy along with blanks for listing other factors. Respondents agreed that the firm's investment opportunities, the availability and cost of alternative sources of capital, and constraints on dividend payments (e.g., cash availability, bond indentures) were important factors in the determination of dividend policy. Respondents did not list any other factors that appeared to be unique to the Philippines.

CAPITAL STRUCTURE POLICY: BACKGROUND

Modigliani and Miller (1958) advanced the proposition that, based upon several simplifying assumptions, capital structure has no effect on the value of a firm. However, recognizing the impact of taxes, bankruptcy, agency costs, and asymmetric information, capital structure theory has evolved to acknowledge that the use of debt does affect the value of a firm. Modern theories of capital structure can be classified into two categories: "static trade-off models" and the "pecking-order hypothesis." Static trade-off models imply an optimal debt-equity mix which is determined by a trade-off between the benefits and costs of debt (i.e., balancing the tax advantages of debt against the risk of bankruptcy and agency costs). The pecking-order hypothesis implies a hierarchy in raising funds, in which the firm prefers internal to external financing and, if it obtains external funds, debt to equity. This empirically motivated hypothesis, which has been theoretically justified on the basis of asymmetric information Myers and Majluf (1984), is consistent with Donaldson's (1961) classic description of actual financing practices in which he observed that firms prefer internal financing and have an aversion to issuing common stock.[9]

In their survey of 176 Fortune 500 firms in the United States, Pinegar and Wilbricht (1989) found that the financing hierarchy implied by the pecking-order hypothesis is more descriptive of actual practice than the static trade-off model. Accordingly, executives ranked internal equity (retained earnings) as their first choice of long-term financing, following by debt and then new common stock. Moreover, they found that capital structure policy is less binding than either the firm's investment decisions or dividend policy, a result that is consistent with survey findings of Pruitt and Gitman (1991).

CAPITAL STRUCTURE POLICY: SURVEY RESULTS

To assess executive views on capital structure policy, an adaptation of Pinegar and Wilbricht's questionnaire was used. In an attempt to identify determinants of capital structure policy that may be unique to the countries in the Asia-Pacific region, the questionnaires also included open-ended questions asking executives to identify the major factors affecting the capital structure policies of their firms.

The survey results in Australia, Hong Kong, Indonesia, Malaysia, the Philippines, and Singapore are compared to the results of the capital structure policy survey conducted in the United States by Pinegar and Wilbricht (1989).[10]

Target Capital Structure Versus Financing Hierarchy

The first question of the capital structure portions of the questionnaires asked respondents to indicate whether, in raising new long-term funds, firms should "maintain a target capital structure by using approximately constant proportions of several types of long-term funds simultaneously" or "follow a financing hierarchy in which the most advantageous sources of long-term funds are exhausted before other sources are used." As shown in Table 10.4, which summarizes the responses to these questions, executives in Australia expressed a slight preference for maintaining a target capital structure. However, executives in the other five Asia-Pacific countries, as well as the United States, expressed a

Table 10.4. Target Capital Structure Versus Financing Hierarchy

Preferred Capital Structure Policy	Aus- tralia	Hong Kong	Indo- nesia	Malay- sia	Philip- pines	Singa- pore	United States
Maintain target capital structure	52.8%	21.6%	21.2%	22.1%	10.0%	26.6%	31.2%
Follow financing hierarchy	47.2%	78.4%	78.8%	77.9%	90.0%	73.4%	68.8%

strong preference for following a financing hierarchy, and the results are consistent with the pecking-order hypothesis. However, as Ang, Fatemi, and Rad (1995) point out, preference for a financing hierarchy alone does not constitute sufficient support of the pecking order hypothesis which, as previously noted, also requires the presence of asymmetric information.[11]

Financing Hierarchy

Respondents who expressed a preference for the financing hierarchy were asked to rank various sources of long-term funds in order of preference for financing new investments, including internal equity (retained earnings), new common stock, bank loans, bonds, convertibles, and preferred stock. Table 10.5 compares the mean rankings of executives all seven countries. Since the specific securities listed in the survey questionnaires varied according to the country surveyed, the comparability of the rankings is limited. For each source, the percentage of responses within each rank, the percentage of respondents who did not rank the source, and the mean of the rankings are shown. Higher means indicate higher preferences.

As indicated, 64% of the respondents in Australia (who expressed a preference for following a financing hierarchy) ranked internal equity (retained earnings) as their first choice of financing. Internal equity was also ranked first by 65.5% of Hong Kong executives, 82.9% of Indonesian executives, 81% of Malaysian executives, 80.6% of Philippine executives, and 89.3% of Singaporean executives. By way of comparison, internal equity was ranked first by 84.3% of the respondents of Pinegar and Wilbricht's survey of U.S. executives.

These results are consistent with the pecking-order hypothesis, in which firms prefer internal to external financing. However, the pecking-order hypothesis further implies that if the firm raises external funds, debt is preferred to new common stock. As previously mentioned, U.S. executives responding to Pinegar and Wilbricht's survey ranked debt (both straight and convertible) higher than new common stock. However, only executives in Australia and the Philippines ranked debt (bank loans in both cases) higher than new common stock. However, they ranked bank loans ahead of new common stock and bonds below new

Table 10.5. Comparative Mean Rankings of Preference Rankings of Long-Term Funds Among Firms That Follow a Financing Hierarchy[a]

Sources of Long-Term Funds	Australia	Hong Kong	Indonesia	Malaysia	Philippines	Singapore	United States
Internal equity (retained earnings)	1	1	1	1	1	1	1
Straight debt[b]	–	–	–	–	–	–	2
Bank loans	2	3	4	3	2	3	–
Bonds	5	7	5	4	5	4	–
Convertibles, warrants, and options							
Convertible bonds	–	–	6	–	6	–	3
Convertible preferred stock	–	–	–	–	–	–	6
Warrants	–	6	–	–	–	–	–
Options or convertible notes	7	–	–	–	–	–	–
External equity (new shares)[c]	3	2	–	–	–	–	4
New common stock (to public)	–	–	2	5	4	5	–
New common stock (rights issue)	–	–	3	2	3	2	–
Preferred stock	7	4	7	6	6	6	5
Loans from affiliated companies	6	5	–	–	–	–	–
Dividend reinvestment plans (DRPs)	4	–	–	–	–	–	–
Other	–	–	–	7	–	7	–

[a]Using Pinegar and Wilbricht's method, mean rankings are calculated by multiplying the percentage in each category with assigned scores of 7 through 1 for rankings from 1 through 7, respectively. A score of 0 is assigned when a score is not ranked.

[b]Only one category of debt, "straight debt," was included in the U.S. survey. Two debt categories, "bank loans" and "bonds," were listed in the other surveys.

[c]Only one category of common stock, "external equity (new shares)" was listed on the surveys of Australian, Hong Kong, and U.S. executives.

common stock. Executives in both Hong Kong and Indonesia ranked new common stock higher than debt. The results in Malaysia and Singapore were mixed. Malaysian and Singaporean executives ranked new common stock sold to the public after debt; however, they ranked new common stock sold through rights issues ahead of debt. (Only one category of new common stock was listed in the questionnaires used in Australia, Hong Kong, and the United States).

Dividend reinvestment plans (DRPs), which were ranked fourth by Australian executives, have become an important source of equity financing in Australia. In fact, DRPs constituted the largest single source of new equity capital for listed companies during 1994-1995.[12]

The low rankings of convertibles and warrants in all six of the Asia-Pacific countries are not surprising, given the low importance of these securities in these countries. Preferred stock was ranked fourth by executives in Hong Kong and fifth or sixth by executives in the other Asia-Pacific countries.

Relative Importance of Various Financial Planning Principles

The next question elicited ratings, on a scale of 1 to 5 (where 1 = unimportant and 5 = important) of the relative importance of various financial planning principles affecting a firm's financing decisions. The comparative rankings for the seven countries are shown in Table 10.6.

Ensuring the long-term survivability of the firm is the most important consideration affecting a firm's financing decisions in all seven countries. The second most important consideration in all of the Asia-Pacific countries except Australia was maintaining financial flexibility. Maintaining financial independence as ranked second by Australian executives.

Maintaining long-term relationships with banks was ranked third by Indonesian executives. However, it was ranked fifth by executives in Hong Kong and Malaysia, and sixth in Australia, the Philippines, and Singapore.

The maximization of security prices, which was ranked fourth by Australian and U.S. executives, was not ranked as an important factor governing a firm's financing decisions by executives in the Philippines and Singapore, where it was ranked fifth, and Hong Kong, Indonesia, and Malaysia, where it was ranked sixth. This result is consistent with the findings of Stonehill et al. (1974) from their survey of the financial executives of 87 firms in five countries (France, Japan, the Netherlands, Norway, and the United States), where they found that not a single country's financial executives, not even those in the United States, ranked maximization of the market value of shares as their first or even second most important financial goal.

Empirical evidence in the capital structure literature suggests the existence of an industry effect.[13] However, the need to maintain comparability with firms in the same industry was ranked least important by executives in all seven countries. Apparently, they do not attach a high level of importance to adhering to industry norms, at least relative to other factors affecting financial decisions.

Table 10.6. Comparative Rankings of Financial Planning Principles by Order of
     Perceived Importance[a]

Planning Principle	Aus-tralia	Hong Kong	Indo-nesia	Malay-sia	Philip-pines	Singa-pore	United States
Ensuring long-term survival of firm	1	1	1	1	1	1	1
Maintaining financial flexibility	5	2	2	2	2	2	1
Maintaining predictable source of funds	3	4	5	4	3	4	3
Maximizing prices of publicly traded securities	4	6	6	6	5	5	4
Maintain financial independence	2	3	4	3	4	3	5
Maintaining a high debt rating	–	–	–	–	–	–	6
Maintaining long-term relationships with banks	6	5	3	5	6	6	–
Maintain comparability with firms in same industry	7	7	7	7	7	7	7

[a]Respondents were asked to indicate the relative importance of the financial planning principle on a scale of 1 to 5, where 1 = unimportant and 5 = important. Using Pinegar and Wilbricht's method, the rankings are based upon mean ratings of each financial planning principle, which are calculated by multiplying the percentage of responses in each category with values of 1 through 5. A score of 0 is assigned when not ranked.

Relative Importance of Capital Structure

Another question examined the importance of capital-structure decisions relative to other decisions. When presented with an attractive new growth opportunity that could not be taken without departing from the target capital structure or financing hierarchy, cutting the dividend, or selling off other assets, the majority of the respondents in each country (ranging from 56.8% in Hong Kong to 78.8% in Australia and 82.4% in the United States) indicated that they would deviate from their target capital structure or financing hierarchy rather than forgo the opportunity, sell off other assets, or cut common dividends. Only 4.6% of executives in Singapore, 5.4% in Hong Kong, and 5.8% in Australia would cut dividends. A higher 9.7% of Philippine, 15% of Malaysian, and 19.2% of Indonesian executives indicated they would cut dividends. These results, which are summarized in Table 10.7, are consistent with the survey results in the United States, suggesting that capital structure decisions in all seven countries are less binding than either investment or dividend decisions.

Table 10.7. Relative Importance of Capital Structure

Likely Action to be Taken in Response to Growth Opportunity	Aus-tralia	Hong Kong	Indo-nesia	Malay-sia	Philip-pines	Singa-pore	United States
Forgo the opportunity	1.9%	16.2%	3.9%	7.0%	12.2%	7.7%	3.4%
Deviate from the target capital structure or financing hierarchy	78.8%	56.8%	67.3%	67.0%	61.0%	76.9%	82.4%
Cut common dividend	5.8%	5.4%	19.2%	15.0%	9.7%	4.6%	1.7%
Sell off other assets	13.5%	21.6%	9.6%	11.0%	17.1%	10.8%	12.5%

The preference for dividend continuity is also consistent with the pecking-order theory and the results of the dividend policy portions of the surveys.

Determinants of Capital Structure Policy

The foregoing questions are based upon Western models of capital structure policy. And, as indicated in the previous sections, there appears to be general agreement on these issues among executives of all countries studied. As in the case of the dividend policy portion of the questionnaire, the capital structure portions of the questionnaires used in Australia, Hong Kong, Indonesia, Malaysia, and Singapore included open-ended questions asking executives to identify the major determinants of their firm's capital structure policy.

By far, the most widely cited factors listed were the level of interest rates and the costs of various sources of funds, which suggest that financial timing is an important consideration in making financing decisions. The firm's debt-to-equity ratio was also cited as an important consideration, even by those expressing a preference for following a financing hierarchy. Apparently, not all respondents view maintaining a target capital structure and following a financing hierarchy as being mutually exclusive. Over time, firms that follow a financing hierarchy may adjust toward a target capital structure.[14]

The questionnaire used in the Philippine survey asked respondents to rate, on a scale of 1 to 5 (where 1 = unimportant and 5 = important), specific determinants of capital structure policy. Ratings were elicited for factors internal and external to the firm. The most important internal factors were the financing requirements of future expansion plans, the percentage of control desired by stockholders, stability of income/revenues, and management's policy regarding the use of internally generated funds. The most important external factors were the availability of long-term funds, the firm's investment opportunities, and the level of domestic interest rates. Although the questionnaire used in the Philippines provided blanks for open-ended responses, very few respondents offered any; none seemed unique to the Philippines.

Table 10.8. Perceived Market Efficiency

Percent of Time Firm's Securities are Believed to be Fairly Priced	Aus-tralia	Hong Kong	Indo-nesia	Malay-sia	Philip-pines	Singa-pore	United States
More than 80% of the time	43.1%	10.8%	18.9%	14.7%	17.9%	4.8%	47.2%
Between 50 and 80% of the time	51.0%	51.4%	52.8%	48.0%	51.3%	52.4%	40.3%
Less than 50% of the time	5.9%	37.8%	28.3%	37.3%	30.8%	42.8%	11.9%

Perceived Market Efficiency

A concern often expressed by foreign investors in the security markets of less developed countries, especially thinly traded markets, is the question of market efficiency. The research evidence to date about market efficiency in the countries of the Asia-Pacific region is generally inconclusive. In addition to thinness in trading, a problem inherent in research on Asia-Pacific financial markets is the lack of sufficient historical data, which in some cases reaches back less than ten years.

To assess executive views of market efficiency, the questionnaire included the question: "Approximately what percent of the time would you estimate that your firm's outstanding securities are priced fairly by the market?" As shown in Table 10.8, which compares the responses to this question among all seven counties, only 4.8% of the executives in Singapore, 10.8% in Hong Kong, 14.7% in Malaysia, 17.9% in the Philippines, and 18.9% in Indonesia, as compared to 47.2% in the United States, believed that their firms' securities were priced fairly by the market "more than 80 percent of the time."

Conversely, 42.8% of executives in Singapore, 37.8% in Hong Kong, 37.3% in Malaysia, 30.8% in the Philippines, and 28.3% in Indonesia indicated that their securities were correctly priced less than 50% of the time, as compared to 11.9% of U.S. executives. Only Australian executives perceived a level of market efficiency comparable to that of the United States, with 43.1% believing that their firms' securities were price fairly by the market "more than 80 percent of the time" and only 5.9% believing that their securities were correctly priced less than 50% of the time.

Therefore, with the exception of Australia, executives of the Asia-Pacific countries surveyed appear to be rather skeptical regarding the level of market efficiency in their countries.

LIMITATIONS

Before making any concluding comments, it is important to note several limitations of this study. The survey was limited to listed firms. The views on dividend and capital structure were (presumably) obtained only from CEOs or CFOs. Obviously, they are not the only ones involved in dividend and capital structure decisions.

The comparisons among the countries must also be approached cautiously. First, the degree of similarity (size, industry, public versus private ownership, and so forth) among the companies surveyed in the Asia-Pacific region can be questioned. There are also significant differences in the size, volume, and liquidity among the smaller developing financial markets in the six Asia-Pacific Countries and the developed U.S. financial market.[15]

It may be that the questionnaires themselves caused a nonresponse bias in the results. The survey results may largely reflect the responses of executives familiar with Western models and theories.[16] Those who did not believe that Western models were useful or relevant may have not responded. This would certainly help explain the high levels of agreement among the executives who did respond. However, it is not possible to determine from the survey results if such a source of nonresponse bias exists.

A potentially significant limitation is that while the surveys in the Asia-Pacific countries were conducted in the early to mid-1990s, the U.S. dividend and capital structure policy surveys were conducted in the mid-1980s. At the time of the U.S. surveys, the leverage "boom" of the 1980s was in high gear. Since capital structure moves in cycles, comparisons of surveys conducted at different times (and in different countries) must be limited in terms of conclusions.

With these limitations in mind, several conclusions can be drawn about the implications of the results of these surveys for theory and practice.

CONCLUSIONS

The survey responses on dividend policy suggest that Lintner's empirically motivated model is a relevant description of actual firm practice not only in the United States, but also in the surveyed countries of the Asia-Pacific region. Executives in the surveyed countries also believe that dividend policy does affect share prices and they seem to be aware of signaling and clientele effects.

The responses of executives in five of the six Asia-Pacific countries to the survey questions on capital structure policy indicate a preference for following a financing hierarchy rather than adhering to a target capital structure. Adhering to a target capital structure was preferred only by Australian executives. Executives in all six countries ranked internal equity as their first choice for long-term financing, a result that is consistent with the pecking-order hypothesis. However, the results were mixed regarding the preferred choice of external financing. Only executives in Australia and the Philippines ranked debt higher than common stock, a result consistent with the preference of U.S. executives and the pecking-order hypothesis.

Executives in the six Asia-Pacific countries agreed with U.S. executives that ensuring the long-term survival of the firm is the most important consideration affecting a firm's financing decisions. Maintaining comparability with firms in the same industry was ranked least important in all seven countries.

Executives in all six Asia-Pacific countries appear to believe that a firm's investment and dividend decisions are more binding than capital structure decisions.

Despite the cultural, political and size differences, the foregoing results suggest a generally high level of agreement among executives in all seven countries on most issues related to dividend and capital structure policy. However, it must be again be pointed out that the survey questionnaires used in this study were inherently limited in scope, adapted from surveys based upon Western models of corporate financial policy, which are in turn based upon stringent underlying assumptions about market conditions and firm behavior. While such an approach lends itself to comparisons among executives in different countries, it implies a level of universality that may not exist. Further research is needed, perhaps using qualitative methods, to discover whether there are other significant issues related to corporate financial policy that are unique to the countries of the Asia-Pacific region.[17]

NOTES

1. The views of U.S. executives on issues related to dividends and capital structure policy are derived from the survey results of Baker, Farrelly, and Edelman (1985) and Pinegar and Wilbricht (1989), respectively. The results of the surveys in Singapore and Hong Kong were previously reported by Kester, Chang, and Tsui (1994).

2. The "stickiness" of dividends was also noted by Donaldson (1961) in a study of the financing practices of a sample of large U.S. corporations. He observed that although firms adapt target payout ratios to their investment opportunities, they do so gradually, trying to avoid sudden changes in dividends.

3. The clientele effect was originally suggested by Miller and Modigliani (1961). However, they argued that one clientele is as good as another, thus concluding that its existence did not imply that one dividend policy is better than another.

4. Two possible reasons for the clientele effect in the United States are different investor tax brackets and differences in perceived riskiness of dividends and retained earnings. See, for example, Elton and Gruber (1970), Litzenberger and Ramaswamy (1979), and Pettit (1977) for empirical evidence of the clientele effect in the United States; Brown and Walter (1986) in Australia; and Lakonsihok and Vermaelen (1983) in Canada. See Ariff and Johnson (1990) for empirical evidence of the clientele effect in Singapore.

5. For empirical studies of the information content of dividends using U.S. data, see Aharony and Swary (1980), Asquith and Mullins (1986), Dielman and Oppenheimer (1984), Kwan (1981), Pettit (1972), and Watts (1973). See Pang, Leong, and Low (1986) and Ariff and Finn (1989) for empirical evidence in Singapore.

6. Baker, Farrelly, and Edelman's survey (1985) of 562 firms listed on the New York Stock Exchange yielded 318 usable responses (56.6% response rate), which were divided among three industry groups: 114 utilities (35.8%), 147 manufacturing firms (46.2%), and 57 wholesale/retail firms (17.9%).

7. Baker, Farrelly, and Edelman (1985) also examined the determinants of dividend

policy by asking U.S. executives to indicate the importance of each of 15 factors in determining their firm's dividend policy. The most highly ranked factors were the anticipated level of the firm's future earnings, the pattern of past dividends, the availability of cash, and concern about maintaining or increasing share price.

8. A few of the respondents in Malaysia cited the availability of Section 108 tax credits and the need to maintain the trustee status of their firms' stock as important factors affecting dividends. Section 108 of the Malaysian Income Tax Act, 1967, requires setting up a notional account to which a credit entry is made in the amount of the current year's corporate income tax payable (currently 30% of taxable income). A tax deduction of (currently) 30% of gross dividends declared is debited to the account. In the full imputation tax system practiced in Malaysia, companies generally do not declare dividends beyond the amount allowed by the available Section 108 credit balance. The classification of a stock as trustee or nontrustee and the amounts that trust funds can invest in trustee and nontrustee stocks is governed by the trustee laws. For listed companies, trustee status is administered and determined by the Kuala Lumpur Stock Exchange. Among the requirements for trustee status is that the company must maintain regular dividend payments for at least five consecutive years. If a dividend is missed for any given year, the company loses its trustee status. In general, investors regard the stock of trustee companies to be of higher investment-grade quality. Therefore, trustee companies are quite reluctant to lose their trustee status.

9. See Baskin (1989) for a review of evidence and additional findings supporting the pecking-order theory.

10. It should be noted that Pinegar and Wilbricht (1989), whose survey yielded 176 responses (35.2% response rate), surveyed the CFOs of Fortune 500 firms listed in Fortune magazine. The Fortune 500 includes only industrials; utilities and financial firms are not included. Due to the small number of responses obtained in the Asia-Pacific countries, we do not compare the results with those of Pinegar and Wilbricht by examining only the industrial firms. All responses to the surveys are included. The effects of industry differences on the results, if any, are unknown.

11. In another survey of Indonesian executives, Ang, Fatemi, and Rad (1995) also found that retained earnings is the preferred source of financing over a variety of scenarios. However, they concluded that this observation alone does not constitute sufficient support for the pecking-order hypothesis, since the contextual nature of the responses to other items in their questionnaire suggested that asymmetric information is not a significant problem in Indonesia. Ang and Jung (1993) similarly failed to find support for the pecking-order hypothesis in a survey of the executives of large South Korean firms.

12. See Chan, McColough, and Skully (1992) for a discussion of DRPs in Australia.

13. See Aggarwal (1990) for an empirical study of the influences of country, size, and industry effect on the capital structure of large Asian companies. See Ariff and Johnson (1989, pp. 289-295) for empirical evidence of an industry effect in Singapore, and Ip and Hopewell (1987) for that in Hong Kong.

14. Myers (1984) points out that, although there is some evidence that firms adjust toward a target capital structure, models based upon this partial adjustment process explain only a small part of actual firm behavior.

15. See Rhee, Chang, and Ageloff (1990) for a comprehensive overview and comparison of the equity markets of the Asia-Pacific region.

16. A number of executives in various Asia-Pacific countries received their education at Western universities. Western models and theories are also taught in the univer-

sities in the Asia-Pacific region, often using Western finance textbooks.

17. See McGoun and Kester (1994) for a commentary on the focus of Asia-Pacific financial research and the universality of Western financial models.

REFERENCES

Aggarwal, R., 1990. Capital structure differences among large Asian companies, *ASEAN Economic Bulletin* 7(1), July, 39-53.

Aharony, J. and I. Swary, 1980. Quarterly dividend and earnings announcements and stockholders' returns: an empirical analysis, *Journal of Finance* 35, 1-12.

Ang, J.S., A. Fatemi, and A.T. Rad, 1995. Capital structure and dividend policies of Indonesian firms. Paper presented at Seventh Annual Pacific-Basin Finance Conference, Manila.

Ang, J.S. and M. Jung, 1993. An alternate test of Myers' pecking-order theory of capital structure: the case of South Korean firms, *Pacific-Basin Finance Journal* 1, 31-46.

Ariff, M. and F.J. Finn, 1989. Announcement effects and market efficiency in a thin market: an empirical application to the Singapore equity market, *Asia Pacific Journal of Management* 6, 243-267.

Ariff, M. and L. Johnson, 1989. Dividend policy in Singapore, Proceedings of the Academy of International Business Meeting, Singapore.

Ariff, M. and L. Johnson, 1990. *Securities Markets and Stock Pricing: Evidence from a Developing Capital Market in Asia.* Singapore: Longman Singapore Publishers, 308-320.

Asquith, P. and D.W. Mullins, 1986. Signalling with dividends, stock repurchases, and equity issues, *Financial Management* 15, 27-44.

Baker, H.K., G.E. Farrelly, and R.B. Edelman, 1985. A survey of management views on dividend policy, *Financial Management* 14, 78-84.

Baskin, J., 1989. An empirical investigation of the pecking-order hypothesis, *Financial Management* 18, 20-25.

Black, F. and M. Scholes, 1974. The effects of dividend yield and dividend policy on common stock prices and returns, *Journal of Financial Economics* 1, 137-146.

Brown, P. and T. Walter, 1986. Ex-dividend day behavior of Australian share prices, *Australian Journal of Management* 2, 139-148.

Chan, K.K.W., D.W. McColough, and M.T. Skully, 1992. Dividend reinvestment plans in Australia, Working paper no. 93/2. Monash University, Melbourne.

Chateau, J-P.D., 1979. Dividend policy revisited: within- and out-of-sample tests, *Journal of Business Finance and Accounting* 3, 355-372.

Dielman, T.E. and H.R. Oppenheimer, 1984. An examination of investor behavior during periods of large dividend changes, *Journal of Financial and Quantitative Analysis* 19, 197-216.

Donaldson, G., 1961. Corporate debt capacity. Division of Research, Graduate School of Business Administration, Harvard University, Cambridge, MA.

Elton, E.J. and M.J. Gruber, 1970. Marginal stockholders' tax rates and the clientele effect, *Review of Economics and Statistics* 52, 135-149.

Fama, E.F. and H. Babiak, 1968. Dividend policy: an empirical analysis, *Journal of the American Statistical Association* 63, 1132-1161.

Gordon, M.J., 1959. Dividends, earnings and stock prices, *Review of Economics and Statistics* 41, 99-105.

Ip, Y.K., and M.H. Hopewell, 1987. Corporate financial structures in Hong Kong, *Hong Kong Journal of Business Management*, 27-31.

Kester, G.W., R.P. Chang, and K.C. Tsui, 1994. Corporate financial policy in the Pacific-Basin: Hong Kong and Singapore, *Financial Practice and Education* 4, 117-127.

Kwan, C.C.Y., 1981, Efficient market tests of the information content of dividend announcements: critique and extension, *Journal of Financial and Quantitative Analysis* 16, 193-206.

Lakonsihok, J. and T. Vermaelen, 1983. Tax reform and ex-dividend day behavior, *Journal of Finance* 38, 883-889.

Lintner, J., 1956. Distribution of incomes of corporations among dividends, retained earnings, and taxes, *American Economic Review* 46, 97-113.

Lintner, J., 1962. Dividends, earnings, leverage, stock prices and the supply of capital to corporations, *Review of Economics and Statistics* 44, 243-269.

Litzenberger, R.H. and K. Ramaswamy, 1979. The effect of personal taxes and dividends on capital asset prices: theory and empirical studies, *Journal of Financial Economics* 7, 163-196.

McGoun, E.G. and G.W. Kester, 1994. A commentary on financial research in the Asia Pacific region, *International Review of Financial Analysis* 2, 113-123.

Miller, M.H. and F. Modigliani, 1961. Dividend policy, growth, and the valuation of shares, *Journal of Business* 34, 411-433.

Miller, M.H. and M.S. Scholes, 1978. Dividends and taxes, *Journal of Financial Economics* 6, 333-364.

Modigliani, F. and M.H. Miller, 1958. The cost of capital, corporation finance, and the theory of investment, *American Economic Review* 48, 261-297.

Myers, S.C., 1984. The capital structure puzzle, *Journal of Finance* 39, 575-592.

Myers, S.C. and N.S. Majluf, 1984. Corporate financing and investment decisions when firms have information that investors do not have, *Journal of Financial Economics* 13, 187-121.

Pang, Y.H., K.S. Leong, and S.S. Low, 1986. The effect of profit and dividend announcements on daily share prices in the Singapore Stock Exchange, *Singapore Accountant* 1, 24-28.

Pettit, R.R., 1972. Dividend announcements, security performance, and capital market efficiency, *Journal of Finance* 27, 993-1007.

Pettit, R.R., 1977. Taxes, transactions costs and the clientele effect of dividends, *Journal of Financial Economics* 5, 419-436.

Pinegar, J.M. and L. Wilbricht, 1989. What managers think about capital structure theory: a survey, *Financial Management* 18, 82-91.

Pruitt, S.W. and L.J. Gitman, 1991. The interactions between the investment, financing, and dividend decisions of major U.S. firms, *The Financial Review* 26, 409-430.

Rhee, S.G., R.P. Chang, and R. Ageloff, 1990. An overview of equity markets in Pacific-Basin countries. In S.G. Rhee and R.P. Chang, eds., *Pacific-Basin Capital Markets Research*. Amsterdam, North Holland: 81-100.

Roy, S.P. and J.K. Cheung, 1985. Target payout and the association between dividends and share prices, *Accounting and Finance* 25, 57-76.

Ryan, T.M., 1974. Dividend policy and market valuation in British industry, *Journal of Business Finance and Accounting* 1, 57-76.

Shevlin, T., 1982. Australian corporate dividend policy: empirical evidence, *Accounting and Finance* 22, 1-22.

Stonehill, A., T. Beekhuisen, R. Wright, L. Remmers, N. Toy, A. Pares, A. Shapiro, D. Egan, and T. Bates, 1974 Financial goals and debt ratio determinants: a survey of practice in five countries, *Financial Management* 4, 27-41.
Watts, R., 1973. The information content of dividends, *Journal of Business* 46, 191-211.

11

Dividend Policy, Management Compensation, and Ownership Structure: Empirical Evidence from the Tel Aviv Stock Exchange

Shmuel Hauser
and June Dilevsky

INTRODUCTION

At first glance, Israel may not appear to be an emerging market. Basic economic indicators, upon which the distinction between emerging and development markets is generally made, show that Israel is no longer a developing nation, and therefore not an emerging market. Other economic and financial indicators tend to support this. Although Israel has a strong social-democratic tradition, it always has been an open economy, for which foreign trade is essential and in which foreign investment is encouraged. Despite government intervention in many sectors of the economy, the development of a vital private sector has traditionally been viewed as an important socioeconomic goal. The capital market in Israel has served as a mechanism for raising equity capital and providing liquidity for investments for several decades. The existence of an organized market for trading in securities in fact predates the establishment of the state.

Despite all this, Israel's capital market more closely resembles capital markets of emerging economies, rather than those characteristics of developed economies in many respects. The structure of financial markets in general, and the securities market in particular, remains highly concentrated. One manifestation of capital market concentration is reflected in the ownership of companies listed on the Tel Aviv Stock Exchange (TASE). Public companies tend to remain closely held firms, even after going public. This fact has grave implications for the development of Israel's securities market, which is often characterized by thin trading, relatively high volatility, and overall illiquidity. Within the context of the study of emerging markets, the Tel Aviv Stock Exchange can be used to gain insights into the behavior of companies and capital markets exhibiting similar characteristics.

Financial literature in recent years views dividend policy as but one component of the firm's overall financial policy that takes into consideration various factors, including: employee compensation, capital structure, and agency costs. Empirical studies on capital market reactions to dividend policy suggest that changes in dividends signal changes in expectations concerning future earnings and profits, and, as a result, changes in investors' assessment of the risk attributed to a company's shares.[1]

The purpose of this study is to examine the relationship between dividend policy, management compensation policy, and the structure of ownership in companies characteristic of emerging markets as evidenced in the Tel Aviv Stock Exchange. The central hypothesis under examination is that dividend and compensation policies adopted by firms are influenced by the opportunity and motivation for management to increase personal welfare at the expense of minority shareholders and that these factors are interdependent. In a large number of companies listed on the TASE, principal shareholders, particularly those who serve as directors and corporate executives, are relatively unencumbered in determining corporate policy at will. This enables them to draw high salaries and other personal benefits and limit the distribution of dividends.[2] The tendency to act in this manner may be restrained by a number of factors. For various reasons, a community of interests between principal and minority shareholders may be created, leading to the adoption of policies designed to optimize decisions in a manner which benefits all shareholders. Hence, the opportunity to exact agency costs is tempered by the motivation of principal shareholders to do so.

This chapter will present the test hypothesis in detail, describe the methodology and data, and present and analyze major findings.

HYPOTHESES

Background

Dividend policy and its implications have been the subject of numerous studies conducted over the last three decades. Black (1976) called the phenomenon "the dividend puzzle," since while there are no apparent advantages to embarking on a policy of dividend distribution, corporate managers place great importance on dividend policy. Empirical studies have shown that, even when taxation favors adoption of a policy of retained earnings, managers prefer distributing dividends, are careful to avoid short-term changes in dividend policy, and tend to adjust dividend distribution rates to long-term earnings expectations.[3] The experience of the United States prior to the 1986 tax reform, for example, indicates that even in cases where capital gains were taxed at a lower rate than dividends, the majority of public companies opted to distribute cash dividends.

The primary explanation for the behavior of companies in developed markets is that companies assess importance to dividend policy that transcends tax considerations. Dividend policy is used as a way of signaling investors as to expectations for future earnings and can be a way of overcoming asymmetric information between "insider" and "outsider" shareholders.[4] It is viewed as a convenient and efficient way in which a company conveys important economic information to its shareholders.[5]

In Israel, while increase in dividend distribution is substantial (see Table 11.1), a culture of regular dividend distribution has not developed, and investors rarely look to dividend announcements as a signal of expected earnings and profits.

Test Hypothesis

Based on studies conducted in other capital markets and on the special conditions which can be attributed to the Israeli capital market we test the following hypotheses:

1. *The opportunity for managers to increase their welfare at the expense of minority shareholders exists in all cases in which the holdings (in capital or voting rights) enables de facto control of the firm. At the same time, however, after control is attained, the incentive to act in this manner is* inversely *related to the degree of ownership.*[6]
2. *In closely held companies, salaries and benefits to managers will tend to be lower for companies that distribute dividends in comparison to firms adopting a policy of non-distribution.*[7]

Table 11.1. Companies Traded on the TASE that Distributed Dividends, 1986-1994

	No. of Companies Listed on TASE	All Companies		No. of Companies Reporting Positive Earnings	Companies Reporting Positive Net Earnings	
		No of Distributing Companies	% of Distributing Companies		No. of Distributing Companies	% of Distributing Companies
1986	263	36	13.7	213	38	17.9
1987	263	44	16.7	213	44	20.7
1988	263	42	16.0	157	42	26.7
1989	240	47	19.6	170	52	30.5
1990	254	61	24.0	157	57	36.3
1991	275	67	24.4	204	67	32.5
1992	370	121	33.7	299	117	39.1
1993	557	149	26.8	455	147	32.3
1994	638	176	27.8	356	158	44.4

Source: Israel Securities Authority.

METHODOLOGY AND DATA

The sample includes all companies traded on the TASE between 1992 and 1994, for which there exist complete data regarding dividend policy and management compensation. Dividend information was collected for the years 1990-94. The following variables have been defined based on this data:

1. $(DIV)_t$ = total dividends distributed in year t;
2. (DIV/NI) = rate of dividend distribution, defined as the ratio between cash dividends and net earnings;
3. (NI/EQUITY) = the rate of return on equity, calculated as the ratio between net earnings to equity;
4. (R_i) = the rate of return on the company's stock;
5. (σ_i) = the standard deviation on the rate of return;
6. (ε_{it}) = abnormal returns on shares calculated as follows:

$$\varepsilon_{it} = R_i - \alpha - \beta R_{mt}$$

where α and β are the regression coefficients and β represents the systematic risk of the stock.[8]

7. $(SIZE)$ = the size of the company as represented by total equity;
8. (% *INSIDE*) = the portion of voting power held by principal shareholders;
9. (% *DIRECT*) = the portion of equity held by corporate directors;
10. (% *CEO*) = the portion of equity held by the CEO and chairman of the board;
11. $(SALARY1)$ = reported salary of the senior manager. (% *SALARY1*) relates to the relative change in salary from the previous year;
12. $(SALARY5)$ = average reported salaries of the five senior managers. (% *SALARY5*) relates to the relative change in share from the previous year;
13. (D/V) = financial leverage, defined as the ratio between long-term debt (D) and total assets (V).

On the basis of these variables, we examined the relationship between dividend policy and ownership structure, as measured by the relative weight of holdings by all principal share holders ($\%INSIDE$),[9] by all board members ($\%DIRECT$), and by the CEO and chairman of the board ($\%CEO$) alone. In a similar fashion, we examined the relationship between dividend policy and management remuneration according to four key variables: reported salary of the senior manager ($SALARY1$), the relative change in salary ($\%SALARY1$), the average salaries of the five senior officers ($SALARY5$), and the relative change in this average salary ($\%SALARY5$). In addition, we examined the relation between dividend policy and corporate profitability, as measured by the return on equity ($NI/Equity$) and the relative change from the previous year, firm size as measured by total equity ($SIZE$), the standard variation of the rate of return on the company's shares (σ_i), the systematic risk of the shares (β_i), and the financial leverage of the firm (D/V). The significance of the correlation between dividend policy and the various independent variables was examined though a standard Chi-square (χ^2) test:

$$\chi^2 = \Sigma_i \, \Sigma_j \, (o_{ij} - e_{ij}) \, / \, e_{ij}$$

with e_{ij} signifying the number of companies that distributed dividends ($i = 1$) or did not distribute dividends ($i = 2$), according to categories j, when $j = 1,2,3$. χ^2 is the statistic following a Chi-square distribution with degrees of freedom.

As a final test to measure the degree to which the various variables (ownership structure, remuneration policy, profitability, and capital structure) affect dividend policy, we performed a multivariable regression, as follows:

$$\begin{aligned} Div_i &= a_0 + a_1 \, (\% \, INSIDE) + a_2 \, (\% \, CEO) + a_3 \, (SALARY1) \\ &+ a_4 \, (\% \, SALARY1) + a_5 \, (NI \, / \, EQUITY) + a_6 \, (SD) + a_7 \, (SIZE) \\ &+ a_8 \, (D \, / \, V) + a_9 \, (AGE) + \varepsilon_i \end{aligned}$$

where the variable (*SIZE*) is calculated as a logarithm of total equity. Because of problems related to data heteroskedacity, we estimate the regression using the generalized least square method. We performed this regression twice, once on those companies traded in 1994 reporting positive net earnings and once on all distributing firms.

RESULTS

The primary findings of the study are presented in Tables 11.2-11.4. Table 11.2 summarizes the correlation between dividend policy, size of the company, and ownership structure. The data presented in this table indicate that the propensity to distribute dividends is positively correlated with firm size. For example, 63% of the group of large firms (the highest third of companies in the sample reporting positive earnings) while only 36% of the group of small firms distributed cash dividends. One possible explanation for this is that the relative cost of raising capital for large firms is lower than for small companies. Another explanation could be linked to possible clientele effects in the Tel Aviv Stock Exchange. Institutional and corporate investors, which are exempt from taxes on dividend income, tend to prefer investments in large firms. Accordingly, the incentive of these firms to distribute dividends is greater.

The proportion of companies that distributed dividends in 1994 was high for companies in which principal shareholders held more than 75% control (as measured by voting rights). For approximately two-thirds of the sample of listed companies, concentration of control exceeds 75%. Of these firms, some 53% distributed dividends. In contrast, only 32% of the firms in which principal shareholders held less than 75% control distributed dividends. Similar results were attained for 1993, although the number of companies with less than 75% control in the hands of principal shareholders was somewhat higher.

Results regarding share ownership by board members and the CEO and chairman of the board are different. The findings listed in Table 11.2 indicate an

Table 11.2. Test of Dependency between Dividend Policy, Firm Size, Overall Concentration of Control, and Ownership by Senior Executives in Companies Reporting Positive Net Earnings, 1994

This table examines the dividend policy of public companies that reported positive net earnings according to various ownership and performance characteristics. Total equity is a proxy for size, which is stratified from highest to lowest into three subgroups of equal sample size. Percentages held by principal shareholdersis based on percentage of total voting rights. Profitability is indicated by return on equity, which is calculated as the ratio between net earnings and total equity. Salaries paid to senior executive include all benefits save distribution of shares and option plans. "Prob" represents the p value for significance of the findings of statistical tests performed to determine the relationship between dividend policy and the other variables.

Classification by	No. Companies	No. Distributing Companies	% Distributing Companies	χ^2	Prob
Percentage Held by Principal Shareholders					
0-75%	112	36	32.1	17.85	0.000
75%+	230	122	53.1		
Percentage Held by CEO & Chairman of the board					
0-10%	206	105	51.0	4.75	0.030
10%+	136	53	39.0		
Percentage Held by Directors					
0-10%	169	93	55.0	9.71	0.002
10%+	168	64	38.1		
Salary of Senior Executive (relative to equity)					
Low salary level	156	81	51.9	2.81	0.094
High salary level	113	47	41.3		
Profitability					
Low profitability	165	53	32.1	25.42	0.000
High profitability	177	105	59.3		
Firm Size					
Upper third	114	41	36.2	20.7	
Middle third	114	45	39.6		
Lower third	114	72	63.1		

inverse correlation between concentrated ownership and dividend policies. Companies in which officers hold less than 10% of the shares tend to distribute dividends. This is consistent with findings of Morck, Schliefer, and Vishny (1988) and others who found a nonlinear relation between the degree of principal shareholder ownership and profitability. One explanation for this is that a relatively small concentration of voting power in the hands of principal shareholders forges common interests between them and the rest of the shareholders. As this concentration rises, opportunities for influencing decisions on allocation of benefits are enhanced and identification with minority shareholders erodes (see Morck, Shleifer, and Vishny, 1988).

Data presented in Table 11.3 draw comparisons regarding the ownership structure, management remuneration policy, profitability, and capital structure between companies that distributed dividends and those that opted for retained earnings. In order to neutralize size effects, we measured salaries as a portion of total equity and examined the relationship between the relative size of salaries, the ownership structure of the firm, and dividend policy. The relative weight of salaries for senior management in firms that did not distribute dividends is higher than for distributing firms. Average concentration of voting rights in the hands of principal shareholders is slightly higher for firms distributing dividends; however, concentration of ownership by top management is significantly higher for nondistributing firms. At the same time, profitability for distributing firms is higher than that of nondistributing firms and nondistributing firms tend to be more highly leveraged.

The findings relating to ownership structure and management compensation are particularly noteworthy. The apparent negative correlation between relative salary levels and higher concentration of voting power in the hands of principal shareholders would tend to support the hypothesis that as the ownership structure of the firm approaches private ownership, principal shareholders have less incentive to increase their personal welfare at the expense of minority shareholders. The apparent positive correlation between concentration of ownership by senior officers of the firm, on one hand, and salary levels, on the other hand, is consistent with the contention of Jensen and Meckling (1976) and others that as ownership by corporate officers increases, mutual interest between them and minority shareholders declines. The combination of these two sets of findings suggests that the relationship between ownership structure, and dividend and salary policies is complex and not monotonic. The findings of this study are similar to those of Morck, Schleifer, and Vishney (1988).

When the proportion of holdings by professional senior officers (specifically the CEO and chairman of the board) is relatively low, mutual interests between them and all shareholders are created. As their holdings grow, this community of interest is broken. One possible explanation for this is that as holdings grow, professional managers tend to identify themselves more closely as owners of the firm in partnership with principal shareholders, rather than agents operating on the shareholders' behalf. In Israel, where professional officers typically hold as much as 15% of the voting power in the firm, this appears

Table 11.3. Comparative Analysis of Ownership Structure, Remuneration Policy, Profitability, and Capital Structure for Companies Distributing Cash Dividends and No-Dividend Companies, 1992-1994

Comparisons drawn between the various factors are based on data for companies distributing cash dividends and no-dividend companies. The sample includes only those firms that reported positive net income. Salary variables are adjusted for company size and are calculated as a percentage of total equity (per million NIS equity). The percentage held by principal shareholders (and key officers) is based on the percentage in total voting rights rather than equity participation (approximately 30 companies had dual share capitalization). Return on equity is calculated as the ration between net earnings and total equity.

Variable	Distributing Companies	No-Dividend Companies	F	Prob.
No. of Companies	156	177		
Ownership Structure				
% Held by Principal Shareholders	81.0	76.0	10.92	0.001
% Held by CEO & Chairman of the board	12.61	20.45	9.93	0.002
% Held by All Directors	21.37	30.30	8.04	0.005
Salary Policy (relative to equity)	12.67	18.42	5.35	0.021
Avg. Annual Change in Senior Executive's Salary	25.9%	49.9%	2.58	0.110
Avg. Salary of 5 Top Officers	7.96	11.47	8.3	0.004
Avg. Annual Change in Top 5 Salaries	20.9%	31.9%	1.16	0.283
Control Variables				
Profitability – Return on Equity	11.52	10.03	1.05	0.306
Abnormal Returns – ε_{it}	0.022	-0.038	4.95	0.009
Size ('000 NIS)*	335,915	112,552	12.08	0.001
Standard Deviation on Share Price Returns	7.66%	10.10%	10.8	0.001
Systematic Risk of Shares (β)	1.045	1.207	7.92	0.005
Financial Leverage	0.353	0.447	1.18	0.278

*Average exchange rate for the relevant period = NIS 2.6 / $1.00.

to be the case. The findings indicate that relatively high agency costs, represented by high salaries,[10] are incurred in firms in which senior officers enjoy high levels of ownership or control.[11] Profitability, as measured by return on equity and stock performance, is generally higher for firms in which the average level managerial ownership is lower.

A regression was performed on a sample of all companies distributing dividends (see Table 11.4). The results support the test hypotheses and indicate that the tendency to distribute dividends is positively correlated to the level of

Table 11.4. Results from Cross-Sectional Regression Examining the Impact of Various Factors on Dividend Policy: All Companies Distributing Cash Dividends, 1994

Regression coefficients were calculated using the generalized least squares (GLS) method. Holdings of principal shareholders and senior officers are based on percentage of voting rights. Salaries are adjusted for firm size and represent a percentage of total equity. Risk is measured by the standard deviation of weekly rates of return. Profitability refers to the change in net earnings over the previous year. Firm size is measured as the natural logarithm of the book value of equity. Financial leverage is defined as the ratio between long-term debt and total assets. Mature companies are those whose shares have been publicly traded for at least three years.

Independent Variables	Dependent Variable			
	Div	Prob	Div/NI	Prob
Constant	3.225	0.006	1.881	0.000
% Held by Principal Shareholders	0.588	0.037	0.027	0.669
% Held by CEO & Chairman of the Board	-0.011	0.043	-0.001	0.212
Salary of Senior Executive	-0.015	0.929	-0.059	0.032
Annual Change in Salary of Senior Executive	-0.079	0.663	-0.074	0.296
Profitability	0.129	0.009	0.030	0.079
Risk (standard deviation)	-21.67	0.000	-2.365	0.015
Firm Size	0.688	0.000	0.051	0.047
Financial Leverage	-0.061	0.069	-0.007	0.370
Maturity	0.893	0.000	0.144	0.019
R^2	61.9%		16.02%	
F	14.96		1.76	
(Prob)	(0.088)		(0.000)	

ownership concentration of all principal shareholders, profitability, size, and maturity of the firm (a_1, a_5, a_7, and $a_9 > 0$), and negatively correlated to managerial ownership, high salaries, risk, and financial leverage (a_2, a_3, a_6, and $a_8 < 0$).

CONCLUSIONS

The propensity to distribute dividends in Israel is positively related to unusually high concentrations (75%+) of control in the hands of principal shareholders, but negatively related to high levels of senior management ownership. Distributing firms are typically larger, more profitable, more mature, and less risky than nondistributing firms. Remuneration levels to corporate officers in distributing firms tend to be lower than in nondistributing firms. These findings suggest that agency costs are less likely in companies distributing cash dividends in which the ownership structure is most highly concentrated. This is reflected, *inter alia*, in lower salaries and benefits paid to senior executives, higher profitability, and the like.

NOTES

1. See, for example, Jensen and Meckling (1976), and more recently, Smith and Watts (1992), Gaver and Gaver (1993), and Sant and Cowan (1994).

2. For a more detailed analysis regarding the impact of control structure, see Dann and DeAngelo (1988).

3. See, for example, Lintner (1956), Miller and Modigliani (1961), Ambarish, John, and Williams (1987), and Sant and Cowan (1994).

4. See, for example, Ross (1977), Bhattacharya (1979, 1980), Ambarish, John, and Williams (1987), Asquith and Mullins (1986), Gaver and Gaver (1993), and Miller and Rock (1982).

5. Venkatesh (1989) argues that dividend policy serves as an efficient mechanism for conveying information and that changes in dividend policy can affect shareholder expectations regarding expected future earnings and the stock's risk-return profile. Unexpected changes in the rate of dividend distribution will be considered signals to investors. Brennan and Kraus (1987) and others argue that signaling through changes in dividend policy incurs agency and other costs that result in a tendency toward a suboptimal allocation of resources. Others argue that the use of dividend policy to bridge asymmetric information reduces agency costs. Rozeff (1982), for example, argues that the distribution of dividends can serve as an efficient instrument through which the actions of principal shareholders and managers can be regulated. See also Pervaiz and Walton (1995).

6. This hypothesis is supported by contentions made by Morck, Shleifer, and Vishny (1988), who demonstrate that the relationship between ownership structure and profitability cannot be described as a monotonic function. They find that profitability increases as these holdings reach a critical level, declines at a mid-range and begin to rise again when these holdings are more substantial. Jarrel and Poulson (1988) also show that the performance of firms with principal ownership of 30-50% is significantly lower than that of other companies.

7. Support for this hypothesis can be found in Gaver and Gaver (1993), who found that in high-growth firms dividends tend to be lower and salaries higher than for mature companies. Moreover, Easterbrook (1984), Rozeff (1982), and Smith and Watts (1992) argue that all costs of contractual arrangements, such as remuneration to senior management, are contingent on the overall financial policy of the firm, which includes: capital structure, dividend policy, employee remuneration, bonus policy, and stock option plans, and so on.

8. β was calculated on the basis of weekly data for the years 1990-94 using the following regression: $R_{it} = \alpha + \beta R_{mt} + \varepsilon_{it}$.

9. Of the 45 companies for which the degree of ownership was less than 50%, only 6% distributed cash dividends. Because of the low incidence of these cases, the sample was divided into two subgroups: companies with less than 75% principal shareholder control and companies with 75% or more.

10. These results are mitigated somewhat by the fact that nondistributing firms tend to be substantially smaller than those that distribute dividends. For some companies, the decision to retain earnings and offer high salaries may well be linked more directly to overall growth strategy rather than ownership structure.

11. These results are supported by Morck, Schleifer, and Vishney (1988), who argue that ownership and control structure can have a significant impact on the profitability of the firm.

REFERENCES

Ambarish, R., K. John, and J. Williams, 1987. Efficient signaling with dividends and investments, *Journal of Finance* 42, 321-343.

Bhattacharya, S., 1979. Imperfect information, dividend policy and the "the bird in the hand" fallacy, *Bell Journal of Economics* 10, 259-270.

Bhattacharya, S., 1980. Nondissipative signalling structures and dividend policy, *Quarterly Journal of Economics* 95, 1-24.

Black, F., 1976. The dividend puzzle, *Journal of Portfolio Management* 3, 5-8.

Brennan, M. and A. Kraus, 1987. Efficient financing under asymmetric influences, *Journal of Finance* 42, 5.

Dann, L. and H. DeAngelo, 1988. Corporate financial policy and corporate control: a study of defensive adjustments in asset ownership structure, *Journal of Financial Economics* 20, 87-127.

Easterbrook, F., 1984. Two agency cost explanations of dividends, *American Economic Review* 74, 650-659.

Gaver, J.J. and K.M. Gaver, 1993. Additional evidence on the association between the investment opportunity set and corporate financing, dividend, and compensation policies, *Journal of Accounting and Economics* 16, 125-160.

Hauser, S. and I. Shohat, 1990. Dividend policy of companies traded on the Tel Aviv Stock Exchange (in Hebrew), Israel Securities Authority.

Jensen, M.C. and W.H. Meckling, 1976. Theory of the firm: managerial behavior, agency costs and ownership structure, *Journal of Financial Economics* 3, 305-360.

Lintner, J., 1956. Distribution of incomes of corporations among dividends, retained earnings and taxes, *American Economic Review,* May, 97-113.

Miller, M. and F. Modigliani, 1961. Dividend policy, growth and the valuation of shares, *Journal of Business*, October, 411-433.

Miller, M. and K. Rock, 1982. Dividend policy under asymmetric information part I, working paper, University of Chicago.

Morck, R., A. Shleifer, and R.W. Vishny, 1988. Management ownership and market valuation: an empirical analysis, *Journal of Financial Economics* 20, 293-315.

Pervaiz, A. and K. Schuele Walton, 1995. Information asymmetry and valuation effects of debt financing, *The Financial Review* 30, 289-311.

Ross, S., 1977. The determination of financial structure: the information signaling approach, *Bell Journal of Economics*, Spring, 23-48.

Rozeff, M.S., 1982. Growth, beta and agency costs as determinants of dividend payout ratios, *Journal of Financial Research* 5, 249-259.

Sant, R. and A.R. Cowan, 1994. Do dividends signal earnings? the case of omitted dividends, *Journal of Banking and Finance* 18, 1113-1133.

Smith, C.W. and R.L. Watts, 1992. The investment opportunity set and corporate financing, dividend and compensation policies, *Journal of Financial Economics* 32, 263-292.

Venkatesh, P.C., 1989. The impact of dividend initiation on the information content of earnings announcements and returns volatility, *Journal of Business* 62, 175-1979.

12

Asymmetric Information, Collateral, and Interest Rate: The Case of Taiwan

Hai-Chin Yu

INTRODUCTION

Secured loans comprise approximately 70% of total bank loans in the United States, according to one empirical study (Berger and Udell, 1990). And in Taiwan, empirical research has recently shown that a high 91.4% of the country's banks require collateral for medium-term loans.[1] Visible collateral clearly plays a central role in the loan market. In recent years the function of collateral has been attracting much attention from researchers working with financial contract theory, and the literature has emphasized the relationship between collateral and loan quality.

Traditional financial theorists postulate that if the borrower's risk is identifiable, then the higher the risk a borrower represents, the more collateral that borrower will offer in order to obtain a loan. Under these circumstances, there is a negative relationship between the amount of collateral and the quality of the borrower. However, information-economics theorists propose that in credit markets, borrowers and lenders are typically in an asymmetric-information situation where the borrower's risk class is not necessarily identifiable. When the risk class of the borrower cannot be ascertained, there is a high likelihood of adverse selection and moral hazard problems occurring (Stiglitz and Weiss, 1981, 1983; Bester, 1985, 1987; Besanko and Thakor, 1987a).[2] Hence banks are faced with a pressing need to design a new type of loan contract that will, by means of the self-selection mechanism proposed in agent theory, reduce the potential conflicts outlined above.

Stiglitz and Weiss (1981, 1983) suggest that even in a competitive commercial environment, adverse selection will still occur if lenders and borrowers in the credit market are in a situation of asymmetric information and at the same time loan contracts are designed to evaluate and classify applicants solely on the basis of interest rates or collateral offered. Bester (1985) considers that in a situation where collateral is a complete substitute for interest and its provision incurs no costs for the borrower, adverse selection can be eliminated with loan contracts which link collateral and interest rates in a range of configurations. Under these circumstances the high-risk borrower will select a contract that matches low collateral with high interest, and the low-risk borrower will choose a combination of high collateral and low interest. Besanko and Thakor (1987a, 1987b) as well as Bester and Hellwig (1987) have reaffirmed the beneficial role played by collateral in reducing adverse selection under asymmetric information.

Most of the contract designs put forward in the studies referred to above assume a fully competitive commercial environment; however, with the local banking industry closed to newcomers, banking cartels have become a major force in Taiwan. In this chapter we would like to see the relationship between collateral and interest rate for different types of borrowers in Taiwan. Taiwan's local banks often use the prime rate: banks must base all loans on this figure, then adjust interest upward or downward on the basis of the borrower's credit rating and the amount of collateral offered. Therefore, in terms of the loan contract, interest rates and collateral are not independent of each other as assumed in the existing literature, but rather the one is a function of the other. Furthermore, owing to the tendency of Taiwan's less-than-ideal accounting systems to generate financial statements which are typically unreliable in many aspects, banks generally require companies to provide collateral to a value exceeding the amount of the loan. This situation again differs from that found abroad, where collateral value is usually lower than the amount of the loan. Therefore it is essential to understand the existing credit system as a model contract which is better suited to local conditions and which can provide a reliable basis for credit operations.

This chapter will investigate the potential incentive conflicts (adverse selection) which asymmetric information generates between banks (the principal) and borrowers (the agent) in the secured-loan market. Furthermore, the conclusions drawn from existing theoretical models are used to examine the actual situation of Taiwan's banks, and general conclusions are put forward.

THE BANKING SYSTEM IN TAIWAN

Taiwan's financial institutions can be classified into two groups: banking or monetary institutions, and nonbanking or nonmonetary institutions. The scope of business that a bank may be authorized to conduct shall be prescribed by the central competent authority—that is, the Ministry of Finance, within the scope of the Banking Law.

Banking System and Content

The Domestic Banks

The domestic banks have been the backbone of the banking system in Taiwan. By the end of 1994, there were 33 domestic commercial banks with 17 old domestic commercial banks and 16 new domestic commercial banks, and in total there have 877 branches.

In 1992, about 66.6% of the domestic banks' assets were held in the form of loans and discounts and of these NT\$3,222 billion, or 83.0%, were made to private enterprises. Of the total loans, 0.6% were in the form of discounts, 0.1% in advances on imports, 35.4% in short-term loans and overdrafts, and the remaining 63.9% in medium- and long-term loans. It is interesting to notice that medium- and long-term loans extended by the local banks far exceeded short-term loans. Approximately 61.9% of the banks' loans were secured.

In terms of funding, deposits of various forms, particularly savings, time, and passbook deposits, comprise 56.6% of the banks' liabilities and net worth. Although as yet not an important source of funding, the domestic banks have also raised some funds overseas in the form of Eurodollar borrowings, floating rate notes, and certificates of deposit.

Foreign Banks

Foreign banks are allowed to establish branches or representative offices in Taiwan. By the end of 1991, 36 foreign banks had established 47 branches. They are authorized to handle foreign exchange transactions and extend loans to customers. They may also accept local currency deposits, up to 15 times their local paid-in capital. These funds are supplemented by interbank borrowings and foreign currency pre-export lendings.

At the end of 1991 foreign banks held only 1.7% of deposit accounts, 5.4% of lending of banking institutions, and about 24% of foreign exchange transactions. However, they have been actively participating in personal financial management, consumer financing, and introducing overseas trust funds. The revised Banking Law provides foreign banks national treatment, enabling them to accept savings deposits, extend long-term credits, and engage in some investment banking activities.

Medium-Business Banks

Under Article 96 of the Banking Law, medium-business banks' main functions consist of extending medium and long-term credit to improve machinery and equipment, financial structure, management, and business operations of medium and small-sized business enterprises. Traditionally the mutual loans and savings companies were a major source of funds for small businesses. At the end of December 1991, the medium-business banks had assets of NT\$848 billion, 73.3% of which were in loans and 12.5% in securities.

Cooperatives

As with much of Taiwan's financial system, the first credit cooperative was established during the Japanese occupation in 1908. The are now three types: credit cooperative associations, the credit departments of farmers' associations, and the credit departments of fishery associations. At the end of December 1991, there were 74 credit cooperative associations with 425 branches mainly in the urban areas of Taiwan. They may accept deposits and grant loans only to their members and offer some banking services such as checking accounts, passbook deposits, and time savings accounts. At the end of December 1991, credit cooperatives had assets of NT$1,030 billion, 55.6% of which were loans to members and 42.2% deposits with other financial institutions.

Interest Rate Deregulation

Financial deregulation is a long-term process. The first major step taken to deregulate interest rates was the establishment of the money market in 1976. The Central Bank of China adopted a series of measures to relax controls on interest rates, beginning with money-market interest rates and later including interest rates on deposits and loans, following the promulgation of Essentials of Interest Rate Adjustment in November 1980. All controls over interest rates were abolished following the implementation of the revised Banking Law in July 1989. It took about 14 years to completely deregulate the interest rates after the money market was established.

The government promulgated the Fair Trade Law in February 1991, prohibiting manipulation of prices, including interest rates and fees charged by the banks. Banks will not be allowed to use their monopoly power to enforce uniform prices and other collective practices. With new private commercial banks approved by the Ministry of Finance in June 1991 that have now begun operations, the banking market in Taiwan has become very competitive.

Deregulation of the Banking System

Many of the recent arguments surrounding financial deregulation have focused on the licenses awarded to new private commercial banks. Minimum paid-in capital has been set at NT$10 billion (approximately $360 million), at least 20% of which will be raised through public share subscription. In addition, new banks have to recruit senior staff whose banking experience is commensurate with their new responsibilities. The Ministry of Finance received a total of 19 bank applications, and granted 15 licenses in June 1991.

Of the major domestic commercial banks, 12 are state-owned and subject to onerous regulations from numerous government agencies. The most troublesome regulations are very demanding standards and procedures for writing off unqualified loans. Small mistakes can cost a loan officer an administrative penalty in the civil service appraisal system; he or she also may be liable to repay bad loans. An effective credit apparatus must entail risk-taking and must provide room for the extension of credit to borrowers in the face of adversity. Some losses are an inevitable part of risk-taking, which in turn is part of the process of economic development. These state-owned banks, facing keen competition from the newly chartered banks and the loss to them of some well-trained staff, will have to be privatized.

EXPERIMENT DESIGN AND EMPIRICAL RESULTS

Hypothesis and Definition of the Problem

Taiwan's banking industry tended toward a oligopolic competitive structure. Because there are only 24 old-established banks, the desire for price parity leads to a highly homogenous commercial structure with interest rates differing only slightly between banks. For this reason the entire banking system can be seen, for the purposes of this study, as a single principal (the banks) that handles the applications of many agents (the borrowers).

This chapter is a discussion of similarities and differences between loan contracts for discrete borrowers, so in order to clarify the relevant relationships, the contrasting situations existing when banks deal with two different types of borrowers (type 1 and type 2) will be discussed.[3] Differences in the financial status of these two types of borrowers refer to the quality or otherwise of their corporate financial structures: the operating conditions and financial structure of the type 2 borrower are superior to those of the type 1 borrower.

From the conclusions of Besanko and Thakor (1987b), we know that in a loan market affected by asymmetric information, and when the collateral constraint is binding, lenders cannot sort borrowers out based on their collateral choice alone. We must use the interest rate also.

This design would motivate financially vulnerable applicants to provide the bank with accurate information, and to work toward improving their financial circumstances; it also provides a greater incentive for financially sound applicants to further improve their circumstances rather than tending toward a less favorable financial structure.

Owing to the design principles of these two self-selection contracts, the two types of applicants can be clearly differentiated. All applicants will select the contract type that should apply in their particular case, and will supply the bank with accurate information. In this way, no-one will jeopardize others by selecting a contract designed for another type of applicant; hence a separating equilibrium is achieved.

It can be seen from the above that if information access in the loan market is asymmetric in such a way that the banks have less information than the borrowers, then the former must make use of self-selection mechanisms so that the latter will first assess the price they are willing to pay and the utility they will attain by investing the borrowed money, then decide, in view of their own financial structure, how much collateral they must offer to borrow the required sum. The banks may then view the amount of collateral offered as a "signal" which indicates the applicant's type, and may be used to set an appropriate interest rate for the loan. This interest rate must act as an incentive for the borrowers to willingly reveal actual information. Reducing the problem of asymmetric information in the market by means of incentives which encourage borrowers to willingly reveal accurate information will minimize conflicts between and maximize satisfaction for the two parties involved.

Under the asymmetric information circumstances the financially sound borrower pays a lower interest rate and collateral than the financially vulnerable borrower. This indicates what is known as the second-best contract. Furthermore the relationship between collateral and interest rates under the above conditions is a functional rather than an independent one. We enable the following three hypotheses to be established:

H_1: There are significant differences in the interest rates applicable to financially sound and financially vulnerable applicants: the more vulnerable an applicant is financially, the higher the rate.

H_2: There are significant differences in the collateral requirements applied to financially sound and financially vulnerable applicants: the more vulnerable an applicant is financially, the higher the collateral.

H_3: Differences in financial circumstances translate into disparities in two of the variables in the loan-terms picture: interest rates and amount of collateral.

H_{3-1}: Differences in financial circumstances are associated with discrepancies in the terms of short-term loans (for two variables: interest rates and collateral).

H_{3-2}: Differences in financial circumstances lead to discrepancies in the terms of medium and long-term loans (for two variables: interest rates and collateral).

Under these circumstances interest rates and collateral continue to play as dependant variables, because if they are independent analytical variables the results are similar to H_1 and H_2, and if they are not mutually independent variables, superior test performance is attained.

Sampling

Sampling Methods

The sample for this study came from two sources: the top 500 companies on the "ROC Large Corporations List" published by the ROC Credit Information Office, and all the companies on the "List of Corporations in Taiwan." A total of 500 companies—250 from each of the above two sources—were selected at random as targets for a postal questionnaire, which could be filled in only by the person in charge of the organization's accounting or finance department.

Another sample consisted of 24 old domestic banks, with three branches of each bank being selected at random from each of Taiwan's northern, central, and southern regions. This provided a total of 216 targets for postal questionnaires. Since the export-import bank has only two branches, the effective sample is 209.

Data Collection

The data collected for this study consisted of primary and secondary data.

Primary Data. Postal questionnaires were used to collect the primary data. The lending behavior of the companies was explored in a three-part survey, which included basic data, loan data, and whether or not the company had access to perfect information. The basic data consisted of the type of industry, capital, ownership, and so on. Lending data included the type of collateral provided for loans, loan ratio, interest rates, the term of loans, and whether the interest rates were floating or fixed.[4] As for banks, the questionnaires asked, in relation to the same topics, about mortgage information and the completeness of the information.

Secondary Data. The secondary data for this study consisted of the companies' financial reports and nine separate average financial ratios over the last three years: (1) current ratio, (2) acid ratio, (3) debt ratio, (4) accounts receivable turnover rate, (5) inventory turnover rate, (6) total asset turnover rate, (7) gross margin, (8) return on assets, and (9) return on equity.

There were 83 valid questionnaires returned by companies, and 82 returned by banks.

The Asymmetric Nature of Information in the Local Banking Market

The phenomenon referred to in this chapter as asymmetric information is defined as meaning that although banks do not have complete information about financial states of individual companies, they know on the basis of past information of the applicants. On a scale of 1 to 5, banks were asked to score their confidence about the financial statements from excellent (score 5) to poor (score 1). The average score is 3.5 which demonstrates the possible asymmetric information between banks and firms even using past information.

Answers to the same question by different respondents (banks and companies) revealed a huge gap between the two groups in terms of knowledge about credit, thereby confirming the possible existence of the asymmetric information phenomenon.

Personal interviews conducted in coordination with the survey results showed the asymmetric information problem is mainly caused by current regulations and systems. The problem is a result of: (1) partial or incomplete information provided by the Unioned Credit Rating Center; (2) outdated information; (3) borrowers do not need to provide financial information to the center if the amount borrowed is less than NT$30 million (equivalent to $1.2 million); (4) the Unioned Credit Rating Center enters data into its computer in a format which omits part of the raw data.

Clustering of Loan Customers by Type

The application of the self-selection mechanism is an ex ante model; however, empirical studies must rely on actual ex post data for testing and verification. The above analysis shows there is a significant problem in terms of incomplete information between the bank and its loan customers. Not knowing precisely how a bank (the principal) differentiates its borrowers (the agent) and provides different loan terms, this study has attempted to take the role of outside observer-collecting customer data, evaluating the standpoint of the banks, and carrying out separation procedures for pooled borrowers. This study also tested whether, after clustering, the customers' loan terms correlated with the conclusions drawn from the theoretical models and whether a separating equilibrium was reached.

To separate companies into two groups according to type, the nine financial ratios can be used as a basis. For this study, financial reports from the last three years for respondent companies were indirectly researched, and nine representative financial ratios were calculated for the basis for clustering.

Factor Extraction, and Degree of Correlation Between Financial Ratios

Table 12.1 shows the results of analysis of the relevant matrices for the companies' nine average financial ratios. It is evident from the table that there is a high correlation between some of the variables: for ROE and ROA the correlation coefficient is 0.7326; for current ratio and acid ratio it is 0.6650; and for X3 and X9 it is 0.5055.

Table 12.1. Relevant Matrices for the Nine Financial Ratios

Relevant Coefficients	X1	X2	X3	X4	X5	X6	X7	X8	X9
X1	1.0000	0.4649	0.5163	-.0371	0.0102	-.0220	0.1700	0.3745	0.4328
X2	0.4649	1.0000	0.6650*	-.1510	0.2861	0.1353	0.2588	0.4075	0.3394
X3	0.5163	0.6650	1.0000	-.1824	0.2683	0.1098	0.1145	0.4032	0.5055
X4	-.0371	-.1510	-.1824	1.0000	0.0625	-.0248	0.2295	-.0713	0.0534
X5	0.0102	0.2861	0.2683	0.0625	1.0000	0.4152	-.2362	0.1828	0.4035
X6	-.0229	0.1353	0.1098	-.0248	0.4152	1.0000	-.2374	0.1507	0.2321
X7	0.1700	0.2588	0.1145	0.2295	-.2362	-.2374	1.0000	0.1099	0.0637
X8	0.3745	0.4075	0.4032	-.0713	0.1828	0.1507	0.1099	1.0000	0.7326
X9	0.4328	0.3394	0.5055*	0.0534	0.4135	0.2321	0.0637	0.7326*	1.0000

*Denotes a high relevant coefficient. X1 = equity ratio; X2 = current ratio; X3 = acid ratio; X4 = accounts receivable turnover rate; X5 = inventory turnover rate; X6 = total asset turnover rate; X7 = gross margin; X8 = return on equity (ROE); X9 = return on assets (ROA).

To eliminate the high degree of correlation between the various coefficients, factor analysis was carried out for the nine financial ratios. Factor extraction was carried out through principal component analysis, in order to select factors with an eigenvalue of more than one. A total of three factors were extracted, the accumulated explained variation was 66.53%. Next, the factor oblique method was used to select the original factors. Coefficients in the factor pattern matrix with loading of more than 0.4 were selected and named. See Table 12.2 for details.

Table 12.2 shows that factor 1 denotes high return on equity, high current ratio, and high rate of return; to highlight the attributes of this factor, it was named the "high profitability and high probability-of-repayment factor." Factor 2 can denote high turnover rate and high rate of return on assets; as this ratio is used to evaluate the efficacy of company management, it was named the "high efficacy factor." Factor 3 represents the accounts receivable turnover rate, and so was named the "high cash-collection factor."

Clustering on the Basis of the Three Factor Scores

The factor coefficients of the three factors for each company were converted into three percentage scores. These three factor scores were used for cluster analysis in order to further test whether there was a marked discrepancy between the different types of borrowers regarding loan terms. The surveyed borrowers were clustered into two groups, and the results are shown in Table 12.3.

Table 12.3 shows that the for group 1 the factor 1 and factor 3 scores were quite high, indicating that these customers represent high profitability, high probability of repayment, and high cash collection. In terms of the theoretical models, this group should have a high likelihood of success, hence it was named "financially sound." Group 2 had fairly high scores for factor 2, while its scores for factors 1 and 3 were correspondingly low, showing that while the companies in this group had high turnover rates, their profitability and cash collection were less than ideal. In terms of the theoretical models, the group's chances of success should be correspondingly low, hence it was named "financially vulnerable." It can be seen from Table 12.3 that the F value reached 47.93 after dividing the companies into two groups, showing that the discrepancy between the two groups was significant. Furthermore the similar number of samples (45 and 38) for the two groups is helpful for statistical inference.

The Relationship Between Financial Situation and Loan Terms

To compare and contrast the loan terms for different types of borrowers, "t-test" analysis was used. The two groups of borrowers acted as the predictor (the independent variable), and the companies' responses to inquiries in the questionnaire about collateral and short/medium/long-term interest rates were used as the dependent variable. The source of the discrepancies between the two

**Table 12.2. Factor Analysis of the Companies' Financial Ratios:
Factor Loading and Explained Variation**

Factor Variable	Commondity	Factor Loading Coefficient Factor 1	Factor 2	Factor 3
X1	0.574	0.727*	-.106	0.041
X2	0.634	0.781*	0.089	0.066
X3	0.710	0.812*	0.152	0.129
X4	0.846	0.105	0.032	0.894*
X5	0.671	0.275	0.799*	0.099
X6	0.579	0.110	0.760*	0.024
X7	0.670	0.313	0.534	0.519*
X8	0.571	0.727*	0.276	0.185
X9	0.733	0.745	0.459*	0.301
Total	5.990			
Eigenvalue		3.17	1.63	1.19
Individual explained variation		35.2%	18.1%	13.2%
Accumulated explained variation		35.2%	53.3%	66.5%
Factor name		high profitability high repayment	high efficacy	high cash collection

*These factors are greater than 0.4 and can be named.

**Table 12.3. Results of Cluster Analysis for the Three Factor Scores after Clustering
into Two Groups**

Group Number	Number of Samples	Cluster Name	Cluster Mean (standard deviation) Factor 1	Factor 2	Factor 3	Central Distance
Group 1	45	Financially vulnerable	34.05 (12.07)	51.16 (14.15)	41.45 (11.13)	37.94
Group 2	38	Financially sound	68.27 (14.81)	44.83 (19.33)	56.55 (14.23)	37.94
F value	47.93		$R^2 = 0.62$	$R^2 = 0.04$	$R^2 = 0.27$	Overall $R^2 = 0.37$

groups was analyzed in terms of the average figure that this variable represented for each group.

The results obtained through the t-test for the loan terms applied to each of the two groups are presented in Table 12.4.

From Table 12.4 it can be seen that there are marked differences between financially sound and financially vulnerable borrowers in terms of interest rates for short-term and medium/long-term loans. Calculating average interest rates for short- and medium/long-term loans by financially vulnerable borrowers yields rates of 10.12% and 10.49%, respectively; figures which are higher than the averages of 9.32% and 8.86% for financially sound borrowers. This result supports H_1, which states that different interest rates apply to borrowers who are in different financial circumstances, and the more vulnerable an applicant is financially, the higher the rate.

Table 12.4 also shows that there are marked differences in the collateral provided by financially sound and financially vulnerable borrowers for short-term and medium/long-term loans; however the differences only become marked when $\alpha = 0.1$ for short-term collateral, and when $\alpha = 0.05$ for medium/long-term collateral. From average collateral values it is evident that banks request more collateral from financially sound borrowers than from financially vulnerable borrowers (the average values for the former were 1.38 and 1.46, and those for the latter were 1.27 and 1.28). This phenomenon is consistent with the conclusions drawn from the theoretical models and supports hypothesis H_2, which states that collateral requirements are different for applicants with different financial circumstances, and the more financially vulnerable a borrower

Table 12.4. T-Test Results for the Effect of Financial Circumstances on Loan Terms

Loan Terms	Mean Financially Sound (N = 38)	Financially Vulnerable (N = 45)	t Value	Significance
Short-Term Collateral†	1.27	1.38	1.74*	0.0858
Medium/Long-Term Collateral	1.28	1.46	2.77**	0.0128
Short-Term Interest Rate‡	9.32	10.12	2.33**	0.0222
Medium/Long-Term Interest Rate	8.86	10.49	5.27***	0.0001

*p < 1; **p < 0.05; ***p < 0.01.
†This collateral has been converted; the numbers in the table indicate the amount of collateral which must be offered for every dollar loaned.
‡The unit here is a percentage.

is, the more collateral is provided. The reason is that the chance of bankruptcy is higher for financially vulnerable applicants, so to protect its rights as a creditor the bank naturally wants access to more real assets in order to guarantee liquidation value after deducting transaction costs. Finally, the fact that average collateral values were greater than 1 shows that local banks require collateral to a value higher than the amount of the loan, a situation that is different from banks abroad.

The Relationship Between Loan Terms and Type of Borrower After Eliminating Covariants

ANCOVA analysis was used to eliminate the effect of other categories of variables—including covariants such as type of industry, collateral, and ownership—on the loan terms for the two groups. Hypotheses H_1 and H_2 were re-tested, and the results remained unchanged. The test results are shown in Tables 12.5 and 12.6. For both groups, one of the covariants, capitalization, has a significant influence on both collateral value and interest rates for short-term and medium/long-term loans. The p values were 0.0032, 0.0077, and 0.0077, respectively, showing that banks require different amounts of security and different long-term interest rates from companies with more or less capital.

This phenomenon may be because companies with a high capital tend to have a lower debt ratio, which indicates they have strong leverage capacity. Hence banks tend to give them more favorable interest rates and request less collateral. Companies with less capitalization, on the other hand, are often excessively leveraged, with the result that their debt ratio tends to be high. Therefore banks require higher interest rates and more collateral for undertaking a high-risk loan. Comparison of Tables 12.4 and 12.6 shows that after adding the covariants the significance levels of the two groups for short-term collateral rose from 0.0858 to 0.0593, and for medium/long-term collateral, it rose from 0.0128 to 0.0054. Thus adding covariants raises the level of significance for the two groups in terms of collateral provided.

However it is evident from Tables 12.4 and 12.5 that adding covariants worsens the level of significance for the two groups: it goes from 0.0222 to 0.0239 for short-term interest rates, and drops to 0.3341 for all variants. This shows that short-term interest rates are not affected by the type of industry, amount of capital, ownership, or type of collateral. For short-term loans, banks are concerned about the financial status of the individual company rather than any other factor, hence the deliberate introduction of these covariants not only fails to eliminate other interference, but actually degrades the results because of reduced degree of freedom. For medium/long-term loans, it can be seen that the borrower's level of capitalization has a significant influence on the interest rate they pay, and it is therefore evident that for medium/long-term loans, banks are particularly concerned about not only the company's financial circumstances, but also about its level of capitalization.

Table 12.5. Financial Status and Loan Terms: Results of ANCOVA Analysis

Source of Variation	Short-Term Interest Rate		Medium/Long-Term Interest Rate	
	F Value	Significance	F Value	Significance
Financial Status	5.36**	0.0239	3.29***	0.0001
Industry	0.69	0.6579	1.41	0.2283
Capitalization	1.17	0.3313	3.89***	0.0077
Ownership	1.17	0.3171	0.42	0.6599
Type of Collateral	0.81	0.5450	0.46	0.8039
All Variables	1.14	0.3341	3.29***	0.0004

$*p < 0.1; **p < 0.05; ***p < 0.01$

Table 12.6. Financial Status and Collateral Value: Results of ANCOVA Analysis

Source of Variation	Short-Term Interest Rate		Medium/Long-Term Interest Rate	
	F Value	Significance	F Value	Significance
Financial Status	3.70*	0.0593	8.43***	0.0054
Industry	2.02*	0.0789	1.50	0.1962
Capitalization	4.53***	0.0032	3.89***	0.0077
Ownership	0.16	0.8566	0.14	0.8739
Type of Collateral	0.83	0.5361	0.10	0.7549
All Variables	2.13**	0.0171	2.38**	0.0119

$*p < 0.1; **p < 0.05; ***p < 0.01$

The Relationship Between the Type of Borrower, Collateral, and Interest Rate

The two variables of collateral and interest rate are not mutually independent, so in order to increase the accuracy of the test results for hypotheses H_1 and H_2, MANOVA analysis was used to test H_3 using interest and collateral as criteria, and financial circumstances as the predictor. The results are shown in Tables 12.7 and 12.8.

Table 12.7 shows that the results of marginal testing for the two criteria were significant with F values equal to 0.01 and 0.05. The Wilks' value of 0.91 had a significance level of 0.0353. This shows that there are significant differences in the terms of short-term loans among companies which differ in regard to financial circumstances. This phenomenon is a confirmation of Hypothesis H_{3-1}.

Table 12.7. Financial Status and the Terms of Short-Term Loans:
Results of MANOVA Analysis

Criteria	Predictor	Financially Sound Mean	Financially Vulnerable Mean	Wilks	F Value	Signif-icance
Marginal Test	Short-Term Collateral	1.27	1.38		2.85*	0.0959
	Short-Term Interest	9.32	10.15		4.59**	0.0355
Total Test				0.91**	3.51**	0.0353

*$p < 0.1$; **$p < 0.05$; ***$p < 0.01$

Table 12.8. Financial Status and the Terms of Medium/Long-Term Loans:
Results of MANOVA Analysis

Criteria	Predictor	Financially Sound Mean	Financially Vulnerable Mean	Wilks	F Value	Signif-icance
Marginal Test	Medium/Long-Term Collateral	1.35	1.43		6.53**	0.0128
	Short-Term Interest	9.85	11.38		29.73***	0.0001
Total Test				0.68	15.77***	0.0001

*$p < 0.1$; **$p < 0.05$; ***$p < 0.01$

Table 12.8 reveals that the marginal testing results for the two criteria were significant with $P = 0.05$ and $P = 0.01$. The level of significance for the Wilks' value of 0.68 the test total was 0.0001, a result which shows that the terms of medium/long-term loans differ among companies with different financial circumstances. This result supports Hypothesis H_{3-2}. As a means of ensuring the reliability of the results, four covariants were added (type of industry, capitalization, ownership, and type of collateral) and MANCOVA analysis was carried out again to test Hypotheses H_{3-1} and H_{3-2} and see whether the conclusions obtained were in agreement with the conclusions drawn without the covariants. The results are shown in Tables 12.9 and 12.10.

**Table 12.9. Financial Status and the Terms of Short-Term Loans:
Results of MANCOVA Analysis**

	Criteria	Predictor (Covariance)	F Value	Signif-icance	Wilks
Marginal Test	Short-Term Collateral	Financial Circumstances	3.70*	0.0597	
		Industry	2.02*	0.0789	
		Capitalization	4.53***	0.0032	
		Ownership	0.16	0.8566	
		Type of Collateral	0.83	0.5361	
	Short-Term Interest	Financial Circumstances	4.71**	0.0346	
		Industry	0.85	0.5346	
		Capitalization	1.78	0.1473	
		Ownership	1.20	0.3078	
		Type of Collateral	0.67	0.6483	
Total Test	Short-Term Collateral and Short-Term Interest	Financial Circumstances	3.41**	0.0406	**0.88*** (P<0.05)
		Industry	1.51	0.1338	0.73
		Capitalization	2.33**	0.0241	0.72**
		Ownership	0.77	0.5475	0.94
		Type of Collateral	0.73	0.6913	0.87

*$p < 0.1$; **$p < 0.05$; ***$p < 0.01$

Tables 12.9 and 12.10 show that the results of MANCOVA analysis support Hypotheses H_{3-1} and H_{3-2}. The Wilks' values are 0.88 and 0.69, respectively, and the significance levels are 0.0406 and 0.0001: these results are not only consistent with the MANOVA analysis results in Tables 12.7 and 12.8, but also support Hypotheses H_{3-1} and H_{3-2}.

CONCLUSIONS

This study has examined the relationship between the type of borrower and the collateral and interest rate required in the loan contract. Here are the resultant findings and conclusions in Taiwan:

1. The better the borrower's financial circumstances, the lower the interest rate required by the bank.

2. The worse the borrower's financial circumstances, the more collateral the bank requires. The reason is that there is a higher risk of bankruptcy for applicants who are financially vulnerable, so to protect its interests the bank requests more collateral from the financially vulnerable borrower.

3. Interest rates and the amount of collateral vary significantly between companies that have different financial circumstances.

Table 12.10. Financial Status and the Terms of Medium/Long-Term Loans: Result of MANCOVA Analysis

	Criteria	Predictor (Covariance)	F Value	Signif-icance	Wilks
Marginal Test	Medium/ Long-Term Collateral	Financial Circumstances	8.72*	0.0581	
		Industry	1.51*	0.0758	
		Capitalization	3.91***	0.0021	
		Ownership	0.13	0.8578	
		Type of Collateral	0.11	0.5378	
	Medium/ Long-Term Interest	Financial Circumstances	38.28**	0.0321	
		Industry	1.89	0.5367	
		Capitalization	4.68	0.1489	
		Ownership	0.22	0.3078	
		Type of Collateral	1.32	0.6483	
Total Test	Medium/Long-Term Collateral and Medium/ Long-Term Interest	Financial Circumstances	11.22***	0.0001	**0.69** (P<0.01)
		Industry	1.57	0.1127	0.71
		Capitalization	3.31***	0.0021	0.63
		Ownership	0.18	0.9459	0.99
		Type of Collateral	0.69	0.5985	0.9477

*p < 0.1; **p < 0.05; ***p < 0.01

It is evident from the above that in Taiwan, price factors (interest rates) and nonprice factors (collateral) not only play a very important role in loan contracts, but also act as a key indicator. The amount of collateral applicants are willing to provide in order to borrow and invest the sum they want varies between individual borrowers, so banks can use it as a "signal" which allows them to deduce the applicant's financial circumstances and thereby set a rational interest rate. Hence under asymmetric information and in the oligopoly structure of Taiwan's bank loan market, the financially sound borrower should be offered loan terms which combine low collateral with low interest, and the financially vulnerable borrower should be offered loan terms which combine high interest with high collateral. Under such loan terms, the problem of adverse selection should be eliminated.

The more important collateral is, the stronger the case for the existence of asymmetric information in the local loan market. Because when banks are unable to identify the financial circumstances of their borrowers, they will use collateral to protect their interests, and in these circumstances the ability to provide sufficient collateral becomes the factor that decides whether a loan will be granted or refused.

NOTES

1. See Yu, Hai-Chin (1992a).

2. The problem of adverse selection arises under these circumstances because when banks are faced with a demand for funds which outstrips the supply, they increase interest rates in order to counteract the excessive demand. In this situation loan quality decreases because the low-risk borrower is gradually driven from the market, leaving only high-risk borrowers. Moral hazard problems arise because raising interest rates encourages borrowers to opt for high-risk investment projects, and not to work hard. This situation leads to higher bankruptcy rates and is detrimental for banks.

3. Most of the writings of Bester (1985), and Besanko and Thakor (1987a, b) discuss the relative risks that the two types of borrowers comprise. This chapter is concerned not with the borrowers' type of risk, but rather with their financial circumstances.

4. The questionnaire was pretested and revised before it was posted out. The data it surveyed was not nominal scales, but rather actual borrower data, such as interest rates and loan ratio; hence validity testing was not necessary. The questionnaire format used to collect this kind of data is a limitation of this study.

REFERENCES

Barro, R.J., 1976. The loan market, collateral, and the rate of interest, *Journal of Money, Credit and Banking* 8, 439-56.

Berger, A.N., 1988. Collateral, loan quality, and bank risk. Salomon Brothers Center for the Study of Financial Institutions,Working Paper Series 502, 1-17.

Berger, Allen N. and Gregory F. Udell, 1990. Collateral, loan quality, and bank risk, *Journal of Monetary Economics* 25, 21-42.

Besanko, David and Anjan V. Thakor, 1987a. Competitive equilibrium in the credit market under asymmetric information, *Journal of Economic Theory* 42, 167-82.

Besanko, David and Anjan V. Thakor, 1987b. Collateral and rationing: sorting equilibria in monopolistic and competitive credit market, *International Economic Review* 28, 671-89.

Bester, Helmut, 1985. Screening vs. rationing in credit markets with imperfect information, *American Economic Review* 75, 850-55.

Bester, Helmut, 1987. The role of collateral in credit markets with imperfect information, *European Economic Review* 31, 887-99.

Bester, Helmut and Martin Hellwig, 1987. *Moral Hazard and Equilibrium Credit Rationing: An Overview of the Issues, Agency Theory, Information, and Incentives*, ed. by G. Bamberg and K. Spremann. Heidlberg: 136-66.

Clemenz, Gerhard, 1986. *Credit Market with Asymmetric Information*. Berlin and New York: Springer-Verlag, 47.

Fried, J. and P. Howitt, 1980. Credit rationing and implicit contract theory, *Journal of Money, Credit and Banking* 12, 471-87.

Greenbaum, S.I., G. Kanatas, and I. Venezia. 1989. Equilibrium loan pricing under the bank-client relationship, *Journal of Banking and Finance* 13(2), 221-235.

Grossman, H.I., 1979. Adverse selection, dissembling, and competitive equilibrium, *Bell Journal of Economics*, 336-43.

Grossman, S.J. and O.D. Hart, 1983. An analysis of the principal-agent problem, *Econometrica* 51, 47-63.

Harris, M. and A. Raviv, 1979. Optimal incentive contract with imperfect information, *Journal of Economic Theory* 20, 231-59.

Hillwig, Martin, 1987. Some recent developments in the theory of compensation in markets with adverse selection, *European Economic Review* 31, 319-25.

Igawa, Kazuhiro and George Kanatas, 1990. Asymmetric information, collateral, and moral hazard, *Journal of Financial and Quantitative Analysis* 25, 469-89.

Jaffee, D. and F. Modigliani, 1969. A theory and test of credit rationing, *American Economic Review* 59, 850-72.

Jaffee, D. and F. Modigliani, 1976. A theory and test of credit rationing: reply, *American Economic Review* 66, 918-20.

Jaffee, Dwight and T. Russell, 1976. Imperfect information and credit rationing, *Quarterly Journal of Economics* 90, 651-66.

Stiglitz, Joseph E. and Andrew Weiss, 1981. Credit rationing in markets with imperfect information, *American Economics Review* 76, 393-410.

Stiglitz, Joseph and Andrew Weiss, 1985. Credit Rationing with Collateral, Bell Communications Research Inc. Economic Discussion Paper 12.

Yu, Hai-Chin, 1992a. The empirical survey of Taiwan's local bank loan market under asymmetric information, *Journal of Business and Banking* 16(2), 1-9.

Yu, Hai-Chin, 1992b. The local bank loan market under asymmetric information, National Chengchi University Ph.D. Dissertation, Taiwan.

13

An Analysis of the Capital Guaranteed Trust and Its Innovation in Taiwan

Paul W.K. Chen, Ming-Chong Chiang, and Edward H. Chow

INTRODUCTION

Financial engineering in the last couple of decades has intrigued academicians and practitioners tremendously. However, many of the financial engineered products may not qualify as financial innovations in the views of, for example, Van Horne (1985), Ross (1989), Miller (1986), and Merton (1990, 1995). Not only does a financial innovation have to improve on trading process or security design, it also needs to provide benefits in at least one of the following areas: reduction of transaction cost, circumvention of regulations, saving of taxes, mitigation of the adverse effect of asymmetric information, and making the market more complete. Taiwan as an emerging market has so many capital flow restrictions, prohibitions on financial products, tax loopholes, and the like, that it is prone to financial innovations.[1] In this chapter we evaluate the financial innovation value of the Jardine Fleming Japan Capital Guaranteed Trust (CGT) in Taiwan, which in March 1995, was made available for subscription in Taiwan, Hong Kong, and Europe by Jardine Fleming Unit Trust Management Corporation, Hong Kong.

The CGT guarantees a nonnegative return and offers investors the opportunity to participate in the upward movements in the Japanese stock market. From an investor's perspective the Japan CGT can be considered as a combination of a zero coupon bond and an Asian call option on the Nikkei 300 index. The option is in the money if the average value of the eight quarter-end Nikkei 300 indices are greater than the index value on the first day (the first dealing day) when the trust starts.

The CGT is a financial innovation for Taiwan's residents, who have very limited channels to trade options. Taiwan does not have futures or options exchanges, nor are over-the-counter (OTC) derivatives legally allowed to be marketed by local financial institutions.[2] Investors can only trade foreign-exchange-listed options or OTC contracts inconveniently through the branches or offices of foreign institutions. The minimum investment amounts for OTC products are usually so prohibitively high that only few wealthy individuals can afford them. In addition, it is quite difficult for local investors to register directly with a foreign broker for the purpose of trading derivatives because of language barrier and credit risk. Therefore, the investment portfolios of Taiwan's investors consist mainly of local financial and real assets, with very little, if any, leverage in foreign assets. The minimum investment for the CGT is less than US$400, which is viable for individual investors who are the primary participants of Taiwan's financial markets.[3] By investing in the CGT, Taiwan's investors hold long-dated OTC options which are otherwise unavailable and participate in Japanese equity market with leverage.[4]

The CGT was initiated by Jardine Fleming Taiwan Limited (JFT), co-designed by JFT and Jardine Fleming Hong Kong Limited (JFHK), issued by JFHK and marketed by the branches of Jardine Fleming throughout the world. The total commitments of JFT to the CGT is 25% of the global subscriptions. The JFT staff in Taiwan identified a local demand for a principal guaranteed product through surveys and customer contacts. Since the local Security and Exchange Commission (SEC) had not approved of any such products before, the CGT had to be issued by JFHK in order to be sold in Taiwan. The success of the CGT is an example of how financial markets circumvent regulations to benefit their participants.

Other equity-linked debt securities similar to the CGT have been around as well. These instruments in general provide investors with the opportunity to participate in the returns linked to the performance of some equity indexes, while guaranteeing the return of their principal invested. McConnell and Schwartz (1986) examined a type of corporate equity-linked debt security called LYON (liquid yield option notes), which has features of a zero coupon convertible bond and stock call and put options. Chance and Broughton (1988) and Chen and Kensinger (1990) examined the structure and pricing of MICDs (market-index certificates of deposits) introduced by Chase Manhattan Bank in 1987. MICDs provide a nonnegative yield which is related to some equity index. Chen and Sears (1990) analyzed a stock-index-linked debt, called SPINs (Standard & Poor's 500 index subordinated notes), which may be considered as a combination of a coupon note and a call option on the S&P 500 stock index. Finnerty (1993) studied a new security called SIGNs (stock index growth notes), which is a zero coupon bond with the single payment linked to the S&P 500.

Bennett, Chen, and McGuinness (1996) examined two Capital Guaranteed Funds (CGF), Citi-Asia and Citi-Latin America, introduced by CitiBank Groups in 1994. These two CGFs provide a nonnegative yield which is related to stock index returns in Asia and Latin American, respectively. Bennett et al. found that the actual offering prices are higher than the theoretical values of both funds by about 15% on the initial day. They argued that the overpricing appeared reasonable due to transaction costs associated with the construction of the products and the incomplete market in stock index options.

This chapter evaluates the CGT from its initial day, April 7, 1995, until one year later, April 10, 1996. We show that the CGT is actually a combination of a zero coupon bond and an average rate option. Applying the Monte Carlo approach to obtain the theoretical value of the average rate option, we are able to assess the financial innovation value of the CGT to Taiwan's investors. We argue that the innovation value can be represented by the subscription and managing fees and the difference between the theoretical value and the net asset value (NAV), which is the cost investors bear for subscribing the CGT and withdrawing prematurely.

The chapter proceeds as follows: the key features of the CGT are analyzed and a portfolio replicating the CGT is presented; the data and the methodology for pricing the CGT are discussed; the simulated CGT values are compared to actual NAV values, which is helpful in our discussion of the CGT's innovation value; in addition, analyses are conducted to check the sensitivity of the simulation results to changes in volatility and dividend ratio assumptions.

AN ANATOMY OF THE CAPITAL GUARANTEED TRUST

The CGT is a unit trust designed to provide investors with the opportunity to participate in the returns linked to the performance of the Japanese Nikkei 300 index while guaranteeing the return of the initial investment if the investors hold their units until maturity. At maturity, the unitholders will receive (1) the initial capital invested plus (2) the Nikkei index rate of return times initial capital invested times participation rate. If the index return is negative, the unitholders will receive their initial capital invested only. The participation rate is 125%.

The rate of return on the Nikkei 300 index will be equal to the average of the closing level of the index on July 7, 1995, and the seven index values on the 10th day of the last month of each of the seven quarters subsequent to the initiation of the trust, minus the closing index level on April 7, 1995 (the index level on the initial day), divided by the initial index. Units will be sold at a price of US$10 per unit. Early redemption is subject to a charge of 2% of NAV before April 1, 1996, and 1% after April 1, 1996, before maturity.

The CGT is denominated in U.S. dollars. The investment policy of this trust is to invest all of the funds raised in the money market instruments (fixed income securities), including fixed-rate U.S. Treasuries and U.S. Treasuries through repurchase agreements, and the like. The interest received on the money market instruments will be exchanged, through a swap agreement, for a return based on the performance of Nikkei 300 index.

The payoff of investing in the capital guaranteed trust at maturity can be written as:

$$TP = F + \lambda F Max [0, (A_T - I_0 / I_0)],$$ \hfill (1)

where TP = total payoff at maturity, F = capital invested, λ = participation rate, A_T = average value of the eight quarter-end Nikkei 300 indices, and I_0 = the index value on the first day when the fund starts.

Apparently, the payoff at maturity of the CGT can be replicated by a portfolio consisting of a zero coupon bond and a call option. For our purpose the strike price has been scaled as 10 to be comparable to the subscription price of \$10 per unit.[5]

At any given time, the value of the replicating portfolio can be computed as

$$V_t = B_t + \lambda * C_t,\tag{2}$$

where V_t is the value of replicting portfolio at time t, B_t is the value of the zero coupon bond at time t maturing at T. C_t is the value of the average rate call option at time t maturing at T. For our purpose, we shall call $\lambda * C_t$ the option component of the value of the CGT.

Computing the value of the zero coupon bond is standard and straightforward. However, the valuation of the option component is somewhat complicated. Since the distribution of the arithmetic average rate is not lognormal, there is not a generally accepted closed-form solution (e.g., Black and Scholes [1973] option pricing model) for the arithmetic average rate option. Numerical approaches are most common in the valuation of these options. Kemna and Vorst (1990) propose a Monte Carlo approach to valuate arithmetic average rate options, which employs the corresponding geometric average rate option as a control variate. Turnbull and Wakeman (1991) apply the Edgeworth series expansion around the lognormal distribution to value the arithmetic average rate option. They provide an algorithm to compute moments for the arithmetic average. Levy (1992), however, develops a closed-form analytical approximation for valuing the arithmetic average rate option on foreign exchange rates based on a defined Wilkinson approximation.

These approximation methods all adopt some regularity restrictions to approximate the true values of the average rate options. These restrictions more or less save computation time but involve drawbacks. For example, Levy's (1992) approach relies on the assumption that the distribution of the sums of the log normal variates is itself well approximated at least to the first and second order by the log normal. However, the accuracy of the pricing formula deteriorates as volatility increases as Levy indicates. Thus, other than assuming that the Nikkei 300 index average is lognormally distributed, we impose no additional restrictions to generate the entire path of the future index average before maturity. Through Monte Carlo simulation, we calculate the value of the option component. Our method is intuitively appealing and seems appropriate for our purpose.

DATA AND METHODOLOGY

The daily net asset values of the CGT for the period April 7, 1995, through April 10, 1996, are obtained from Jardine Fleming Taiwan Limited. The total number of NAVs for the sample period is 236. We take from the *Asia Wall Street Journal* the yield on the U.S. Treasury Strips which have the maturity date closest to that of the CGT as zero coupon rates to estimate the bond value.

The risk-free rate is proxied by the yield to maturity of the April 1997 Treasury Note, which has a maturity date closest to the maturity of the CGT. The volatility of the Nikkei 300 index returns is estimated from the daily closing index levels for the period one year before the date for which the theoretical value of the CGT is computed.[6] As will be explained later, the theoretical value of the CGT is simulated for all the dates for which we have the NAV values. Thus, the volatility is estimated each day for the sample period through the same method. Daily closing indices are obtained from Reuters.

The dividend yield for the Nikkei 300 index is computed by subtracting the value-weight market return without cash dividend from the one with dividend. The 1994 dividend yield is adopted for our simulation because of the availability of the data when this research started. The data are obtained from PACAP (Pacific-Basin Capital Markets) data bank.

The Estimation of the Zero Coupon Bond Component of the CGT

The implied yield from Treasury Strips are used as the proxy for the zero coupon bond yield to estimate the zero coupon bond component of the CGT using the following standard bond valuation model:

$$B_t = F / (1 + r_B / 2)^{2(T-t)}, \tag{3}$$

where F = face value of coupon bond ($10 per unit), B_t = value of the zero coupon bond component at time t, r_B = the zero coupon bond yield, and T-t = time to maturity for the zero coupon bond.

The Estimation of the Average Rate Option

The value of the option component is computed using Monte Carlo simulation. For each day in our sample we compute the value of the option component in equation (2) to obtain what we dubbed as the theoretical value of CGT, which is then compared to the actual NAV. To compute the value of the option component for each day, we first generate a sequence of stock indexes I_{t+1} for t = 1, 2 ... N given I_t by using the following risk-neutral stochastic process expression, where N is the number of trading days before maturity:

$$I_{t+1} = I_t e^{(r - \delta - 0.5\sigma^2) \Delta t + \sigma z \sqrt{\Delta t}}, \tag{4}$$

where I_t = index level at time t, r = risk-free rate, δ = annual dividend yield, σ = standard deviation (volatility) of the Nikkei 300 index return, z is a standard normal distribution, $z \sim N(0,1)$, and Δt stands for one business day annualized in this simulation. According to the payoff function of the CGT, the terminal option value, C_T, can be expressed as:

$$C_T = Max\ (0, A_T - 10),\tag{5}$$

where A_T is the quarterly average of the index level. Under the risk-neutral assumption which is common in the literature (for example, Cox and Ross, 1976), we discount the terminal option value to obtain the call value at time t as

$$C_t = e^{-r\ (T-t)}\ C_T,\tag{6}$$

This procedure is repeated 5,000 times. The average value of these 5,000 calls is taken as the value of the option for day t. We then repeat the simulations to obtain the option value for each day t. As noted in the previous section, the volatility figure used in the simulation is updated for each day t.

EMPIRICAL RESULTS

Figure 13.1 plots the estimated value of the option component, bond component, and the theoretical value of the CGT. The value of the bond component is very stable, while the value of the option component is volatile, which implies that the change in the value of the CGT is driven mostly by the option component. Both values tend to increase as time passes, but the increase in the option value is relatively more pronounced, mainly due to the positive performance of the Nikkei 300. Figure 13.2 plots the NAVs and the theoretical values of the CGT. Figure 13.3 shows the difference in percentage between the NAV and the theoretical value of the CGT. In general the NAVs are lower compared to the theoretical values of the CGT. On average, the NAV is .51% lower than the theoretical value for the one-year period April 7, 1995, to April 10, 1996. The instances in which NAV is higher than the theoretical value are concentrated in the early period of the Trust.

Table 13.1 presents the estimated values of the option component, bond component, and theoretical values of the CGT for five selected dates. These five days include the initial day and four quarterly days whose Nikkei 300 index levels are used to calculate A_T. On the initial day (April 7, 1995), the offering price ($10) is slightly higher than the theoretical value of the CGT by 1.21%. The subscription fee of the CGT is 2.5% of the amount of investment if purchased from the trust department of a bank, for which the investors do not have direct ownership of the investment, or 5% if from Jardine Fleming Taiwan, for which the investors are the registered owners. The managing fee is 1.35% per annum of the net assets of the trust on the initial day. Since an investor invests in a trust whose theoretical value is lower than its subscription price, the difference can also be considered to be a cost for obtaining the CGT. Thus, the total cost the investor bears for the investment is at least 6.41% (2.5% + 1.35% + 1.35% + 1.21%) for the duration of the trust. Given the trust was sold out in Taiwan within a week, the cost can be thought of as the innovation value for Taiwan's investors.[7]

Figure 13.1. The Theoretical Values of the CGT, Bond Component, and Option Component

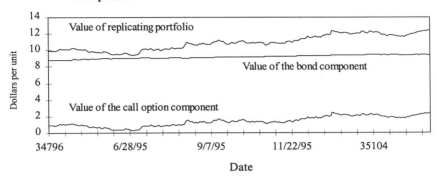

Figure 13.2. The Net Asset Value of the CGT and the Value of the Replicating Portfolio for the Period April 7, 1995, to April 10, 1996

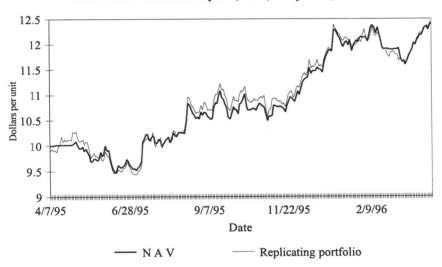

In addition, although on average CGT's theoretical values are only slightly higher than the NAVs for the sample period, some large price discrepancies exist. Since the NAVs after the trust starts are the basis of early withdrawal, investors, if withdrawing before the trust's maturity, are imposed a cost in the case in which the theoretical value is greater than NAV. Thus, the withdrawal cost before maturity is the difference between the theoretical value and NAV. Note that there is also a redemption charge as mentioned before. This additional withdrawal cost, 0.5% on average, plus redemption charge of 1% to 2% should also be considered as innovation value. Therefore, added to the withdrawl cost, the innovation value of the CGT is at least 7.91% (6.41%+1.5%).

Figure 13.3. Percentage Difference Between NAV and the Theoretical Value of the CGT

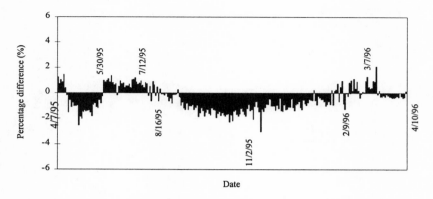

Table 13.1. The Theoretical Value of the CGT for Selected Dates

	Dates				
	4/7/95	7/10/95	10/11/95	1/10/96	4/10/96
NAV (A)	10.00	10.12	10.70	12.13	12.41
Value of bond	8.77	9.08	9.19	9.38	9.45
Value of option	0.89	0.80	1.36	2.25	2.36
Participation rate	1.25	1.25	1.25	1.25	1.25
Value of option component	1.11	0.99	1.71	2.81	2.95
Value of replicating portfolio (B)	9.88	10.08	10.90	12.19	12.40
Price difference [(A) - (B)] %	1.21%	0.42%	-1.82%	-0.5%	0.12%
Nikkei 300 index	239.72	243.34	267.24	303.37	310.12

SENSITIVITY ANALYSIS

Because the simulated theoretical value of the option component is influenced by the magnitudes of dividend yield and the volatility of Nikkei 300 index returns, an analysis of the sensitivity of CGT's value to changes in these two inputs are performed. The analysis is done only for the first trading day. Four estimates of volatility (σ = 15.8%, 14.3%, 13.6%, and 12.9%) are used, which are estimated using historical daily closing data 360 days, 240 days, 150 days, and 90 days before the initial day (April 7, 1995). Table 13.2 presents the values of the option component and the theoretical values of the CGT for the initial day based on the four different volatility estimates. One can see that while changes in volatility can have significant impacts on the value of the option component, they have small impacts on the value of the CGT, which is dominated by the bond component. For example, if the volatility changes from 15.8% to 12.9% (a decrease of 20%), the value of the option component decreases by 11%, while the value of CGT decreases by only 1.3%. This is because the option component only accounts for around 12% of the value of the CGT.

This study also finds that changes in dividend yield have much less impact on the values of the option component and CGT (results are available upon request). For instance, if the dividend yield changes from 1% to 1.2% (an increase of 20% as well), the value of option decreases by about 2%, while the value of CGT decreases by .3%, much less than the sensitivity to volatility changes. Thus it appears that although the volatility measure affects the value of the CGT to some extent, our discussion about the innovation value is not significantly affected.

CONCLUSION

This chapter examines the Japan Capital Guaranteed Trust offered by the Jardine Fleming Group. The payoff of CGT can be replicated by a zero coupon bond with $10 face value and an average price call option whose underlying security is the Nikkei 300 index. By utilizing Monte Carlo simulation, we find that the offering price ($10 per unit) on April 7, 1995, is higher than the theoretical value of the replicating portfolio by 1.2%. Since investors invest in a trust whose theoretical value is lower than its offering price, we consider the difference an innovation value. We add this value to subscription and managing fees

Table 13.2. Sensitivity Analysis: Effect of Volatility on the Value of CGT on the Initial Day (April 7, 1995)

	Volatility of Index Return			
	$\sigma = 0.158$	$\sigma = 0.143$	$\sigma = 0.136$	$\sigma = 0.129$
NAV (A)	10.00	10.00	10.00	10.00
Value of bond	8.77	8.77	8.77	8.77
Value of option	0.89	0.81	0.80	0.80
Participation rate	1.25	1.25	1.25	1.25
Value of option component	1.11	1.02	1	1
Value of replicating portfolio (B)	9.88	9.79	9.77	9.77
Price difference [(A) - B)] %	1.21	2.15	2.34	2.33

to obtain the innovation value of CGT (6.41%) on the initial day. Moreover, over the sample period the theoretical value is on average lower than NAV by 0.5%, which means that on average investors' redemption value before maturity is less than the value of the CGT by 0.5%. Thus, taking into account the redemption charge of 1-2%, the total innovation value for investors who redeem before maturity may be as high as 8%. We believe that this figure is higher than the transaction costs of most mutual funds offered to retail investors.

Our discussion with the staff at Jardine Fleming Taiwan indicates that, because of the success of the CGT, Jardine Fleming Taiwan is designing other similar products for the Taiwan market. Between the end of 1994 and mid-1996 there were nine CGT-type trusts offered by different financial institutions in Taiwan. The nature of the guarantee provided by the products are quite similar. Therefore, our simulation method can be applied to the valuation of the other eight products. Since the minimum investment ranges from $10,000 to $50,000, affordable to individual investors in Taiwan, the products are essentially designed for individuals. In Taiwan, where individuals dominate institutions in trading, a financial product can succeed only if individuals perceive value. Since the product is well received at a pretty high transaction cost, it seems to us that the CGT products provide value to Taiwan's residents that was not available before. In this regard, it is a financial innovation that will have lasting impacts on the local market in the future. Because of the CGT, Taiwan's investors have the opportunity to participate in the foreign equity markets by way of financially engineered options.

NOTES

1. For example, Chow and Liu (1996) argue that the Treasury bond margin contract (TBMC) in Taiwan created by local dealers is a true financial innovation because it provides regulation arbitrage, tax arbitrage, and other profit opportunities that are otherwise unavailable without TBMC.

2. The Security Exchange Commission plans to allow stock warrants to be traded on the Taiwan Stock Exchange (TSE). But as of the completion of this chapter, warrants are yet traded on the TSE.

3. More than 90% of the equity trading in Taiwan is contributed by individual investors.

4. It is difficult and costly, if not impossible, for small retail investors to replicate an average rate option on the Nikkei 300 index. There is no exchange-traded average rate option on the Nikkei 300 index. Vanilla Nikkei 300 index options are traded on the Singapore International Monetary Exchange (SIMEX) and the Chicago Board Option Exchange (CBOE), and Nikkei 300 LEAPS (long-term equity anticipation securities) options are traded on the CBOE. However, these options are European-style and have payoffs different from the average rate option. In addition, trading volumes for these two options have been very thin.

5. The investment amount is in ten thousands of NT$.

6. Previous researches use implied standard deviation (ISD) from option prices as the estimate of return volatility. However, both the Nikkei 300 index options traded on the SIMEX and CBOE and Nikkei 300 LEAPS traded on the CBOE are not Asian

options and have very thin trading volume. It is improper to use the ISDs from these two infrequently traded option contracts as estimates of index volatility.

7. Strictly speaking, the innovation value should be net of transaction cost reduction, regulation arbitrage, tax benefits, and so on. For the CGT, there is no obvious tax benefit compared to other funds issued by foreign institutions in Taiwan. Since replicating the CGT for investors in Taiwan is practically infeasible, we do not consider transaction cost reduction. Furthermore, the benefit of regulation arbitrage is difficult to estimate.

ACKNOWLEDGMENTS

The authors gratefully acknowledge the data provided by Jardine Fleming Taiwan Investment Management Limited. We benefitted a great deal from the discussions with Frances Chang and Wen-Hua Chuang at Jardine Fleming Taiwan Investment Management Limited.

REFERENCES

Bennett, J.A., A.H. Chen, and P. McGuinness, 1996. An analysis of capital guaranteed funds, *International Review of Economics and Finance* 259-68.

Black, F. and M. Scholes, 1973. The pricing of options and corporate liabilities, *Journal of Political Economy* 637-654.

Chance, D.M. and J.B. Broughton, 1988. Market index depository liabilities: analysis, interpretation, and performance, *Journal of Financial Services Research* 1(4), 335-352

Chen, A.H. and J.W. Kensinger, 1990. An analysis of market-index certificates of deposit, *Journal of Financial Services Research* 4(2), 36-47

Chen, K.C. and R.S. Sears, 1990. Pricing the SPIN, *Financial Management* 19(2), 36-47.

Chow, E.H. and P. Liu, 1996. The creation of Treasury bond margin contract in a market absent of futures—on the financial engineering of Taiwan's OTC bond trading, 1997. CBOT Research Symposium Proceedings.

Cox, J.C. and S.A. Ross, 1976. The valuation of options for alternative stochastic processes, *Journal of Financial Economics* 3(1/2), 145-166.

Finnerty, J.D., 1993. Interpreting SIGNs, *Financial Management* 34-47.

Kemna, A.G.Z. and A.C.F. Vorst, 1990. A pricing method for options based on average asset values, *Journal of Banking and Finance*, 113-129.

Levy, E., 1992. Pricing European average rate currency options, *Journal of International Money and Finance* 14(1), 474-491.

McConnell, J.J. and E.S. Schwartz, 1986. LYON taming, *Journal of Finance* 41(3), 561-576.

Merton, R.C., 1990. The financial system and economic performance, *Journal of Financial Services Research* 4(3), 263-300.

Merton, R.C., 1995. A functional perspective of financial intermediation, *Financial Management*, 23-41.

Miller, M.H., 1986. Financial innovation: The last twenty years and the next, *Journal of Financial and Quantitative Analysis* 21(4), 459-471.

Ross, S.A., 1989. Institutional markets, financial marketing, and financial innovation, *Journal of Finance* 44(3), 541-556.

Turnbull, M. and L.M. Wakeman, 1991. A quick algorithm for pricing European average options, *Journal of Financial and Quantitative Analysis* 26, 377-389.

Van Horne, J.C., 1985. Of financial innovations and excesses, *Journal of Finance* 40(3), 621-631.

14

Market Structure and Performance in the Greek Banking System

George Hondroyiannis, Sarantis Lolos,
and Evangelia Papapetrou

INTRODUCTION

The relationship between market structure and performance has been studied by using two alternative approaches: the structure-conduct-performance and the efficient-structure hypothesis. The structure-conduct-performance (SCP) hypothesis asserts that banks gain higher profits in concentrated markets and consequently profitability depends on industry concentration. Banks are able to extract monopolistic rents in concentrated markets by offering low deposit rates and charging higher loan rates. On the contrary, the efficient-structure (EFS) hypothesis argues that differences in firms' efficiency within markets create unequal market shares and high levels of concentration. Efficient firms increase in size and market share as a result of their ability to generate higher profits, which usually leads to higher market concentration.

The SCP hypothesis has been studied extensively for the United States (Rhoades, 1982; Gilbert, 1984; Berger and Hannan, 1989, 1992; Calem and Carlino, 1989; Hannan 1991) and to some extent for European banking (Lloyd-Williams, Molyneux, and Thornton, 1994; Molyneux, 1995; Goldberg and Rai, 1996). Other researches have studied the EFS hypothesis (Smirlock, 1985; Shepherd, 1986; Rhoades, 1982; Timme and Yang, 1991). However, there is still no consensus regarding the relationship between structure and performance.

The purpose of this chapter is to extend the earlier work by implementing tests to find whether there exists a statistical relationship between profitability and market structure in Greece. Our study attempts to ascertain whether the conclusions reached for other countries can be extended to a medium-sized country like Greece. Currently, the Greek banking system is undergoing major changes. The need for a modern, flexible, and market-oriented financial system has initiated efforts toward the deregulation of the financial system. Further, in recent years banking activity in Greece was decisively affected by the harmoni-zation of national regulations within the European Union-that is, with the enact-ment of the Second Banking Directive of 1992, the elimination of capital con-trols, and capital movement liberalization. However, to the present, the Greek banking system has not been studied extensively due to data deficiency. As a result there is lack of market power and efficiency structure explanation of the profit-structure relationship in the Greek banking system. This chapter uses for the first time data that help shed light on this important relationship.

The chapter is organized as follows: the institutional structure of the Greek banking system is outlined; the SCP and EFS hypotheses are discussed and the previous empirical work on market structure is reviewed; the empirical model is presented and empirical results are discussed; finally, the results are summarized and implications for banking activity in Greece are analyzed.

STRUCTURE AND REGULATORY ENVIRONMENT OF THE GREEK BANKING SYSTEM

A major structural feature of the Greek banking system has been its institutional specialization required by law rather than dictated by market forces. The regulation and control of the banking system was carried out through a complex system of credit rules in an environment of administrative fixed interest rates.[1] Credit and interest rate policy are aimed at influencing the asset structure of the credit system, in a way conducive to the government's economic policy priorities, such as export expansion, promotion of small and medium-sized enterprises, financing of state-owned firms, and the like.

Commercial banks have been the dominant group in the Greek credit system (see Table 14.1). Although the depth of the capital and money markets has increased considerably in recent years, the relative weight of banking in the Greek financial system is still very high.[2] In 1995, besides the Central Bank, there were 52 credit institutions established and operating in Greece. The commercial banking system comprises 20 commercial banks and 20 branches of foreign banks, of which 12 are EU based.[3] Also there are seven specialized credit institutions, namely two investment banks, three real-estate banks, a savings bank, a specific purpose bank, as well as four credit cooperatives. In addition, the Agricultural Bank which, although it is classified as a specialized credit institution, has been operating as a commercial bank since 1991.

The specific feature of the Greek finance-credit system, which involves the smallest number of credit institutions in the European Union, is the decisive presence of the state at a level that is rare in other Western economies. In par-ticular, all specialized credit institutions plus nine[4] of the commercial banks, including three of the larger ones, are directly or indirectly state-controlled.[5] Another characteristic of the Greek commercial banking system is the dominant role of a few large banks, which have considerable market power. Finally, the share of foreign banks is rather limited, given that 20 banks hold just over 15% of the commercial banking market.

Table 14.1. The Greek Credit System in Terms of Assets

Institutions	Billion Drs			Percentage Shares		
	1993	1994	1995	1993	1994	1995
Commercial Banks	16,925	18,709	22,305	67.9	67.9	68.6
Greek Banks *of which:*	14,199	15,405	18,113	56.9 100.0	55.9 100.0	55.7 100.0
Four large banks	11,868	12,516	14,681	47.6 83.6	45.4 81.2	45.1 81.0
Smaller banks	2,331	2,889	3,432	9.3 16.4	10.5 18.8	10.6 19.0
Foreign Banks *of which:*	2,725	3,304	4,192	10.9	12.0	12.9
EU Banks	1,710	1,948	2,365	6.9	7.1	7.3
non-EU Banks	1,016	1,355	1,826	4.1	4.9	5.6
Specialized Credit Institutions	8,011	8,862	10,214	32.1	32.1	31.4
Agricultural Bank	2,680	3,037	3,515	10.7	11.0	10.8
Other Institutions	5,331	5,825	6,699	21.4	21.1	20.6
Total Assets	24,936	27,571	32,519	100.0	100.0	100.0

Source: Banks' Balance Sheets (1993-95).

The complicated system of direct controls, although frequently modified, essentially remained in place until the late 1980s. Over the last decade, the process of deregulation of the banking system was carried out at an accelerating pace.[6] The implementation into Greek Law (1992) of the EC Council Directives that establish a common financial market resulted in further liberalization and deregulation of the Greek banking system. Also, in 1992, the Own Funds and the Solvency Ratio of the credit institutions directive were enacted into Greek legislation and foreign exchange controls concerning current transactions were lifted, while capital movements were completely liberalized in May 1994.

Financial liberalization enabled new, mainly small, private banks to establish operations and led to an increase in the number of branches, resulting in a decline in the high concentration ratio of the commercial banking sector. In particular, over the period 1993-95, the presence of four of the largest banks, in terms of assets, in the Greek banking system declined from 83.6% in 1993 to 81% in 1995. A similar decline was registered in the share of the four largest banks in the whole commercial system (from 70.1% in 1993 to 65.8% in 1995). Also, the Herfindahl index (HE) (i.e., the sum of the squares of market shares calculated over bank deposits of the Greek banking system) decreased from 0.32 in 1993 to 0.27 in 1995.[7] The Herfindahl index can also be viewed in terms of an equivalent number of n symmetric firms (where $n = 1/HE$). In this case the number of symmetric firms increased from 3.3 in 1993 to 3.7 in 1995. Finally, over the period under consideration, the state presence in the commercial banking system, in terms of institutions' assets, fell from 67.8% in 1993 to 61.8% in 1995, while for the whole Greek banking system these assets fell from 80.8% to 67.1%.

On the other hand, financial liberalization has not led to any significant increase in a foreign presence in the banking sector in the 1990s in terms of number of banks.[8] Further, it appears that major foreign banks do not have plans to create an extensive network in Greece. However, the offering of banking products and services on a cross-border basis will certainly have intensified international competition.

In Greece, the financing of the large budget deficits has been traditionally carried out principally by the large state-controlled banks (especially the National Bank) through purchasing of government securities. It should be noted that until the beginning of 1991 the banking system had to keep a high proportion (40%) of its portfolio in government securities, on a compulsory basis. Although the obligatory purchasing of new treasury bills was gradually reduced in subsequent years, the high stock of public debt held by the banking system still remains. This situation leads to the determination of high interest rate margins between loans and deposits, which are set by the main holders of public bonds (large banks), while the accrued profits are enjoyed by the whole banking system. However, the interest rate margins are expected to fall along with the gradual reduction of budget deficits and the liberalization of the banking system. This development will put pressures on banks' profits and is expected to lead to structural changes in the Greek banking market. Indeed, recent empirical evidence showed that there has been a gradual shift of the banking system away from conditions of monopoly to those of monopolistic competition.[9]

In the years to come, major changes are expected as a result of government measures and the dynamics of domestic and EU financial and credit markets. The government seems set to reduce the state's presence in a controlled way. At the moment, the government's declared interest is to privatize two small banks, namely the Bank of Central Greece and Cretabank, but there is no hint of the possibility of mergers between large state-owned banks or of the privatization of some of them. In the private sector, Eurobank, the third largest private bank, is in the process of unification with Interbank, a small private bank, in order to compete with the other two major private banks (Alpha Credit and Ergobank).

THE SCP HYPOTHESIS, THE EFS HYPOTHESIS, AND RELATED STUDIES

There have been many empirical studies examining bank performance and market concentration. According to the SCP paradigm, market structure influences the conduct of firms and ultimately their prices and profits. Rhoades (1982) concluded that most of the previous studies found a positive relationship between concentration and bank performance. Gilbert (1984) found that only 27 of 56 studies have identified the relationship itself.

A number of reasons have been put forward to explain the inconsistencies of the theory. Rhoades (1982) claimed that many of the equations are mis-specified, thus biasing the estimated coefficients on the concentration measure. Clark (1986) argued that risk and profitability should be determined simultaneously. Evanoff and Fortier (1988) argued that differences in entry barriers between markets affect the impact of structure on profits.

The SCP theory has been criticized as containing too many inconsistencies (Brosen, 1982; Gilbert, 1984). Gale and Branch (1982) have argued that an industry's structure may be the result of the greater production efficiency of some firms that enables them to increase their market share and ultimately enlarge market concentration. Thus, it is firm efficiency, not collusion, that leads to higher profits. Brosen (1982), Evanoff and Fortier (1988), Smirlock (1985), Timme and Yang (1991), and Berger (1995) find that firm-specific efficiency is the important factor explaining profitability. However, researchers such as Shepherd (1986) question the conclusions of this theory, and Shepherd argues that the market share variable is a proxy of efficiency of larger firms rather than a measure of market power.

The bulk of the studies examining bank performance and market concentration have focused on U.S. banking markets.[10] Empirical work using non-US data is limited. In particular, Lloyd-Williams et al. (1994) examined the market structure and performance in Spanish banking, while Molyneux (1995) studied the SCP and EFS hypotheses for a sample of European banks. Also, Goldberg and Rai (1996), by incorporating two measures of efficiency in the model, examined the correlation between profitability and concentration for eleven European countries. Their results contrast with previous studies that seem to support the SCP hypothesis.

THE EMPIRICAL MODEL AND DATA

Following Smirlock (1985), Lloyd-Williams et al. (1994), Molyneux (1995), and Goldberg and Rai (1996) the model for obtaining the tests for the traditional and efficient structure hypothesis, for the ith firm, is given by the following linear profit function:

$$\delta_i = f(HE, MS_i, Z_i) + \mathring{a}_i \tag{1}$$

where δ_i is a profit measure, HE is a measure of market structure (a concentration ratio), MS_i is a measure of market share, Z_i is a vector of control variables that account for firm-specific and market-specific characteristics, and $\mathring{a}_i$ is a random error variable. The SCP hypothesis implies that the coefficient of the HE variable is positive and statistically significant and the coefficient of the MS variable is zero. The EFS hypothesis implies that the coefficient of the MS variable is positive and statistically significant and the coefficient of the HE variable is zero.

The following equation is used to test the two hypotheses:

$$INTPROF = \hat{a}_0 + \hat{a}_1 HE + \hat{a}_2 MS + \hat{a}_3 ASSET + \hat{a}_4 BR +$$
$$\hat{a}_5 PL + \hat{a}_6 PF + \hat{a}_7 PK + \hat{a}_8 RISKASS \qquad (2)$$

where *INTPROF* = net interest revenue over bank total assets
       HE = Herfindahl index on bank deposits
       MS = market share measure
       ASSET = bank total assets
       BR = number of branches to total number of branches
       PL = personnel expenses to total assets (unit price of labor)
       PK = capital expenses to fixed assets (unit price of capital)
       PF = ratio of interest expenses to own funds (unit price of funds)
       RISKASS = provisions to total assets[11]

The dependent variable *INTPROF* is used as a measure of performance. Berger and Hannan (1992), and Goldberg and Rai (1996) have argued that if the SCP hypothesis reflects anticompetitive pricing, then banks are able to charge lower deposit rates and charge higher loan rates. Thus, net interest margin captures the pricing ability of banks and their power to charge lower deposit rates and higher loan rates. We used the *INTPROF* (net interest income over assets) variable and not the widely used return on assets (ROA) variable (which includes noninterest income) as it provides a better measure of bank performance for the Greek banking system. Since a basic structural characteristic of the Greek banking system is the traditional high spread which banks enjoy and from which they make significant profits, an accurate measure of bank profitability is considered to be the *INTPROF* variable rather than ROA.

The independent variables include firm-specific and market specific variables similar to those used in other studies (Smirlock, 1985, Lloyd-Williams et al. 1994; Molyneux, 1995; and Goldberg and Rai, 1996). The Herfindahl index is used as a measure of concentration, defined as the sum of squared market shares of deposits of all Greek commercial banks. Different measures of concentration are also used. In particular, we used various Herfindahl indices calculated on banks' loans and banks' deposits including *REPOS*. The market share variable (*MS*) is defined as bank deposits divided by total deposits in the Greek banking market assets.

To account for firm-specific risk we used the variable risk capital to assets ratio (*RISKASS*) and we expect it to be positively correlated to the dependent variable since higher provisions should lead to higher bank revenue. The *ASSET* variable is included in our analysis to account for possible economies of scale, given the wide range of bank asset sizes in the Greek banking system. The *BR* variable is used as a proxy for bank size.

The *PL* variable is included as a proxy for the cost of labor. This is generally expected to have a negative impact on profitability. However, Molyneux and Thornton (1992) have identified a strong positive relationship between staff expenses and profitability. Their findings imply that high profits earned by firms in a regulated industry may be appropriated in the form of higher payroll expenditures, and this possibly suggests evidence of expense preference behavior. The *PK* variable is used to account for cost differences between banks, the proxy for the cost of capital. It is expected to have a negative impact on profitability. The *PF* variable is included as a proxy for the cost of funds and is used to account for cost differences between banking institutions. We expect this variable to have a negative impact on bank performance as increased funding cost would reduce profitability.

The data used in the analysis cover 19 banks for the years 1993, 1994, and 1995 and they have been collected from the annual bank reports. The linear relationship between the variables is estimated following two different methods, since the data are cross-section and time-series. In the first method a time-series/ cross-section estimation is employed to estimate equation (2). We used the error-component method and, to allow for heterogeneity across the examined banks, we assume that individual error components are uncorrelated with each other and are not autocorrelated (across both cross-section and time-series units). The estimation is done in two steps. In the first step ordinary least squares is run on the entire pooled data to estimate the variance components (weights), while in the second step the estimated weights are used to estimate the generalized least-squares parameters. In the second method, equation (2) is estimated separately for each year using the method of ordinary least squares.[12] Employing the second method we can investigate the evolution of the profit-structure relationship in the Greek banking system over the period 1993 to 1995.

REGRESSION RESULTS

Pool Estimation

Table 14.2 reports the pooled time-series estimates of the SCP and EFS hypotheses. All estimated coefficients except that for the market share coefficient are statistically significant at 1% and 5% level of significance, while there is no evidence of multicollinearity among the independent variables.[13] We performed a variety of tests to check for serial correlation, for normality of the residuals, for heteroskedasticity, and for the functional form. All tests confirm the good fit of the model. The estimated regression equation explained 97.7% of the variability in profits.

The empirical results support the SCP proposition and reject the competing efficiency hypothesis. The estimated coefficient of the concentration ratio variable (*HE*) is positive and statistically significant at a 1% level of significance, while the estimated coefficient of the market share variable is negative but not statistically significant.

The estimated coefficient for the assets variable (*ASSET*) is positive and statistically significant. This suggests that size-induced differences between banks, in terms of assets, may lead to higher profits, implying that larger banks

Table 14.2. Regression Results of the SCP Relationship and Efficiency Hypothesis for Greek Banks, Panel Data, 1993-95

Independent Variable	INTPROF
HE	11.24**
	(20.89)
MS	-2.41
	(-1.83)
ASSET	8.28E-08**
	(2.89)
BR	-5.16*
	(-2.45)
PL	21.43**
	(3.76)
PF	-0.31**
	(-6.53)
PK	-0.80**
	(-7.04)
RISKASS	24.49**
	(3.6)
Weighted R^2	0.98
Weighted F-statistic	284.5**
Number of Observations	57

Note: Values in parentheses are the *t*-statistics. The symbols * and ** denote levels of significance at 5 and 1 percent, respectively.

seem to be more efficient in generating profits compared to smaller banks. The branches variable (*BR*) is negative and statistically significant, suggesting that banks with many branches are less profitable. This last result may be attributed to the liberalization process of the banking system, where the expansion of the interbank market and the development of new financial products (*REPOS*) diminishes the relative importance of bank branching in raising funds (Georgoutsos et al., 1994). The estimated coefficients for the three unit cost variables—labor, capital, and funds—are statistically significant. The sign of the unit cost of fund and capital is negative, suggesting that an increase in the cost of funds decreases profits. However, the sign of the estimated coefficient of the unit cost of labor is positive. This result indicates that high profits earned by banks may be appropriated in the form of higher payroll expenses. Finally, the risk variable (*RISKASS*) is positive and statistically significant, indicating that banks with higher provisions to assets in their balance sheet generate higher profits.[14]

Year-by-Year Estimation

The regression equations for each of the three years 1993, 1994, and 1995 using the ordinary least squares method are reported in Table 14.3. The estimated coefficient for the market share variable is not statistically significant for all the estimated regression equations, while there is no evidence of multicollinearity among the independent variables.[15] For all the years we performed a variety of tests to check for serial correlation, normality of the residuals and heteroskedasticity, and for the functional form. All tests confirm the good fit of the model. The estimated regression equations explained from 60% to 90% of the variability of the profitability during the periods under examination. Thus, the empirical results for the yearly data, 1993 through 1995, also support the traditional approach.

Table 14.3. Regression Results of the SCP Relationship and Efficiency Hypothesis for Greek Banks, Year by Year Estimation, 1993-95

Independent Variable	INTPROF 1993	INTPROF 1994	INTPROF 1995
Constant	3.99**	3.64**	3.45**
	(4.54)	(5.47)	(10.89)
MS	41.34	123.26	123.19
	(1.02)	(1.02)	(1.38)
ASSET	-3.46E-06	-8.71E-06	-7.24E-06
	(-1.06)	(-1.02)	(-1.41)
BR	10.29	6.54	3.73
	(0.54)	(0.35)	(0.47)
PL	15.07	-3.19	12.53*
	(0.45)	(-0.10)	(2.07)
PF	-0.87*	-0.46**	-0.41**
	(-2.75)	(-3.19)	(-5.04)
PK	-0.69	-1.01*	-0.12
	(-0.80)	(-2.31)	(-0.10)
RISKASS	25.86	57.68	21.84**
	(0.77)	(1.512)	(3.6)
R^2	0.61	0.79	0.91
F-statistic	2.44	5.96**	14.89**
Number of Observations	19	19	19

Note: Values in parentheses are the *t*-statistics. The symbols * and ** denote levels of significance at 5 and 1 percent, respectively.

It should be noted, finally, that the results for Greece are similar to those obtained for Spain (Lloyd-Williams et al., 1994) and for European banking (Molyneux, 1995) but are in contrast with the work of Goldberg and Rai (1996) for European banking and the studies related to the U.S. banking industry which has favored the efficiency hypothesis. This may be due to the different methods of estimation employed in these studies.

CONCLUDING REMARKS

In this chapter we test for two competing hypotheses—the structure-conduct-performance hypothesis and the efficiency hypothesis—using data for Greek banks over the period 1993-95. The empirical evidence seems not to support the efficiency hypothesis. Given the structural features of the Greek banking system, mainly related to government interventions in the functioning of the banking system, it appears that concentration has been a main determining factor of bank profitability.

The liberalization of the Greek banking system initiated in 1992 with the enactment of the Second Banking Directive, the elimination of capital controls, and the liberalization of capital movements has intensified international competition among banks. Further, Greek banking institutions need to have an adequate size in order to compete effectively in international markets, especially in Balkan countries where they have been very active recently. Under this new changing environment, a policy of prohibiting bank mergers and aquisitions so as to reduce, or at least restrict, the monopoly power of these banks is not justified. Further work might provide limitations on bank mergers and acquisitions and provide reasons of encouraging market concentration in certain circumstances.

NOTES

The views expressed in this chapter are those of the authors and not necessarily of the Bank of Greece.

1. For a detailed discussion on the regulatory framework and actual policies pursued, see Halikias (1978), Courakis (1981), and Lolos (1988).

2. For example, in the decade 1985-94, the number of credit institutions increased from 41 in 1985 to 50 in 1994, the number of mutual funds increased from 2 to 98, and the number of brokerage firms increased from 28 to 62 (Central Banking, 1995/6).

3. In addition, the representative offices of 20 foreign banks are established in Greece.

4. In 1996 the small Bank of Attica was privatized and sold to the Pension Fund for Engineers and Contractors of Public Works and to the State Fund for Trusts and Loans.

5. For example, although the chief shareholders of the National, the Commercial, and the Ionian Banks are insurance and pension funds and legal entities of the wider public sector, the government is represented by the finance minister in the stockholders' meeting and appoints their top-level management.

6. For a presentation of the deregulation measures of the Greek banking system, see Gortsos (1995) and *Central Banking* (1995/6).

7. The picture does not change if the Herfindahl index is calculated over banks' loans (1993: 0.22, 1996: 0.19), or if REPOS are included in banks' deposits (1993: 0.31, 1996: 0.25).

8. For a review of the forms of operation of foreign banks in Greece, see Hondroyiannis and Papapetrou (1996).

9. See, Hondroyiannis et al. (1997).

10. See Smirlock (1985), Timme and Yang (1991), Berger (1995), Rhoades (1982), Gilbert (1984), Berger and Hannan (1989), Hannan (1991).

11. For a detailed presentation of the variables used in the model, see the Appendix to this chapter.

12. In addition, given the small sample, we employ the jackknife technique (Efron, 1982), which is robust in the face of problems associated with small numbers of outlying observations. The estimated coefficients are very similar to those obtained from OLS.

13. The covariance between the estimated parameters is small in absolute values, indicating that multicollinearity is not associated with the independent variables used in the regression equation.

14. The results, not reported here, seem to be invariant to the different measures of concentration used.

15. See footnote 13, above.

APPENDIX: DEFINITION OF VARIABLES

ASSET = Bank total assets. *Total Assets* include cash on hand and deposits with the Bank of Greece, government and other securities acceptable for refinancing with the Bank of Greece, loans and advances to credit institutions and customers less provisions, bonds and other fixed income securities, shares and other variable-income securities, participation in affiliated and nonaffiliated companies, intangible assets, tangible fixed assets and other assets, as well as prepaid expenses and accrued income.

PL = Personnel expenses to total assets (unit price of labor). *Personnel Expenses* include wages and salaries, social security contributions, contributions to pension funds and other related expenses.

PK = Capital expenses to fixed assets (unit price of capital). *Capital Expenses* refer to depreciation expenses on a historical cost-basis balance sheet. *Fixed Assets* include tangible fixed assets (land, lots, buildings and installations, furniture, office equipment, etc., less depreciation), as well as intangible fixed assets (goodwill, software, restructuring expenses, research and development expenses, minority interests, formation expenses, underwriting expenses, etc.).

PF = Ratio of annual interest expenses to own funds (unit price of funds). *Interest Expenses* include interest paid on deposits and commission expenses and payments under Law 128/75 (which refers to obligations of commercial banks to finance priority sectors at preferential interest rates; note that these are payments to the Bank of Greece, but they are also included in the interest income as revenues). *Own Funds* include share capital, reserves (regular, extraordinary, and special), subordinated debt, reserves paid in excess of par value, and balance carried forward.

RISKASS = Provisions to total assets. *Provisions* include provisions for contingent liabilities and other provisions, such as staff pensions, depreciation of fixed assets and of previous year's expenses, and so on.

BR = Number of branches to total number of branches. The ratio of a bank's number of branches to the number of branches of the whole banking system.

INTPROF = Net interest revenue to total assets. *Net Interest Revenue* is defined as interest revenue minus interest expenses. *Interest Revenue* includes revenue received from loans and advances, as well as other interest income (long-term claims, claims on banking activity, government securities, special deposits with the Bank of Greece, deposits, etc.).

HE = Measure of market concentration. This uses either a *Herfindahl index*, defined as the sum of squared market shares of deposits of all Greek commercial banks, or a *four-firm concentration ratio*, defined as the share of four-bank assets to total assets of the Greek banking system. Alternatively, different measures of concentration are also used, employing bank loans and bank deposits plus REPOS.

MS = Measure of market share, defined as bank deposits divided by total deposits in the Greek banking market. Alternatively, different measures of market share are also used in the analysis, employing bank assets, bank loans and bank deposits plus REPOS.

REFERENCES

Berger, A.N., 1995. The profit-structure relationship in banking: tests of market-power and efficient-structure hypotheses, *Journal of Money, Credit and Banking* 227(2), 404-431.

Berger, A.N. and T. Hannan, 1989. The price-concentration relationship in banking, *The Review of Economics and Statistics* 71, May, 291-299.

Berger, A.N. and T. Hannan, 1992. The price-concentration relationship in banking: a reply, *The Review of Economics and Statistics* 74 (February), 376-379.

Brosen,Y., 1982. *Concentration, Mergers, and Public Policy*. New York: Macmillan.

Calem, P.S. and G.A. Carlino, 1989. The concentration/conduct relationship in bank deposit markets, *Federal Reserve Bank of Philadelphia Working Paper* 89-26.

Central Banking, 1995/6. Special feature: the bank of Greece, *Central Banking* 6(3) (Winter), 55-85.

Clark, J.A., 1986. Single-equation, multiple-regression methodology: is it an appropriate methodology for estimation of the structure-performance relationship in banking? *Journal of Monetary Economics* 18(3), 295-312.

Courakis, A.S., 1981. Financial structure and policy in Greece: retrospect and prospect, *Greek Economic Review* 3(3), December, 205-244.

Efron, B., 1982. The jackknife, the bootstrap, and other resampling plans, CBMS-NSF Regional Conference Series on Applied Mathematics, No. 18. Society for Industrial and Applied Mathematics, Philadelphia.

Evanoff, D. and L. Fortier, 1988. Revaluation of the structure-conduct-performance paradigm in banking, *Journal of Financial Services Research* 1(3), 277-294.

Gale, B.T. and B.S. Branch, 1982. Concentration versus market share: which determines performance and why does it matter? *The Antitrust Bulletin* 27(1), 83-105.

Georgoutsos, D., S. Lolos, D. Moschos, St. Pantazidis, Ch. Stamatopoulos and N. Zonzilos, 1994. Alternative sources of fund raising in Greece: recent developments and prospects, mimeo, Hellenic Industrial Development Bank, Athens (in Greek).

Gilbert, A., 1984. Studies of bank market structure and competition: a review and evaluation, *Journal of Money, Credit and Banking* 16, 617-644.

Goldberg, L.G. and A. Rai, 1996. The structure-performance relationship for European banking, *Journal of Banking and Finance* 20, 745-771.

Gortsos, C.V., 1995. The *Greek Banking System.* Athens: Hellenic Bank Association.

Halikias, D.J., 1978. *Money and Credit in a Developing Economy: The Case of Greece.* New York: New York University Press.

Hannan, T.H., 1991. Bank commercial loan markets and the role of market structure: evidence from surveys of commercial lending, *Journal of Banking and Finance* 15, 133-150.

Hondroyiannis, G., S. Lolos, and E. Papapetrou, 1997. Assessing competitive conditions in the greek banking system, mimeo, Bank of Greece.

Hondroyiannis, G. and E. Papapetrou, 1996. International banking activity in greece: the recent experience, *Journal of Economics and Business* 48, 207-215.

Lloyd-Williams, D.M., P. Molyneux, and J. Thornton, 1994. Market structure and performance in spanish banking, *Journal of Banking and Finance* 18, 433-443.

Lolos, S., 1988. The development of reserve requirements in Greece, *Hellenic Bank Association Bulletin* 20 (September), 3-14 (in Greek).

Molyneux, P., 1995. Co-operation and rivalry in European banking, *Research in International Business and Finance* 12, 3-23.

Molyneux, P. and J. Thornton, 1992. Determinants of European bank profitability: a note, *Journal of Banking and Finance* 16, 1173-1178.

Rhoades, S., 1982. Structure-performance studies in banking: an updated summary and evaluation, Staff Study No. 119, Board of Governors of the Federal Reserve System.

Shepherd, W.G., 1986. Tobin's q and the structure-performance relationship: comment, *American Economic Review* 76, 1205-1210.

Smirlock., M., 1985. Evidence on the (non) relationship between concentration and profitability in banking, *Journal of Money, Credit and Banking* 17(1), 69-83.

Timme, S. and W. Yang, 1991. On the use of a direct measure of efficiency in testing structure-performance relationships in U.S. commercial banking, Working Paper, Georgia State University.

PART V

Financial Issues
in Transitional Economies

15

Commercial Bank Development in Asian Transitional Economies

Paul M. Dickie

INTRODUCTION

Commercial banking is being developed from a very low base in Asian transitional economies. The People's Republic of China (PRC) initiated the gradual development of a modern banking system in 1983. Viet Nam and Lao People's Democratic Republic (PDR) followed with their first banking reforms in 1988. For most economies, the process has been under way only during the 1990s. Not only has the reform been under way for a relatively short period, but the development of commercial banking has been complicated by the fact that banking under the former command structures consisted largely of a Treasury function in support of implementing the economic plan.[1] Moreover, the soft budget constraints[2] characteristic of intragovernmental credit under the command system are not easily replaced by the financial discipline required for market-based banking systems. Adding to these difficulties, the institutional infrastructure of a market economy needed to be developed, involving, for example, the legal framework for banking transactions that supports hard budget constraints. These factors in combination with the lack of market-based skills has meant that the banking systems of transitional economies have been subject to repeated crisis.

The common solution that has been proposed is tightened regulation and improved central bank oversight. The basis for this approach comes from the success of the G-10 countries (Belgium, Canada, France, Germany, Italy, Japan, the Netherlands, Sweden, Switzerland, the United Kingdom, and the United States) in forging agreements through the Basel Committee on Banking Supervision relative to supervisory responsibility and capital adequacy (IMF, 1996). The extension of this approach to emerging economies is seen as the solution to their banking crises. While such measures certainly are supportive, they do not address the fundamental challenges facing transitional economies in developing sound, market-based commercial banking better able to withstand the inevitable shocks.

This review will first look at the evolution and importance of banking in transitional economies and then provide a functional assessment of banking performance in these economies. Based on an analysis of the regulatory systems in use and on the assumption that hard budgetary constraints and the needed market institutions can be put in place, the future reform path for banks in these economies is posited. The coverage of the transitional economies includes the PRC, Mongolia, the Greater Mekong economies of Cambodia, Lao PDR, and Viet Nam, as well as the Central Asian economies of Kazakhstan, Kirghiz Republic, and Uzbekistan which are members of the Asian Development Bank.[3]

THE EVOLUTION OF BANKING REFORMS

The banking systems in transitional economies have evolved from systems structured to serve the command economy. The principal function of these banking systems was to make and receive payments on behalf of the central government, the local government entities, and the state-owned enterprises (SOEs). Most of these receipts and payments were for current transactions and principally involved tax receipts and transfer payments. In addition, investment financing to meet the plan targets took place through the banking system, in the form of grants or loans. The loans were primarily used to finance investments of SOEs and since they were, in effect, intragovernmental transfers, they were subject to soft budget constraints. The only area where these banking systems came into contact with market-based financial systems was through the financing of foreign trade with market economies.

The evolution to banking structures more appropriate to market-based economies began in the PRC with the dismantling of the monobank structure in 1983 into a central bank and four specialized banks focused on the sectors of agriculture, industry, construction, and foreign trade.[4] Under this new structure it was not envisaged that there would be competition between the specialized banks and there were few efforts to impose hard budget constraints on bank lending or to separate government directed or policy lending from commercial-based lending.

During the following decade, overlapping of financial functions increased and competition intensified. Six new national banks as well as several regional banks and a large number of nonbank financial institutions, including trust and investment corporations, insurance and leasing companies, began operations. Inadequate spreads within the controlled interest rate structure created incentives for the misuse of interbank lending for the highly profitable real estate development and for equity investments on the Shenzhen and Shanghai stock exchanges established in 1990 and 1991.

A program of administrative controls (the 16-Point Program) was promulgated in 1993 to restore order to the financial system and this was followed in 1995 with new central bank and commercial banking laws. Policy lending was separated from commercial banks with the setting up of three policy banks to take over government-directed lending. There were also important steps to impose hard budget constraints in the form of a new company law, a new securities law, and continued efforts to revise the bankruptcy law.

Nevertheless, social considerations in the PRC have still not permitted the imposition of hard budget constraints on the SOEs given the widespread unemployment that would be expected from the ensuing bankruptcies should overdue loan repayments be demanded. As a result of these social considerations, there has been more progress in the PRC on the regulatory framework than on the fundamental reforms needed to move to a market-based financial system.

With some variations, the same pattern of banking reforms has been evident in the other Asian transitional economies. All have broken up their monobanks into a central bank and commercial banks. Except for Viet Nam and Cambodia, where such laws are under preparation, all transitional economies have recently adopted modern central bank and commercial banking laws. This is the same top-down reform approach that has been advocated by the International Monetary Fund and has also been observed in relation to the banking reforms in Central and Eastern Europe (Long and Rutkowska, 1995).[5] While this approach can be justified on the basis of the systemic changes required, the restructuring of the individual banks and the training of bank officers in the best practices of commercial banking have been neglected under the top-down approach. Only in the case of Mongolia and the Kirghiz Republic where resource constraints are very binding and government officials are most open to reforms, has a meaningful start been made in introducing hard budget restraints. The ongoing reform programs in these two economies take a more bottom-up approach to bank restructuring and this is integrated with enterprise reform. The program objective is that only well-capitalized banks dedicated to commercial banking best practices will constitute the banking systems over the medium term. The strong preference of most transitional economies is to avoid the imposition of hard budget constraints that is accompanied by the need to restructure the state banks with their portfolios of intractable state-owned enterprise debt and their weak banking cultures. To address the lack of banking services, the transitional economies have favored permitting the entry of new banks to better serve the emerging small and medium enterprise sectors.

COMMERCIAL BANK PERFORMANCE

Commercial banks in the Asian transitional economies are charged with managing a relatively simple financial intermediation function. Once access to government budgets was discontinued with the breakup of the monobanks, the commercial banks had the role of soliciting savings from the household sector and onlending those funds to the state-owned enterprises. The involvement of government in directing those loans to certain state-owned enterprises has been difficult to phase out. Even in PRC and Kazakhstan, where government directed loans are to be channeled through government agencies at the national level, the continuing financing needs of the SOEs, more often at the local level, may result in continued government pressure on the commercial banks to make available the needed working capital financing even when the SOEs are insolvent. The portfolio structure of commercial banks in the PRC illustrates the common structure where almost 66% of the deposits emanate from the household sector while over 90% of the loans appear to go to the SOEs.[6]

The commercial banking skill levels are generally rudimentary in the state-owned banks created from the breakup of the monobanks. It is understandable that officials who have been involved primarily in Treasury functions in fulfillment of the economic plan would not have the skills necessary for commercial banking in a market-based economy. The one exception to this is in the external departments of the monobanks where officials were involved in international trade financing and benefited from training from overseas correspondent banks. Banks such as the National Bank of Uzbekistan that evolved from the monobanks' external departments are in excellent shape in serving the needs of a market economy and are prospering. So too are the newer banks—private as well as public—that are not encumbered with SOE debt. The management of these banks is attuned to the market and utilizes hard budget constraints as a natural part of their functions.

The available commercial banking services are new and at a rudimentary level in the transitional economies. Efficient payment and settlement systems are only now being developed and it will take at least another five years for national payment systems to be put in place.[7] Probably within that time frame, payments will be able to be settled nationally through systems being developed within the more progressive nationwide banks. The range of financial instruments is also at a rudimentary level and does not go much beyond deposits, short-term working capital loans, and standard trade financing instruments such as letters of credit. However, it can be expected that as their market economies develop, the newer banks will quickly broaden the range of new financial instruments to meet the basic financial requirements.[8]

Where hard budget constraints have begun to be applied, bankruptcies of banks have caused major problems. During 1996 in the Kirghiz Republic two large bank bankruptcies accounting for about 55% of the banking system were undertaken during their ongoing bank restructuring program.[9] Also during 1996 in Mongolia, three banks accounting for about 40% of the banking system went through bankruptcy. While these bankruptcies have been difficult, they really only constitute a recognition of the costs previously incurred in keeping unviable SOEs in operation.

INTRODUCTION OF MARKET FORCES IN THE FINANCIAL SECTOR

The status of opening of the financial sector to market forces is outlined in Table 15.1. Market forces were first introduced in setting the exchange rate, a key price for the domestic financial sector. All transitional economies in Asia now have floating exchange rates, either in a managed or independently determined

Table 15.1. Status of Introduction of Market Forces in Financial Sectors

Transitional Economy	Commercial Bank Ownership	Capital Adequacy	Reserve Require-ment	Credit Controls	Restrictions on Investment Banks	Interest Rate	Treasury Bills	Current Account Convert-ibility[a]	FX Rates
Cambodia	Public Private	None	None[b]	No	No	Market	None	No	Managed floating
PRC	Public[c]	8%	13%[d]	Yes	Yes	Fixed	Auction	Yes	Managed floating
Kazakhstan	Public/Private	8%	20%	Yes	Yes	Fixed	Auction	No	Independently floating
Kirghiz Republic	Public/Private	8%	13.5%	Yes	No	Market	Auction	Yes	Managed floating
Lao PDR	Public/Private	8%	5%	Yes	No	Fixed	Auction	No	Managed floating
Mongolia	Public/Private	8%	13.7%[e]	Yes	Yes	Market	Auction	Yes	Independently floating
Uzbekistan	Public	2%	25%	Yes	No	Fixed	Auction	No	Managed floating
Viet Nam	Public/Private	None	None	Yes	Yes	Fixed	Auction	No	Managed floating

[a] Acceptance of Article VIII status at the International Monetary Fund.

[b] Administrative requirements on an informal basis.

[c] One private bank, the Minsheng Bank, began operations in 1996.

[d] A minimum of 13% of a commercial bank's local currency deposits are placed with the People's Bank of China (PBC), the central bank. In addition, PBC may require a commercial bank to place a further 7-10% of its local currency deposits with it to meet its payment requirements to PBC. PBC also requires all commercial banks to place with it in reserves 5% of the commercial bank's FCY deposits.

[e] Weighted average of reserve ratios set in relation to industrial commercial banks.

regime. Current account convertibility has also been achieved in three of the eight economies and most recently by the PRC in December 1996.

Market forces have been introduced much more slowly in the operations of the domestic financial sectors. Treasury bills are auctioned in all economies except Cambodia, and this is generally the most important interest rate set by the market. Bank interest rates, on the other hand, are generally fixed with the noticeable exception of the Kirghiz Republic and Mongolia which have been very progressive in adopting market-based reforms. Restrictions are likewise retained in most economies to limit the entry of private banks, again with the noticeable exception of the Kirghiz Republic and Mongolia. Monetary policy control is exercised through reserve requirements and direct credit controls, with credit controls predominating, especially in circumstances where there is a need to bring an excessive credit expansion under control. The PRC used such credit controls with great success to engineer a soft lending for the economy during the 1994-96 period while bringing inflation under control.[10]

As the Treasury bills market develops, most transitional economies are committed to developing indirect monetary controls through open market operations. This policy shift will allow reducing or eliminating the reserve requirements on commercial banks so as to allow them to be competitive with the nonbank financial institutions which are still in their infancy in the transitional economies (Edwards and Mishkin, 1995).

REGULATORY APPROACHES

Regulation in general and banking regulation in particular need to be reflective of policy and adapted to the existing market structures. Over time, policies and market structures will be compatible as the structures gradually reflect the financial-sector policies that are being pursued. The deficiencies in the banking sectors of transitional economies are often confused with the lack of regulation.

In light of the inadequate role being played by the financial sector in Asian transitional economies, policymakers are focusing on approaches that promote financial deepening. To engender financial deepening, consumer confidence in the banking system as a safe repository of household savings is a crucial starting point. At present such confidence is very high in China where domestic savings in the 1990-95 period averaged over 40% of GDP with a large proportion of such savings intermediated through the banking sector. In terms of these fundamentals, the PRC is comparable to East Asian market economies. On the other hand, confidence in the banking system of most of the Central Asian Republics (CARs) and in the Mekong transitional economies tends to be very fragile and, together with the prevailing low savings rates, the banks have not yet been able to play an effective intermediation role. Moreover, some flight from local currencies to the U.S. dollar is seen in economies such as Viet Nam, Lao PDR, and Cambodia. The status of financial intermediation in the Asian transitional economies is shown in Table 15.2.

Table 15.2. Status of Financial Intermediation, 1995 (in percent)

	Bank Liabilities (M2) to GDP	Nongovernment Commercial Bank Credit to GDP
Cambodia	9.0	4.2
Kazakhstan	11.5	13.4
Kirghiz Republic	14.3	15.8
Lao PDR	12.6	11.4
Mongolia	23.0	15.8
People's Republic of China	105.2	89.4
Uzbekistan	12.9	2.6
Viet Nam	21.2	19.0

Source: ADB Key Indicators, International Monetary Fund.

There have also been misplaced attempts to create confidence in the commercial banks through legal requirements for deposit insurance. In Mongolia, the initial commercial banking law required banks to provide deposit insurance for their customers. However, commercial banks were unable to find insurance companies willing to provide such cover. When the law was amended in September 1996, this provision was dropped without major efforts to find alternative sources of insurance because of the moral hazard created by deposit insurance (Keeley, 1990). Deposit insurance detracts from the incentives for bank management to improve performance and yet improved management is the only way to restore depositors' confidence in banks' custodianship of their savings.

The transitional economies in Asia are moving toward regulatory regimes that promote competition within the financial sector. For example, in 1995 the PRC set up a regulatory framework with new central banking and commercial banking laws that envisaged full competition between the commercial banks, the separation of government-directed lending into these new policy banks, and the separation of investment banking from commercial banking.[11]

In Lao PDR, the banking system is compartmentalized on a geographical basis. Vientiane is well served (eleven commercial banks, three state-owned, two private banks, and six branches of Thai banks) and while there are provisions allowing operations elsewhere, they are subject to central bank consent which is not currently forthcoming. As a result the state-owned Agricultural Promotion Bank, which has offices throughout Lao PDR, is protected for the time being from full competition (Bond, 1996). At the same time the state-owned banks are being encouraged to become more competitive so as to withstand the emerging competition.

In Mongolia and the CARs, full competition is encouraged through a regulatory regime that generally places no restrictions on banking activities in terms of geographical location or customer base.

In building competitive banking markets, the regulatory structures emerging in the Asian transitional economies rely very heavily on Bank for International Settlement (BIS) capital adequacy requirements that tend to promote less risky portfolios and to address the moral hazard issues of the lender of last resort facilities provided by central banks (Furlong, 1992). The BIS capital adequacy rules are adapted in most of these economies.[12] However, with the prevalence of SOEs in these economies, most commercial banks have large portfolios of bad debt that have not yet been recognized on their books. Often, as in the case of the PRC, these debts are several multiples of the capital of commercial banks. As a consequence, a large number of commercial banks in the Asian transitional economies are insolvent and the governments will need to stand ready to recapitalize these banks in order to maintain a stable banking system.[13]

SUMMARY

Commercial banking is at a rudimentary stage in the Asian transitional economies. The task of transforming the monobanks of the previous command systems into commercial banks that are able to serve a market economy has proved to be very difficult. The top-down approach of improved regulation and closer central bank supervision can address systemic issues but will not serve to create the viable commercial banks that are needed to provide the full range of banking services for a market economy.

The most desirable reform approach is through imposing hard budget constraints on the banking sector within an environment where the needed institutional support for market transactions has been created. It is not just sufficient to have the basic legal requirements such as the bankruptcy law enacted; there must be the institutions' support in the form of specialized courts and related agencies to adjudicate these laws. The reluctance of the Asian transitional economies to impose hard budget constraints is largely based upon the expected social disruptions of increased unemployment arising from SOE bankruptcies. Only in the resource constrained economies of Mongolia and the Kirghiz Republic has meaningful progress in this direction been achieved. Under their reform programs, the emphasis had to be on bottom-up reforms involving basic restructuring in both the banking and enterprise sectors. Under these programs, the costs incurred from inappropriate support through the banking system of unviable SOEs have to be recognized and managed. It is then possible for commercial banks to begin to develop the skills necessary to serve a market economy while building the capital base to help protect against future shocks. It is not possible to have healthy banks without healthy enterprises and vice versa.

NOTES

1. The monobank was in charge of implementing the cash as well as the credit plans which were the counterparts of the overall physical plan.

2. For example, the lack of penalties for nonrepayment of loans.

3. While Cambodia did not have the command structure that characterizes the other transitional economies, its public ownership and the underdeveloped nature of its banking system result in many of the same challenges.

4. For an overview of the chronology and an assessment of the financial reforms in PRC, see Mehran et al. (1996).

5. Long and Rutkowska (1995) also noted that this top-down reform of banking was in marked contrast with the bottom-up approach taken in respect to enterprise restructuring.

6. In 1995, on the liability side, 31.9% of total commercial bank deposits represents deposits by SOEs themselves and a further 3.5% in deposits by Treasury and government departments; 64.6% appears to come directly or indirectly from the household sector. On the asset side, 6.6%t of the loans are to urban and township collectives, individual proprietors, and joint ventures; 93.4% of the loans appear to be to state-owned enterprises in sectors such as industry and construction. Statistics are from *China Financial Outlook* (1996).

7. Wherever justified, there will be modern, real-time gross settlement systems (RTGS). One such RTGS system is under pilot testing in the PRC during 1997.

8. For example, in late 1996, Viet Nam initiated a leasing industry in cooperation with Japanese leasing companies and with the support of the Asian Development Bank and the International Finance Corporation as a new instrument to help small and medium enterprises to acquire capital goods.

9. The program is being supported by the World Bank with a financial-sector development credit of SDR 31.2 million approved in May 1996.

10. In light of an inflation rate that rose to 22% in 1994, an increasingly restrictive monetary policy was imposed, largely through direct credit controls. Inflation was brought down to 15% in 1995 and to 6% in 1996. At the same time GDP growth was only moderated from 14% in 1992 and 1993 to 9.7% in 1996.

11. This separation of investment banking from commercial banking is akin to the Glass-Steagall Act of the United States and appeared to be intended to restrict the range of activities of commercial banks as the level of perceived abuses had been increasing. For a full review of these new laws, see Mehman et al. (1996, pp. 22-23).

12. One principal modification is generally adopted, namely, treating their own government paper is accorded a zero credit risk rating. Under BIS rules, only OECD countries are extended the zero risk credit rating. See Committee on Banking Regulations and Supervising Practices (1988).

13. For example, the PRC has set aside 30 billion yuan ($3.7 billion) to help the commercial banks absorb the bad loans of the state-owned enterprises that will be permitted to wind up in 1997 (*China Daily*).

REFERENCES

Bernabe, B. and M. Gertler, 1987. Banking and macroeconomic equilibrium. In W.A. Barnett and K.J. Singleton (eds.), *New Approaches to Monetary Economics*. Cambridge: Cambridge University Press.

Bhattacharya, S. and A.V. Thakar, 1993. Contemporary banking theory, *Journal of Financial Intermediation* 3, 2-50.

Bond, Marian, 1996. Reforming the financial sector in the Lao PDR, Asian Development Bank, Manila.

Chant, John, 1992. The new theory of financial intermediation. In K. Dowd and M. Lewis (eds.), *Current Issues in Financial and Monetary Economics*. London: Macmillan.

China Daily, 1997. March.

China Financial Outlook, 1996, 1996. People's Bank of China, April, Table 7, p. 95.

Committee on Banking Regulations and Supervising Practices, 1998. *International Convergence of Capital Measurement and Capital Standards*, July, p. 24.

Edwards, Franklin R. and F.S. Mishkin, 1995. The decline of traditional banking: implications for financial stability and regulatory policy, *Economic Policy Review* 1(2), 27-45.

Furlong, F.T., 1992. Capital regulation and bank lending, *Economic Review*, Federal Reserve Bank of San Francisco, No. 3, 23-33.

Huh, Chan and Sun Bau Kim, 1994. Financial regulation and banking sector performance: a comparison of bad loan problems in Japan and Korea, *Economic Review*, Federal Reserve Bank of San Francisco, No. 2, 18-29.

International Monetary Fund, 1996. Managing risks to the international banking system, *Finance and Development* 33(4), 26-28.

Jacklin, Charles, 1993. Bank capital requirements and incentives for lending, Working Paper 93-07, Federal Reserve Bank of San Francisco.

Keeley, M.C., 1990. Deposit insurance, risk and market power in banking, *American Economic Review* 80, 1183-1200.

Long, M. and I. Rutkowska, 1995. The role of commercial banks in enterprise restructuring in Central and Eastern Europe, Policy Research Working Paper 1424. Washington, DC: World Bank.

Mehran, H., M. Quintyn, T. Nordman, and B. Laurens, 1996. Monetary and exchange system reforms in China: an experiment in gradualism, Occasional Paper 141. Washington, DC: International Monetary Fund.

16

Conditional Variance and Nonlinearity in the Polish Emerging Market

Sunil Poshakwale
and Douglas Wood

INTRODUCTION

One of the main barriers to investing in emerging markets is that they are generally perceived as highly volatile and informationally inefficient compared to the developed markets. This is partly because developed stock markets have relatively better infrastructure for ensuring efficient dissemination of information and transparency of transactions. Also higher capitalization in developed markets provides a greater choice and higher liquidity of stocks. The emerging markets generally lack these advantages due to inferior infrastructure, tendency of institutional investors to participate only in blue-chip stocks, lack of appropriate regulations, inadequate accounting information disclosure standards, and the like.

The degree to which the market is informationally efficient has important implications for practitioners, policymakers, and academic researchers. The more informationally inefficient the market, the more likely it is that corporate managers can manipulate stock prices by creative accounting practices and false signalling. Informationally inefficient markets provide the opportunity to technical traders who can identify and exploit persistent patterns.

Although first established in 1817, the Polish stock market is regarded as an emerging market, opening in its new guise in April 1991 after a 52-year hiatus. The new legal and regulatory framework of the market was developed after a thorough review of several contemporary securities markets. As a result the Polish stock market is one of the most up-to-date with computerized and paperless trading. Within just five years the Warsaw Stock Exchange has a capitalization of $8 billion. There are 83 listed stocks with an average daily turnover of $35 million in 1996. The market capitalization accounts for 7% of GDP in 1996 and with further privatization of public companies it is estimated to achieve a level of 30% of GDP as in Germany.[1] Individual members constitute the majority of investors, although the share of institutional investors is rising. Foreign investors are estimated to account for 20% of the turnover. Measured by securities transactions, the Warsaw Stock Exchange has very rapidly become one of the most active European stock exchanges and is the largest among the emerging markets of Central and Eastern Europe. Since the Warsaw Stock Exchange is modern in infrastructure and regulation, it is potentially interesting to investigate volatility and informational efficiency of stock prices in the Polish emerging market. Table 16.1 provides major characteristics of the Polish market.

This chapter investigates behavior of daily returns and their volatility in the Polish emerging market. First the chapter tests daily returns for conditional variance and investigates whether this is priced. Second, the returns are examined for nonlinear dependencies. The martingale hypothesis that future changes of the daily stock prices are independent of the past available information is tested using Generalized Autoregressive Conditional Heteroskedasticity (GARCH) models.

Several papers have examined the intertemporal relationship between stock market volatility and expected returns in developed stock markets using Autoregressive Conditional Heteroskedasticity (ARCH) models developed by Engle (1982) and later generalized by Bollerslev (1986). A number of these studies reported that variance of returns in time shows strong correlations with prior innovations (see for example, Geyer, 1994; Errunza, Hogan, Kini, and Padmanabhan, 1994; and others). Pindyck (1984) suggested an increase in volatility as

Table 16.1. Major Market Characteristics of the Warsaw Stock Exchange, 1996

Structural Characteristics	Description
Types of Securities	Equities, warrants, corporate bonds, government securities.
Market Capitalization (US$b)	8
Avg. Turnover per Session (US$m)	35
Trading Volume (US$m)	580
Number of Companies Listed	83
Trading System	Screen-based system.
Settlement and Transfer System	Settlement and transfer on DVP and T+3 basis. Securities are cleared through National Depository of Securities.
Brokerage Commissions	Not fixed by the WSE and range from 0.8% to 1.2%.
Taxes	For institutions, the basic tax rate is 40%. Dividends are taxed at 20%. Personal income from stock investment is not taxed.
Securities Lending	Securities lending is not available in Poland.
Regulatory Agency	National Securities Commission regulates the activities.

Source: Euromoney Guide to Central and Eastern European Equities 1997.

the reason for decline in stock prices during 1970s in the United States. Bollerslev, Engle, and Wooldridge (1988) reported that the conditional volatility significantly affects expected returns, although Baillie and DeGennaro (1990) found a weak relationship. There are, however, fewer studies providing evidence of relationship between volatility and expected returns in markets other than the United States. For instance, Theodossiou and Lee (1995) investigated daily returns in ten industrialized countries and found presence of significant conditional heteroskedasticity but no relationship between conditional volatility and returns. Heteroskedasticity, where it exists, has numerous implications. If the data-generating process underlying returns contains heteroskedasticity, then it needs to be explicitly accounted for when testing for market efficiency. Capital asset pricing as well as option pricing models is based on the assumption that markets are efficient and returns are homoskedastic. However, evidence suggests that asset pricing models based on the Efficient Markets Hypothesis (EMH) do not fully capture the pricing dynamics (Brock et al., 1990).

Evidence of linear and nonlinear dependence in returns is reported by a number of studies. Lo and MacKinlay (1988) and Fama and French (1988), for instance, reported significant correlation in stock returns and stock indices. D. Hsieh (1991) and Scheinkman and LeBaron (1989) suggested that significant nonlinear dependencies exist in returns from the S&P index. The presence of nonlinear dependence implies that the underlying process is nonlinear and that returns are not described by a normal distribution. D. Hsieh (1989) found that a GARCH model explained a large part of the documented nonlinear dependencies. In the context of emerging markets, Sewell et al. (1993) document evidence of nonlinear dependence in weekly returns in five Asian stock markets and the United States. Grassberger and Procaccia (1983), Brock and Malliaris (1989), Brock, Hsieh, and Lebaron (1991), and D. Hsieh (1991) addressed the potential importance of nonlinearity in economic and financial modeling and the corresponding tests used in detecting its presence. Since the exposition of these papers is comprehensive, only a brief discussion of their contents is presented below.

A chaotic time series has two characteristics. First, as the time series evolves, no point is ever reached twice, although in actual data this may not be strictly true because of rounding. Second, the evolutionary pattern of time series is extremely sensitive to the system's initial conditions. The key concept in determining whether a process is chaotic is the correlation dimension, a statistic which helps obtain topological information about the underlying system generating the data without knowing (or assuming) a particular structural model. For truly random data, the correlation dimension monotonically increases with the dimension of the space within which these data are contained. This latter dimension is called the embedding dimension. In contrast, for chaotic data the correlation dimension remains small even when the embedding dimension increases. In other words, the correlation dimension measure indicates the "non-linear degrees of freedom" or complexity of a time series. As suggested by Hsieh (1991), if the dynamics of asset prices were linear in nature, their conditional densities could be obtained in a straightforward manner. An empirical finding that the dynamics of asset prices are nonlinear, however, may complicate substantially the estimation of their conditional densities.

Wood, Poshakwale and Dasgupta (1996) reported significant nonlinearity in daily returns from the Warczawski Indeks Gieldowy (WIG) 20 index in the Polish stock market. One of the objectives of this chapter is to determine the cause of the rejection of independent and identical distribution (IID) in the Polish stock market. Rejection of IID is consistent with the notion that the time series is nonstationarity (i.e., the series is generated by a nonlinear stochastic system), or that low-dimension chaotic behavior is present in the time series. We investigate nonstationarity as one of the possible explanations by using daily returns from the Warsaw General Index, WIG-20 Index, and Equally Weighted Portfolio of 17 securities in the Polish stock market.

In developed markets, such as the United Kingkom or the United States, which are informationally efficient, the reasons for rejection of IID could be the complex dynamics. However, in an emerging market like Poland continuous structural changes such as abolition of exchange controls, increasing number of market participants, deregulation, and such may also cause rejection of IID. Also in emerging markets, information is typically not available to all traders simultaneously, and these informational asymmetries may cause nonlinear dependencies. In the presence of nonlinearities, market participants look for alternative ways of developing models which can provide above-average performance and a higher degree of explanation for market movements. For example, Brock et al. (1990) use technical analysis based on several transformations of time series and moving averages to predict equity returns and find above-average performance, which is inconsistent with the EMH, random walk theory, and linear statistical models such as autoregression. There is a growing evidence that volatility in the financial markets is not only time varying but also predictable. The nonlinear dependencies in the Polish stock market documented previously by Wood, et al. may exist because the returns are nonlinear-in-variance. If this is the case, a GARCH model should capture these nonlinearities and the residuals from a GARCH model should be IID. In other words, where conditional heteroskedasticity causes rejection of IID, the series is best described by a nonlinear stochastic system.

Increasing interest in emerging stock markets such as Poland provides the main motivation for this study, which documents an empirical evidence on this relatively new emerging market and addresses two important issues. The first is whether high volatility, which generally characterizes emerging stock markets, is a permanent feature and whether it is priced. The second is whether nonlinearity in returns is caused by conditional heteroskedasticity. The results suggest that significant conditional heteroskedasticity exists in the Polish market, indicating presence of volatility clustering in daily returns, however, it is not priced. There is the evidence of significant nonlinear dependencies and the GARCH model appears to capture these nonlinear dependencies. Though daily returns contain conditional heteroskedasticity and nonlinear dependencies, the actual amount of dependence is too small to be important in explaining expected returns. We conjecture that sharp reduction in the conditional volatility observed after June 1995 may be due to stabilization of exchange rates and improved correlation of the Polish market with the German and U.K. markets.

The chapter is organized as follows. The data and methodology are explained; empirical results are discussed; and main conclusions are given.

THE DATA AND METHODOLOGY

The data used in this study are the daily closing stock prices from the Warsaw General Index and WIG-20 index. An equal weighted portfolio of the 17 actively traded stocks on the market is also used in investigating the behavior of returns and volatility. The daily price data cover the period January 1, 1994, to June 30, 1996, except for the WIG-20 index which commences on April 16, 1994.

The ARCH specification introduced by Engle (1982) is used. As suggested by Sumel and Engle (1994), the ARCH appropriately accounts for volatility clustering in the error terms that are serially uncorrelated and have fat tailed distributions. The ARCH process and its generalization due to Bollerslev (1986) are widely used in explaining the stochastic characteristics of financial time series. The evidence suggests that conditional heteroskedasticity can well represent time-varying stock return volatility and fat-tailed distribution parsimoniously, while incorporating autocorrelation (see Bollerslev, Chou, and Kroner, 1992) for a comprehensive literature review.

Model selection in this chapter is based on three criteria: the Log Likelihood Ratio (LR) statistic, the Akaike Information Criterion (AIC), and the Shwartz Bayesian Criterion (SBC). All three statistics are based on the log likelihood value at the estimated vector. The LR ratio of the restricted to the unrestricted model is distributed as χ^2 (k) where k is the number of restricted parameters. In this chapter, we estimate models with one restriction imposed at a time, and thus use the LR test as a comparison between two models, with $k = 1$. The AIC and SBC are functions of the log likelihood values as well as the number of free parameters in estimation. They incorporate a penalty for a large number of parameters, which gives us a bias toward more parsimonious specifications. If a model contains k free parameters, the AIC is $(2 / T) * (LogL + 2K)$ and the SBC is $(2 / T) * (LogL + (LogL / 2)K)$.

According to McCurdy and Morgan (1988), the martingale hypothesis assumes that changes in stock prices from period t-1 to period t are innovations or forecast errors which are orthogonal to the information available at period t-1. The estimation equation is expressed as:

$$\Delta P_t = \gamma_0 + \sum_{i=1}^{n} \gamma_i \Delta P_{t-i} + \sum_{j=1}^{m} \delta_j D_{tj} + \varepsilon_t \tag{1}$$

where ΔP_t is defined as the difference in logarithms of daily stock price index (or daily stock returns), D is a seasonal dummy variable which takes the value of 1 for a given day of the week and 0 otherwise. Under the null hypothesis that changes in daily stock prices are independent of the previous available information, parameters γ_i and δ_j are expected to equal 0, and errors ε_t uncorrelated with a 0 mean, but are not necessarily homoskedastic.

The conditional variance of daily stock returns h_t is specified as a linear function of its own lagged p conditional variances and the lagged q squared residuals—that is, the GARCH (p,q) specification—is characterized as:

$$h_t = \alpha_0 + \sum_{i=1}^{q} \alpha_i \varepsilon^2_{t-1} + \sum_{j=1}^{p} \beta_j h_t \tag{2}$$

where α and β are parameters to be estimated. For $p = 0$ (2) becomes the ARCH (q) process, and for $p = q = 0$ the variance of daily stock returns is simply a white noise process. In this linear GARCH (p,q) procedure, shocks to the current volatility of stock returns persist if $\sum \alpha_i + \sum \beta_j = 1$. This process is called the integrated GARCH or IGARCH (Engle and Bollerslev, 1986). Given the IGARCH process, Bollerslev, Chou, and Kroner (1992) conclude that as in the martingale model for conditional means of stock returns, current information remains important for forecasts of the conditional variance for all horizons.

The GARCH model can be extended to be the "GARCH in mean" or GARCH-M specification. By including $h^{1/2}$ in (1), the conditional variance given the available information at time t-1:

$$\Delta P_t = \gamma_0 + \sum_{i=1}^{n} \gamma_i \Delta P_{t-i} + \sum_{j-1}^{m} \delta_j D_{tj} + \theta \sqrt{h_t} + \varepsilon_t \tag{3}$$

where the conditional variance h_t is defined by (2). Engle, Lilien, and Robins (1987) introduced this model to examine the relationship between risk and return. Bollerslev, Engle, and Wooldridge (1988) used a multivariate GARCH-M model to test time-varying risk premiums. Yu (1996) employed the GARCH-M model to assess the risk premium assumption in the Chinese stock markets. Bollerslev, Engle, and Wooldridge (1988) used a multivariate GARCH-M model to test time-varying risk premiums. In the absence of daily information for nominal risk-free returns, empirical testing for the risk premium hypothesis is indirect. Since the GARCH-M connects conditional volatility and expected returns, equation (3) is used as a proxy for risk premium for testing the hypothesis of time-varying risk premium.

We use the Brock, Dechert, and Scheinkman (1987) (BDS) test for investigating nonlinearities. As suggested by Hsieh (1991), the BDS test can detect many types of departure from independent and identical distribution, such as nonstationarity, nonlinearity, and deterministic chaos, any of which imply that the conditional distribution is different from the unconditional distribution. The BDS test has also been shown to have good finite sample properties.

The BDS test proves or disproves the hypothesis that the data are identically and independently distributed. If this hypothesis is rejected, there is a high probability that the time series is nonlinear or has chaotic characteristics. The concept of correlation dimensions (CD) proposed by Grassberger and Procaccia (1983) is the basis of the BDS test. The CD technique is designed to reveal evidence of nonlinear structure in data embedded in phase space. This technique involves embedding overlapping subsequences of length *(l)* of a data series in *m*-dimensional space for various embedding dimensions *m*. Truly random data will create a region of *m* space for any *m*, deterministically generated data will only show geometric structure for sufficiently large *m*.

Given a time series $\{Z_t : t = 1, \ldots T\}$ of *D* dimensional vectors, the correlation integral *C(l)* is defined as

$$C(l) = \lim_{T \to \infty} \frac{2}{T(T-1)} \sum_{i<j} I_l(Z_i, Z_j) \tag{4}$$

where $I_l(x,y)$ is an indicator function that equals 1 if $\|x - y\| < l$, and 0 otherwise, where $\| \ \|$ is the sup-norm. The correlation integral measures the fraction of pairs of points of $\{Z_t\}$ that are within a distance of *l*, from each other. The CD of $\{Z_t\}$ is thus defined as:

$$v = \lim_{l \to 0} \left[\frac{\log C(l)}{Log l} \right], \text{ if the limit exists.} \tag{5}$$

If $\{Z_t\}$ were independently and identically distributed, then BDS tests the null hypothesis that $C_m(l) = C_1(l)^m$. Brock et al. (1990, 1991) show that the test statistic is asymptotically a standard normal distribution and that the asymptotic distribution is a good approximation of the finite sample distribution when there are more than 500 observations. Further, they recommend that *l* should be between one-half to two times the standard deviation and that the accuracy of the asymptotic distribution deteriorates for high embedding dimensions of 10 or above.

EMPIRICAL RESULTS AND THE PRICING OF VOLATILITY

Daily returns and squared daily returns computed from the Warsaw General Index, WIG-20 index, and equally weighted portfolio are tested for the presence of autocorrelation and stationarity. Panel A of Table 16.2 reports descriptive statistics for all three return series. The returns as well as the squared returns exhibit significant skewness with a kurtosis much higher in squared returns from all three series. The autocorrelations and the Ljung-Box statistics in Panel B show that except for the squared returns from the equally weighted portfolio, the Q statistic is significant in the rest. The coefficients in the squared return series are much larger for Warsaw General and WIG-20 indices. However, squared daily returns from the equally weighted portfolio are not autocorrelated. The null hypothesis of no serial correlation and homoskedastic daily

Table 16.2. Descriptive Statistics and Autocorrelations of Daily Returns

Panel A — Descriptive Statistics of Daily Returns

	Eqport	EqportSq	Wargen	WagenSq	WIG20	WIG20Sq
Mean	0	0	0	0	0	0
Median	0	0	0	0	0	0
Maximum	0.15	0.25	0.15	0.04	0.15	0.02
Minimum	-0.5	0	-0.19	0	-0.1	0
Std. Dev.	0.04	0.01	0.03	0	0.03	0
Skewness	-3.61	23.34	-0.53	7.18	-0.03	5.83
Kurtosis	47.7	575.49	7.89	80.44	6.2	55.07
Jarque-Bera	55434.97	8921559.32	678.27	167733.84	245.24	68098.2
Probability	0	0	5.18	0	0	0
Observations	649	649	649	649	574	574

Panel B — Autocorrelation Coefficients of Daily Returns

Lags	Eqport	EqportSq	Wargen	WagenSq	WIG20	WIG20Sq
1	0.08**	0.02	0.17**	0.09**	0.15**	0.13**
2	0.02	0.01	0.04**	0.19**	0.05**	0.24**
3	0.01	0.01	0.02**	0.14**	-0.02**	0.24**
4	0.09**	0.01	0.07**	0.03**	0.11**	0.07**
5	-0.05**	0.01	-0.05**	0.3**	-0.03**	0.34**
6	-0.02	0	0**	0.04**	0**	0.09**
7	-0.01	0	0.02**	0.21**	-0**	0.05**
8	0.01	0	0.06**	0.13**	0.08**	0.04**
9	0.01	0	0.01**	0.03**	0.03**	0.05**
10	0	0.01	0.08**	0.13**	-0.01**	0.06**
11	0	0	-0.01**	0.02**	-0.03**	0.04**
12	0.01	0	-0.02**	0.08**	-0.05**	0.07**
13	0.06	0	0.08**	0.06**	0.03**	0**
14	-0.03	0	-0.02**	0.09**	-0.05**	0.05**
15	-0.08	0.03	-0.07**	0.19**	-0.06**	0.06**
16	0.02	0.01	-0.04**	-0.04**	-0.05**	0.01**
17	0.03	0.01	0.02**	0.12**	0.02**	0.14**
18	0.08	0.01	0**	0.01**	-0**	0.02**
19	0.01	-0.01	-0**	-0.01**	-0.01**	0.03**
20	-0.03	0	-0.05**	0.15**	-0.14**	0.1**
21	0	0	-0.04**	-0.01**	-0.07**	0.09**
22	-0.04	0.01	-0.01**	0.23**	0.05**	0.07**

Significant at **5%. Eqport = Equally weighted portfolio, Wargen = Warsaw General Index, WIG-20 = WIG-20 Index. Sq = Squared returns.

returns (uncorrelated squared returns) is rejected at the 5% level for the returns from the Warsaw General Index and WIG-20. As first suggested by Diebold (1986), these characteristics of high kurtosis and the variance clustering seen in the autocorrelation coefficients (ACF) suggest that the ARCH specification provides a good approximation to the structure of conditional variance. This suggests that the ARCH process is appropriate for capturing time series characteristics of the daily returns in the Polish emerging equity market.

To compare performance of a linear model with a nonlinear one in removing nonlinear dependencies, we first use Autoregressive Integrated Moving Average (ARIMA) models. As suggested by Hsieh (1991), the BDS test can detect linear dependence easily and therefore to employ BDS as a test for nonlinearity, we must remove any linear dependence in the data. In our sample significant first-order autocorrelation is a common feature among all three return series, which suggest Autoregressive Moving Average (1,0) (ARMA) as a good specification to characterize the daily returns in all three series. However, as suggested by Box and Jenkins (1976), ARIMA models should only be applied to a stationarity series. Therefore, a unit root test for testing stationarity developed by Dickey and Fuller (1979) is applied to the returns. Panel A of Table 16.3 presents unit root test results according to which the logarithmic forms of the daily stock returns are not integrated. The ARMA (1,0) model can therefore be applied to the series. Panel B shows the estimates of ARMA (1,0) model. The coefficient for the first order autoregression is significant in all three series. Among the three, highest log likelihood ratio is obtained for the Warsaw General Index returns series.

To test whether the ARMA model removes heteroskedasticity, the ARCH-LM test is applied to the residuals. The ARCH-LM procedure tests for ARCH. The test is based on the regression of squared residuals on lagged, squared residuals. The statistic is distributed as χ^2, and provides a test of the hypothesis that the coefficient of the lagged squared residuals are all zero—that is, no ARCH. The statistic is the outcome of a Lagrange multiplier (LM) test and has an asymptotic distribution with degrees of freedom equal to the number of lagged, squared residuals. The ARCH-LM statistic indicates presence of heteroskedasticity in the Warsaw General and WIG-20 indices, suggesting that the ARMA (1,0) model does not remove heteroskedasticity in returns.

To test whether ARMA (1,0) removes nonlinear dependence, the BDS test is applied on the residuals for embedding dimensions 2 to 10 and epsilons ranging from half to two times the standard deviation. Table 16.4 provides the test results which indicate significant BDS statistics for all three series. The results exhibit presence of low dimension nonlinearity and suggest that the ARMA (1,0) model does not fully capture nonlinear dependencies in returns.

The results of the ARCH-LM test, which shows significant heteroskedasticity in the residuals in daily returns from the ARMA (1,0) model in the Warsaw General and WIG-20 indices together with the evidence of nonlinear characteristics indicated by the BDS test, give rise to the possibility that the return-generating process may be explained by an ARCH model.

Table 16.3. Augmented Dickey-Fuller Test Statistics and ARIMA (1,1,0) Estimates

Panel A — Augmented Dickey-Fuller (ADF) Test Statistic

	Eqport		Wargen		WIG-20	
	C	C&T	C	C&T	C	C&T
ADF Test Statistic	-10.86***	-10.88***	-10.98***	-11.05***	-6.63***	-7.36***
AR 1	-0.87***	-0.87***	-0.81***	-0.82***	-0.37***	-0.48***
D[SER1(-1)]	-0.04	-0.04	-0.01	0	-0.49***	-0.41***
D[SER1(-2)]	-0.03	-0.03	0	0	-0.37***	-0.31***
D[SER1(-3)]	-0.04	-0.03	0	0.01	-0.23***	-0.19***
D[SER1(-4)]	0.06	0.06	0.08	0.08**	-0.27***	-0.25***
C	0	0	0	0	0***	0***
Trend		5.87		7.75		-1.17***

Panel B — ARIMA (1,1,0) Estimates

	Eqport	Wargen	WIG-20
C	-0.002	-0	0
	(1.47)	(0.24)	(0.31)
AR 1	0.082	0.172	0.151
	(2.10)**	(4.45)***	(3.68)***
Adjusted R2	0.005	0.028	0.021
ARCH LM Statistic	0.05	0.08	0.12
Log likelihood	1196.796	1358.618	1261.897
	(1.16)	(2.11)**	(2.95)***

Significant at ***1%, **5%. *t*-statistics are in parentheses. C = Constant; T = Trend. Lags in brackets. Eqport = Equally weighted portfolio, Wargen = Warsaw General Index, WIG-20 = WIG-20 Index.

Table 16.5 provides the results of the OLS and ARCH procedures with dummy variables accounting for day of the week effects in daily returns for the full period. Equation 1 reports the OLS results with dummy seasonals for the Warsaw General Index returns while equation 3 reports the results without seasonal dummies. The estimates as indicated by the Log Likelihood Ratio marginally improve when dummies representing days of the week are included. The coefficients for the Tuesday's dummy are found highly significant, while the dummy for Friday is significant at 10%. The coefficient for the first-order autoregression is also found highly significant in both series.

Equations 2 and 4 report the parameter estimates from the ARCH procedure. The LR improves considerably in both equations and the Q statistic also declines, confirming that the ARCH process is appropriate. Because the ARCH procedure successfully accounts for the volatility clustering in returns and yields a higher log likelihood function, it is superior to conventional OLS estimation.

Table 16.4. BDS Test Statistic for Standard Residuals from ARIMA (1,1,0) Model

M	Warsaw Gen	WIG-20 Index	Eqw Portfolio
2	0.34	0.528	0.337
3	0.5	1.115	0.577
4	0.39	1.36	0.549
5	0.26	1.332	0.396
6	0.18	1.235	0.276
7	0.11	1.084	0.181
8	0.07	0.916	0.114
9	0.05	0.741	0.071
10	0.03	0.609	0.045
2	0.54	0.314	0.545
3	1.28	0.401	1.365
4	1.59	0.298	1.892*
5	1.65*	0.182	2.135**
6	1.58	0.111	2.235**
7	1.45	0.068	2.206**
8	1.3	0.04	2.111**
9	1.11	0.023	1.937*
10	0.93	0.013	1.773*
2	0.45	0.555	0.339
3	1.38	1.401	0.993
4	2.17**	2.087**	1.686*
5	2.78**	2.507**	2.267*
6	3.17***	2.764***	2.776***
7	3.45***	2.931***	3.17***
8	3.6***	2.965***	3.445***
9	3.61***	2.883***	3.599***
10	3.55***	2.762***	3.682***
2	0.22	0.354	0.154
3	0.88	1.089	0.513
4	1.59	1.826*	0.962
5	2.25**	2.445*	1.357
6	2.83***	2.957***	1.786*
7	3.35***	3.435***	2.174**
8	3.77***	3.78***	2.523**
9	4.12***	4.021***	2.827***
10	4.39***	4.183***	3.079***

Significant at ***1%, **5%, and *10%.

Table 16.5. OLS and ARCH Estimates With and Without Dummy Variables

	Warsaw General Index				WIG-20 Index				EW Portfolio			
	Eq. 1	Eq. 2	Eq. 3	Eq. 4	Eq. 5	Eq. 6	Eq. 7	Eq. 8	Eq. 9	Eq. 10	Eq. 11	Eq. 12
γ_0	0.0039	0.0009	-0.0003	-0.0003	0.0037	0.003	0.0003	0.0007	-0.0021	-0.0007	-0.0022	-0.0011
	(1.359)	(0.265)	(-0.240)	(-0.256)	(1.343)	(1.556)	(0.311)	(0.961)	(-0.413)	(-0.267)	(-1.485)	(-1.168)
γ_i	0.1813	0.2232	0.1723	0.2182	0.1592	0.2142	0.1513	0.2096	0.0834	0.3966	0.0824	0.429
	(3.73***)	(5.097***)	(3.514***)	(4.99***)	(2.972**)	(4.52***)	(2.819***)	(4.40***)	(1.166)	(2.125**)	(1.187)	(2.047**)
D_{Tue}	-0.01				-0.0077	-0.0031			-0.0037	-0.0045		
	(-2.42***)				(-1.978**)	(-1.027)			(-0.602)	(-1.231)		
D_{Wed}	-0.0027				-0.0032	-0.0038			0.0018	0.0038		
	(-0.746)				(-0.884)	(-1.497)			(0.323)	(0.948)		
D_{Thu}	-0.0017				0.0001	-0.0009			0.0032	-0.006		
	(-0.419)				(0.016)	(-0.356)			(0.530)	(-0.940)		
D_{Fri}	-0.006				-0.0058	-0.0038			-0.0017	0.0047		
	(-1.889*)				(-1.80*)	(1.591)			(-0.310)	(0.733)		
Constant		0		0.0001		0		1.793		0.0002		0.0002
		(1.611)		(1.527)		(2.046**)		(2.074)		(3.028***)		(2.638***)
α		0.248		0.2631		0.1601		0.1507		0.6822		0.6375
		(1.912*)		(1.799*)		(4.04***)		(3.984*)		(1.950***)		(1.693*)
β		0.7308		0.7136		0.8076		0.8209		0.501		0.5309
		(6.526***)		(5.66***)		(20.3***)		(21.71*)		(5.345***)		(5.136***)
Adj. R^2	0.0389	0.0236	0.0282	0.0215	0.0276	0.0125	0.0214	0.0125	0.0032	-0.1189	0.0053	-0.1202
Log likelihood	1363.483	1446.528	1358.618	1443.815	1265.71	1357.017	1261.897	1355.063	1198.1473	1253.7137	1196.7963	1243.9748
Q(10)	15.583	4.6868	13.978	4.9151	15.3847	12.9449	12.9458	12.4894	8.716	9.6426	8.198	11.572
Q(36)	41.197	29.7985	36.012	28.8092	47.8382	35.1643	44.0399	34.019	41.179	35.5722	39.207	42.046
Skewness	-0.566	-0.753	-0.559	-0.77	-0.146	-0.03	-0.1	-0.016	-3.62	-2.956	-3.603	-3.67
Kurtosis	8	10.8	8.26	10.93	6.535	4.08	6.58	4.01	48.62	33.45	48.21	45.32

Significant at ***1%, **5%, and *10%. *t*-statistics are in parentheses. Q = Ljung-Box statistic. Observations = 649 and 573 (for WIG-20 index). D is dummy variable.

Equations 5 and 7 display the OLS estimates and Equations 6 and 8 show the estimations of the ARCH model for daily returns from the WIG-20 index. Once again the LR improves significantly for the ARCH models and also reduces the skewness and kurtosis. The inclusion of seasonal dummies marginally improves the estimation, although the coefficients remain insignificant. Equations 9, 11, 10, and 12 are estimated for the daily returns from the equally weighted portfolio. The estimates suggest that the ARCH model overfits since the variance estimates exceed unity.

The variance estimates for Warsaw General Index and WIG-20 Index show significant ARCH and GARCH effects with $\Sigma \alpha_i + \Sigma \beta_j = 1$ close to unity and therefore the ARCH model is said to be integrated in variance. Analogous to a unit root in conditional mean, this process is characterized by a high degree of persistence in conditional variance. Consequently, the high aggregate value of α's in the ARCH indicates that shocks to variance have substantial persistence. The computed asymptotic t-statistic shows that the prior day's return or variance has a significant effect on the current daily return.[2] This suggests market inefficiency in the Polish stock market. The Ljung-Box statistics show that the ARCH model captures autocorrelations in the conditional variance, although skewness and kurtosis present in residuals indicate that the ARCH procedure does not explain leptokurtosis.

Notably, for both OLS and GARCH models, low adjusted R^2 are obtained. This suggests that though daily returns contain conditional heteroskedasticity duly accounted for by the GARCH procedure, these models do not provide high explanation for the expected volatility. Thus, although successive price changes may not be strictly independent, the actual amount of dependence is too small to be important for predicting future volatility.

Although the ARCH procedure does not normalize the residuals, it is interesting to investigate whether the residuals, even though not normal, are identically and independently distributed and are free from nonlinearity. The residuals from the OLS and ARCH procedures are, therefore, tested for nonlinearity using the BDS test procedure. The results in Table 16.6 show a significant statistic for the residuals from the OLS procedures. The significant BDS statistic occurs at epsilon one and half and two times the standard deviation and is larger for the higher embedding dimensions. Nonlinearity, however, is not present once the ARCH process is applied. This suggests that the nonlinearity occurs due to volatility clustering, which is accounted for in the ARCH procedure.

The conditional volatility of daily returns from the Warsaw General Index and WIG-20 Index is shown in Figure 16.1 and a cyclical pattern and a clear downward trend are evident. This suggests that the risk premium required by the investors for undiversifiable risk should be time varying. The conditional volatility for daily returns from the Warsaw General Index also shows significant regime changes and a similar although more prominent cyclical pattern. The conditional volatility of daily returns in the Polish market appears to have declined considerably over the whole window and notably after June 1995.

Table 16.6. BDS Test Statistic for the Residuals from OLS and ARCH Estimations

M	WGOLS	WGARCH	WIGOLS	WIGARCH	EWOLS	EWARCH
2	0.337	-0.062	0.312	0.042	0.229	-0.059
3	0.482	-0.004	0.379	0.057	0.348	-0.029
4	0.398	0.005	0.279	0.04	0.288	-0.014
5	0.276	0	0.165	0.014	0.172	-0.009
6	0.191	0.001	0.095	0.005	0.097	-0.002
7	0.119	0.001	0.051	0	0.05	0
8	0.07	0	0.026	-0.001	0.024	0
9	0.039	0	0.012	-0.001	0.012	-0.001
10	0.021	0	0.005	0	0.006	0
2	0.487	-0.17	0.504	0.045	0.517	-0.271
3	1.175	-0.104	1.04	0.132	1.296	-0.323
4	1.516	-0.06	1.278	0.202	1.776*	-0.289
5	1.618	-0.044	1.253	0.178	1.979**	-0.268
6	1.585	-0.007	1.156	0.153	2.05**	-0.217
7	1.47	0.019	1.01	0.122	1.998**	-0.145
8	1.149	0.033	0.842	0.082	1.882*	-0.086
9	1.146	0.023	0.672	0.045	1.7	-0.063
10	0.963	0.01	0.545	0.024	1.53	-0.043
2	0.375	-0.162	0.543	0.004	0.409	-0.243
3	1.242	-0.168	1.361	0.067	1.127	-0.359
4	2.035**	-0.166	2.042**	0.211	1.819*	-0.391
5	2.659***	-0.166	2.439**	0.277	2.362**	-0.431
6	3.113***	-0.138	2.665***	0.311	2.814***	-0.438
7	3.47***	-0.105	2.813***	0.333	3.125***	-0.385
8	3.693***	-0.052	2.823***	0.305	3.306***	-0.315
9	3.786***	-0.03	2.724***	0.245	3.359***	-0.271
10	3.783***	-0.026	2.585***	0.193	3.355***	-0.217
2	0.198	-0.095	0.348	-0.018	0.167	-0.094
3	0.802	-0.129	1.071	0.016	0.55	-0.188
4	1.474	-0.173	1.828*	0.103	1.019	-0.263
5	2.095**	-0.214	2.443**	0.144	1.434	-0.366
6	2.659***	-0.237	2.947***	0.188	1.879*	-0.488
7	3.171***	-0.266	3.424***	0.239	2.284**	-0.552
8	3.602***	-0.264	3.761***	0.237	2.644***	-0.611
9	3.966***	-0.243	3.982***	0.207	2.947***	-0.636
10	4.249***	-0.232	4.118***	0.176	3.191***	-0.62

Significant at ***1% and **5%. Marginal significance level of the statistics for a two-tailed test is 2.576 (1%) and 1.960 (5%). WGOLS = Warsaw General Index OLS residuals, WGARCH = Warsaw General Index ARCH residuals, WIG = WIG-20 Index, and EW = equally weighted portfolio.

Figure 16.1. Conditional Volatility

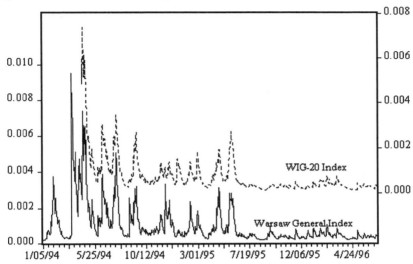

The sharp reduction in the conditional volatility after June 1995 seen in Figure 16.1 requires further investigation. We therefore examine the exchange rate of the Polish zloty with the German mark over this period. We find that annualized volatility of exchange rate which was 12.64% before June 1995 decreased to 2.80% after June 1995. This suggests stabilization of the Polish economy reflected in lower volatility of exchange rate (and inflation) after June 1995 that might have led to the marked decline in investor's risk perceptions toward the Polish market.

As an alternative explanation, we computed the correlation of the Polish stock market with the German Dax 100 Performance index and the U.K. FTSE 100. Again we find a significant increase in the correlation of the Polish market with the German and U.K. markets post-June 1995 reaching 89% and 64%, respectively, compared to 45% and 50% for the period January 1994 to June 1995. This increased correlation after June 1995 suggests that stabilization of the inflation (reflected by the exchange rate) may reflect a "coming of age" of the Polish market. Figure 16.2 displays the stock market trends which show improvement of correlation of the Polish market with the German market over the years.

For testing the hypothesis that conditional volatility is priced in the Polish emerging market, we use equation 3. In Table 16.7 the estimates of the GARCH in mean (GARCH-M) model are given. The estimation has been done with and without inclusion of lagged values and dummy variables. The LR improves with the inclusion of lagged returns and dummy variables for the Warsaw General Index as well as for the WIG-20 index. The inclusion of lagged returns removes autocorrelations of residuals. The estimates suggest that the conditional volatility

Figure 16.2. Correlation of Warsaw General Index with German Dax

is not priced as the coefficients (θ) of conditional volatility $h^{1/2}$ are small and in-significant. This means that the GARCH-M model does not connect time-vary-ing volatility to the mean of daily stock returns. The hypothesis that conditional volatility is priced in the Polish market is therefore rejected.

CONCLUSIONS

This chapter provides empirical evidence on the nature of stock market volatility in the Polish emerging market by investigating daily returns from the Warsaw General Index, WIG-20 Index, and an equally weighted portfolio of 17 stocks. The results suggest that the daily stock return's volatility in the emerging Polish market can be best specified as a process of conditional heteroskedas-ticity. The GARCH models perform better than the conventional OLS models in Warsaw General and WIG-20 indices and the GARCH-M further improves the estimations for WIG-20 index. GARCH models do not perform well on daily returns from the equally weighted portfolio. Although an ARMA (1,0) model fits well for this series, it does not remove nonlinear dependencies. Seasonal regularities reflected in significantly higher or lower returns on certain days of the week commonly found in most markets do not appear to be present in the Polish stock market.

Volatility seems to be of a persistent nature in the Polish market, however, as measured by a GARCH-in-mean model, this does not seem to be priced. The findings suggest marked decline in conditional variance over the sample period. This indicates that prior to June 1995 the investors perceived the Polish stock market as highly risky and required a higher risk premium to compensate for

Table 16.7. GARCH in Mean Estimates

	Warsaw General Index				WIG-20 Index				EW Portfolio			
	GARCH-M	WDM	WAR-1	WDMAR-1	GARCH-M	WDM	WAR-1	WDMAR-1	GARCH-M	WDM	WAR-1	WDMAR-1
θ	0.0063	0.001	0.0036	-0.0108	-0.086	-0.083	-0.0819	-0.0827	-0.0629	-0.0631	0.2502	0.2757
	(0.06)	(0.01)	(0.033)	(-0.104)	(-0.758)	(-0.761)	(-0.66)	(-0.66)	(-0.759)	(-0.761)	(1.911*)	(2.247**)
γ_i			0.2186	0.2232		0.2143	0.219	-0.0001			0.4662	0.4111
			(4.972***)	(5.064)		(4.41***)	(4.524***)	(-0.046)			(2.056**)	(2.034**)
γ_0	-0.0003	0.0008	-0.0004	0.0011	0.003	0.0048	0.0025	0.0046		0	-0.0082	-0.0083
	(-0.122)	(0.20)	(-0.136)	(0.268)	(1.275)	(1.75*)	(1.10)	(1.595)		(-0.013)	(1.869*)	(1.729*)
D_{Tue}		-0.0036		-0.0044		-0.0026		-0.0031		-0.0008		-0.0048
		(-1.074)		(-1.318)		(-0.793)		(-1.008)		(-0.0138)		(1.391)
D_{Wed}		-0.0024		-0.0019		-0.0038		-0.0033		-0.0013		-0.0013
		(-0.631)		(-0.481)		(-1.454)		(-1.30)		(-0.235)		(0.547)
D_{Thu}		0.0012		0.0016		-0.0006		-0.0003		0.0009		-0.0052
		(0.245)		(0.309)		(-0.21)		(-0.105)		(0.212)		(1.001)
D_{Fri}		-0.0002		-0.0008		-0.0034		-0.0037		0.001		0.0069
		(-0.038)		(-0.186)		(-1.378)		(-1.536)		(0.192)		(0.953)
C	0.0001	0	0.0001	0	1.80	2.063	0	0	0	0	0.0002	0.0002
	(1.435)	(1.518)	(1.457)	(1.539)	(1.78*)	(1.77*)	(1.794*)	(1.78*)	(-0.013)	(-0.006)	(2.739**)	(3.433***)
α	0.2451	0.234	0.2597	0.2445	0.162	0.1736	0.1361	0.1432	0.0724	0.0714	0.7643	0.7982
	(1.914*)		(1.765*)	(1.866*)	(3.91***)	(4.02***)	(4.23***)	(4.25***)	(3.45***)	(3.49***)	(1.709*)	(1.946**)
β	0.7214	0.736	0.7174	0.7339	0.819	0.8032	0.844	0.8336	0.9425	0.9429	0.4433	0.4015
	(5.90***)	(6.70***)	(5.61***)	(6.43***)	(19.75***)	(18.62***)	(25.66***)	(24.02***)	(81.06***)	(78.82*)	(3.287***)	(3.287***)
Adj. R^2	-0.0067	-0.007	0.0198	0.0225	-0.0047	-0.0062	0.0126	0.0134	-0.0059	-0.012	-0.1319	-0.1249
Log likelihood	1434.0586	1436.092	1442.3091	1445.0598	1338.038	1339.7995	1342.7216	1344.5361	1276.5165	1276.8752	1245.5771	1257.1331
Q(10)	27.07*	27.50*	4.772	4.5652	43.6806*	44.8364*	10.085	10.6899	12.0402	11.929	11.6213	8.95
Q(36)	51.35*	52.64*	28.8702	30.1814	66.7787*	68.4564*	30.726	32.1214	35.8326	36.054	41.7366	33.535
Skewness	-0.77	-0.743	-0.8	-0.77	0.1654	0.151	0.288	0.279	-3.02	-3.033	-3.11	-2.476
Kurtosis	10.58	10.434	11.07	10.92	4.329	4.349	5.403	5.482	35.72	36.05	36.267	25.517

WDM = GARCH-M model with dummy variables, WAR-1 = GARCH-M model with AR1, WDMAR-1 = GARCH-M Model with dummy variables and AR1. Significant at ***1%, **5%, and *10%. t-statistics are in parentheses. Q = Ljung-Box statistic. Observations = 649 and 573 (for WIG-20 index). D is dummy variable.

bearing undiversifiable risk. In effect, international investors did not diversify into the Polish market and Polish investors were unable to diversify externally. The volatility of the exchange rate may have been the proximate cause of the lack of integration of the Polish and global market. However, possibly increasing interest shown by the international investors after June 1995 appears to have reduced the risk premium. This is reflected by a significant decline in the variance of Polish zloty's exchange rate with the German mark and significant increase in correlation of the Polish market with the German and U.K. markets in the period after June 1995.

The chapter also presents evidence of nonlinearity in daily returns. The nonlinear dependencies appear to have been captured by the GARCH models. This suggests that nonlinearity caused by shocks or discontinuous events is reflected in the heteroskedastic behavior. Based on the empirical evidence, the martingale hypothesis that future changes of the daily stock prices in the Polish stock markets are orthogonal to the past information is significantly rejected. Though daily returns contain conditional heteroskedasticity and nonlinear dependencies, the actual amount of dependence is too small to be important for explaining expected volatility.

NOTES

1. Euromoney Guide to Central and Eastern European Equities 1997, pp. 7-9.
2. The procedure was repeated accounting for the lagged returns up to the eleventh day. For none of the lags was the log-likelihood ratio higher than the reported estimates with one-day lagged returns.

REFERENCES

Baillie, R. and R. DeGennaro, 1990. Stock returns and volatility, *Journal of Econometrics* 31 (April), 307-327.
Bollerslev, T. 1986. Generalized autoregressive conditional heteroskedasticity, *Journal of Econometrics* 31, 307-327.
Bollerslev, T., R. Chou, and K. Kroner, 1992. ARCH modelling in finance: a review of theory and empirical evidence, *Journal of Econometrics* 52, 5-59.
Bollerslev, T., R. Engle, and J. Wooldridge, 1988. A capital asset pricing model with time varying variance, *Journal of Political Economy* 96 (Feb.) 116-131.
Box, G. and M. Jenkins, 1976. *Time Series Analysis: Forecasting and Control*, rev. ed. San Francisco: Holden-Day.
Brock, W., W. Dechert, and Scheinkman, 1987. A test for independence based on the correlation dimension, mimeo, University of Chicago.
Brock, W., D. Hsieh, and B. Le Baron, 1991. *Nonlinear Dynamics, Chaos, and Instability: Statistical Evidence and Economic Evidence*. Cambridge, MA: MIT Press.
Brock, W., J. Lakonishok, and B. LeBaron, 1990. Simple technical trading rules and the stochastic properties of stock returns, Social Systems Research Institute Workshop Series no. 9022, University of Wisconsin-Madison.
Brock, W. and A. Malliaris, 1989. *Differential Equations Stability and Chaos in Dynamic Economics*, Amsterdam: North Holland.

Chou, R., 1988. Volatility persistence and stock valuations: some evidence using GARCH, *Journal of Applied Econometrics* 3, 279-94.

Diebold, F., 1986. Temporal aggregation of ARCH processes and the distribution of asset returns, Special Studies Chapter 200, Federal Reserve Board, Division of Research and Statistics, Washington DC.

Dickey, D. and W. Fuller, 1979. Distribution of the estimators for autoregressive time series with a unit root, *Journal of the American Statistical Association* 74, 427-431.

Engle, R., 1982. Autoregressive conditional heteroskedasticity with estimates of the variance of United Kingdom inflation, *Econometrica* 50, 987-1007.

Engle, R., D. Lilien, and R. Robins, 1987. Estimating time varying risk premia in the term structure: the ARCH model, *Econometrica* 55, 391-408.

Engle, R. and T. Bollerslev, 1986. Modelling the persistence of conditional variances, *Econometric Reviews* 5, 1-50.

Errunza, V., K. Hogan, O. Kini, and P. Padmanabhan, 1994. Conditional heteroskedasticity and global stock return distribution, *The Financial Review* 29(3), 293-317.

Euromoney Guide to Central and Eastern European Equities, 1997, 7-9.

Fama, E., 1970. Efficient capital markets: A review of theory and empirical work, *Journal of Finance* 25, 383-417.

Fama, E., 1976. *Foundations of Finance*. New York: Basic Books.

Fama, E., 1991. Efficient capital markets II, *Journal of Finance* 46(5), 1575-1615.

Fama, E. and K. French, 1988. Permanent and temporary components of stock prices, *Journal of Political Economy* 96, 246-273.

Geyer, A., 1994. Volatility estimates of the Vienna stock market, *Applied Financial Economics* 4, 449-455.

Grassberger, P. and I. Procaccia, 1983. Characterization of strange attractors, *Physics Review Letters* 50, 346-358.

Hsieh, C., 1993. Some potential applications of artificial neural system in financial management, *Journal of Systems Management* 44(4), 12-15.

Hsieh, D., 1989. Testing for non-linear dependence in daily foreign exchange rates, *Journal of Business* 62(3), 339-368.

Hsieh, D., 1991. Chaos and non-linear dynamics: application to financial markets, *Journal of Finance* 46(5), 1839-1877.

Hsieh, D., 1993. Using non-linear methods to search for risk premia in currency futures, *Journal of International Economics*, 35(1-2), 113-132.

Hsieh, D., 1993. Implications of non-linear dynamics for financial risk management, *Journal of Financial and Quantitative Analysis* 28(1), 41-64.

Lo, A. and A.C. MacKinlay, 1988. Stock market prices do not follow random walks, evidence from a simple specification test, *Review of Financial Studies*, 1(1), 41-66.

McCurdy, T. and I. Morgan, 1988. Testing the martingale hypothesis in Deutsche Mark futures with models specifying the form of heteroskedasticity, *Journal of Applied Econometrics* 3, 187-202.

Pindyck, R., 1984. Risk, inflation and stock market, *American Economic Review* 74 (June), 335-351.

Satchell, S. and A. Timmermann, 1992. An assessment of the economic value of nonlinear foreign exchange rate forecasts, Discussion Chapter in Financial Economics, Birkbeck College, University of London FE-6/92, 1-38.

Scheinkman, J. and B. LeBaron, 1989. Nonlinear dynamics and stock returns, *Journal of Business* 31, 1-337.

Sewell, S., R. Stansell, I. Lee, and Ming-Shun Pan, 1993. Nonlinearities in emerging foreign capital markets, *Journal of Business Finance and Accounting* 20(2), 237-248.

Sumel, R. and R. Engle, 1994. Hourly volatility spillovers between international equity markets, *Journal of International Money and Finance* 13, 3-25.

Theodossiou, P. and U. Lee, 1995. Relationship between volatility and expected returns across international stock markets, *Journal of Business Finance and Accounting* 22(2), 289-301.

Wood, D., S. Poshakwale, and B. Dasgupta, 1996. Investigating the dynamics of Polish WIG-20, Modelling and Analysing Economies in Transition, September, Polish Academy of Sciences, Warsaw.

Yu, Q., 1996. A conditional variance model for daily stock returns in China's emerging stock markets: Empirical evidence on the Shanghai and Shinzhen exchanges, *Journal of International Financial Markets, Institutions and Money* 6(4), 1-19.

17

Developing Financial Markets in Russia: The Russian Securities Industry in Comparative Perspective (With Special Reference to Derivatives)

Val Samonis and Oleg Bondar

INTRODUCTION

In the communist period, financial markets and their underlying institutions were seen as the quintessential embodiment of capitalism with all its unpredictability and irrationality, so badly comparing with socialism based on firm, scientific foundations developed by communist parties. After the collapse of communism, many Central European reformers were tempted to desecrate the headquarters of communist parties by establishing stock exchanges there; that's what actually happened in Poland! The development of financial markets is the crucial dimension of the postcommunist transformation. However, due to legacies of the communist system and precommunist underdevelopment, this is one of the most difficult and time-consuming processes, which was started only in 1997.

FINANCIAL MARKETS IN RUSSIA: ORIGINS, DETERMINANTS, AND DEVELOPMENT STRATEGIES

A brief postcommunist history of Russian financial markets goes back to 1988-1990, when the centralized system of wholesale trade (Gossnab) began to rapidly disintegrate. Various commodity exchanges spontaneously sprang up in the old system's place. They of course traded in commodities but subsequently provided a home for securities trading as well. The single biggest factor working for the development of the securities markets was the nature of Russian privatization. In an attempt to create people's capitalism and sidestep barriers imminent to classical privatization, Russian and other reformers (e.g., Czech, Lithuanian) based their privatization strategy on vouchers issued by the government to the population. Countries which use the voucher method are, on average, more advanced in building their securities markets than those (like Hungary) which, at least in the beginning, opted for classical privatization methods (initial public offerings, etc.).

When the Russian voucher-based privatization ended in 1994, it had produced some 40 million shareholders! Large amounts of enterprise shares were supposed to hit secondary markets. However, to neutralize the opposition to privatization, insiders (workers and managers) were granted special privileges in this big "sell-in" of Russian assets. These privileges are jealously guarded by insiders; they do everything to keep outsiders "where they properly belong"— that is, out of the enterprise and its shares. As a result, many shares are tied up inside newly privatized enterprises, with a rather modest spillover to the larger local, regional, or national markets which therefore suffer from the shortage of liquidity and transparency. Still, insiders are legally free to sell their shares.

Consequently, the consolidation of equity started almost immediately after the workers had received their shares. Shares which have been purchased from workers now comprise the main source of increases in the stakes of both management and outside investors. Usually workers sell their shares cheaply to brokers, who then resell consolidated packages to large investors at a premium. Investment funds that spring up spontaneously serve as catalysts for these processes and contribute to the development of securities markets in Russia. True, the level of trading skills and ethics in these funds is low; in many cases, they run schemes which would not be tolerated in the West (e.g., the pyramid by Sergei Mavrodi). For the most part, these funds went totally unsupervised in Russia and helped give something of a new bad name—*dikiy kapitalism*, that is, "wild capitalism"—to a market economy among the confused population.

Securitization of large domestic inter-enterprise debts could have further contributed to the development of securities markets, but no such schemes were implemented or even seriously attempted in Russia. However, there seems to be a trend to develop a market for debt of bankrupt enterprises and banks—such as TAIGA bonds (short-term government). With the Russian government debt trading at anything from 20% up to 75% of the nominal value in 1996 (it actually soared to 75% in 1997 at the news of President Yeltsin recovering from heart surgery), there is a huge potential for foreign debt-for-equity swaps which can be implemented through debt securitization and downloading onto the secondary markets. However, perhaps due to the political sensitivity of the matter, no such schemes were devised or even officially discussed by 1997 (Samonis, 1993; Rinaco Plus, 1996; Vash Finansovy Popechitel, 1996).

Trading in Russian securities occurs mainly on stock exchanges and over-the-counter (OTC—see Appendices 1 and 2). Russian security markets are very thin, separated regionally and sectorally, not transparent, and illiquid, except perhaps for short-term government securities. Moreover, Russian markets, especially in the beginning, were skewed in favor of new bank stock. By 1997, they were skewed primarily in favor of government paper (GKO and other short-term obligations of state) issued to help domestically finance the budget deficit (75% of the deficit in 1995), and to help ailing banks because they carry very high yields, some 3-6% in real terms in 1996. The ruble return on GKOs reached 80% when inflation in 1996 was about 27%. The crowding-out effect of such government behavior was particularly high in 1996.

All this contributes to the weakness of the company securities market. The national market has developed only for about 100 of the largest and most interesting enterprises, especially those that were sold at the all-Russia interregional auctions. Demand for their shares comes from both domestic and international investors. A liquid market for these shares in the major financial centers has developed. The capitalization of the Russian market was just over $20 billion in 1996, according to Dmitri Vasiliev, head of the Federal Commission on Securities and the Capital Market, established in 1994. A large part of the Russian stock market is dependent on foreign money, which is very sensitive to volatile Russian politics and wars (e.g., in Chechnya). According to government estimates, Russian domestic savings were largely not invested but tucked away in large U.S. bills in mattresses and reached well over $20 billion in 1996. According to some estimates, Russian savings rates at one-third of GDP are no worse than in other emerging markets (e.g. China, India) but investment rates are two times less. The challenge, therefore, is to close this gap by attracting money from the predominantly small Russian savers—that is, to turn them into domestic investors. This would also send powerful signals which would help stem and even reverse the capital flight from Russia; over $50 billion is legally or illegally "parked" in offshore accounts according to some estimates (e.g., "Russia's Emerging Market," 1995). Such a reversal would "feed" the new private sector starved for capital. These are ingredients of the most promising strategy for securities markets development in Russia. Weak bankruptcy laws and processes, a virtual lack of distortions of debt-based control mechanisms (e.g., nonexistent collateral laws, weaknesses, and the "incestuous" nature of commercial banking), point to the important role for securities markets in Russia.

Securities deliver equity-based control mechanisms which can supplement debt-based control mechanisms. Both are needed in a transition economy like Russia's. Especially so, that efficient securities markets can serve as a vehicle for correction of the flaws of Russian privatization (e.g., insider bias, excessive ownership dispersion, etc.). For the majority of privatized enterprises, a secondary share market existed only for a short time immediately after privatization. After the consolidation of capital into the hands of the new owners (especially *nomenklatura*) little trading is done. As a result of the securities markets operation, property rights should consolidate into the most capable hands, corporate governance should be improved, thereby increasing the efficiency of the national economy. To implement such a strategy for securities markets development, necessary financial instruments (or products) and institutions need to be developed.

DEVELOPING SECURITIES MARKETS IN RUSSIA

Starting from zero or rather below it in a sense, the Russian stock market has been rising in the erratic, volatile manner typical of emerging markets. It lost about half its U.S. dollar value in 1994-95 due to the surge in inflation and the collapse of the MMM-type pyramid schemes. However, it rapidly regained its value in 1996, largely in anticipation that Boris Yeltsin would win the presidential election. In general, Russian assets are grossly underpriced (10-20 times or more) compared to similar Western assets. According to the Russian Privatization Center, the average value of Russian manufacturing companies was less than $1,000 per employee in 1994, compared to about $100,000 per employee in the United States. Such low valuations are partly due to the specifics of Russian privatization.

High combined stakes of the Russian government (residually) and employees (by compromise if not design) in the privatized enterprises tend to discourage outside investors. This is so because outside investors have grounds to fear that these enterprises may favor job retention and higher wages over dividends which, additionally, may be siphoned off by government (e.g., via taxes, bureaucratic rent-seeking, etc.). These low valuations also reflect the fact that the company performance paradigm is undergoing (or should do so) such a radical shift in transition economies like Russia's (from fulfillment of quantitative plan targets to a profit-based goal function).

Past performance is a very poor indicator of what the future holds, given that enterprises need to be radically restructured in many cases. Under such circumstances, it is extremely difficult to predict company performance and, consequently, the value of its stock. Risks here are extremely high, both for companies and investors. The crucial problem for newly privatized Russian companies and investors is managing high risks stemming from the unstable transition economy environment. The level of risk-management skills is particularly low in Russian companies emerging from the system which tried to eliminate risk.

Therefore a case can be made for a possible use of derivative securities in a transition economy like Russia's. Derivatives are financial instruments (products) which derive their value from more basic underlying variables such as stocks, bonds, commodity contracts, and interest rates. Derivative instruments may include, but would not be limited to, futures contracts, options, forward contracts, and swaps. In essence, they boil down to transferring risk from market players who want to hedge their exposure (or isolate a particular kind of risk) to other players who are willing to take this risk. The risks to be replaced are those which a particular nonfinancial company finds difficult to handle on its own (e.g., exchange rate risk). Thanks to derivatives, such risks tend to be downloaded onto financial markets which, presumably, should be able to better handle them. More complex, customized derivatives are usually designed and handled by banks. Such instruments carry still not researched or not well understood risks of their own which may have contributed to financial problems rather than solved them as in the well publicized cases of derivative-related losses by Baring's or Orange County. Simpler forms of derivatives are easier to understand and price and tend to be traded on stock exchanges. In the West, the growth of derivatives markets has led to increasing involvement by institutions and individuals for investment purposes. Derivatives research is the fledgling field of economic, business, and financial research that examines, on a scholarly basis, the use of derivative instruments as an investment vehicle.

There are two major general problems with using derivatives. Their originally intended use was hedging (i.e., ensuring the payoff, forfeiting part of desired profit as an insurance payment). They are still used for this purpose by owners of commodities and other risk-averse people. But derivatives allow players to take positions in the market by investing a small fraction of the money they would need to invest in stocks (e.g., derivatives allow a player to take a position in a $100 stock by purchasing a $2 option on it). Therefore, for the most part derivatives are used by speculators foreseeing any significant change in the value of the underlying asset. So the first problem is that derivatives are very highly leveraged instruments. There is nothing wrong with this, but a player may buy several million options, turning exchange trading into big-time legal gambling. Most major losers, though, lost money writing derivatives.

The second major problem is difficulty of pricing derivative securities. There is some high-level mathematics involved and the complexity of many instruments is astonishing. This field is highly computerized, and there are very complex derivative pricing software packages dynamically linked to stock market databases. The purpose of these packages is to price derivatives based on underlying stock, interest rates, and the like, and, at the same time, to look for any discrepancies. These discrepancies could allow a possibility of a riskless profit. By 1997, there was little such research done on the possibilities or limitations of derivatives within the environment of a transition economy.

POSSIBILITIES FOR USING DERIVATIVES
ON THE RUSSIAN MARKET

The use of derivative products is taking an increasing role in the world economy. Commodity futures and options have been around for nearly a century in the United States; however, they were mostly used by a small segment of the market dealing with some commodities, such as grain. Futures and options were used primarily for hedging. When the United States abandoned the gold standard in 1972, the currencies were allowed to float and that opened possibilities for introducing financial futures (e.g., interest rate derivatives). Since then there has been a tremendous growth in use of derivatives and now about a half of the world volume of derivatives trading happens outside the United States (Kilcollin and Frankel, 1993).

In the 1990s, the use of derivatives has been exploding in emerging markets, most formidably in Latin America and Asia, but also in Eastern Europe. The reason for this is a growing investment in emerging markets. Investors are attracted by higher returns and growth potential of these markets. Some of the market participants want to hedge, others want to leverage their investments. Some investors would like to use derivatives as a means of avoiding local regulations of the capital markets. This is usually done by synthetically replicating a restricted instrument. A variety of other derivative uses show up in emerging markets. Of course, obviously helpful are currency forwards and swaps for protection from the volatile local currency fluctuation. Many un-hedged companies in Mexico suffered a great deal as a result of the peso crisis of 1994, when they had to face huge nonlocal currency debts and most of their cash flow was in pesos. Interest rate floors, caps, and other derivatives could be used to take care of interest rate changes.

The increase of joint venture investment gives rise to such corporate needs as repatriation of earnings, currency convertibility guarantees, and dollar return on equity. There are instruments to meet such needs (e.g., convertibility insur-ance and deliverable currency forwards). Many investors have found that derivatives could be the most efficient and cost-effective way to invest into an emerging market (e.g., Nicholls, 1996). For example, out-of-the-money options are an inexpensive way to cap losses if a disastrous price or interest rate move happens in a highly volatile market.

So far most of the derivatives' activity in Eastern Europe is OTC, small in scale and in most simple forms ("plain vanilla"). The derivatives are not even marketed as derivatives, but used as a part of a financing package in, say, fixed income or equity issues. Recently issued Russian Eurobonds have a great poten-tial to develop the derivatives market, but there are already some instruments depending on the Russian yield curve. J.P. Morgan makes markets in several options on Ministry of Finance papers and on nonperforming Vneshekonom-bank debt. On July 8, 1996, Salomon Brothers launched a multicurrency series of European-style call warrants on a Russian equity basket. The warrants with a December 1997 expiry date were offered in deutchmarks, U.S. dollars, Swiss francs, and Portuguese escudos to widen the distribution network (Nicholls, 1996).

We would like to consider the possibilities and limitations on the use of derivatives on the Russian market, to compare the situation in Russia to that in economically similarly structured countries like Mexico or Brazil, and to consider the possibilities and limitations on the use of Western derivative markets by Russian brokerages.

ADVANTAGES OF EXCHANGE-BASED MARKETS AND EFFECTS OF USING DERIVATIVES

Price Stability. Active trading of a product gives a constant reassessment of its true value, therefore providing the market with the most up-to-date information, which is then used for appropriate resource allocation. The active derivative market tends to make the underlying cash market prices more stable in most cases. Overall, high market liquidity contributes to overall stability in the economy.

Hedging and Speculating. Derivatives' markets provide a basis for risk management. Risk-averse players have an opportunity to hedge, making the outcome more certain. Hedging transfers the risks to the other group of players—speculators. They are willing to take higher risks for a chance of higher profits. Also arbitrageurs (players looking for any meaningful discrepancies in prices between a derivative and an underlying asset to get a riskless profit) perform a very important function, making sure that prices everywhere are at the same level, contributing therefore to the price stability.

Dealing with Credit Risk. Another advantage of exchanges is a presence of a clearinghouse, which makes sure that counterparties fulfil their liabilities, thereby allowing transactions between players with very different credit ratings. This system is very effective and works with the help of clearing and maintenance margins.

Liquidity and Depth. Centralization of trading makes sure that there always is a buyer and a seller for a given product, so depth and liquidity increase.

Standardization of Operations. Transactions, information, and procedures are standardized, thus reducing costs and probability of inefficiency.

GENERAL LIMITATIONS ON THE USE OF DERIVATIVES IN TRANSITION ECONOMIES

General limitations can be summarized into several categories outlined below.

Awareness and Understanding of Derivative Products. These products are relatively new and fairly complicated. In Eastern Europe there are few specialists and a very low awareness among the general public. For a very long time under centrally planned economies there was no need to hedge against risks, so most institutions still do not see the need for the use of derivatives or do not understand potential benefits. On the other hand, new firms operating several years in turbulent Russian conditions simply consider many risks natural and unavoidable. These factors prevent higher use of derivative products.

Legal Obstacles. As any new initiative, introduction of derivatives into new markets meets many legal obstacles. Legal institutions see potential problems with derivatives before their potential usefulness, so for the most part they impede the process.

Problems with Broker Services. Most major brokerage firms do not rush to enter East European markets, or if they enter they limit their clientele to a few established local companies. There are several major problems for brokerage firms. Costs of entering a new market are quite significant. There are up-front costs of learning the market, local customs and laws, and establishing contacts. This is especially true in Russia, where many business deals are done based on personal or political contacts and outsiders are kept out. And, of course, costs of running a brokerage office could be significant. Then there is the issue of two major types of risk. One is country risk arising from lack of political and economical stability. The second is a credit risk which is common even in established market economies. Credit information is either not completely available or less reliable than it should be, and also regulations and legal institutions do not seem to be of much help when the client does not meet its financial obligations. Most Western institutions working in Russia seem to rely on their own credit information. The next problem is lack of an appropriate infrastructure. Telecommunications are notoriously bad and unreliable, banking services are not reliable either and often are very slow. This is true for Russia; in other countries of the Confederation of Independent States (CIS) the situation is even worse. The problem of a small customer base is disappearing rapidly in Russia, although it is still persistent in other CIS countries.

POSSIBILITIES AND LIMITATIONS OF USING DERIVATIVES ON THE RUSSIAN MARKET: MAIN CONCLUSIONS

The attempts to use derivatives in transition economies run against many obstacles. First of all, securities markets are thin, illiquid, and fragmented as argued above; therefore there is not much (stocks, bonds, etc.) from which to derive anything. By 1997, the best base for derivatives in Russia was provided by government zero coupon bonds (GKO) and other government securities. There were some derivatives on GKO trading in 1997. The Russian government has not defaulted on any GKO/OFZ issues and yields are extraordinarily high by Western standards. Foreign investment in GKO is limited to 10% in each issue. But foreign investors can purchase "synthetic GKOs," derivatives that replicate GKO/OFZ yields but do not offer direct control of these bonds. This strategy was used before the 1996 presidential elections and these products were sold through Western banks. The dollar return of 19% was guaranteed and the government expected a significant inflow of foreign money. However, investors considered this not nearly as good as real GKOs and the inflow was not large enough.

After Yeltsin's reelection a new type of investment, the so-called S account, was set up, allowing foreigners to buy directly from a Russian bank. However the government forces foreigners to convert the ruble profits into dollars using a three-month forward rate set by The Central Bank of Russia, which again reduces prices to about 19%. The ruble corridor was maintained effectively for about two years but was relaxed in July 1996. Generally, investors have no confidence in its stability but can hedge their GKO investment using futures and forwards. Unfortunately, this is limited by the small size of the forward and futures market and its low liquidity. Counterparty risk is also substantial; if there is a collapse of the value of the ruble, exchanges may go bankrupt and banks may renege on forward contracts.

The currency futures market is liquid—that is, with a sufficient number of participants and volume. Currency futures are traded on several exchanges in Moscow with trade volume of approximately $12 million a day. Forward contracts can be established with large banks for sums up to $10 million. The rates are similar to corresponding futures rates. There are some arbitrage opportunities based on discrepancy between the two rates, but the possible profit is small because of low liquidity. Several major multinational banks are going to offer currency forwards in the near future. The Moscow Inter-Bank Currency Exchange (MICEX) announced the development of a market in government securities as one of its goals.

INFRASTRUCTURE

The institutional infrastructure is weak. The crucial institution of a clearinghouse is almost nonexistent; without it there is no efficient mechanism to insure against defaults. True, there were attempts in Russia to use commodity exchanges as clearinghouses, but they were not successful. In October 1994, the Moscow Central Stock Exchange division dealing with these instruments went bust because it ran out of capital to cover defaulting brokers when the ruble lost much of its value (e.g., Valencia, 1995). Skills in this area of finance are practically nonexistent. Therefore, some circulate proposals that a clearinghouse for East Central Europe should be based in some Western city like Vienna rather than in any capitals of former communist countries. Others counter that this would deprive these countries of profits which properly belong to them.

What also needs to be done is a proper prudential regulation and supervision of the Russian banking system and investment funds. Russian securities laws are not numerous, which may not be a bad thing. However, and this is much worse, most of them are violated most of the time. A new Law on Securities was signed by President Yeltsin on April 22, 1996, which established a structure for market regulation based on the Federal Commission on Securities and the Capital Markets and self-regulatory organizations of market participants. It affirmed that the Securities Commission will continue to have the status of a ministry, and will be responsible for implementing the government's capital market policies in the area of corporate securities. However, the Commission's standing was effectively downgraded by placing it under the auspices of the Ministry of Finance in late 1996.

The Commission is responsible for regulating the activities of professional market participants, establishing rules for securities issues and trading, and licensing all types of professional market activities. The law grants the Commission authority to file lawsuits seeking the liquidation of companies that violate capital market regulations. The law defines various types of corporate equities that can be traded on the Russian market, and also various types of professional market activities. The law also establishes procedures for registering securities issues and for proving ownership of a security. It includes requirements for issuing prospectuses and for information disclosure about securities issues. Unfortunately, the law does not contain a clear definition of responsibility for violations of capital market laws and regulations. However, the Russian government intends to address this through amendments and additions to the Criminal Code of the Russian Federation and through the issue of other normative acts, as outlined in the Complex Program on the Protection Investors' and Shareholders' Rights adopted in 1996 (see Appendix 3).

As argued above, the regulation and supervision aspect of reform has been rather neglected in Russia, confirming McKinnon's (1991) predictions about the perils of financial markets liberalization. In 1995, a presidential decree authorizing the creation of so-called unit mutual funds was issued. The Federal Commission on Securities and the Capital Market was entrusted with the creation of the regulatory frame and licensing. Only licensed funds are to be allowed; they are subject to minimum capitalization of 1 billion rubles, independent auditing, and are required to disclose information to normal international standards for regulators and investors (prospectus, mutual fund rules). There are two types of Russian mutual funds. Open funds are required to redeem shares within 15 days of request. Interval funds are required to redeem shares at least once a year. Foreign investors can invest in Russian mutual funds.

With regard to financial markets institutions, Central and East European countries are developing solutions which are developing their own unique mixes of German/European and American/Anglo-Saxon traditions. The Czech Republic, for example, has a stock market which, measured by market capitalization as a percentage of GDP (35% in 1996), is bigger than Germany's. At 4-5% of GDP in 1996, Poland and Hungary have small stock markets but they are relatively liquid and transparent compared to both the Czech and Russian markets. Russia in its unique way will rely on both banks and stock exchanges for the institutional underpinning of its financial markets. One of the most important features of this Russian way are financial-industrial groups led by major banks. They are being formed along the lines which resemble the German practice and the Asian practice (Korean chaebols, Japanese keiretsu).

APPENDIX 1: THE RUSSIAN TRADING SYSTEM

The Russian Trading System (RTS), an electronic OTC system based on NASDAQ, links about 30 Russian cities. In 1996, some 150 brokers used the system. About 40% of OTC trading in Moscow, which dominates the market, is carried out on the RTS. Moreover, the RTS has become the primary pricing mechanism for OTC securities. As of January 1996, there were 104 issues listed on the RTS; 21 of these are truly liquid in the Western sense, meaning that they trade at least every three days. The bid-offer spread for these 21 securities is between 3 and 10%.

The RTS is managed by four Russian self-regulatory organizations of market participants, including the Moscow-based Professional Association of Market Participants (PAUFOR), the St. Petersburg-based Fund of Securities Market Participants, the Urals Association of Financial Brokers/Dealers, and the Association of Siberian Stock Brokers. In November 1995, a new nationwide organization was created, PAUFOR-Russia, which has over 200 members in 1996.These associations have developed governance, fair practice rules, as well as rules for trading on the system, and each has appointed a compliance officer to oversee enforcement of the rules. There have been several cases of associations taking disciplinary action against members who have violated rules. In addition, a Technical Center has been created, which supervises the technological aspects of the RTS. In January 1996, PAUFOR's disciplinary committee was given new powers, including the right to impose fines and other penalties on RTS participants who violate the rules.

APPENDIX 2: TRADE PROCEDURES IN THE
RUSSIAN STOCK MARKET (Vash Finansovy Popechitel, 1996)

For nonresidents to trade on the Russian stock market they should open an "I" type account with a Russian bank having the special general license for foreign currency operations of the Central Bank of the Russian Federation (RF). All operations with such accounts are to be only in Russian rubles. All settlements in any foreign currency on the territory of the Russian Federation are prohibited. Funds from abroad can be transferred to the account and immediately converted to rubles—the foreign currency would be sold at the Moscow Interbank Exchange (MIBE). The amount in rubles credited on the account would be calculated on the basis of the official rate of exchange announced by the Central Bank as of the date of convertation. The difference between such official exchange rates and MIBE rates has been recently steadily diminishing and today cannot lead to major losses.

Furthermore, by repatriation of incomes from RF, one's own bank would use MIBE exchange rates. Repatriation of incomes from "I" type accounts is allowed upon submitting the relevant certificate of the Russian Internal Revenue Service. Russian law implies in its essence that such "I" type account holders cannot be considered as having "a representation" in Russia, so one should take into account the benefits of the Treaties on Double Tax Exemption of RF (the former USSR) with other countries. Such treaties, for example, grant tax privileges to investors who are residents of Cyprus, the United Kingdom, Switzerland, the United States, and some other countries. To trade using such "I" type accounts, the investors have to provide a large number of documents. They also needs to choose an agent in Russia who could deal with bank transfers and submit required documentation to IRS and other state bodies. To open an "I" type account is reasonable for those investors who decide to trade in the Russian stock market for a period exceeding half a year. To enter into the Russian market, an investor should immediately develop a scheme allowing tax exemption and repatriation of incomes using Russian banks.

"Russian banks" here means all banks established in compliance with Russian law which have the general license for foreign currency operations of the Central Bank of RF. Some well-known Western banks already have subsidiaries in Russia established under the Russian law. Also in the said period the client would choose a depository and clearing firm that could see to stock transfer and settlements. There are a number of world-renowned companies in Russia doing that kind of business. As a rule, share trade is executed both in the Moscow stock market and in the regions. Moscow firms generally sell big blocks of stocks, the price of which is higher than that asked by the regional brokers. But to buy stocks in the regions would take much more time. At the next stage the broker or several brokers on behalf of the investor would support the liquidity of the stocks bought.

APPENDIX 3: COMPLEX PROGRAM ON THE PROTECTION
OF INVESTORS' AND SHAREHOLDERS' RIGHTS

On March 21, 1996, the Russian government announced a major policy initiative aimed at improving legal protections for investors in Russia's fledging capital market. The purpose of this Presidential Decree No. 408 is to improve both legal protections for investors and the enforcement of capital market regulations. The program declares that "Solving the problem of development of financial and capital markets of the Russian

Federation depends in the first instance on the level of protections for the rights and legal interests of shareholders and investors."

The Program calls for a number of legislative initiatives to protect shareholders' rights, including amendments to the Criminal Code of Russian Federation. The proposed amendments, which have to be passed by the Parliament, would establish a list of capital-market-related crimes, such as defrauding investors and operating without a license, and mandatory punishments. For example, some serious types of fraud would be punishable by prison terms of 5-10 years. The Program also calls for drafting and promulgating amendments to the Administrative Code, which would give the Federal Commission on Securities and the Capital Market authority to impose fines on market participants and to file lawsuits on behalf of shareholders. In addition, the Program calls for amendments to the Civil Procedural Code that would create class-action lawsuits. The Program proposes the introduction of new legal procedures making it easier for government agencies to suspend the operations of fraudulent financial companies, to freeze and seize their assets, and to distribute their assets to investors.

In order to strengthen cooperation in the struggle against fraud, the government plans to create a Presidential Commission on the Protection of Investors' and Share-holders' Rights in the Capital and Financial Markets. This Commission is slated to include representatives of the Federal Securities Commission, the Central Bank of Russia, the Ministry of Internal Affairs, and the Procurator's Office. The Program calls for the creation of well-regulated collective investment vehicles, including unit invest-ment funds, credit unions, shareholder investment funds, investment banks, and nonstate pension funds. The Federal Securities Commission is instructed to establish rules for these collective-investment vehicles based on the principles of strong government regula-tion, separation of asset management from custody, and strict information disclosure requirements.

REFERENCES

Kilcollin, T.E. and M.E. Frankel, 1993. Futures and options markets: their new role in Eastern Europe, *Journal of Banking and Finance*, March.
Latin American risk supplement, 1996. *Risk Magazine*, April.
Latin America's Financial Reforms, 1996. Washington, DC: Inter-American Develop-ment Bank.
McKinnon, R., 1991. *The Order of Economic Liberalization*. Baltimore: The Johns Hop-kins University Press.
Melkumov, I., 1996. Personal communication with Dr. Ian Melkumov, Senior Expert, Federal Commission on Securities and the Capital Market of the Russian Federa-tion.
Nicholls, M., 1996. Curtain raiser, *Risk Magazine*, August.
Rinaco Plus, 1996. Materials from the brokerage house Rinaco Plus, Moscow.
Russia funds soar as economy improves, 1997. *Chicago Tribune*, January 12.
Russia's emerging market: a survey, 1995. *The Economist*, April 8.
Samonis, V., 1993. Western capital's role in privatizing the post-communist economies: the issue of debt-for-equity swaps in Eastern Europe. MOST-MOCT: *Economic Journal on Eastern Europe and the Former Soviet Union*, No. 2.
Samonis, V., 1996. From plan to market: towards the theory of the postcommunist trans-formation. In R. Hill, ed., *Proceedings of the V World Congress of Central and East European Studies*. London: St. Martin's Press.

Samonis, V., and A. Voronova, 1996. Western bank strategies for entering the markets of transition economies: the case of Ukraine, *Journal of Emerging Markets*, Summer.

Valencia, M., 1995. Derivatives: a hedge too far, *Business Central Europe*, No. 25.

Vash Finansovy Popechitel, 1996. Materials from the Moscow-based brokerage firm.

PART VI
Asian Emerging Stock Markets

18

Stock Returns and Conditional Variance-Covariance: Evidence from Asian Stock Markets

Thomas C. Chiang

INTRODUCTION

The stock market crash in October 1987 revealed two important market phenomena. First, the risk associated with market volatility needs to be more precisely measured in asset pricing. Second, stock market volatility appears to be a global occurrence. In response to these two phenomena, empirical research has developed in the following two paths.

The first approach attempts to examine the intertemporal relation between risk and expected returns, with particular attention given to the cause and modeling of risk. For instance, French et al. (1987) showed evidence that the expected market risk premium of the stock portfolio is positively related to the predictable volatility of stock returns. Lee and Ohk (1991) and Glosten et al. (1993) employing ARCH-M and GARCH models, respectively, found a significant negative relationship between risk and return for the U.S. data.[1]

The second line of approach emphasizes the significance of co-movements of international stock indices. Researchers such as Jeon and Chiang (1991) and Kasa (1992) tackled the issue of international stock linkages by exploring time series factors that are commonly shared by individual national markets. By employing multivariate cointegration tests, Jeon and Chiang and Kasa found evidence to support the existence of a common stochastic trend in a system formed by the major stock exchanges.

Moreover, attention has been directed to examine the nature and the lead and lag patterns of international stock returns. For instance, in their investigation of an international transmission mechanism in stock market movements, Eun and Shim (1989) found that innovations in the U.S. market are rapidly transmitted to the rest of the world. King and Wadhwani (1990) also demonstrated a contagion effect—in that price changes in one market can be transmitted to other markets through information assessment and inference. Hamao et al. (1989) reported that price volatility spills over across markets. Theodossiou and Lee (1993) and Chiang and Chiang (1996) concluded that national stock market volatility is caused mainly by U.S. stock return volatility. In sum, the accumulated evidence indicates that international linkages and inter-actions among international stock markets have increased in the postcrash era, indicating that national markets have grown more interdependent (Koutmos and Booth, 1995).

Despite a substantial amount of empirical research analyzing stock market behavior, most of the studies concentrate on a few major developed stock markets. There has hardly been any comparable research work devoted to the newly industrial countries such as Taiwan, Hong-Kong, South Korea, and Singapore. In this chapter we present an integrated model using recently developed time series techniques to analyze behavior in these Asian stock markets.

Built on the well-established empirical evidence derived from the advanced countries, it is important to highlight the features of international interacting and time-varying volatility. Thus, in modeling national stock behavior, the return equation is assumed to be explained by its own lags, the cross correlation term, and possibly an error correction term; while the variance equation is assumed to follow a bivariate GARCH (1,1) process.

DATA AND TIME SERIES PROPERTIES

Data

In this chapter, we employ daily data for the period from January 4, 1988, through January 15, 1997. The stock market indices are for Taiwan, Hong Kong, South Korea, Singapore, Japan, and the United States. The stock returns are defined as the natural log-difference of daily stock prices. All of the indices are expressed in U.S. dollar values and are obtained from Morgan Stanley Capital International.

Autocorrelation and Cross Correlation

To obtain some basic information in relation to the time series properties for each stock return variable, R_t^i (superscript i refers to the indices for Taiwan, Hong Kong, South Korea, and Singapore), we calculate the autocorrelation function (ACF) for each market with 10-day lags and cross correlation, respectively, of the stock returns with Japan, R_t^{JP}, and the United States, R_t^{US}, from 5-day leads through 5-days lags. The estimated statistics of the autocorrelation function (not reported) were found to be significant for Taiwan, Singapore, and Japan in lag one; while Hong Kong, Korea, and the United States did not show any statistical significance in the first two orders.

We also investigated the statistics of the cross-correlation functions. The evidence (not reported) shows that all of the stock returns, R_t^i, are contemporaneously correlated with the Japanese market, R_t^{JP}, without having any time lag.

However, with respect to their correlations with the U.S. market, the effect is dominated by a one-day lag, although some of the coefficients in the current day are also significant.

Unit Root and Cointegration Tests

It is generally recognized that a precondition for applying the two-step procedure estimating error correction model (ECM) is that all the time series variables in the cointegrating equation are nonstationary and must be of the same order of integration. Thus, each national stock index involved in the cointegrating equations is tested for first-order integration employing univariate Dickey-Fuller (DF) and Augmented Dickey-Fuller (ADF) tests. The null hypothesis is that the variable under investigation has a unit root, against the alternative that it does not. The test statistics (not reported) show that the null hypothesis of a unit-root for the price levels cannot be rejected at the 5% level, indicating that in general the levels of the stock prices are nonstationary.[2] However, the null is strongly rejected for the first difference on the price levels, suggesting that the differenced series, the return series, are themselves stationary.

In addition, unit-root tests were performed on the residuals of the equations for each market cointegrating with either Japan or the United States. The evidence shows that the hypothesis of nonstationarity is rejected, especially in the case of cointegrating with the Japanese market. That is, the residuals, $u_t s$, are I(0), suggesting that the markets for Taiwan and Korea are likely to cointegrate with that of Japan.[3]

To inquire into the nature of cointegration, it is of importance to test for the presence of a common growth factor among stock prices. Thus, an analysis of common stochastic trends is performed employing the multivariate model developed by Johansen (1988, 1991) and Johansen and Juselius (1990). A multiple-dimensional vector autoregressive model with Gaussian errors can be expressed by:

$$X_t = A_1 X_{t-1} + A_2 X_{t-2} + \cdots + A_k X_{t-k} + \varepsilon_t, \qquad t = 1, 2, \ldots, T. \tag{1}$$

where $X_t = [R_t^i, R_t^j]$ and ε_t is IID N $(0, \Sigma)$; the index i refers to the stock returns for Taiwan, Hong Kong, Korea, or Singapore; the index j refers to the stock returns for Japan or the United States. By taking first differencing on the vector level, we write the model in error correction form as:

$$\Delta X_t = \Gamma_1 \Delta X_{t-1} + \Gamma_2 \Delta X_{t-2} + \cdots + \Gamma_{k-1} \Delta X_{t-k+1} - \Psi X_{t-k} + \varepsilon_t \tag{2}$$

where $\Psi = I - A_1 - A_2 - \ldots - A_k$. This Ψ matrix conveys information about the long-run relationship between the X variables (R_t^i and R_t^j) and the rank of Ψ is the number of linearly independent and stationary linear combinations of R_t^i and R_t^j. Thus, testing for cointegration involves testing for the rank of the Ψ matrix, r, by examining whether the eigenvalues of Ψ are significantly different from zero.

Johansen (1988, 1991) and Johansen and Juselius (1990) propose two statistics for testing the number of cointegrating vectors: the trace (λ_{trace}) and maximum eigenvalue (λ_{max}) statistics. The results of Johansen's multivariate cointegration tests for stock returns are reported in Table 18.1.[4] Both the trace test and the maximum eigenvalue test produce similar results. As presented in Panel C, the four-dimensional cointegration tests for stock prices—Taiwan, Hong Kong, Korea, and Singapore—indicate that the null for no cointegration is rejected. Yet, when the Japan market was added to the system, the five-dimensional cointegration tests in Panel B suggest that there are at least two cointegrating vectors. If we replace Japan with the United States (Panel D), there is only one common cointegrating vector. Therefore, the Japanese market appears more significant than the United States in influencing Asian markets.

We also conducted bivariate cointegration tests for each Asian country with Japan and the United States. The test results (not reported) indicate that the null hypothesis of no cointegrating vector ($r = 0$) with Japan is rejected at the 5% level for Taiwan and around 10% level for Korea. However, the results with the U.S. market show that the null can only be rejected at the 10% level for Taiwan, while Hong Kong and Korea are marginally significant around the 10% level. Thus, our evidence suggests that there is one common cointegrating vector with Japan in the cases of Taiwan and Korea, but the cointegrating relationship with the United States is relatively weak. The testing results present very little evidence in favor of the cointegration of Singapore and Hong Kong with either Japan or the United States.

Our tests conclusively show that the stock markets for Taiwan and Korea are cointegrated with Japan, and perhaps with the United States in a moderate degree.[5] This suggests that these markets have a meaningful equilibrium relationship such that stock prices do not tend to move too far away from each other.

THE STOCK RETURNS IN AN ERROR CORRECTION REPRESENTATION

Having exploited the time series properties, we write the stock return process as follows:

$$R_t^i = \beta' Z_{t-1}^i + \varepsilon_t^i, \tag{3}$$

$$h_t^i = h_0^i + A(L) \ \varepsilon_t^i \varepsilon_t^i + B(L) \ h_t^i, \tag{4}$$

where R_t^i is the daily stock return for market index i (i applies to Taiwan, Hong Kong, Korea, and Singapore), ε_t^i is an error term from the return equation, $h_t^i = \mathrm{E}$ ($\varepsilon_t^i \varepsilon_t^i$) is a conditional variance, and L is the lagged operator.[6] Equation (3) states that the stock return is a linear function of information set defined by Z_{t-1}^i. The evidence from the studies of the advanced countries suggests that market returns depend on a set of information variables, Z_{t-1}^i, such as dividend yields, interest rates (term structure relationships), and risk factors (Glosten et al., 1993; Longin and Solnik, 1995).

Table 18.1. Multivariate Cointegration for Stock Indices Using the Johansen Procedures

Panel A – All Countries (U.S., Japan, Taiwan, Korea, Hong Kong, and Singapore)

H_0	Trace Tests	Trace (0.95)	Trace (0.90)	H_0	λmax Tests	λmax (0.95)	λmax (0.90)
$r = 0$	105.13**	102.14	97.18	$r = 0$	33.95	40.30	37.45
$r \le 1$	71.1	76.07	71.86	$r = 1$	30.86	34.40	31.66
$r \le 2$	40.32	53.12	49.65	$r = 2$	19.80	28.14	25.56
$r \le 3$	20.52	34.91	49.65	$r = 3$	12.45	22.00	19.77
$r \le 4$	8.06	19.96	17.85	$r = 4$	5.90	15.67	13.75
$r \le 5$	2.16	9.24	7.52	$r = 5$	2.16	9.24	7.52

Panel B – Asian Countries (Japan, Taiwan, Korea, Hong Kong, and Singapore)

H_0	Trace Tests	Trace (0.95)	Trace (0.90)	H_0	λmax Tests	λmax (0.95)	λmax (0.90)
$r = 0$	81.71**	76.07	71.86	$r = 0$	33.37*	34.40	31.66
$r \le 1$	48.34	53.12	49.65	$r = 1$	29.18**	28.14	25.56
$r \le 2$	19.16	34.91	49.65	$r = 2$	9.26	22.00	19.77
$r \le 3$	9.90	19.96	17.85	$r = 3$	5.46	15.67	13.75
$r \le 4$	4.44	9.24	7.52	$r = 4$	4.44	9.24	7.52

Panel C – Asian Countries except Japan (Taiwan, Korea, Hong Kong, and Singapore)

H_0	Trace Tests	Trace (0.95)	Trace (0.90)	H_0	λmax Tests	λmax (0.95)	λmax (0.90)
$r = 0$	51.38*	53.12	49.65	$r = 0$	31.93**	28.14	25.56
$r \le 1$	19.45	34.91	49.65	$r = 1$	10.87	22.00	19.77
$r \le 2$	8.59	19.96	17.85	$r = 2$	4.70	15.67	13.75
$r \le 3$	3.89	9.24	7.52	$r = 3$	3.89	9.24	7.52

Panel D – Asian Countries except Japan with the U.S. (U.S., Taiwan, Korea, Hong Kong, and Singapore)

H_0	Trace Tests	Trace (0.95)	Trace (0.90)	H_0	λmax Tests	λmax (0.95)	λmax (0.90)
$r = 0$	71.14	76.07	71.86	$r = 0$	32.69*	34.40	31.66
$r \le 1$	38.45	53.12	49.65	$r = 1$	19.98	28.14	25.56
$r \le 2$	18.47	34.91	49.65	$r = 2$	8.82	22.00	19.77
$r \le 3$	9.64	19.96	17.85	$r = 3$	7.50	15.67	13.75
$r \le 4$	2.14	9.24	7.52	$r = 4$	2.14	9.24	7.52

Note: * and ** indicate statistical significance at the 10% and 5% levels, respectively. Trace (0.95) and Trace (0.90) are the critical values for trace statistics at 5% and 10% significance levels, respectively. λmax (0.95) and λmax (0.90) are the critical values for λmax statistics at the 5% and 10% significance levels, respectively. The critical values are taken from Osterwald-Lenum (1992).

Since daily observations for these variables are not readily available from the markets under investigation, we instead specify that Z^i_{t-1} consists of the information derived from time series patterns, cross-correlation with other stock return series, and the element of dynamic adjustment implied by the cointegrated markets. Specifically, we define that Z^i_{t-1}: $\{R^i_{t-p}, R^j_{t-k}, u^{i-j}_{t-1}, h^i_t\}$, where R^i_{t-p} is the autocorrelation term for stock market i in pth order; R^j_{t-k} captures the cross-correlation with the stock returns from market j with the kth order (j applies to Japan or the United States); u^{i-j}_{t-1} is an error correction term between indices i and j.

The variance equation in (4) is assumed to follow a finite GARCH process. Notice that in a standard GARCH-M model, a conditional variance term is usually treated as an independent argument included in the return equation. The idea behind this is to capture the traditional two-parameter asset pricing models by relating the means to the variances (or standard deviations). Since the experience from finance literature suggests that the GARCH (1,1) is sufficient to describe the conditional volatility (Bollerslev et al., 1992) and our empirical experiment also indicated that the conditional variance variable produces statistical insignificance, the variance equation seems reasonably to be specified in a GARCH (1,1) process.

A drawback of the univariate GARCH (1,1) process such as equation (4) is that the model fails to take into account the information of covariance between national stock returns. In their recent research chapter, Longin and Solnik (1995) showed that the correlation matrix of international asset return provides useful information in forming an optimal international portfolio. Moreover, the knowledge of covariance between national stock markets can be employed as an important input in formulating international investment strategy. To highlight this feature, the stock return equations in the next section will be estimated jointly with a vector GARCH (1,1) process.

THE ESTIMATIONS OF STOCK RETURNS USING MULTI-VARIATE CONDITIONAL VARIANCE-COVARIANCE MODEL

Using the methodology similar to Engel and Rodrigues (1989) and Chan et al. (1992), we write a time-varying conditional covariance model as follows:

$$R^i_t = \beta_0 + \beta_1 R^i_{t-1} + \beta_2 R^{JP}_t + \beta_3 u^{i-JP}_{t-1} + \varepsilon^i_t, \tag{5}$$

$$R^{JP}_t = \gamma_0 + \gamma_1 R^{JP}_{t-1} + \gamma_2 R^{US}_t + \gamma_3 R^{US}_{t-1} + \gamma_4 u^{JP-US}_{t-1} + \varepsilon^{JP}_t, \tag{6}$$

$$h^i_t = h^i_0 + d_1 \varepsilon^i_{t-1} \varepsilon^i_{t-1} + d_2 h^i_{t-1}, \tag{7}$$

$$h^{JP}_t = h^{JP}_0 + e_1 \varepsilon^{JP}_{t-1} \varepsilon^{JP}_{t-1} + e_2 h^{JP}_{t-1}, \tag{8}$$

$$h^{i,JP}_t = h^{i,JP}_0 + f_1 \varepsilon^i_{t-1} \varepsilon^{JP}_{t-1} + f_2 h^{i,JP}_{t-1}. \tag{9}$$

(5) and (6) are return equations, (7) and (8) are variance equations, while

equation (9) is a covariance equation. Our earlier empirical evidence suggests that the national market "*i*" in equation (5) is co-integrated with the Japanese market, and that in equation (6) the Japanese market is cointegrated with the U.S. market. The orders of autocorrelation and cross-return in the return equation for market *i* and Japan are based on the statistical significance of autocorrelation and cross-correlation functions. To be specific, the autocorrelation function displays an AR (1) model for Taiwan, Singapore, Hong Kong, and Japan, while South Korea follows a random walk process. As far as the cross-correlation function is concerned, we found that all of the newly industrial Asian markets are contemporaneously correlated with Japan, while the coefficients are significantly correlated with the U.S. market on the following day.

The error correction term is denoted by u_{t-1}^{i-JP} in equation (5) and by u_{t-1}^{JP-US} in equation (6), respectively. According to the error correction theory, the sign for these two error correction terms should be negative. This variable measures to some extent the divergence of the two national stock prices, which then can be used to predict the subsequent stock price changes.[7]

Next, equations (7) and (8) are conditional variance for market "*i*" and Japan, respectively, while equation (9) is the conditional covariance between markets "*i*" and Japan. The covariance term in (9) is assumed to be a function of the product of past innovations and covariance.

Ideally, the system in equations (5) through (9) should be estimated in a multivariate GARCH (1,1) fashion. However, since the estimations would consist of six markets and involve many mean and variance equations, and the resulting large numbers of parameters would make the iteration process very tedious. For this practical reason, the model has been estimated on the bivariate GARCH (1,1) process. That is, the estimations were conducted based on Japan and an "Asian" market.

THE EMPIRICAL RESULTS

The estimated results of the return equations are reported in Table 18.2. The evidence in Panel A shows that, with the exception of the Korean market, the return equations follow an AR (1) process and the estimated coefficients for the AR terms are statistically significant. The correlation with the Japanese market is significant at the current period, suggesting that Japanese stock returns play a major role in dictating stock price changes toward each Asian market. Consistent with the theoretical anticipation, the error correction terms for Asian markets uniformly display a negative sign. The evidence shows that the error correction terms based on an equilibrium condition with the Japanese market are statistically significant for Taiwan, Korea, Hong Kong, and Singapore. This means that the state of disequilibrium between the two national stock price indices tends to be corrected in the subsequent trading day. Thus, the error-correcting term reflecting the deviation of a national stock price from the Japanese price can be used to predict price changes on the following day.

Table 18.2. Estimation of National Stock Returns Cointegrated with the Japanese Market

Country	Taiwan	Hong Kong	Korea	Singapore
A. Return Equation for National Stock Returns				
Constant	0.114***	0.099***	0.013	0.033
	(2.95)	(3.84)	(0.46)	(1.37)
R^i_{t-1}	0.046**	0.123***		0.105***
	(2.08)	(7.26)		(5.20)
R^{JP}_t	0.180***	0.329***	0.171***	1.119***
	(4.49)	(24.44)	(4.11)	(11.52)
$u^{i\text{-}JP}_{t-1}$	-0.799***	-0.079**	-0.769***	-0.145**
	(6.17)	(2.36)	(3.97)	(3.30)
B. Return Equation for the Japanese Stock Returns				
Constant	0.033	-0.013	0.032	0.015
	(1.51)	(0.61)	(0.46)	(0.68)
R^{JP}_{t-1}	0.083***	0.049**	0.080***	0.002
	(3.70)	(2.60)	(3.89)	(0.12)
R^{US}_t	0.028	0.069***	0.039*	0.030**
	(1.36)	(3.29)	(1.91)	(2.08)
R^{US}_{t-1}	0.237***	0.364***	0.231***	0.252***
	(8.08)	(14.34)	(8.01)	(9.31)
$u^{JP\text{-}US}_{t-1}$	-0.403***	-0.153	-0.386***	-0.039
	(3.45)	(1.31)	(3.33)	(0.43)

Notes: The estimated equations are: $R^i_t = \beta_0 + \beta_1 R^i_{t-1} + \beta_2 R^{JP}_t - \beta_3 u^{i\text{-}JP}_{t-1} + \varepsilon^i_t$ and

$$R^{JP}_t = \beta_0 + \beta_1 R^{JP}_{t-1} + \beta_2 R^{US}_t + \beta_3 R^{US}_{t-1} - \beta_4 u^{JP\text{-}US}_{t-1} + \varepsilon^{JP}_t$$

***, **, and * indicate statistically significant difference from zero at the 1% (=2.62), 5% (=1.98), and 10% (=1.65) levels for the t-ratios. The critical value for $\chi^2(10)$ is 18.31 at the 5 levels for the $Q^2(10)$ test.
The numbers in the parentheses are the absolute values of the *t*-statistics.

Panel B gives the results of the estimation of the Japanese market based on the U.S./Japan relationship. The evidence from Panel B reveals that the parameters appear more significant and stable when the Japanese market is estimated jointly with the Taiwan or Korean market, but the error-correcting terms are not significant when the estimations are made jointly with Hong Kong or with Singapore. The evidence shows that the Japanese market is positively and significantly correlated with the U.S. market, especially with a one-day lag caused by different time zones in relation to different trading days.

Table 18.3 gives the estimated results of the variance-covariance equations. The estimated results strongly indicate that the stock return series for the Asian markets have been experiencing nonconstant variance. All of the coefficients in

Table 18.3. Variance and Covariance Equations in a Bivariate GARCH Process

Country	Taiwan	Hong Kong	Korea	Singapore
A. Variance Equation for National Stock Returns				
h_0^i	0.233***	0.428***	0.147***	0.223***
	(8.69)	(27.14)	(7.15)	(7.18)
$\varepsilon_{t-1}^i \varepsilon_{t-1}^i$	0.092***	0.363***	0.102***	0.120***
	(8.78)	(17.64)	(9.61)	(12.16)
h_{t-1}^i	0.852***	0.349***	0.833***	0.775***
	(62.17)	(30.86)	(57.53)	(46.34)
B. Variance Equation for the Japanese Stock Returns				
h_0^{JP}	1.260***	0.067***	0.079***	0.160***
	(7.09)	(8.52)	(10.00)	(12.46)
$\varepsilon_{t-1}^{JP} \varepsilon_{t-1}^{JP}$	0.071***	0.096***	0.138***	0.139***
	(6.49)	(12.71)	(12.37)	(17.27
h_{t-1}^{JP}	0.237**	0.859***	0.821***	0.763***
	(2.49)	(82.08)	(71.49)	(64.52)
C. Covariance Equation between National and Japanese Stock Returns				
$h_0^{i\,JP}$	-0.004	-0.156***	-0.004	-0.146***
	(1.20)	(12.47)	(1.30)	(7.41)
$\varepsilon_{t-1}^i \varepsilon_{t-1}^{JP}$	0.009	-0.028**	0.013**	0.125***
	(1.61)	(2.19)	(2.15)	(15.52)
$h_{t-1}^{i\,JP}$	0.967***	0.537***	0.966***	0.778***
	(46.17)	(13.51)	(57.57)	(59.43)

Notes: The estimated equations are: $h_t^i = h_0^i + d_1 \varepsilon_{t-1}^i \varepsilon_{t-1}^i + d_2 h_{t-1}^i$,

$$h_t^{JP} = h_0^{JP} + e_1 \varepsilon_{t-1}^{JP} \varepsilon_{t-1}^{JP} + e_2 h_{t-1}^{JP},$$

$$h_t^{i\,JP} = h_0^{i\,JP} + f_1 \varepsilon_{t-1}^i \varepsilon_{t-1}^{JP} + f_2 h_{t-1}^{i\,JP}.$$

***, **, and * indicate statistically significant difference from zero at the 1% (=2.62), 5% (=1.98), and 10% (=1.65) levels for the t-ratios. The critical value for $\chi^2(10)$ is 18.31 at the 5 levels for the $Q^2(10)$ test.
The numbers in the parentheses are the absolute values of the *t*-statistics.

Panels A and B show significant GARCH (1,1) effects for all countries. Interestingly, the conditional covariances in Panel C, with one exception in the case of Taiwan, are found to be significantly explained by the cross-product of past shocks and covariance, indicating that the covariances are time varying. This evidence is consistent with the findings by Engel and Rodrigues (1989) in that the time-varying conditional variance-covariance process should be more explicitly built into international asset pricing models.

Further analysis involved placing a conditional variance or conditional covariance term on the right side of the return equations. However, when significance tests were conducted on the coefficients of the conditional mean and conditional covariance, the null could never be rejected at the conventional significance levels. Our study concludes that the model represented by equations (5) through (9) is more consistent with the data than the vector GARCH (1,1) in mean or the standard univariate GARCH (1,1) model.

CONCLUSION

In this chapter we employ time series techniques to analyze behavior in various Asian stock markets. This chapter explores three important aspects that have not been investigated simultaneously in previous research. First, cointegration tests indicate that stock price movements for the four markets examined have a much closer relationship with the Japanese market than with the U.S. market. Thus, the signal derived from the Japanese market may carry information pertinent to the U.S. market.

Second, both the levels and the differences of the stock prices are incorporated explicitly into the model. It follows that the stock return equations contain not only short-run dynamics, but also information regarding the long-run equilibrium relationship with the Japanese market. Thus, Japanese stock price movements provide important information to predict other Asian market movements.

Third, the model has been estimated in the framework of a bivariate GARCH (1,1) process. The results derived from this chapter indicate that both variance and covariance terms are time-varying. This suggests that, in pricing international assets, the conditional variance-covariance process should be explicitly built into the model in order to account for the time-varying risk.

NOTES

1. The conflict sign for the relationship between return and risk does not seem to be consistent with standard portfolio theory. This is reconciled by arguing that the investor may want to save more in the current period against the uncertainty of the future. As a result, a lower risk premium is demanded.

2. The test results will be available upon request.

3. This means that the series for Taiwan and Korea are in agreement with an error correction suggested by Engle and Granger (1987).

4. The results reported in Table 18.1 are based on the fifth-order lag in the Johansen test.

5. Due to lack of daily risk-free asset returns in these markets, which prevented us from using excess return variable in the return equation (Baillie and DeGennaro, 1990; Kim and Kon, 1994; Choudhry, 1996).

6. The error term may be specified as an MA (1) process to capture the effect of non-synchronous trading (Ballie and DeGennaro, 1990).

7. In our estimation, we shall follow the two-step procedure outlined by Engle and Granger (1987). The reason for using a two-step approach rather than a Vector Autoregressive (VAR) model is due to the difficulty that a uniform order of lag is required for VAR specification. This may not be consistent with the dynamic structure associated with a particular country.

REFERENCES

Baillie, Richard and Ramon DeGennaro, 1990. Stock returns and volatility, *Journal of Financial and Quantitative Analysis* 25, 203-214.

Bollerslev, Tim, 1986. Generalized autoregressive conditional heteroskedasticity, *Journal of Econometrics* 31, 307-327.

Bollerslev, Tim, Ray Chou, and Kenneth Kroner, 1992. Arch modeling in finance: a review of the theory and empirical evidence, *Journal of Econometrics* 52, 5-59.

Chan, K.C., A.G. Karolyi, and R. Stulz, 1992. Global financial markets and the risk premium on U.S. equity, *Journal of Financial Economics* 32, 137-169.

Chiang, Thomas C. and Jeanette J. Chiang, 1996. Dynamic analysis of stock return volatility in an integrated international capital market, *Review of Quantitative Finance and Accounting* 6, 5-17.

Choudhry, Taufiq, 1996. Stock market volatility and the crash of 1987: evidence from six emerging markets, *Journal of International Money and Finance* 15, 969-981.

Dickey, David A. and Wayne A. Fuller, 1979. Distribution of the estimators for autoregressive time series with a unit root, *Journal of the American Statistical Association* 74, 427-431.

Dickey, David A. and Wayne A. Fuller, 1981. Likelihood ratio statistics for autoregressive time series with a unit root, *Econometrica* 49, 1057-1072.

Engel, C. and A.P. Rodrigues, 1989. Test of international CAPM with time-varying covariances, *Journal of Applied Econometrics* 4, 119-138.

Engle, Robert F. and Cliff W.J. Granger, 1987. Co-integration and error correction: representation, estimation, and testing, *Econometrica* 55, 251-276.

Eun, C.S. and S. Shim, 1989. International transmission of stock market movements, *Journal of Financial and Quantitative Analysis* 24, 241-256.

French, Kenneth, G. William Schwert, and Robert Stambaugh, 1987. Expected stock returns and volatility, *Journal of Financial Economics* 19, 3-29.

Fuller, Wayne A., 1976. *An Introduction to Statistical Time Series.* New York: John Wiley.

Glosten, Lawrence, Ravi Jagannathan, and David Runkle, 1993. On the relation between the expected value and the volatility of the nominal excess return on stocks, *Journal of Finance* 48, 1779-1801.

Hamao, Y., R. Masulis, and V. Ng, 1989. Correlations in price changes and volatility across international stock markets, *Review of Financial Studies* 3(2), 381-3307.

Jeon, Bang Nam and Thomas C. Chiang, 1991. A system of stock prices in world stock exchanges: common stochastic trends for 1975-1990? *Journal of Economics and Business* 43, 329-338.

Johansen, Soren, 1988. Statistical analysis of cointegration vectors, *Journal of Economic Dynamics and Control* 12, 231-254.

Johansen, Soren and Katarina Juselius, 1990. Maximum likelihood estimation and inference on cointegration–with applications to the demand for money, *Oxford Bulletin of Economics and Statistics* 52 (2), 169-210.

Johansen, Soren, 1991. Estimation and hypothesis testing of cointegration vectors in Gaussian vector autoregressive models, *Econometrica* 59 (6), 1551-1580.

Kasa, Kenneth, 1992. Common stochastic trends in international stock markets, *Journal of Monetary Economics* 29, 95-124.

Kim, Dongcheol and Stanley Kon, 1994. Alternative models for the conditional heteroscedasticity of stock returns, *Journal of Business* 67, 563-598.

King, M.A. and S. Wadhwani, 1990. Transmission of volatility between stock markets, *The Review of Financial Studies* 3, 5-33.

Koutmos, Gregory and G. Geoffrey Booth, 1995. Asymmetric volatility transmission in international stock markets, *Journal of International Money and Finance* 14, 747-762.

Lee, Sang and Ki Ohk, 1991. Time-varying volatilities and stock market returns: international evidence. In Ghon Rhee and Rosita Chang, eds. *Pacific-Basin Capital Markets Research*, Vol. II. Amsterdam: North-Holland.

Longin, Francois and Bruno Solnik, 1995. Is the correlation in international equity returns constant: 1960-1990? *Journal of International Money and Finance* 14, 3-26.

Osterwald-Lenum, Michael, 1992. A Note with quantiles of the asymptotic distribution of the maximum likelihood cointegration rank test statistics, *Oxford Bulletin of Economics and Statistics* 54, 461-471.

Roll, Richard, 1989. Price volatility, international market links, and their implications for regulatory policies, *Journal of Financial Services Research* 3, 113-246.

Schwert, G. William, 1989. Why does stock market volatility change over time? *Journal of Finance* 44, 1115-1153.

Theodossiou, P. and U. Lee, 1993. Mean and volatility spillovers between international equity markets: further empirical evidence, *Journal of Financial Research* 16, 337-350.

19

The Behavior of
Chinese Stock Markets

Dongwei Su

INTRODUCTION

The extraordinary expansion and rapid growth of the Chinese stock markets in the past six years have been accompanied by some difficulties. Problems include high initial public offering (IPO) underpricing, market segmentation, and high stock-market return volatility. This chapter deals with these problems.

This chapter will begin with an overview of Chinese stock markets with emphasis on the institutional details related to the above questions. Then the basic pattern of the risk and return behavior in Chinese stock markets will be laid out. A Generalized Autoregressive Conditional Heteroskedasticity (GARCH) model to examine the predictability of stock market returns when they exhibit temporal dependence and volatility clustering will be formulated and estimated. An intertemporal Capital Asset Pricing Model (ICAPM) will be used to explain the difference in prices and the variation of expected returns between classes of shares that can be bought by Chinese citizens and foreign investors, respectively. And existing theoretical analysis will be adopted to consider the peculiarities of the IPO process and to explain the extraordinarily high IPO underpricing that characterizes domestic Chinese stock markets.

OVERVIEW OF CHINESE STOCK MARKETS

Institutional Background

China's stock markets emerged in December 1990 when the Shanghai Securities Exchange was inaugurated, listing eight A-share stocks. A shares can be purchased and traded only by domestic investors. A second market, the Shenzhen Securities Exchange in the Special Economic Zone just north of Hong Kong, was inaugurated in April 1991, with six A-share stocks listed. Dual listing is not allowed across the two exchanges. Two nationwide trading systems, the Securities Trading Automated Quotations System (STAQS) and the National Electronic Trading System (NETS), were launched by a professional team of foreign trainees in April 1991. A stock market regulatory committee, the China Securities Regulatory Commission (CSRC), was established to supervise stock listing and trading activities.

The aggregate amount of new shares issued each year is determined by a quota set by the security regulatory authorities, namely—the State Planning Commission, the People's Bank of China (the central bank), and the CSRC. The quota is then distributed among individual provinces. The stated criteria used for allocation of new issues among provinces reflect the central security regulatory authorities' perceived regional development needs and provincial differences in production structure and industrial base.

When a firm is selected for going public, there are a number of steps it must take before its shares are listed and traded in the secondary markets. Some typical steps include: (1) publication of a prospectus in major newspapers and selection of underwriters; (2) setting the IPO price and choosing an offering mechanism; (3) purchasing of application forms by prospective investors; (4) conducting the IPO using the predetermined offering mechanism; (5) delivering of shares to lottery winners after payments are made.

A firm can issue five types of shares: (1) government shares, which are retained in the state institutions and government departments and are non-tradable; (2) legal entity shares, or C shares, which can only be held by other state-owned enterprises;[1] (3) employee shares, which are nontradable until the firm allows their convertibility; (4) ordinary domestic individual shares, or A shares, which can only be purchased and traded by private Chinese citizens in the two official exchanges in China; and (5) foreign individual shares, which can only be purchased and traded by the foreign investors in security exchanges in China (B shares), in Hong Kong (H shares), or on the New York Stock Exchange (NYSE) (N shares).

China's stock markets opened to international investors on February 21, 1992, when the Shanghai Vacuum Electronics began issuing B shares in the Shanghai Securities Exchange. This was quickly followed by the listing of China Southern Glass B shares in the Shenzhen Securities Exchange on February 28, 1992. For each company, A and B shares are entitled to the same rights and dividends. However, B shares are generally sold and traded at substantially lower prices than A shares (see Figure 19.1). The average daily discount of B shares relative to A shares prices over the period analyzed is 62.26%, with the spreads in Shenzhen only half of those in Shanghai. Discounts for H and N shares are equally persistent, but smaller.

The offering mechanism adopted by most Chinese firms going public is quite different from those observed in other countries. The offer price is typically chosen months before the market trading starts, and in the great majority of offerings there is no feedback mechanism through market demand that allows adjustment in the offer price.[2] The lottery mechanism, which remains the

Figure 19.1. Equal-Weighted Average Weekly Prices for A and B Shares

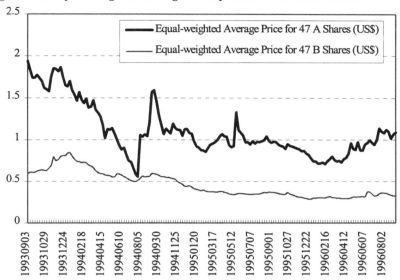

primary method of share allocation, has undergone several substantial changes. Before 1992, a lottery system based on a preannounced fixed number of application forms was used. Each retail investor was allowed to purchase a limited number of lottery forms. Lottery winners were entitled to a certain number of shares per winning form. In 1993 the security regulatory authorities introduced two new lottery mechanisms: One mechanism was based on an unlimited number of application forms. The other was based on savings deposit certificates. In 1994 two kinds of auction mechanisms were introduced. Under the first auction mechanism, an issuer set an initial price and investors were required to bid for the price and quantity. The final offer price was set at the level where the cumulative quantities demanded by investors equaled the total number of new shares available. Under the second auction mechanism, the IPO price was fixed and investors were invited to bid for the quantity of shares. In case of oversubscription, all investors were guaranteed a certain amount of shares and the remaining shares were distributed on a *pro rata* basis. Lottery mechanisms as described above remain as options, however, so firms can choose either a lottery method of distributing IPO shares or an auction mechanism. The proceeds from the lottery belong to the state banks that sell shares for the firms.

Risk and Return Behavior

Table 19.1 presents some sample distributional statistics (all in U.S. dollar terms) for A- and B-share indices for Shanghai and Shenzhen and stock-indices for Morgan Stanley Capital International (MSCI) world market, NYSE, and

Table 19.1. Distributional Characteristics of Chinese Stock Markets
and Other World Equity Markets Returns

	Shanghai A share	Shanghai B share	Shenzhen A share	Shenzhen B share	MSCI World	NYSE Index	Hong Kong Hang Seng
Daily retn	0.1%	0.023%	0.11%	0.06%	0.053%	0.041%	0.1%
Std. dev.	4.38%	1.18%	3.69%	2.06%	0.52%	0.45%	1.58%
Shape ratio	1.54%	-0.52%	2.1%	1.34%	6.73%	5.11%	5.19%
Minimum	-18.43%	-12.88%	-26.74%	-9.36%	-3.25%	-3.99%	-10.06%
Maximum	82.75%	12.59%	20.18%	15.44%	3.13%	6.58%	13.51%
Skewness	6.27*	0.8*	1.37*	1.69*	-0.156*	-0.313*	0.54*
Kurtosis	33.21*	8.97*	13.01*	21.69*	2.3*	3.86*	7.24*
Ljung-Box Q (12)	25.374*	83.016*	31.17*	90.5*	21.41†	21.456†	19.408
Weekly retn	0.513%	0.121%	0.522%	0.305%	0.262%	0.204%	0.485%
Std. dev.	10.69%	4.93%	7.57%	5.59%	1.18%	1.23%	3.34%
Shape ratio	3.28%	-0.83%	4.76%	2.56%	14.58%	9.27%	11.83%
Minimum	-20.7%	-14.09%	-29.07%	-17.37%	-2.79%	-3.81%	-9.62%
Maximum	113.04%	29.31%	57.43%	29.23%	3.43%	4.58%	10.63%
Skewness	5.96*	2.216*	2.36*	2.09*	-0.1467	-0.3467*	0.187*
Kurtosis	28.36*	10.89*	16.5*	10.1*	0.0538	1.2*	0.743*
Ljung-Box Q (12)	6.952	12.388†	14.6†	22.95*	10.82	13.7	15.91

*Statistically significant at the 5% level
†Statistically significant at the 10% level
Source: Su and Fleisher (1998a).

Hong Kong Stock Exchange. The daily market indices are based on value-weighted portfolios of securities and do not reflect dividends. Statistics include risk-unadjusted sample mean returns, Sharpe ratio, coefficients of skewness and kurtosis, and Ljung-Box portmanteau statistics.

I characterize the stock market return and volatility pattern as follows: (1) Mean returns for A shares in Shanghai and Shenzhen are higher than the U.S., Hong Kong, and MSCI world indices, but the standard deviations of returns are also higher. (2) Risk-adjusted mean excess returns (Sharpe ratios) are lower in Chinese stock markets. (3) Mean returns on B shares are lower than those on A shares, but the volatility of returns is also smaller. Risk-adjusted mean returns are lower for B shares. (4) The skewness parameters are significantly positive, indicating that the stock market returns are not symmetrically distributed. (5) Coefficients of kurtosis are generally higher in Chinese stock markets, suggesting that extreme return volatility exists in both exchanges. (6) Ljung-Box Q (12) statistics are highly significant, indicating that returns are positively autocorrelated to greater extent in Chinese stock markets than in developed markets.

I conclude that higher average returns are associated with larger exposure to risks in Chinese stock markets, which is consistent with traditional asset pricing theory and previous findings for other emerging markets by De Santis and İmrohoroğlu (1995) and Bekaert and Harvey (1997).

PREDICTABILITY OF STOCK MARKET RETURNS

Since there is strong evidence of time-varying volatility change in the stock-market returns in China, Su and Fleisher (1998a) formulate a GARCH (1,1) model that relates the time series of weekly stock market returns for A and B shares, $r_{j,t}$, to a set of local and global information variables ($Z_{j,t-1}$) in the conditional mean equation and formulate the conditional variance process using three error generation processes. The purpose of this specification is to examine whether shocks common to world financial markets have predictable influences on Chinese stock markets.

$$r_{j,t} = \delta'_j Z_{j,t-1} + \varepsilon_{j,t}, \tag{1}$$

$$\varepsilon_{j,t} = \sigma_{j,t} z_{j,t}, \tag{2}$$

$$z_{j,t} | \Omega_{t-1} \sim \phi(0,1,v), \tag{3}$$

$$\sigma^2_{j,t} = \omega_j + \alpha_j \sigma^2_{j,t-1} + \beta_j \varepsilon^2_{j,t-1}, \tag{4}$$

where $\sigma^2_{j,t}$ is the conditional variance,[3] $z_{j,t}$ is the standardized residual formed by dividing the residual, $\varepsilon_{j,t}$, by the standard deviation, $\sigma_{j,t}$, Ω_{t-1} is the set of information available at the beginning of time t, $\phi(\cdot)$ denotes a conditional density function, and v denotes a vector of parameters besides conditional mean and conditional variance that may be needed to fully characterize the probability distribution.

The following three error distributions are assumed:

- Normal distribution,

$$z_{j,t} | \Omega_{t-1} \sim N(0,1), \tag{5}$$

- Standardized distribution,

$$z_{j,t} | \Omega_{t-1} = \Gamma(\frac{v+1}{2}) \Gamma(v/2)^{-1} (v-2)^{-1/2}$$
$$\times (1 + z^2_{j,t} (v-2)^{-1})^{-(v+1)/2}, \qquad v > 2, \tag{6}$$

- Stable distribution,

$$\varepsilon_{j,t} = (\sigma^2_{j,t})^{1/v} z_{j,t}, \tag{7}$$

$$\log[E(e^{iXt})] = -|t|^v, \qquad (v \in (0,2)) \tag{8}$$

Local information variables include lagged market return ($r_{j,t-1}$), lagged change in the exchange rate between the Chinese yuan and U.S. dollar ($\Delta RMBUS_{t-1}$), lagged change in the exchange rate between the Hong Kong dollar and U.S. dollar ($\Delta HKUS_{t-1}$), and lagged change in weekly turnover rate ($\Delta TO_{j,t-1}$). World information variables include lagged MSCI world return in excess of the 30-day U.S. Treasury bill rate ($MSCI_{t-1}$), lagged Hong Kong Hang Seng return in excess of the 30-day U.S. T-bill rate (HS_{t-1}), lagged NYSE return in excess of the 30-day U.S. T-bill rate ($NYSE_{t-1}$), lagged change in term structure spread (TS_{t-1}, the yield on long-term U.S. government security minus the 30-day U.S. T-bill rate), and lagged change in the 30-day U.S. T-bill rate (ΔTB_{t-1}).

First, parameter estimates are obtained for the GARCH (1,1), TGARCH (1,1) and SGARCH (1,1) models with only local information variables in the conditional mean equation (1). In doing this, markets are treated as fully segmented in the sense that common shocks to world equity markets do not influence the stock market returns in China and there are no covariance dynamics. To test the hypothesis that global as well as local factors influence the conditional mean returns in Chinese stock markets, the GARCH (1,1), TGARCH (1,1) and SGARCH (1,1) models are reestimated with both local and world information variables in the conditional mean equation. The Constrained Maximum Likelihood (CMLE) application module with Sequential Quadratic Programming method is used to estimate these models. Both BFGS (Broyden, Fletcher, Goldfarb and Shanno) and NR (Newton and Raphson) algorithms have been implemented to obtain the maximum likelihood estimates. Through a battery of residual diagnosis tests, including the Ljung-Box Q-statistics and the likelihood ratio test statistics, Su and Fleisher (1998a) find that the SGARCH (1,1) model fits the data best. The parameter estimates for SGARCH (1,1) model are presented in Table 19.2.

Among the factors that influence the stock market returns in China, the coefficient for lagged one-week return is significant in all cases. This is probably due to nonsynchronization of trading and clearing and thinness of the market. The lagged change in the U.S. dollar-Hong Kong dollar exchange rate, the lagged MSCI, NYSE, and Hong Kong Hang Seng returns are significant in various cases, suggesting that stock market returns in China are correlated with international markets to varying degrees. However, the lagged market turnover rate and international interest rate changes do not seem to influence stock market returns in China. A likelihood ratio test fails to reject the null hypothesis that global information variables are jointly zero except for the Shanghai B-share market, where the null hypothesis is rejected at the 5% level of significance. This indicates that the degree of correlation among Chinese stock markets and international equity markets is weak.

Su and Fleisher (1998a) also test the hypothesis that the government's stock market liberalization policies adopted in May 1992 led to increased stock market volatility. They add a policy dummy variable in the SGARCH (1,1) formulation, so that the conditional variance equation become

$$\sigma^2_{j,t} = \omega_j + \eta_j P_{j,t} + \alpha_j \sigma^2_{j,t-1} + \beta_j \varepsilon^2_{j,t-1}, \tag{9}$$

where $P_{j,t}$ is a policy dummy variable,

Table 19.2. Maximum Likelihood Estimates of the SGARCH (1,1) Model

	Shanghai A Shares	Shanghai B Shares	Shenzhen A Shares	Shenzhen B Shares	Shanghai A Shares	Shanghai B Shares	Shenzhen A Shares	Shenzhen B Shares
Constant	-0.007	-0.005	-0.01	0.002	-0.004	-0.006	-0.007	-0.004
$r_{j,t-1}$	0.268*	0.191*	0.153*	0.242*	0.287*	0.202*	0.15*	0.291*
$\Delta RMBUS_{t-1}$	-0.012	-0.018	-0.036	-0.036	-0.013	-0.012	-0.037	-0.002
$\Delta HKUS_{t-1}$	0.342*	0.071	0.744*	0.32*	0.266	0.57	0.152	0.237
ΔTO_{t-1}	0.004	0.001	0.014	-0.001	0.006	-0.001	0.018	-0.002
$MSCI_{t-1}$	0.03	0.198	0.345*	-0.002				
HS_{t-1}	-0.06	-0.29*	0.094	0.087				
$NYSE_{t-1}$	-0.31*	-0.22	-0.35*	-0.074				
TS_{t-1}	0.433	-0.094	0.175	-0.239				
ΔTB_{t-1}	-5.937	0.03	-12.22	1.233				
$\hat{\omega}_j$	0.033*	0.004	0.011*	0.02*	0.018*	0.003	0.024*	0.017*
$\hat{\alpha}_j$	0.619*	0.552*	0.688*	0.732*	0.615*	0.318*	0.74*	0.743*
$\hat{\beta}_j$	0.121*	0.164*	0.169*	0.224*	0.107*	0.189*	0.214*	0.205*
v	1.506*	1.493*	1.7666*	1.567*	1.551*	1.54*	1.676*	1.58*
Mean log likelihood	1.322	1.828	1.311	1.887	1.309	1.769	1.296	1.845

$$r_{j,t} = \delta'_j Z_{j,t-1} + \varepsilon_{j,t} \qquad \varepsilon_{j,t} = (\sigma^2_{j,t})^{1/v} z_{j,t} \qquad \log[E\,(e^{i\lambda t})] = -|t|^v \qquad \sigma^2_{j,t} = \omega_j + \alpha_j\,\sigma^2_{j,t-1} + \beta_j\,\varepsilon^2_{j,t-1}$$

$z_{j,t-1}$ includes lagged one-week market return ($r_{j,t-1}$), lagged change in the exchange rate between Chinese yuan and U.S. dollar ($\Delta RMBUS_{t-1}$), lagged change in exchange rate between Hong Kong dollar and U.S. dollar ($\Delta HKUS_{t-1}$), lagged change in weekly turnover rate (ΔTO_{t-1}), lagged MSC world index return in excess of the 30-day U.S. Treasury Bill rate ($MSCI_{t-1}$), lagged Hong Kong Hang Seng index return in excess of the 30-day U.S. T-Bill rate (HS_{t-1}), lagged NYSE index return in excess of the 30-day U.S. T-Bill rate ($NYSE_{t-1}$), lagged change in term structure spread (TS_{t-1}) and lagged change in the 30-day U.S. T-Bill rate (ΔTB_{t-1}). *Denotes 5% level of significance according to the Wald Confidence Limits.

Source: Su and Fleisher (1998a).

$$P_{j,t} = \begin{cases} 0: \text{Before the removal of the 5\% daily price change limit.} \\ 1: \text{After the removal of the 5\% daily price change limit.} \end{cases}$$

The unconditional variance of $\varepsilon_{j,t}$ is equal to $\omega_j\,/\,1 - \alpha_j - \beta_j$ before the market liberalization policies were announced, and is equal to $\omega_j + \eta_j\,/\,1 - \alpha_j - \beta_j$ after the announcement. Su and Fleisher find that the null hypothesis $\hat{\eta}_j = 0$ can not be rejected at a reasonable level of significance for both Shanghai and Shenzhen A shares. They conclude that the stock market return volatility in China may have been increased by market liberalization.

OWNERSHIP RESTRICTIONS, MARKET SEGMENTATION, AND B SHARES DISCOUNTS

It is widely documented that ownership restrictions and market segmentation result in price differentials among classes of shares in many emerging stock markets. For example: Hietala (1989) studied investment restrictions in Finland;

Bailey and Jagtiani (1994) examined the effects of investment barriers in Thailand; Johnson (1995) studied the Swedish case; and Stulz and Wasserfallen (1995) investigated ownership restrictions and IPO price differentials for the Swiss case.

In China, foreign-owned shares are usually sold and traded at various discounts relative to A shares.[4] Su (1997) uses an Intertemporal Capital Asset Pricing Model to analyze the economic factors that determine domestic Chinese and foreign investors' portfolio choices under ownership restrictions to explain these discounts.

Assume that there are two countries in the world, the domestic country D and the foreign country F. Each domestic firm i ($i = 1,2, ..., N$) issues a single stock, but in two types of shares: A and B shares. Each foreign firm j ($j = 1,2, ..., M$) issues a single type of stock: C shares. A risk-free debt instrument exists in each country. Risk-free rates (r_D, r_F) are assumed to be time-invariant across countries. The following ownership restrictions exist in the world economy: (1) Domestic investors are prohibited from buying B and C shares. (2) Foreign investors are prohibited from buying A shares. (3) Investors in each country can not hold the other country's safe asset.

Assume that there is no arbitrage across A and B shares that would undermine these restrictions and that stock price follows a diffusion process with constant mean and variance. Then the stock price is log-normally distributed and the rate of return is

$$r_{h,i}(t) = \mu_{h,i}\, dt + \sigma_{h,i}\, dz_{h,i}(t), \tag{10}$$

where $r_{h,i}(t)$ is the rate of return for type h stock i, $\mu_{h,i}$ and $\sigma^2_{h,i}$ are the mean and variance of the stock returns and $dz_{h,i}(t)$ is a standard diffusion (Wiener) process.

A domestic composite consumer-investor maximizes her expected utility from wealth over an infinite horizon, such that

$$V(W^D,t) = \max_{\{C^D(t), w_{a,i}(t)\}} E_0 \left[\int_{t=0}^{\infty} e^{-\rho t}\, U(C^D,t)\, dt \right] \tag{11}$$

subject to

$$dW^D(t) = \sum_{i=1}^{N+1} w_{a,i}(t)\, W^D(t)\, dr_{a,i}(t) - C^D(t)\, dt. \tag{12}$$

Foreign composite consumers-investors also maximizes their expected utility from wealth over an infinite horizon,

$$V(W^F,t) = \max_{\{C^F(t), w_{b,i}(t),\, w_{c,j}(t)\}} E_0 \left[\int_{t=0}^{\infty} e^{-\rho t}\, U(C^F,t)\, dt \right] \tag{13}$$

subject to

$$dW^F(t) = \sum_{i=1}^{N+1} w_{b,i}(t) \ W^F(t) dr_{b,i}(t) + \sum_{j=1}^{M} w_{c,j}(t) \ W^F(t) dr_{c,j}(t) - C^F(t) dt, \qquad (14)$$

where ρ is the rate of pure time preference, $w_{h,i}$ (t) is the fraction of wealth invested in the type h stock i at time t, $W(t)$ is total wealth and $C(t)$ is consumption at time t.

Assume both domestic and foreign investors have state-independent isoelastic utility of consumption with constant relative risk aversion coefficients Γ_D and Γ_F, respectively,

$$U(C^D,t) = \frac{C^D(t)^{1-\Gamma_D}}{1-\Gamma_D}, \quad U(C^F,t) = \frac{C^F(t)^{1-\Gamma_F}}{1-\Gamma_F}.$$

The solution to the domestic investor's maximization problem yields:

$$\mu_{a,i} - r_D = \Gamma_D \frac{\sigma_{a,i,M}}{\sigma_{a,M}^2} \ \sigma_{a,M}^2 = \beta_{a,i,M}(\mu_{a,M} - r_D). \qquad (15)$$

The solution to the foreign investor's maximization problem yields:

$$\mu_{b,i} - r_F = \beta_{b,i,M\Gamma F}\sigma_{b,M}^2 + \beta_{b,i,c,M\Gamma F}\sigma_{c,M}^2. \qquad (16)$$

Combining equations (15) and (16) yields the following testable equation for the difference in expected excess return between A and B shares:

$$(\mu_{a,i} - r_D) - (\mu_{b,i} - r_F) = \beta_{a,i,M}(\mu_{a,M} - r_D) - \beta_{b,i,M\Gamma F}\sigma_{b,M}^2 - \beta_{b,i,c,M\Gamma F}\sigma_{c,M}^2. \qquad (17)$$

Equation (17) implies that the difference in the expected excess returns for the A and B shares is linear in a share's market risk factors as measured by its market betas. The lower the A-share market beta, the higher the B-share market beta, or the higher the beta of an individual B share against international financial market returns, the higher is the foreign investor's required B-share premium.

To test the ICAPM, equation (17), a traditional two-pass estimation methodology (Fama and MacBeth, 1973; Fama and French; 1992) is adopted, with a slight modification of the explanatory variables in the second pass. The data consist of 19 companies listed in Shanghai and 18 companies listed in Shenzhen that have issued both A and B shares and have been traded for at least two years. The Chinese yuan-U.S. dollar and Hong Kong dollar-U.S. dollar exchange rates are used to measure the pricing differences between A and B shares. Additional variables from international financial markets, such as the Hong Kong Hang Seng index, the MSCI world equity index, the NASDAQ index, the NYSE index, and the one-month U.S. Treasury bill returns are used to calculate individual B-share betas against international equity markets.

In the first pass, the beta estimates for each share are obtained from the following time-series regression,

$$r_{j,t} - r_{f,t} = \alpha_j + \beta_{1,j}(r_{1,M,t} - r_{f,t}) + v_{j,t}, \qquad (18)$$

where $r_{j,t}$ is the rate of return for stock j in week t, $r_{f,t}$ is the risk-free interest rate, $r_{l,M,t}$ is the rate of return for lth market index at time t, $\beta_{l,j}$ is the market beta for stock j with respect to type l market, and $v_{j,t}$ is the error term. Six beta estimates are computed for each company: $\beta_{j,A}$, $\beta_{j,B}$, $\beta_{j,NASDAQ}$, $\beta_{j,NYSE}$, $\beta_{j,MSCI}$, and $\beta_{j,HS}$.

In the second pass, the following cross-sectional regression is used to estimate equation (17):

$$\ln\left(1 + \frac{\overline{\Delta P_{a,j,t}}}{P_{a,j,t}}\right) - \ln\left(1 + \frac{\overline{\Delta P_{b,j,t}}}{P_{b,j,t}}\right) = \alpha_0 + \alpha_1 \hat{\beta}_{j,a,M} + \alpha_2 \hat{\beta}_{j,b,M} + \sum_{k=1}^{K} \alpha_k \hat{\beta}_{j,k,b,c,M} + \varepsilon_j \quad (19)$$

where the dependent variable is the difference in the logarithm of one plus the arithmic mean of stock returns between A and B shares.

Table 19.3 presents the parameter estimates associated with the risk factors from the cross-sectional OLS regressions. The results show that: (1) $\hat{\alpha}_1$ is significantly positive (regression iv). The higher the A-share market beta, the higher is the A-share average return; (2) $\hat{\alpha}_2$ is significantly negative. The higher the B-share market beta, the higher is the B-share average return; (3) $\hat{\alpha}_6$ is significantly negative. The higher the B-share beta with respect to the Hong Kong Hang Seng index, the smaller is the difference in average returns between A and B shares. (4) The constant terms are not significantly different from zero. (5) The coefficient estimates for $\hat{\beta}_{NYSE}, \hat{\beta}_{NASDAQ}$, and $\hat{\beta}_{MSCI}$ have the anticipated sign, but they are not significant.

Therefore, the cross-sectional results strongly support the ICAPM formulation. The cross-sectional spread between the A- and B-share expected returns is related to the difference in risk exposure of both shares. The higher the B-share risk exposure to the international financial markets, specifically to the Hong Kong stock market, the higher is the foreign investors' required risk compensation. Moreover, Su (1997) finds that after controlling for the market betas, the variance of returns and the firm size do not appear to affect the cross-sectional differences in expected excess returns.

THE UNDERPRICING OF IPOs

Su and Fleisher (1998b) document that the average degree of IPO underpricing in China, using a sample of 308 firm-commitment IPOs that went public before January 1, 1996, is 948.59% and the median is 231.25%. Define IPO initial return as $IPORETN = (P_1 - P_0) / P_0 \cong \ln P_1 - \ln P_0$. Su and Fleisher (1998b) consider the following three hypotheses: (1) The extraordinary large IPO underpricing in China can be explained by a signaling model in terms of a separating equilibrium under asymmetric information in which underpricing is a strategy for firms to signal their values to investors. (2) Underpricing in China is primarily explainable as a means of bribing public officials by the firms to gain favoritism. (3) Allocating IPO shares by lottery mechanism has been a cause of extreme underpricing. The variables used include:

Table 19.3. Cross-sectional Regression Using the Difference in Logarithm of Average Return as Dependent Variable

$$\ln\left(1 + \frac{\overline{\Delta P_{a,j,t}}}{P_{a,j,t}}\right) - \ln\left(1 + \frac{\overline{\Delta P_{b,j,t}}}{\Delta P_{b,j,t}}\right) = \alpha_0 + \alpha_1\hat{\beta}_{j,A} + \alpha_2\hat{\beta}_{j,B} + \alpha_3\hat{\beta}_{j,NYSE} + \alpha_4\hat{\beta}_{j,NASDAQ}$$

$$+ \alpha_5\hat{\beta}_{j,MSCI} + \alpha_6\hat{\beta}_{j,HS} + \alpha_7 D_j + \epsilon_j$$

where D_j is a location dummy variable,

$$D_j = \begin{cases} 0: \text{If firm } j \text{ is listed in Shanghai.} \\ 1: \text{If firm } j \text{ is listed in Shenzhen.} \end{cases}$$

	$\hat{\alpha}_0$	$\hat{\alpha}_1$	$\hat{\alpha}_2$	$\hat{\alpha}_3$
(i)‡	-0.00256	0.12881	-0.241778	-0.01422
	(-0.0166)	(0.8772)	(-3.0458)	(-0.3707)
(ii)	-0.01593	0.14085	-0.23118*	
	(-0.1067)	(0.9885)	(-2.7841)	
(iii)	-0.01133	0.12523	-0.20686*	
	(-0.0774)	(0.8988)	(-2.5436)	
(iv)	-0.09388	0.19516†	-0.17356*	
	(-0.7508	(1.6589)	(-2.5986)	
(v)	-0.0975	0.18836	-0.18783*	
	(-0.4532)	(1.592)	(-2.7175)	

	$\hat{\alpha}_4$	$\hat{\alpha}_5$	$\hat{\alpha}_6$	$\hat{\alpha}_7$	R^2
(i)					0.1212
(ii)	-0.01323				0.119
	(-0.1729)				
(iii)		-0.04707			0.1429
		(-1.1086)			
(iv)			-0.17593*		0.3844
			(-4.3102)		
(v)			-0.15721*	-0.03024	0.3802
			(-3.3749)	(-0.8433)	

‡Figures in parentheses are *t*-statistics.
*Statistically significant at the 5% level.
†Statistically significant at the 10% level.

$IPOSZ$ =	The monetary price of the portion of the firm initially offered to the investors, or the proceeds for IPO in U.S. dollars.
$PROFIT$ =	Past year's profit at the time of IPO in U.S. dollars.
AGE =	Age of the firm at the date of its IPO.
$TIMEIPO$ =	Number of days elapsed between the announcement of an IPO and the first-day market trading.
$MKTCAP$ =	The sum of IPO proceeds from A- and B-shares offerings, government shares, shares purchased by other state-owned enterprises, and proceeds from all seasoned equity offerings (SEOs) in U.S. dollars.
$AFTRETN1$ =	After-market return between the first day of trading and the end of the second week of trading.
$AFTRETN2$ =	After-market return between the beginning of the third week of trading and the end of the fourth week.
STD =	Standard deviation of after-market returns estimated over a 100-day period after inception of market trading.
EXD =	Stock exchange dummy, $EXD = 1$ for a company that is listed in Shanghai Securities Exchange, $EXD = 0$ for a company that is listed in Shenzhen Securities Exchange.
$\dfrac{IPOSZ}{MKTCAP}$ =	IPO proceeds as a fraction of firm's intrinsic value ($MKTCAP$ is used as a proxy for firm's intrinsic value).
$\dfrac{SEOSZ}{MKTCAP}$ =	Total SEO proceeds as a fraction of firm's intrinsic value.
$SIC(k)$ =	Six industry dummies: durable goods ($SIC1$); nondurable goods ($SIC2$); transportation and public utilities ($SIC3$); finance, insurance, and real estate ($SIC4$); services including restaurants, department stores, and hotels ($SIC5$); and domestic and foreign trade ($SIC6$).
$YEAR(t)$ =	IPO year dummies, $t = 1$ if a firm went public before January 1, 1991; $t = 2 \ldots 5$ for going public in the years 1992 through 1995.

Descriptive statistics for these variables are presented in Table 19.4. Note that in order to study the relationship between subsequent equity offerings and IPO underpricing, I also extract a subsample of firms that went public between December 1986 and June 1994. The June 1994 cutoff allows 548 days for a firm to issue SEOs.

THE SIGNALING HYPOTHESIS

I believe that the conditions for equilibrium underpricing exist in China, and that high underpricing is caused by basic problems derived from the microeconomic uncertainty and information asymmetry inherent in any stock market and probably especially pronounced in China.

Table 19.4. Descriptive Statistics for Variables to Explain IPO Initial Returns

Variable	Description	Mean	Median	Std. dev.	Minimum	Maximum
Full Sample of 308 Firm-commitment during 1987 and 1995						
IPORETN	IPO initial return	948.59%	231.25%	2967.7%	-18.58%	38300%
AFTRETN1	First two-week return after market trading starts	-2.6422%	-5.3967%	24.2801%	-92.6836%	170.3947%
AFTRETN2	Next two-week return after market trading starts	-2.7498%	-4.5075%	18.4111%	-91.7275%	94.4444%
IPOSZ	IPO proceeds (in million US$)	16.8289	11.988	22.5626	0.2892	249.3976
PROFIT	Past year's profit before IPO (in million US$)	466.5848	221.988	98.1307	2.7735	3788.269
lnAGE	Logarithm of firm's age	2.4849	2.7701	0.8929	0.6931	4.4773
STD	Standard deviation of first 100-day returns	5.8895%	4.7398%	5.1073%	0.6512%	51.2719%
MKTCAP	Firm's intrinsic value (in million US$)	161.2268	86.0064	237.4339	2.6145	1856.433
TIMEIPO	Time elapsed between offer and trade dates	260	135	341	3	1868
IPOSZ/MKTCAP	IPO proceeds as a Fraction of firm's value	15.02%	12.6%	11.22%	0.07%	81.25%
Subsample of 269 firm-commitment IPOs during January 1987 and June 1994						
IPORETN	IPO initial return	1043.1%	271.24%	3166.3%	-10%	38300%
AFTRETN1	First two-week return after market trading starts	-2.1446	-5.1389%	25.1854%	-92.6836%	170.3947%
AFTRETN2	Next two-week return after market trading starts	-3.7509%	-4.9375%	16.8386%	-91.7275%	69.3227%
IPOSZ	IPO proceeds (in million US$)	16.8937	11.653	23.6056	0.2892	249.3976
PROFIT	Past year's profit before IPO (in million US$)	430.6412	211.1253	83.6418	2.7735	3788.269
lnAGE	Logarithm of firm's age	2.7743	2.6391	0.9016	0.6931	4.4773
STD	Standard deviation of first 100-day returns	6.0078%	4.7356%	5.42%	0.6512%	51.2719%
MKTCAP	Firm's intrinsic value (in million US$)	160.0253	88.586	236.7245	2.6145	1856.433
TIMEIPO	Time elapsed between offer and trade dates	251	142	306	3	1831
SEOSZ/MKTCAP	Proceeds from all SEOs as a fraction of firm's value	49.93%	43.85%	28.95%	0	99.87%
TIMESEO	Time elapsed between first-day market trading and first SEO date	284	220	217	0	1217

Allen and Faulhaber (1989), Grinblatt and Hwang (1989), Welch (1989), and Chemmanur (1993) have proposed a class of signaling models of IPO underpricing in which issuers have more superior information than investors about the intrinsic value of the firms. In their models, an issuer maximizes the value of the firm through an IPO and subsequent SEOs. Because investors do not have complete information, in the absence of a signal, they can not distinguish between "high value" and "low value" firms. In a separating equilibrium, a "high value" issuer signals its quality by underpricing. It can afford to underprice its IPO because it expects to capture larger revenues through SEOs. In contrast, a "low value" issuer does not signal because it does not expect to recoup its investment in underpricing through after-market SEOs. The best a low-value issuer can do is to "take the money and run" when its stock is initially offered. When a separating equilibrium occurs, the average risk-adjusted IPO return over all new issues will be positive, the quantity of shares demanded for underpriced issues will exceed quantity supplied, and shares will be rationed by a mechanism other than the offer price.

There are three testable implications from the signaling models with a separating equilibrium: (i) The correlation between the degree of IPO underpricing and IPO proceeds is negative. (ii) There is an optimal signaling schedule relating the firm's intrinsic value, the degree of IPO underpricing, and relative IPO size. (iii) Issuers with a larger degree of IPO underpricing are more likely to return to the secondary market and offer larger amount of SEOs more quickly than issuers with lower IPO underpricing.

The alternative to a separating equilibrium is a pooling equilibrium where IPO prices are a weighted average of the present value of high-value and low-value issuers. When information is revealed after market trading starts, price differentiation occurs, but the first-day market price cannot be predicted from the IPO price and there is no risk-adjusted "excess" IPO initial return. In addition, in a pooling equilibrium, high-value firms do issue SEOs, but only in response to market-provided information about their value. If the after-market returns are high, then firms will issue seasoned equities. If they are low, then there are no seasoned issues. No equilibrium signaling schedule exists. This is the so-called Market Feedback Hypothesis.

Su and Fleisher (1998b) estimate the following regression using 2SLS to test empirical implication (i):

$$\ln IPORETN_i = \beta_0 + \beta_1 \ln I\hat{P}\hat{O}SZ_i \beta_2 (I\hat{P}\hat{O}SZ/MKTCAP)_i + \varepsilon_i \qquad (20)$$

where $I\hat{P}\hat{O}SZ$ and $I\hat{P}\hat{O}SZ/MKTCAP$ are fitted values from the first stage where $IPOSZ$ and $IPOSZ/MKTCAP$ are regressed against the exogenous variables $\ln AGE$, $\ln PROFIT$, EXD, $\ln TIMEIPO$, $SIC(k)$ and $YEAR(t)$ respectively.[5]

The estimation results reported in Table 19.5 show that: (1) holding constant the relative size of initial offerings, a 1% decline in the price of initial offering is associated with approximately a 0.8% increase in IPO initial return and that (2) a 1 percentage-point increase in relative IPO size is associated with a 11% decline in IPO return. Both coefficients are highly significant.

**Table 19.5. 2SLS Regression Estimates for the Correlation Between IPO
Underpricing and IPO Price**

Variable	Full Sample	Subsample
Constant	15.1907*	13.9522*
	(23.2712)	(20.1465)
ln $IP\hat{O}SZ$	-0.8612*	-0.7021*
	(-11.3981)	(-8.5542)
$\overline{R}^2$	0.5396	0.5469

The dependent variable is the logarithm of IPO initial return (ln *IPORETN*). The independent variables are the fitted values for the logarithm of IPO proceeds (ln *IPÔSZ*) and the relative size of IPO (ln *IPÔSZ/MKTCAP*), which are obtained by regressing ln *IPOSZ* and *IPOSZ/MKTCAP* on exogenous variables including ln *AGE*, ln *PROFIT*, ln *TIMEIPO*, stock-exchange dummy (*EXD*), industry dummies (*SIC(k)*), and IPO dummies (*YEAR(t)*). Figures in parentheses are *t*-statistics. *Denotes 5% level of significance.
Source: Su and Fleisher (1998b).

To test for the empirical implication (ii), Su and Fleisher (1997b) estimate the following regression using 2SLS:

$$\ln IPORETN_i = \beta_0 + \beta_1 \ln MK\hat{T}CAP_i + \beta_2 \ln IP\hat{O}SZ_i + \beta_3 S\hat{T}D_i + \varepsilon_i \qquad (21)$$

where $MK\hat{T}CAP$ and $S\hat{T}D$ are fitted values for variables representing firm's intrinsic value and standard deviation of returns over the first 100-day period of market trading from the first stage regression.

The estimation results reported in Table 19.6 show that: (1) holding constant the firm's intrinsic value and the project variance, a 1% decrease in the size of IPO is associated with approximately a 2% increase in IPO underpricing; (2) holding constant the size of IPO and the project variance, a 1% increase in the firm's intrinsic value is associated with approximately a 1% increase in the IPO underpricing; and (3) holding constant the firm's intrinsic value and the size of IPO, an increase of one standard eviation in the variation of future returns is associated with almost an 11% increase in IPO underpricing, which implies an elasticity of approximately 0.6 at the mean value of the regressor. All of the coefficients are statistically significant, at the 1% level or less.

To test for the empirical implication (iii), Su and Fleisher follow the spirit of Jegadeesh, Weinstein, and Welch (1993) and first estimate the following logit model,

$$\ln\left(\frac{P_i^{SEO}}{1 - P_i^{SEO}}\right) = 2.0242 + 0.001326\, IPORETN_i + 0.031597\, AFTRETN\, 1_i$$
$$\qquad\qquad (6.5531)\quad (2.1301) \qquad\qquad (2.1831)$$
$$\qquad + 0.014543\, AFTRETN2_i \qquad\qquad\qquad\qquad (22)$$
$$\qquad\quad (0.8885)$$

Table 19.6. 2SLS Regression Estimates for the Correlation Among IPO Underpricing and Issuer's Intrinsic Value, Fractional Ownership, and Project Variance

Variable	Full Sample	Subsample
Constant	-5.1423*	-6.2608*
	(-2.9377)	(-3.1859)
ln $IP\hat{O}SZ$	-1.8383*	-1.7676*
	(-19.9304)	(-17.411)
ln $MK\hat{T}CAP$	1.1406*	1.1646*
	(12.0549)	(10.9617)
$S\hat{T}D$	10.9575*	10.2704*
	(4.0374)	(3.7736)
$\bar{R}^2$	0.6216	0.5967

The dependent variable is the logarithm of IPO initial return (ln *IPORETN*). The independent variables are the fitted values for the logarithm of the size of initial offerings (ln *IPÔSZ*), the logarithm of firm's intrinsic value (ln*MKT̂CAP*), and the project variance (*ST̂D*), which are obtained by regressing ln *IPOSZ*, ln *MKTCAP*, and *STD* on exogenous variables including ln *AGE*, ln *PROFIT*, ln *TIMEIPO*, stock-exchange dummy (*EXD*), industry dummies (*SIC(k)*), and IPO dummies (*YEAR(t)*). Figures in parentheses are *t*-statistics. *Denotes 5% level of significance.
Source: Su and Fleisher (1998b).

where P_i^{SEO} is the probability that the *i*th issuer will issue subsequent equity offerings after the initial sale. Although the slope coefficients for *IPORETN* and *AFTRETN*1 are both significant at the 5% level, the explanatory power of the signaling hypothesis is greater than that of the market feedback hypothesis in the sense that a one standard-deviation increase in IPO return is associated with an increase in the magnitude of the probability of an SEO that is more than five times larger than is a one standard-deviation increase in after-market return over the first two weeks of market trading after the IPO.[6]

Su and Fleisher estimate the following tobit model to test the positive relationship between the degree of IPO underpricing and the size of seasoned equities:

$$
\left(\frac{SEOSZ}{MKTCAP} \right)_i = \begin{cases} 0.4312 + 0.0000309 IPORETN_i \\ (25.8477) \quad (6.127) \\ + 0.002015 AFTRETN1_i \\ (2.6024) \\ + 0.000483 AFTRETN2_i \\ (0.5501) \\ \\ 0 \end{cases} \quad \begin{matrix} \text{if RHS} > 0 \\ \\ \\ \\ \\ \text{otherwise} \end{matrix} \qquad (23)
$$

Again, both the coefficient estimates for *IPORETN* and *AFTRETN*1 are statistically significant. However, the signaling hypothesis has almost twice as much "strength" in explaining SEO relative magnitude than does the market-feedback hypothesis in that a one standard-deviation increase in IPO return and the first two weeks after market return are associated, respectively, with an increase in relative SEO size of 10% and 5.1%.

Su and Fleisher estimate the following tobit model to test the negative relationship between IPO underpricing and the time elapsed between the IPO and the first SEO:

$$
TIMESEO_i = \begin{cases} \begin{aligned} & 291.0871 - 0.00222 IPORETN_i \\ & (22.3196) \quad (-0.5245) \\ & + 1.0864 AFTRETN1_i \\ & (2.2203) \\ & + 0.7852 AFTRETN2_i \\ & (0.9593) \\ \\ & 0 \end{aligned} & \begin{aligned} & \text{if RHS} > 0 \\ \\ \\ \\ \\ & \text{otherwise} \end{aligned} \end{cases} \tag{24}
$$

The slope coefficient (*t*-statistic) for *IPORETN* is -0.00222 (-0.5245), indicating that firms with a higher degree of IPO underpricing tend to return to the secondary market and issue seasoned equity offerings more quickly than do firms with a lower degree of IPO underpricing and larger IPO sizes, although the estimated coefficient of IPO return is not significant at conventional levels. Moreover, the estimated coefficients (*t*-statistic) for *AFTRETN*1 and *AFTRETN*2 are 1.0864 (2.2203) and 0.7852 (0.9593), respectively, which appear to be contradictory to the market feedback hypothesis.

To summarize, there is strong evidence from the Chinese A-share data that supports the signaling models linking IPO underpricing to SEOs. Chinese issuers who underprice their A-share IPOs more heavily are more likely to return to the secondary market and issue larger amounts of after-market equities. The alternative—namely, the market feedback hypothesis—does not fare as well in explaining the high underpricing in the data, although it can not be rejected.

THE BRIBERY AND LOTTERY HYPOTHESES

Because underpriced IPO shares are valuable, issuers may be willing to allocate severely underpriced shares to politicians or bureaucrats who have substantial control over their activities and/or ability to obtain resources in short supply. However, under full information or a pooling equilibrium with asymmetric information among issuers and investors, underpricing IPOs as a means of bribery is much more costly to the issuers than simply transferring funds directly in order to gain favors. Su and Fleisher (1998b) present evidence pertaining to the price-depression effect under the bribery hypothesis. They find that compared to the first-day IPO return, the mean and median IPO under-pricing using first-, second-, third-, and fourth-week market closing prices remain approximately the same. They take this result as evidence that bribes (if they occurred) were not "cashed in" during the first four weeks of market trad-ing. Su and Fleisher also calculate various measurements of the average degree of IPO underpricing for 29 firms that went public before the emergence of formal stock markets when bribery might be fertile. However, they do not find evidence of a large after-market price drop for those issues either.

A team of World Bank specialists argued that offering mechanisms affected the degree of underpricing (World Bank, 1995, p. 96): "the allocation mechanism adopted for the new share issue affects the degree of underpricing. Non-discretionary allocation of shares, by mechanisms such as a lottery, exacer-bate the tendency to underprice."

I disagree with their assertion. It was hypothesized and empirically sup-ported that a lower offer price and smaller IPO size lead to higher IPO under-pricing, which implies an excess demand for shares. Some form of nonprice rationing is necessary to allocate the underpriced shares. Lottery mechanisms and auction mechanisms with only quantity bids are best viewed as simply a means to allocate oversubscribed shares and do not determine the after-market demand for shares and/or the initial supply of shares. Therefore, these mechan-isms themselves do not *cause* IPO underpricing. Auction mechanism with both price and quantity bids does create an offer price that is not predetermined by the issuing firm. Eighteen firms used auction mechanisms in issuing and allocat-ing new shares prior to January 1996. The average IPO underpricing is only 1.04% for these 18 issues. However, it is critically important to note that these firms *chose* the auction method when several lottery mechanisms were avail-able. With the choice of share-allocation mechanism endogenous, it would be difficult to conclude that the auction led to virtually zero underpricing. Rather, the opposite may be inferred—namely, that these firms chose not to signal their quality by underpricing and used the auction mechanism as a means to assure they received the largest possible revenue at the IPO, because they had little nor no intention of returning to the secondary market with SEOs unless they re-ceived a strong after-market signal that SEOs would be successful.

CONCLUSION

In this chapter, I have analyzed the behavior of the emerging Chinese stock markets in terms of (1) the predictability of stock market returns, (2) volatility of stock markets, (3) price differentials among classes of shares, and (4) under-pricing of IPOs. The major findings are:

1. The risk-adjusted mean stock market returns are low and the volatility of returns is high in China relative to developed markets. Moreover, returns are positively auto-correlated to a greater extent than in developed markets.

2. The stock market return volatility is leptokurtotic, time-varying, and mildly persistent. The stock market returns are influenced by world market returns as well as exogenous variables representing government policies.

3. The cross-sectional variability in mean returns for domestic and foreign shares is related to shares' risk exposure as measured by their own market betas and betas against international financial markets in a manner consistent with the ICAPM.

4. The extraordinarily large underpricing of Chinese IPOs is caused by basic problems derived from microeconomic uncertainty and information asymmetry in China and can be understood as rational behavior under signaling models with separating equilibrium. On both theoretical and empirical grounds, bribery and the use of alternative IPO-share allocation mechanisms as causes or explanations of the observed underpricing behavior are rejected.

NOTES

1. C shares cannot be listed in the two official exchanges (Shanghai and Shenzhen Security Exchange), but a very small number are traded on the STAQS and the NETS.

2. In the United States, the "Rules of Fair Practice" of the National Association of Securities Dealers require that new issues must be offered at a fixed price and that a maximum offering price be announced two weeks in advance of the offering. But the actual final offering price need not be established until immediately before the offering date (or the effective date of registration). Underwriters can attempt to obtain indications of interest prior to an issue.

3. Since equation 4 defines a variance, a nonnegativity constraint must be imposed on α and β. Moreover, the sum $\alpha + \beta$ must be less than 1 for the volatility process to be covariance stationary.

4. When a Chinese company issues both A and B shares, the two kinds of stock are equal: They have the same sliver of ownership and voting rights. Yet a company's A-share price may be three times the B-share price. Since the beginning of November 1996, local Chinese investors who could produce the simplest of documents to point to some foreign connection were allowed to purchase and trade B shares. As a result, A- and B-share prices started to converge (Faison, 1996).

5. There are two sources of possible bias if OLS is used in the estimation. Errors-in-variable (EIV) problems may exist if the first-day market price and the price for initial offering are observed with error. In this case, there will be a spurious negative correlation between the observed IPO price and the observed *IPORETN*, even under a pooling equilibrium. Another source of possible bias also exists for the relative IPO size variable. Relative IPO size is constructed using the fraction of the intrinsic value of the firm that is initially offered to the public. A firm's intrinsic value is measured by the variable *MKTCAP*, which is a function of the firm's realized IPO and SEO behavior. Therefore, simultaneous-equation bias may occur if the "raw" measure of relative IPO size is used as a regressor. To correct for the EIV and simultaneity problems, a 2SLS procedure is adopted (see Su and Fleisher, 1998b).

6. To compare the explanatory power of the signaling versus market feedback hypotheses, Su and Fleisher (1998b) calculate $(\partial P^{SEO}/\partial IPORETN) \, dIPORETN$ and $(\partial P^{SEO}/\partial AFTRETN1) \, dAFTRETN1$ and evaluate the two expressions using the standard deviation of the respective regressors, obtaining 4.2 and 0.80, respectively.

REFERENCES

Allen, Franklin and Gerald R. Faulhaber, 1989. Signaling by underpricing in the IPO market, *Journal of Financial Economics* 23, 303-323.

Bailey, Warren, 1993. Risk and return behavior in Chinese stock markets: some preliminary evidence, *Pacific-Basin Finance Journal* 2, 243-260.

Bailey, Warren and Julapa Jagtiani, 1994. Foreign ownership restrictions and stock prices in the Thai market, *Journal of Financial Economics* 36, 57-87.

Bekaert, Geert and Campbell R. Harvey, 1997. Emerging equity market volatility, *Journal of Financial Economics* 43, 29-78.

Bollerslev, Tim, 1986. Generalized autoregressive conditional heteroskedasticity, *Journal of Econometrics* 31, 307-327.

Chemmanur, Thomas J., 1993. The pricing of initial public offerings: a dynamic model with information production, *Journal of Finance* 48, 285-304.

De Santis, Giorgio and Selahattin İmrohoroğlu, 1995. Stock returns and volatility in emerging financial markets, University of Southern California working chapter.

Errunza, V. and E. Losq, 1985. International asset pricing under mild segmentation: theory and test, *Journal of Finance* 40, 105-124.

Eun, C. and S. Janakiramanan, 1986. A model of international asset pricing with a constraint on the foreign equity ownership, *Journal of Finance* 41, 897-914.

Faisan, S., 1996. Out of the darkness and into a shadow, *New York Times*, December 13.

Fama, Eugene F. and Kenneth R. French, 1992. The cross-section of expected stock returns, *Journal of Finance* 47(2), 427-466.

Fama, Eugene F. and James D. MacBeth, 1973. Risk, return and equilibrium: Empirical tests, *Journal of Political Economy* 81, 607-636.

Grinblatt, Mark and Chaun Y. Hwang, 1989. Signaling and the pricing of unseasoned new issues, *Journal of Finance* 44, 393-420.

Hietala, Pekka, 1989. Asset pricing in partially segmented markets: Evidence from the Finnish market, *Journal of Finance* 44, 697-718.

Ingersoll, Jonathan, 1987. *Theory of Financial Decision Making*. Totowz, NJ: Rowman & Littlefield.

Jegadeesh, Narasimhan, Mark Weinstein, and Ivo Welch, 1993. An empirical investigation of IPO returns and subsequent equity offerings, *Journal of Financial Economics* 34, 153-175.

Johnson, Dean L., 1995. Barriers to international investment: stock premiums in Sweden, University of Wisconsin working chapter.

Kim, Dongcheol, 1995. The errors in the variables problems in the cross-section of expected stock returns, *Journal of Finance* 50, 1605-1634.

Loughran, Tim, Jay R. Ritter, and Kristian Rydquist, 1994. Initial public offerings: International insights, *Pacific-Basin Finance Journal* 2, 165-199.

Merton, Robert C., 1973. An intertemporal asset pricing model, *Econometrica* 41, 867-887.

Ritter, Jay R., 1984, The "hot issue" market of 1980, *Journal of Business* 57, 215-240.

Stulz, René M. and Walter Wasserfallen, 1995. Foreign equity investment restrictions, capital flight, and shareholder wealth maximization: theory and evidence, *Review of Financial Studies* 8, 1019-1057.

Su, Dongwei, 1998. Ownership restrictions and stock prices: evidence from Chinese markets, forthcoming *Journal of Economics and Business*.

Su, Dongwei and Belton M. Fleisher, 1998a. Risk, return and regulation in Chinese stock markets, forthcoming *Journal of Economics and Business*.

Su, Dongwei and Belton M. Fleisher, 1998b. An empirical investigation of underpricing in Chinese IPOs, forthcoming *Pacific-Basin Finance Journal* 8.

Viard, Alan D., 1995. The asset pricing effects of fixed holding costs: An upper bound, *Journal of Financial and Quantitative Analysis* 30, 43-59.

Welch, Ivo, 1989. Seasoned offerings, imitation costs and the underpricing of initial public offerings, Journal of Finance 44, 421-449.

World Bank, 1995. China: The Emerging Capital Market, Volumes I and II.

20

Launching Markets for Stock Index Futures and Options: The Case of Korea

Yu-Kyung Kim

INTRODUCTION

The Korea Stock Exchange (KSE) started to look into the feasibility of establishing an equity index futures and options market in the mid-1980s, not long after the first stock index futures market was opened at the Kansas City Board of Trade. In the early part of 1989, the Korea Composite Stock Price Index for the first time recorded 1,000 points and soon after it started to turn southward. As the market movement became volatile, there was a need to equip investors with tools to control market risk. To meet such need the KSE formed an independent blue-ribbon committee whose task was to study whether the Korean financial market was ready to deal with exchange-listed derivatives products, including financial and commodity futures and options.

The committee's in-depth analysis indicated that derivatives based on commodities such as grains, livestock, meat, and metals were not economically feasible. The reasoning was that some of the products were monopolized, had inefficient distribution channels, were under government control, and were lacking clear-cut pricing mechanisms. Additionally, these products were difficult to standardize in terms of quality and trade unit, and many producers were too small in scale to utilize the derivatives market. If one is in dire need to access the market, several foreign markets were available. Therefore, the committee's recommendation was that financial derivatives were more feasible to introduce in comparison to commodity products.

In the area of financial derivatives, the committee investigated whether long-term interest rates, short-term interest rates, currency, and equity index could fulfill the following criteria: market size, price volatility, standardization requirements, and the degree of market liberalization. Out of the four financial product types, the stock index was closest to satisfying the necessary conditions.

As far as interest-rate-related products were concerned, both primary and secondary markets for bonds were not yet in mature stages and a market for government bonds had not been developed. Additionally, the short-term bond market was closed to foreigners and under heavy influence from the government. The market for currency-related products was too small in size and too heavily regulated under the Foreign Exchange Act.

Contrary to the fixed income and currency markets, the Korean stock market fulfilled the above-mentioned necessary conditions. According to the 1989 year-end figures, the market capitalization stood at $119 billion, which represented 68% of the GNP, and the total number of shares outstanding and the trading value were 4.2 billion and $102 billion, respectively. In comparison to some of the countries which were already operating stock index derivatives markets, these quantitative figures indicated that the Korean market had as good a chance to succeed as the benchmark countries, which were Australia, Finland, New Zealand, and Sweden. Additionally, the investor base was steadily increasing. Some 14% of the total population owned at least one stock, while the comparable figures for the United States and Japan were 20% and 17%, respectively. It should be noted that the Korean stock market experienced a significant rise in stock prices in the latter half of the 1980s.

In order to have a successful equity derivatives market, a fair amount of stock volatility is a must. The Korean stock market volatility in 1990 as measured by standard deviation of monthly returns was 2.01%, whereas those of the S&P 500 and Topix were 1.07% and 1.63%, respectively. In conclusion, the Korean stock market had sufficiently large size and volatility and had a good number of market participants, which strongly suggests that there would be strong demand for equity derivatives on the part of institutional investors and individual investors with large portfolios.

The final area of concern was the regulatory environment of the stock market. In many aspects, the equity market was still under strong influence of the government. The view of the Ministry of Finance was that while the market had grown quantitatively, the qualitative aspect of the market was still some years behind that of advanced markets. However, the speed of information dissemination had been quickened, the numbers of professional investors and investment advisory firms had increased, and the market had been rapidly internationalized. All of these changes were forcing the market to be more efficient and self-sustained without the government's strong-arm tactics. Given these analyses, the committee's recommendation was that the stock index was at the best position to succeed in comparison to other financial derivatives.

Having decided on what would be the first-ever exchange-traded derivatives product, it was now time to convince and educate the government authority on how beneficial it would be to have a stock index futures market in the Korean financial system. The points the KSE emphasized were that stock index futures were important tools in managing the systematic risk of stock portfolio investment, they could be used as new investment products in correctly predicting future movements of overall market portfolios, and their prices would allow market participants to anticipate the direction of future cash prices. Therefore, having stock index futures would enrich the overall quality of the stock market by providing a hedging vehicle and, subsequently, would enhance marketability and liquidity in the cash market. In turn, it would augment the quality of the primary market and the overall financial system.

BASIC POLICY GUIDELINES AND LEGAL ASPECTS OF ESTABLISHING A FUTURES AND OPTIONS MARKET

As the Brady Report for developing country debts in 1987 pointed out, stocks, stock index futures, and stock index options all together compose one single market. They are closely linked by their price discovery mechanism, market participants, and trading strategies. This means that the underlying cash and derivatives markets are not two separate and distinct markets but one market. Based upon this single market philosophy, the KSE placed top priorities on minimizing any possible side effect that futures might have on the underlying cash market. At the same time, the KSE emphasized ensuring the operation of the futures and options market to be consistent and harmonized with that of the underlying cash market, while conforming the institutional framework to the international norms. As a result, the trading and settlement rules were modeled after those of the underlying cash market.

INSTITUTIONAL ASPECTS

KOSPI 200

The underlying asset of stock index futures and options contracts is KOSPI 200. This index is composed of 200 leading stocks listed on the KSE. The KOSPI 200 accounts for about 70% of the total market capitalization, and represents all industrial groups in the Korean economy. The selection criteria the KSE used are each firm's market value and trading volume relative to its industry averages. To maintain the index component selection process fairly and independently, a Steering Committee was formed, composed of 11 academics and practitioners. It reviews the content of the index in June of every year, so that if a firm no longer meets the predetermined survival criteria, it can be replaced with other qualified firms.

Safety Features

The KSE established some built-in stabilization measures in order to ensure stable operation of both derivatives and underlying cash markets. The daily price fluctuation in the futures market is limited to 5% of the previous day's closing price, but there is no limit for options contracts. As the new computerized trading system was put in operation in November 1996, the so-called SideCar and Circuit Breaker were introduced. For the SideCar to be kicked in,

futures prices must fluctuate by 3% or more relative to the previous day's closing price and such deviation must last for five minutes or longer. Then, program
trading orders are executed after a five-minute cooling-off period. For the
Circuit Breaker to be triggered, the futures price must fluctuate by 5% or more
from the previous day's closing price and such fluctuation must last for one
minute or more. Then futures and options trading are halted for five minutes.

MARKET ACTIVITIES UP TO DATE

As the KOSPI 200 futures and options markets were opened on May 6,
1996, and July 7, 1997, respectively, available data are limited—especially for
the options contracts, which have been traded only for a few months. Considering that the futures market has been in existence for less than two years at the
time of writing, the consensus in the market is that it has a potential to be a
successful market. As Table 20.1, Panel A indicates, the average daily trading
volume for August 1997 was 11,117 contracts or equivalently around 435 billion
Korean won (KRW). This notional trading value represents around 86% of the
underlying stock market's daily average. The total trading volume for the month
was 277,924 contracts, which was the highest figure since the introduction, and
the daily average open interest was around 11,449 contracts.

As shown in Panels A and B, the trading volume, daily open interest, and
ratio of futures to stock trading value have been increasing steadily. Market
participants are increasingly employing a wide variety of investment techniques
such as position trading and hedge trading. However, as Panel C indicates, they
have been overwhelmingly concentrated by securities companies and individual
investors. These two groups together accounted for more than 90% of the total
trading volume. In particular, retail investors have shown a growing interest in
the futures market with their share increasing to more than 30%. Furthermore, as
the minimum margin requirement was lowered from 50 million Korean won to
10 million won with the opening of the options market, participation by retail
investors in the futures and options market is expected to increase continuously.

To have a successful futures market, the market needs different types of
players: speculators, hedgers, and arbitrageurs. Until recently, most trades were
made for speculative purposes while arbitrage trading accounted for less than
1% of the total trading volume. It is not to criticize that speculative trading is a
bad thing or it is a disturbance to the market. But what is important is having a
right balance of different traders participating in the market. Arbitrage trading
plays such an important role in the futures market that it makes sure the futures
and cash prices do not wander off into different directions. Since April 1997 the
volume of arbitrage trading has been picked up as the fiscal year of most
securities companies ended at the end of March, which has resulted in more
aggressive investment behavior on the part of these companies. Their rationale is
that if they make unprofitable trades, there is some time to make up the differences. Also these securities companies started to adopt an employee compensation scheme that is linked to the employee's contribution to the firm's bottom

Table 20.1. Market Archives

Panel A — Average Daily Trading Volume of Futures and Open Interest, in Number of Contracts

	'96.5	'97.1	2	3	4	5	6	7	8	Average Daily (97)
Trading Volume	3,473	5,790	6,427	6,380	5,963	7,706	7,193	8,743	11,117	7,436
Open Interest	2,054	6,594	8,444	8,558	11,561	11,076	7,725	9,441	11,449	9,369

Figures for trading volume and open interest are average daily trading volumes and average daily open interest for each month, respectively. The record volume of 19,800 contracts was reached on August 29, 1997.

Panel B — Size of Futures Market Relative to Stock Market, in Billion Won, %

	'96.5	'97.1	2	3	4	5	6	7	8	Average Daily (97)
Stock Market	805	478	551	519	608	721	727	586	508	586
Futures Market	182	201	229	206	204	280	294	350	435	276
Ratio	22	42	42	40	34	39	40	60	86	49

The size of each market is measured by an average daily trading value of the market for each given month. The ratio is computed by dividing the size of the futures market by that of the stock market. On September 1, 1997, a record ratio was hit at 157%.

Panel C — Futures Trading Activities by Market Participating Groups, in Percent

	'96.5	'97.1	2	3	4	5	6	7	8	Average (97)
Securities Co.	90	66	73	71	71	72	72	64	63	69
Individuals	3	26	21	20	23	21	20	30	33	24
Institutions	6	4	4	5	3	4	4	3	3	4

Percentage shares by each group are based on the number of futures contracts bought and sold by the group.

line. As a result, the deviation between a futures price and its theoretical price has narrowed significantly.

The trading activities of the KOSPI 200 options market were very sluggish in the beginning but they have picked up recently. The average daily trading volume for the first month was around 1,250 contracts or, equivalently, around KRW 10 billion and the trading value relative to the underlying stock market's daily average was about 3.5%. The average daily open interest was 8,290 contracts. However, in August 1997 the average daily trading volume and open interest increased to 3,730 and 38,720 contracts, respectively.

The trading activities of the options market have been far below expectations. It will take some time to develop as a successful market. The reasons for the sluggishness of the market can be found by analyzing its depth and breadth. It is not an exaggeration to say that a measure of a market's maturity can be determined by its liquidity. A liquid market brings investors, and more investors make the market more liquid. When a market lacks liquidity, it is difficult to draw investors to the market. The KSE needs to step up its effort in providing continuous education on derivatives to both institutional investors and retail investors. The reason why these players are reluctant to actively participate in the market could be due to their cautious and conservative wait-and-see approach, which is influenced by a torrent of derivatives disasters such as at Barings and Sumitomo bank. These two banks and other institutions suffered huge losses stemming from their aggressive derivative positions.

CHALLENGES AHEAD AND CONCLUSION

As far as the future prospects of Korean derivatives market is concerned, the KSE is expected to offer individual stock options in the near future. By the end of 1998 a new futures exchange is scheduled to be established, and traded products are most likely to be interest rate and currency futures.

The KSE has enjoyed over 40 years of monopoly but it seems that for the first time it will have a competitor in the domestic market. As prescribed in the Securities and Exchange Law, currently the KSE has the exclusive right on equity-linked derivatives products. Obviously a responsibility always accompanies a right. On that account, the KSE will do its best to establish itself as a pacesetter in stock, bond, and derivative markets.

REFERENCES

Shim, B.K., 1990. Feasibility study on introducing new products. Seoul: Korean Securities Association.

Brady, N., J. Cotting, R. Kirby, J. Opel, and H. Stein, 1988. *Report of the Presidential Task Force on Market Mechanisms.* Washington, DC: U.S. Government Printing Office.

Brenner, M., M. Subrahmanyam, and J., Uno, 1989a. Arbitrage opportunities in the Japanese stock and futures markets, *Financial Analyst Journal* 46, 14-24.

Brenner, M., M. Subrahmanyam, and J., Uno, 1989b. The behavior of prices in the Nikkei spot and futures markets, *Journal of Financial Economics* 23, 363-383.

Figlewski, S., 1984. Hedging performance and basis risk in stock index futures, *Journal of Finance* 39, 657-699.

McMillan, H., 1991. Circuit breakers in the S&P 500 futures market: their effect on volatility and price discovery in October 1989, *Review of Futures Markets* 10, 248-274.

Miller, M.H., 1993. The economics and politics of index arbitrage in the U.S., and Japan, *Pacific-Basin Finance Journal* 1, 3-11.

Modest, D.M. and M., Sundaresan, 1983. The relationship between spot and futures prices in stock index futures market: some preliminary evidence, *Journal of Futures Markets* 3, 15-42.

Stoll, H.R., 1988. Index futures, program trading and stock market procedures, *Journal of Futures Markets* 8, 391-412.

Weekly reports: futures and options markets. Seoul: Korea Stock Exchange.

PART VII

Emerging Stock Markets in Latin America and Europe

21

The Emerging Markets in Latin America: Prospects and Problems for an Investor

Dilip K. Ghosh
and Edgar Ortiz

INTRODUCTION

Emerging markets have gained currency owing to the growing interests of investors from every part of the globe. Professional analysts and market practitioners alike have focused their attention to such nascent economies for higher-than-average rates of return on investment and diversification of portfolio. A voluminous literature has already come into being, but most of the studies are on Asia-Pacific countries. Singapore, South Korea, Hong-Kong, and the Asian tigers have attracted major financial firms in that region and in those countries. Eastern Europe is also coming on the radar screen of many academic researchers and professional investors.

In the other hemisphere, one may note, quite a number of Latin American countries such as Mexico, Chile, Argentina, and Brazil are coming out strongly on measures of returns. Mature economies such as the United States, Germany, Japan, and the like appear to yield less attractive returns on investment. So investors are on globe-trotting tours with their strategies and funds. Since serious studies abound already on the examination of the emerging markets in Asia, we plan to look into such markets in Latin America in this chapter, and attempt to assess the prospects and problems for an investor.

Research thus far has focused on the opportunities for investing in those emerging markets and on (in)efficiency studies (Leal and Ratner, 1994; Cabello and Ortiz, 1995). There has been an increased interest in emerging market research because of unparalleled growth and exceptionally high returns in these markets. These markets have become very important mechanisms to channel global resources to local corporations, thereupon ending overreliance of developing countries on sovereign borrowing. Yet the performance of these emerging markets has not been free from problems. Erroneous policymaking like sustaining overvalued currencies and high trade deficits, as in the case of Mexico, has led to a dramatic fall in the external value of the currencies and the volume of trade. This situation in Mexico, dubbed as the "tequila effect," has spread to other neighboring countries and created serious problems (Alford, 1995). To overcome the resultant predicament, many macroeconomic policy prescriptions have been put in place.

Growth of the emerging stock markets has been the result of liberalization of financial markets around the world (Cabello, 1997). Deregulation in the developed countries, resulting in the removal of restrictions to invest in the securities of firms from developing countries, has played a major role in this process. Serious economic liberalization policies and financial deregulation by governments of the developing countries have completed the institutional environment necessary for investing in the emerging economies. One may note, for instance, that in the case of Mexico and Brazil, stock exchanges have been about to reach the level of a developed market. By late 1994 total market capitalizations neared $130 billion for Mexico and $189 billion for Brazil. Perspectives for a definitive takeoff into development for these economies have appeared certainly bright. Daring economic reforms, undertaken during the Salinas administration, and the North American Free Trade Agreement (NAFTA) with Canada and United States, have been recognized as the factors which have already led the country into higher stages of development. However, in the midst of such promising developments, mismanagement of the economy has also triggered a profound crisis, strongly linked to foreign portfolio investments in the securities markets (Cabello and Ortiz, 1995).

The markets in Latin America are still at a critical crossroads. Although the stock markets have also grown remarkably, economic recovery has not yet taken a strong hold. However, the region underwent a sharp transformation during the 1980s. Industrial restructuring policies and later comprehensive modernization policies have begun to be implemented in the region. At different rhythms and intensities, governments of the area have opened up the economies to foreign trade and investments, deregulated their markets, and privatized public enterprises. In the process still to be consolidated, the traditional high intervention of the state in the economy has been diminished and replaced by a liberalized market model, where the private sector has become the engine for growth. In addition, by the end of the decade, renegotiation of the foreign debt has started to take better grounds with the application of the Baker and Brady plans that created secondary markets for LDC debts. Thus, by the end of the 1980s, especially since 1989, economic recovery has been in sight in Latin America.

The area has shown positive rates of growth (54.7 [Chile], 49.9 [Colombia], 27.9 [Brazil] percent cumulative growth for 1981-1994). Since 1991, GNP growth has been positive and increasing. Fresh funds from foreign sources have also benefitted the area. In 1992 alone, capital transfers to the area amounted to $27.4 billion. However, patterns of development for the 1989-92 period have not been smooth. On top of the growth being irregular, it has underscored some troublesome facts. Particularly, the external sector turned negative and inflation remained high. The average inflation rate for the region was still very high: 470.0% in 1992.

Growth trends of the Latin American countries have been dissimilar and have not always reflected the overall buoyancy in the region. Argentina and Venezuela have exhibited paths of both crisis and economic recovery. Cumulative GDP growth has been 6.6%—that is, 0.82% in annual terms. The crisis has had severe impact on GDP per capita. It has fallen by -14.6 % (-1.82% per year), a situation similar to that of Argentina. In sharp contrast to these trends stand the cases of Chile and Colombia, as already noted. Chile's cumulative GNP growth increased 16.6% for the 1981-88 period (or 2.07% per year), and since 1989 economic trends have been even more favorable. GNP has increased almost 7% per year, showing a cumulative increase of 49.9%. Colombia has displayed impressive growth rates for the entire 1981-94 period. From 1981 to 1988 GNP averaged an increase of almost 4% per year (31.96% cumulative). This led to GNP per capita increases the average of which amounts to 3.6% per year from 1981 through 1994.

Foreign debt and debt servicing have remained within manageable levels. Hence, the external sector appears to have contributed decisively to the growth of the economy. Brazil stands at its own peculiar crossroads. Both the 1981-88, and 1989-94 periods show trends contrary to the Latin American experience. Resistance to apply adjustment policies has resulted in positive, but irregular, rates of growth from 1981 to 1988.

Unfavorable economic trends have adversely affected, but have not deterred, the development of the Latin American stock markets. The share in market capitalization of the world's emerging markets increased from 3.42% in 1981 to almost 7% by 1992. Their cumulative growth from 1981 to 1994 has been an impressive 318.18%, even though below the average for the emerging markets as a whole.

The remarkable growth of the Latin American capital markets began to take place in the late 1980s, spurred by economic reforms and financial liberalization policies. The promotion of larger and efficient capital markets as a means to increase domestic savings and attract international resources to their economies by way of deregulation of investment restrictions and capital remittances to foreign portfolio holders has caught the attention of global investors. Currently, the stocks from all listed companies are freely available to foreign investors in the markets from Argentina, Brazil, and Colombia. Repatriation of dividends and capital gains is very liberal in these markets. However, a few restrictions on entry and repatriation of income and capital gains still exist in Chile and Venezuela. The institutional setup stands improved with well-defined roles of the regional Securities Exchange Commissions. Better trading and clearing rules are in place now. The exchanges themselves have approved some important self-regulation rules, and have modernized their trading and information systems.

Deregulation and growth of the markets also have led to better and more frequent corporate financial disclosure, and sharp competition in brokerage services has led to better services and lower intermediation costs. At the same time, deregulations of the developed capital markets, allowing institutional investors holding securities issued by firms from foreign countries, have induced these investors to move into the emerging capital markets as an alternative to attain higher returns relative to those in their own domestic markets. Thus by 1992 the Latin American stock markets experienced both rapid growth and rapid internationalization of their services. The growth in market capitalization in the Buenos Aires stock exchange for the 1981-94 period has been largest (1,793.0%). Venezuela has experienced the smallest market capitalization growth of the area during the same time (168.4%, which is slightly less than that experienced by the U.S. equity market). However, it is worth noting that the share of the Latin American stock markets in relation to total market capitalization in Latin America decreased significantly from 62.6% in 1981 to 44.0% in 1992, reflecting the increasing importance of the Mexican securities market in the area. The price/earnings ratios in these economies exhibit upward revision. In 1992 Argentina and Colombia yielded P/E ratios (38.0 and 27.9, respectively)—higher than the P/E ratio in the U.S. market (22.7).

Confirming the extraordinary growth realized by the Latin American stock markets, Table 21.1 shows that from 1989 through 1993 the Latin American markets often generated high returns, although some negative returns at times plagued investors. In 1989 and 1990 three Latin American markets were among the ten best performers in the global economy. In 1991 all six markets have been among the markets yielding the highest returns, but in 1992 only Chile and Colombia joined this select group. Although there are some important exceptions (negative returns), returns from 1989 to 1994 in all these markets have been higher than returns obtained in the U.S. market and the world at large.

Against the general backdrop of the depicted market scenarios we will attempt to examine the risk exposure of foreign investors, and their problems and prospects in view of exchange rate variability, and we discuss how to contain such risk. We will conclude the chapter with some collateral comments pertinent to this piece in the context of a more general study.

RISK AND RETURNS IN EQUITY MARKETS: HEDGED AND UNHEDGED

In this section we present the picture of risk and returns from the equity markets in six Latin American economies and in the United States for the period 1989 through 1993. Here average returns and volatilities in the unhedged situations are first reported in Table 21.1, and then the same items in the hedged conditions are presented in Table 21.2. These tables, originally reported by Soenen and Schrepferman (1997), are reproduced for further scrutiny. The returns are measured here in terms of the currency of the investor concerned. That is, for Mexican investors investing in Venezuela, their average returns are adjusted by the appreciation/ depreciation of Venezuela's currency against the Mexican peso. Along the rows the returns are measured in terms of the common denominator (here, the U.S. dollar is the numeraire), thus adjusting for inflation and highlighting real interest rates. Beyond arithmetic mean (AM), geometric mean (GM) is computed and presented in these tables. Standard deviation (SD), coefficient of variation (CV), and Sharpe index (SI) are presented to highlight risk and return-to-risk measures. Note the extremely high rates of return of average Argentinean and Brazilian investors across the spectrum. But the Sharpe index for an average Brazilian investor is negative for

Table 21.1. Performance of Unhedged Returns in the Latin American and U.S. Equity Markets, 1989-1993

Investor's Perspective		Argentina	Brazil	Chile	Colombia	Mexico	Venezuela	U.S.
					Country of investment			
Argentina	AM	0.2278	0.2932	0.2080	0.2057	0.2211	0.1844	0.1819
	GM	0.1531	0.1041	0.1497	0.1513	0.1624	0.1298	0.1312
	SD	0.5504	0.7358	0.4751	0.4493	0.4724	0.4547	0.4284
	CV	2.4159	2.5091	2.2842	2.1836	2.1363	2.4654	2.3551
	SI	0.3298	0.3356	0.3403	0.3548	0.3701	0.3038	0.3165
Brazil	AM	0.3282	0.3518	0.2793	0.2847	0.2938	0.2688	0.2544
	GM	0.2708	0.2168	0.2670	0.2688	0.2810	0.2451	0.2467
	SD	0.4444	0.6511	0.1843	0.2074	0.1814	0.2501	0.1402
	CV	1.3540	1.8508	0.6599	0.7286	0.6174	0.9303	0.5510
	SI	-1.7294	-1.1443	-4.4351	-3.9154	-4.4262	-3.3112	-6.0083
Chile	AM	0.0793	0.1093	0.0375	0.0421	0.0506	0.0287	0.0192
	GM	0.0383	-0.0059	0.0352	0.0366	0.0466	0.0173	0.0186
	SD	0.3338	0.5435	0.0696	0.1124	0.0921	0.1608	0.0364
	CV	4.2093	4.9699	1.8577	2.6657	1.8198	5.6046	1.8909
	SI	0.8272	0.1703	0.2974	0.2256	0.3671	0.0739	0.0669
Colombia	AM	0.0862	0.1122	0.0429	0.0466	0.0560	0.0335	0.0242
	GM	0.0433	-0.0010	0.0402	0.0417	0.0517	0.0222	0.0235
	SD	0.3431	0.5292	0.0755	0.1077	0.0961	0.1599	0.0360
	CV	3.99817	4.7180	1.7584	2.3112	1.7143	4.7775	1.4900
	SI	0.1821	0.1672	0.2546	0.2126	0.3367	0.0611	0.0129
Mexico	AM	0.0751	0.1040	0.0337	0.0374	0.0463	0.0233	0.0151
	GM	0.0341	-0.0099	0.0310	0.0325	0.0424	0.0132	0.0145
	SD	0.3328	0.5331	0.0743	0.1070	0.0903	0.1506	0.0343
	CV	4.4314	5.1263	2.2060	2.8589	1.9495	6.4648	2.2758
	SI	0.1602	0.1542	0.1598	0.1461	0.2716	0.0099	-0.1962
Venezuela	AM	0.0871	0.1186	0.0461	0.0496	0.0589	0.0345	0.0270
	GM	0.0460	0.0016	0.0429	0.0444	0.0544	0.0249	0.0262
	SD	0.3294	0.5486	0.0820	0.1094	0.0975	0.1462	0.0399
	CV	3.7803	4.6258	1.7793	2.2085	1.6556	4.2405	1.4793
	SI	0.1531	0.1493	0.1146	0.1175	0.2275	-0.0152	-0.2437
U.S.	AM	0.0693	0.0977	0.0280	0.0320	0.0406	0.0179	0.0096
	GM	0.0285	-0.0152	0.0255	0.0269	0.0368	0.0077	0.0090
	SD	0.3292	0.5274	0.0730	0.1077	0.0891	0.1505	0.0334
	CV	4.7516	5.4005	3.3704	3.3704	2.1930	8.3984	3.4792
	SI	0.1965	0.1764	0.3205	0.2544	0.4044	0.0885	0.1496

Key: AM = arithmetic mean; GM = geometric mean; SD = standard deviation; CV = coefficient of variation; SI = Sharpe (performance) index.   *Source:* From Soenen and Schrepferman (1997).

Table 21.2. Performance of Hedged Returns in the Latin American and U.S. Equity Markets, 1989-1993

Investor's Perspective		Country of investment						
		Argentina	Brazil	Chile	Colombia	Mexico	Venezuela	U.S.
Argentina	AM	0.2278	-0.7684	-0.1610	0.6094	0.7632	0.8346	2.2517
	GM	0.1531	-0.9604	-0.3526	-0.1418	0.1256	-0.1805	0.9912
	SD	0.5504	0.5842	1.2454	2.0107	1.9314	1.4840	3.8094
	CV	2.4159	-0.7603	-7.7368	3.3995	2.5305	2.9766	1.6918
	SI	0.3298	-1.3946	-0.1665	0.2801	0.3712	0.3174	0.5789
Brazil	AM	75.2508	0.3518	56.8045	40.5354	58.7652	35.0939	95.0505
	GM	29.6622	0.2168	43.3553	30.0945	40.3877	28.5717	68.8753
	SD	87.7054	0.6511	45.0584	31.2959	53.1281	22.3811	74.5366
	CV	1.1655	1.8508	0.7932	0.7721	0.9041	0.6377	0.7842
	SI	0.8455	-1.1443	1.2363	1.2602	1.0855	1.5190	1.2605
Chile	AM	0.3249	-0.9514	0.0375	-0.2896	0.066	-0.3748	0.6693
	GM	0.1672	-0.9727	0.0352	-0.2437	0.0255	-0.3389	0.7251
	SD	0.5875	0.0701	0.0696	0.2533	0.2886	0.2111	0.4207
	CV	1.8023	-0.0737	1.8577	-1.0246	4.2679	-0.6228	0.5802
	SI	0.5244	-13.8177	0.2974	-1.2096	0.1760	-1.8550	1.5510
Colombia	AM	2.5399	-0.9164	0.1208	0.0466	0.1159	-0.0110	1.0318
	GM	2.3461	-0.9557	0.0874	0.0417	0.0829	-0.0522	1.0084
	SD	0.8312	0.1098	0.2968	0.1077	0.2650	0.2892	0.1520
	CV	0.3273	-0.1198	2.4556	2.3112	2.2875	-26.2123	0.1473
	SI	3.0272	-8.5642	0.3272	0.2126	0.3477	-0.1201	6.6331
Mexico	AM	-0.1050	-0.9354	-0.2079	-0.1724	0.0463	-0.1356	0.6881
	GM	-0.3642	-0.9674	-0.2341	-0.2090	0.0424	-0.2151	0.6631
	SD	0.5517	0.0892	0.2207	0.2511	0.0903	0.3846	0.3001
	CV	-5.2559	-0.0954	-1.0616	-1.4565	1.9495	-2.8352	0.4361
	SI	-0.2298	-10.7266	-1.0408	-0.7734	0.2716	-0.4094	2.2206
Venezuela	AM	0.7680	-0.9135	0.5155	0.1192	0.3629	0.0345	1.4089
	GM	0.0147	-0.9460	0.4340	0.0927	0.2387	0.0249	1.2975
	SD	1.4002	0.0999	0.5371	0.2434	0.6011	0.1462	0.7558
	CV	1.8231	-0.1093	1.0418	2.0416	1.6564	4.2405	0.5365
	SI	0.5223	-9.5128	0.8915	0.3389	0.5427	-0.0152	1.8155
U.S.	AM	-0.4832	-0.9640	-0.5482	-0.5783	-0.5019	-0.5745	0.0096
	GM	-0.6417	-0.8921	-0.5634	-0.5799	-0.5209	-0.5806	0.0090
	SD	0.3258	0.0499	0.1099	0.0892	0.0830	0.1631	0.0334
	CV	-0.6743	-0.0518	-0.2005	-0.1543	-0.1654	-0.2838	3.4792
	SI	-1.4972	-19.3941	-5.0300	-6.5348	-6.1032	-3.5519	0.1496

Key: AM = arithmetic mean; GM = geometric mean; SD = standard deviation; CV = coefficient of variation; SI = Sharpe (performance) index.   Source: From Soenen and Schrepferman (1997).

hyperinflationary situations. Venezuelans investing in the domestic economy and in the U.S. economy find their SI negative, and Mexican investors find themselves in that situation only in the U.S. market.

Perold and Schulman (1988), and Arnott and Henriksson (1989), as many others before and after them have suspected, observe that "on a stand-alone, un-hedged basis, foreign stocks are much riskier than the U.S. market" holds. Jorion (1989) shows that for a period of ten years (January 1978 through December 1988) unhedged foreign stocks outperform U.S. stocks by 710 basis points per annum on average. Yet, as Table 21.1 depicts, since standard deviations in the monthly returns in the Latin American markets are much higher than those in the American market, the former do not dominate U.S. equities for U.S dollar-based investors. However, the observation (by Soenen and Schrepferman, 1997) that, based on the coefficient of variation as the better relative measure of volatility, one can find that a U.S. investor has done well indeed in Mexico, Chile, and Colombia by comparing against the domestic U.S. market for the period of 1983 through 1993 deserves a special recognition. In their study, the Sharpe index shows that from the U.S. investor's perspective, all these Latin American stock markets outperform the U.S. stock market with the exception of Venezuela. However, the caveat should also be in order. In approximately 60% of cases foreign equities seemed to have under-performed, and for investors from Mexico, Brazil, and Chile this result has been overwhelming.

As is often noted, foreign investment is always laced with two additional risks: political and currency. The Business Environment Risk Information (BERI) index is a scale to measure political risk of a country, and by this index, Chile (52) is medium-risk country: Colombia (46), Mexico (46), Venezuela (43), and Argentina (40) high-risk countries; and Brazil is a prohibitively risky country. In this score scale, 100 is the best (no-risk) score, and the further the score is away from 100, the higher becomes the risk level of the country. Diamonte et al. (1995) and others have given a more extensive and useful analyses on the issue of political risk, and it always seems puzzling to recognize the borderline between political risk and investor's prudence.

Exchange risk, on the other hand, is more mundane and more palpable, and every investor involved in overseas transactions must factor in exchange rate move-ments in the calculation of risk and returns, and, if possible, to hedge this risk with available market instruments. A number of studies such as Eaker and Grant (1985), Eun and Resnick (1988), Lee (1988), Thomas (1989), Hauser and Levy (1991), Glen and Jorion (1993), Kritzman (1993), and Aggarwal and DeMaskey (1997) have highlighted the merits of hedging currency risk. Hauser, Marcus, and Yaari (1994), however, contend that "hedging currency risk is beneficial in developed, but not in emerging stock markets."

Before we take issue with any of the positions, it is instructive to reexamine the hitherto-known empirical results on this question. On that score, we take a close look at the performance table of hedged equities by Soenen and Schrepferman (1997), reproduced here in Table 21.1. One can immediately see in this table that hedged foreign investment is certainly inferior to unhedged investment. Upon this recognition it becomes incumbent to check on the hedging device(s) employed in the calculation of the entries in the table. Using a one-month rolling hedge for each stock market, the returns have been computed. In their own words, "currency is hedged through a forward sale of the investment amount at the beginning of each month. That is equivalent to borrowing the foreign currency for one month and swapping this amount into domestic currency of the investor for simultaneous lending in the local market for the same maturity." These statements need further scrutiny for validation or otherwise, and in that context then the pertinent question is: how do you hedge in the emerging markets in Latin America where hedging instruments are virtually conspicuous by their absence?

HOW TO HEDGE IN EMERGING MARKETS?

It should be noted that the number of hedging instruments such as forward, futures, and option contracts, which are so readily available in the developed countries like the United States, the United Kingdom, Japan, Germany, and so on are missing in emerging markets. Folks and Aggarwal (1987) correctly point out in such economies exchange risk may be hedged by holding offsetting positions in appropriate commodities such as gold and other precious metals or in futures and options in those commodities. Aggarwal and Mougoue (1996) further suggest that by holding derivatives in closely related but more liquid developed market currency, an investor may eliminate (or at least reduce) such risk. In a recent work, Aggarwal and DeMaskey (1997) have introduced cross-hedging currency risks in Asian emerging markets by way of using futures and options in hard currencies such as yen, DM, pound, Swiss franc, and have shown that Sharpe index improves through such covered investment design.

Let us design some hedging strategy for U.S. investors who find an unbelievably high rate of return, say 30%, in a country such as Mexico (that is, $r_M = 30\%$), while their home market interest rate is 10% ($r_A = 10\%$). But since the foreign exchange fluctuations can potentially reduce the return from Mexico to, say, 5% or even negative 15%, what can these investors do or have they any option in this environment? Assume, for the sake of analytical development, that 7.8830 pesos = $1 in the spot market (that is, $S = 7.8830$). In this situation, if a U.S. investor borrows $1/1.1 now, sells the dollar amount for pesos and gets $7.8830 \times (1/1.1) =$ 7.1664 pesos, then he can turn that amount into 9.3163 pesos (= $7.8830 \times [1/1.1] \times [1.3]$) at the end of the term by investing at the Mexican rate of 30% per annum.

If the forward market existed on pesos, then under condition of interest rate parity, 9.3163 pesos should have been worth $1 at the end of one year. By selling 9.3163 pesos for $1 by taking a forward contract, the investor should/could have earned 30% on his investment after paying off his borrowed dollar amount 1/1.1 plus the accrued interest cost of 10%. Since the forward rate is nonexistent for all these Latin American countries, the investor should enter into a creative arena of exchange through some form of commodity *vis-à-vis* currency swap.

Under the situation of nonexistent forward markets, the investor should look for an American or British or German importer or the like who needs 9.3163 pesos (or any multiple thereof) to buy the Mexican goods or services. If he finds that in that swap situation 9.3163 pesos ≈ \$1 (or 9.3163 pesos ≈ £λ = \$1, where λ is the forward rate of exchange between the British pound and U.S. dollar) one year from now, he should successfully enter into that contract, and the size of the contract should be suitably tailored to his initial investment. That is, $S(1 + r_M)/(1 + r_A)$ should be somehow swapped for \$1 exactly (or approximately) through intermediaries in the import/export financing houses. Calvo and Nickelsburg (1987) note that for "many of these countries, the majority of their exports are sold in world markets for dollars. . . . With three properties of expatriate dollars: ready availability, low cost information about world economic performance and low cost information about the course of the dollar, U.S dollars are a natural substitute for the domestic money."

Let $S(1 + r_M)/(1 + r_A) = F^c$. If F^c is different from what the import/export houses exchange for \$1 a year from now, there is a scope for covered arbitrage profits. Then as Ghosh (1997a, 1998a) shows, the first-round profits can be magnified by iterative plays in the currency market, and cumulatively the present value of the earnings for the investor through n consecutive iterations can be equal to (π_0^*) 1 where:

$$\pi_0^* = \frac{(1+\theta)M}{(1+r_A)} \left[\frac{F^c}{S}(1+r_M) - (1+r_A) \right] \left[\frac{1-(\alpha\beta)^n}{1-\alpha\beta} \right].$$

Here M is the initial dollar amount of investment, and θ is the proportion of funds borrowed against the investor's equity, $\alpha \equiv 1/(1+r_A)$, and $\beta \equiv (F^c/S)(1+r_M) + \theta[(F^c/S)(1+r_M) - (1+r)]$. With forward contracts on interest rates, and thus rolling over the strategy, which is a variant of what Soenen and Schrepferman (1997) suggest, the investor can potentially multiply his covered returns significantly, as Ghosh demonstrates by his theoretical designs in two works (1997b, 1998b).

One important point should be made now. If r_M is known with certainty at the time of initial investment, then the problem is easy to deal with. If, however, r_M is the rate of return from an equity investment or from a portfolio of investment whose rate of return is known *ex post*, but hardly known *ex ante*, how can the investor enter into a suitable forward contract? An immunized portfolio's return is rather easily ascertained beforehand, and in that case the foreign returns under hedging can be earned without much difficulty. It should be noted that locked-in rates of interest in many of these countries are way above the U.S. interest rate, and hence if an investor invests in CD-type instruments, this hedging scheme is a valid strategy to follow. Investors from other countries such as Chile or Argentina can follow the U.S. investor and mimic his strategies as well.

Many researchers working on Latin America have found that the monetary phenomena in that part of the world fit the currency substitution approach, developed and empirically examined earlier by Melvin (1984), Ortiz (1983), and Ohanian (1986) for Mexico; and so on. Yet the dollar and the Latin American currencies are not perfect substitutes, as Calvo and Nickelsburg (1987) aptly note, for at least two important institutional constraints. As long as Latin Americans do not choose away from domestic money in the midst of liberalization and stabilization processes, investment in emerging markets may not be quite as difficult as one may suspect. A predominant preference for dollarization in the Latin American economy may help U.S. investors significantly, but direction of investment in intra-Latin economies seems to appear mixed.

ACKNOWLEDGMENTS

The authors would like to thank Programa de Apoyo a Proyectos de Investigación e Innovación Tecnológica at the Office of Academic Affairs from Universidad Nacional Autónoma de México (UNAM) for the support received for this work. The work has benefited from the comments from K.P. Fischer, Tom Sanders, and upon discussion with Raj Aggarwal, and Uzi Yaari.

REFERENCES

Aggarwal, R. and R. Leal, 1995. Integration and anomalies in the emerging markets of Asia and Latin America. In J. Doukas and L. Lang, eds., *Advances in International Stock Market Relationships and Interaction*. Westport, CT: Greenwood Press.

Aggarwal, R. and A.L. DeMaskey, 1997. Cross-hedging currency risks in Asian emerging markets using derivatives in major currencies, *The Journal of Portfolio Management* 24, 88-95.

Aggarwal, R. and M. Mougoue, 1996. Cointegration among Asian currencies: evidence of the increasing influence of the Japanese yen, *Japan and the World Economy* 8, 291-308.

Agrawal, A. and K. Tandon, 1994. Anomalies or illusions? evidence from stock markets in eighteen countries, *Journal of International Money and Finance* 13.

Alford, A., 1995. Surviving the tequila hangover: managing transaction exposure in NAFTA countries, Working Paper, Northeastern University.

Arnott, R. and R. Henriksson, 1989. A disciplined approach to global asset allocation, *Financial Analysts Journal*, 45, 17-28.

Avgustinous, P., A.A. Lonie, D.M. Power, and C.D. Sinclair, 1997. The argument for increased investment in emerging markets: a re-examination. In Dilip K. Ghosh and E. Ortiz, eds., *The Global Structure of Financial Markets*. London: Routledge.

Black, F., 1976. Investment policy spectrum, *Financial Analyst Journal* 32(1), 23-31.

Butler, K.C. and S.J. Malaikah, 1992. Efficiency and inefficiency in thinly traded stock markets: Kuwait and Saudi Arabia, *Journal of Banking and Finance* 16.

Cabello, A., 1997. Liberalization and deregulation of the Mexican stock market. In Dilip K. Ghosh and E. Ortiz, eds., *The Global Structure of Financial Markets*. London: Routledge.

Cabello, A. and E. Ortiz, 1995. Debt crisis and economic recovery and performance of the emerging Latin American markets. In H. Peter Gray and Sandra Richard, eds., *International Finance in the New World Order*. New York: Pergamon Press.

Calvo, V.A. and G. Nickelsburg, 1987. *Currency Substitution: Theory and Evidence From Latin America*. Amsterdam and New York: Kluwer Academic Publisher.

Clark, E. and B. Marios, 1997. *Managing Risk in International Business*. New York: International Thompson Business Press.

Clark, E. and S. Schrepferman, 1998. Capital budgeting, political risk, and prudence, *The International Journal of Finance* 10, forthcoming.

Diamonte, R., R. Liew, and R. Stevens, 1995. Political risk in emerging and developed markets. New York: Golddman Sachs, Working Paper.

Eaker, M. and D. Grant, 1985. Optimal hedging of unconstrained long-term foreign exchange exposure, *Journal of Banking and Finance* 9(2), 221-231.

Eun, C. and B. Resnick, 1988. Exchange rate uncertainty, forward contracts, and international portfolio selection, *Journal of Finance* 43(1), 197-215.

Folks, W.R. and R. Aggarwal, 1987. *International Dimensions of Financial Management.* Boston: Kent Publishing Company.

Ghosh, D.K., 1997a. Profit multiplier in covered currency trading with leverage, *Financial Review* 32, 391-409.

Ghosh, D.K., 1997b. Risk-free profits with forward contracts in exchange rates and interest rates, *Journal of Multinational Financial Management*, forthcoming.

Ghosh, D.K., 1998a. Arbitrage with hedging by forward contracts: exploited and exploitable profits, *The European Journal of Finance*, forthcoming.

Ghosh, D.K., 1998b. Covered arbitrage in the foreign exchange market with forward contracts in interest rates, *The Journal of Futures Markets* 18, forthcoming.

Glen, J.D. and P. Jorion, 1993. Currency hedging for international portfolios, *Journal of Finance* 48, 1865-1886.

Hartmann, M.A. and D. Khambata, 1992. Emerging stock markets' investment strategies of the future, *The Columbia Journal of World Business* 28.

Hauser, S. and H. Levy, 1991. The effect of exchange rate and interest rate risk on international currency and fixed income security allocation, *Journal of Economics and Business* 43, 375-388.

Hauser, S., M. Marcus, and U. Yaari, 1994. Investing in emerging stock markets: is it worthwhile hedging foreign exchange risk? *The Journal of Portfolio Management* 20(3), 76-81.

Jorion, P., 1989. Asset allocation with hedged and unhedged foreign stocks and bonds, *The Journal of Portfolio Management* 15(4), 49-54.

Kritzman, M., 1993. Optimal currency hedging policy with biased forward rates, *The Journal of Portfolio Management* 19, 94-100.

Leal, R. and M. Ratner, 1994. Inefficiencies in the emerging stock markets of Latin America and Asia. In A.Z. Vazquez-Parraga, ed., 1994 BALAS Proceedings, College of Business, Florida International University.

Lee, A., 1988. International asset currency allocation, *The Journal of Portfolio Management* 14(1), 41-57.

Melvin, M., 1984. The dollarization of Latin America: a market enforced monetary reform, mimeo, Arizona State University.

Ohanian, L., 1985. Currency substitution and prices in Latin America: what have we learned from the evidence? mimeo, Security Pacific Bank, Los Angeles.

Ortiz, G., 1983. Currency substitution in Mexico, *Journal of Money, Credit and Banking* 15, 173-185.

Ortiz, E., 1993. Emerging capital markets and development. In K. Fatemi and D. Salvatore, eds., Foreign Exchange Issues, *Capital Markets and Banking in the 1990s.* Washington, DC: Taylor and Francis.

Ortiz, E. and V.R. Errunza, 1995. Los mercados de capital emergentes y la globalización financiera; retos para las finanzas modernas. in A. Giron, E. Ortiz, and E. Correa, eds., *Integracion Financiera y TLC: Retos y Perspectivas.* Mexico, D.F.: Siglo XXI.

Ortiz, E. and Grocio Soldevilla, 1997. A GARCH analysis of risk and returns in the South American emerging equity markets, mimeo, Universidad Nacional Autónoma de México.

Perold, A. and E. Schulman, 1988. The free lunch in currency hedging implications for investment policy and performance standards, *Financial Analysts Journal* 44, 45-50.

Soenen, L. and S. Schrepferman, 1997. Benefits from diversification and currency hedging of investments in Latin American capital markets. In Dilip K. Ghosh and E. Ortiz, eds., *The Global Structure of Financial Markets*. London: Routledge.

Thomas, L., 1989. The performance of currency hedged foreign bonds, *Financial Analysts Journal* 45, 25-31.

22

Potential Gains from International Diversification Across Latin American Stock Markets

Yochanan Shachmurove

INTRODUCTION

This chapter examines the strategy of investing in Latin American markets and the risk-return trade-off that is associated with such a strategy. An optimal portfolio is derived through historic observations and is subsequently evaluated utilizing performance measures. International investment gradually increased during the late 1980s and the early 1990s with the emergence of markets in the newly industrialized countries of Latin America such as Mexico, Brazil, Argentina, Peru, Colombia, Venezuela, and Chile. Investors willing to assume the additional risk present in these markets have been well compensated. Yet, many market analysts have indicated that such markets are somewhat of an abnormality, in that they tend to be characterized as thin, narrow, and driven by poorly informed individuals rather than by fundamentals.

It cannot be assumed, however, that investing in emerging stock markets is more dangerous than investing in more progressive countries, given the expected returns. The average investors may increase their returns if they hold portfolios which include foreign stocks. Since stock markets are not highly correlated and consequently do not fluctuate in tandem, diversifying leads to a higher return for a given risk. To accurately measure the performance of Latin American stock markets, several standards may be employed. They include yearly rates of return, market capitalization, and volume of shares traded. While the rate of return on the Latin American regional index was down for 1994, primarily due to the collapse of the Mexican peso, both market capitalization and volume of shares traded grew substantially.

The International Finance Corporation's (IFC) regional index for Latin America, which includes Mexico, Argentina, Brazil, Chile, Venezuela, Peru, and Colombia, performed poorly in 1994, falling 10.9% in U.S. dollar terms. The collapse of the Mexican peso in December 1994, in part a result of massive capital outflows, led to large decreases in the Mexican stock market index: the IFC reported a 39.7% decline for the year. Comparable losses were experienced by investors in the stock markets of Argentina and Venezuela, which declined by 26.0 and 16.4%, respectively. Not all Latin American markets, however, posted such dismal results. The IFC index for Brazil was up 64.9% for the year. Peru's market gained 47.5%, as did both Chile's and Colombia's, with increases of 42.3 and 25.9%, respectively.

While the overall level of Latin American stock market performance was mixed in 1994, these exchanges were still able to outperform their counterparts in other developing regions. After solid results in 1993, the IFC Investable Composite Index (IFCI) for stocks in developing countries was off by 13.8% in dollar terms in 1994. Asia was down 14.6%, while the Europe, Middle East, and Africa (EMEA) Index fell 30%. Even Poland, the best performer in 1993, posted losses of 42.6%. Similarly, China lost 49.2% and Turkey realized a drop of 42.7%.

Capitalization in Brazil grew from $99.4 billion in 1993 to $190.6 billion in 1994, an increase of 91.8%. Similar growth was recorded in the markets of Peru, Colombia, and Chile, with increases of 63.5, 60.7, and 59.6%, respectively. Capitalization in Mexico, however, shrank by 2.3% in 1994, to $196.1 billion. The overall level of capitalization growth for the seven Latin American countries included in the IFC index—Mexico, Brazil, Chile, Colombia, Venezuela, Argentina, and Peru—expanded by 28% between December 1993 and November 1994. Likewise, volume of shares traded experienced substantial increases. Colombia reported the largest gains, with an increase of 206.6%. Brazil expanded by 142.9%, Peru 101.9%, and Chile 91.6%. Only Venezuela suffered a decrease, falling 35.9% for the period.

While the aforementioned data indicate that the Latin American markets are attractive investment opportunities, they are not without their drawbacks. Among their deficiencies, the phenomenon of dollarization has been persistently observed in these economies.[1] Dollarization adversely affects the domestic economy because it intensifies the inflationary effects of a given fiscal deficit. Moreover, dollarization thwarts the ability of authorities to implement independent economy-wide monetary and fiscal policies because the foreign currency component of the total money supply is not subject to their control. The methods by which firms in emerging markets secure funding and capital in the domestic financial markets is an issue that concerns international investors. In most developing countries, lack of funding is often the main obstacle to growth in the private sector. Banking systems are frequently unable to provide the required funds and capital markets have in the past failed to secure the desired instruments, both in terms of required quantities and preferred maturities. Moreover, government controls often restrict the types of instruments available and regulate the issuing and pricing of such tools.

However, with the advent of recent market reforms, firms in emerging countries are currently experiencing an increase in the choice of financing options. For many firms, the criterion that is used to determine the most desirable option available is a combination of minimized cost and minimized risk. In other words, cheaper financing is usually the first to be used and management is wary of overburdening the firm with debt secured financing due to of the possibility of bankruptcy.[2]

The dynamic linkages among the world's major markets have been studied since the late 1960s (e.g., Grubel, 1968; Granger and Morgenstern, 1970; Levy and Sarnat, 1970; Grubel and Fadner, 1971; Agmon, 1972; Bertoneche, 1979; Hilliard, 1979), with increased scrutiny emerging in the last decade (e.g., Schollhammer and Sands, 1985; Eun and Shim, 1989; Meric and Meric, 1989; Von Furstenberg and Jeon, 1989, 1991; Hamao, Masulis, and Ng, 1990; Koch and Koch, 1991; Birati and Shachmurove, 1992; Chan, Gup, and Pan, 1992; Malliaris and Urrutia, 1992; Roll, 1992, Friedman and Shachmurove, 1996; and Shachmurove, 1996). While some have studied the Latin American economies (e.g., Bhagwati, 1993; Alonso, 1994; Gwyne, 1994), this study is among the first to investigate the dynamic linkages across national stock indexes of the seven newly emerging markets of Latin America.

Determining which country occupies the leading position in market size depends on how well each country's stock market and currency are performing at a given time. Hence, this process is not of great significance. Yet, the classification presented in Table 22.1 is true for the period studied in this chapter. The Mexican stock market is the largest exchange, followed by the Brazilian, Chilean, Argentinean, Colombian, Peruvian, and Venezuelan markets. This chapter will discuss theoretical issues and present empirical results.

THEORETICAL CONCEPTS

This section briefly surveys the theoretical concepts employed in this chapter: optimization algorithms and portfolio evaluation techniques. Optimization algorithms are mathematical procedures that solve multiple variable problems simultaneously. The results are optimal given the information provided in the formulation of the problem. The allocation of funds into different investments is accomplished in such a way as to maximize returns and minimize variability. In order to screen investments according to their return and risk characteristics, several statistical measures are used. These statistics include the geometric mean, variance, beta, and lower partial moment (LPM).[3] These procedures are employed to measure the return and risk inherent in investment. The ranking of assets by their risk/return statistics provides an initial screen of individual assets.

Optimization algorithms, however, provide only trade-offs between risk and return. There will be optimized high return-high risk portfolios, optimized medium return-medium risk portfolios and optimized low return-low risk portfolios. At this point the owner of portfolio has to decide which portfolio maximizes her utility. Evaluation techniques are applied to assess the optimal solutions derived by comparing them to other investment alternatives such as the

Table 22.1. Overview of Emerging Latin American Markets (as of November 1994)

Country	Number of Companies	Market Capitalization ($ billions)	Value of Shares ($ billions)
Mexico	198	196.10	78.50
Brazil	542	190.60	81.60
Chile	304	71.20	4.70
Argentina	168	41.60	9.90
Colombia	90	14.80	2.00
Peru	215	8.40	2.80
Venezuela	93	3.70	1.10
Total	1,610	526.40	180.60

Source: International Finance Corporation, Emerging Markets Database.

S&P 500, or a portfolio consisting of equally weighted initial allocations of the assets present in the derived optimal portfolio.

Optimization Algorithms

Optimization algorithms are mathematical tools that solve multiple-variable problems using quadratic programming. In portfolio theory a dollar of investment is allocated among different securities in order to maximize return and minimize variability. In this case, the budget constraint requires that all allocations sum up to 100% of the available total investment. In addition to the variance, both beta and LPM statistics can be formulated and used in quadratic programming analysis.

As with any limited resource that is to be apportioned, decisions have to be taken regarding the division of these endowments. The construction of portfolios assumes two such decisions: choosing between asset classes such as stocks, bonds, foreign currency, and the like (strategic optimization), and choosing between securities in any given asset class (tactical optimization). The majority of investors prefer to participate in the former kind of allocation, mainly to optimize across asset classes. Few, however, optimize within a given asset class, omitting tactical optimization. This despite the fact that there is evidence to support the concept of tactical optimization. For example, an equity market index with optimized allocations will outperform indices with equal or value weighted allocations (Haugan, 1990a, 1990b). In this chapter the Markowitz Variance-Covariance Analysis and the Lower Partial Moment Analysis are employed to derive the optimal portfolio.[4]

Markowitz Variance-Covariance Analysis

Markowitz (1959) developed the basic variance-covariance analysis. Low or negative correlations between assets are used to reduce the overall variability or risk of the portfolio. The variance of the portfolio is calculated as follows:

$$V_p = \sum_{i=1}^{k} \sum_{j=1}^{k} X_i X_j \, Cov_{ij}, \tag{1}$$

where V_p is the portfolio variance, k is the number of assets in the portfolio, X is the share of asset i or j within the portfolio, and Cov_{ij} is the covariance between assets i and j. It is calculated by:

$$Cov_{ij} = \sigma_i \, \sigma_j \, r_{ij}, \tag{2}$$

where σ_i is the standard deviation for asset i and r_{ij} is the correlation coefficient between assets i and j.

The expected return of the portfolio is determined by:

$$E_p = \sum_{i=1}^{k} X_i \, E\,(R_i), \tag{3}$$

where E_p is the expected return of the portfolio and $E(R_i)$ is the expected return for asset i.

Using the preceding formulas, a quadratic programming method is constructed to maximize return and minimize variance as follows:

$$Min \; z = V_p - \lambda \cdot E_p \tag{4}$$

$$s.t., \; \sum_{i=1}^{k} X_i = 1,$$

where λ is the slope of the objective function. The term λ may be varied from zero to infinity in order to solve for various points on the efficiency frontier.[5] The outcome of these calculations is that the results map the efficiency frontier, where each point corresponds to a portfolio, which in turn represents the lowest risk for a given return or the highest return for a given risk (Markowitz, 1959).

Lower Partial Moment Analysis

In lower partial moment analysis, the variance is replaced with the lower partial moment or the semivariance, which is a special case of lower partial moment with $n = 2$. The same expected return and risk equations hold true as does the following quadratic formulation:

$$LPM_{2,p} = \sum_{i=1}^{k} \sum_{j=1}^{k} X_i X_j \, SD_i \, SD_j \, r_{ij} \tag{5}$$

$$Min \; z = LPM_{2,p} - \lambda \cdot E_p, \tag{6}$$

where $LPM_{2,p}$ is the semivariance of portfolio p, k is the number of assets, SD_i is the semideviation (square root of the semivariance) for asset i, and r_{ij} is the correlation between assets i and j (e.g., Bawa, 1975; Fishburn, 1977; Nawrocki, 1991).

Portfolio Evaluation

After the selection of a portfolio, its performance is then evaluated. Performance measures that account for both risk and return need to be computed. Portfolio evaluation measures consist of Terminal Wealth; Sharpe's Utility Measure, Sharpe, Treynor, and Jensen Measures; Reward to Semivariance; and Stochastic Dominance.

Terminal Wealth

The Terminal Wealth measure replies to the following query: How much money did the investor make? It is a ratio that indicates the amount of money generated for each dollar of initial investment. Terminal Wealth is the k-th power of the geometric mean, or simply the product of the individual returns. It is the only important, long-term evaluation performance measure. This is because risk-return measures are not accurate, since as the investment horizon increases, the importance of liquidity risk decreases. Terminal Wealth is given by the following expression:

$$Terminal\ Wealth = \prod_{i=1}^{k}(R_t) \qquad (7)$$

where $\prod$ is the multiplication operator, k is the number of periods and R_t is the rate of return at time period t.

Sharpe Utility Measure

The Sharpe (1966) Utility Measure employs an estimate of the investor's risk tolerance rather than the riskless rate of return as an indicator of the portfolio holder's utility function. The risk tolerance ranges from zero to one. The higher the risk tolerance, the higher the proportion of the portfolio invested in the riskier assets (Sharpe and Alexander, 1990). The measure is defined as follows:

$$Utility = Return - (Variance/Risk\ Tolerance) \qquad (8)$$

Risk tolerance is defined as the level of risk an investor is disposed to bear. This characteristic is unique for each individual investor. Investors who are risk-averse accept only low amounts of risk compared to their risk-neutral and risk-loving counterparts. Risk-averse investors penalize the expected rate of return of a risky investment by a certain percentage to reflect the inherent danger. Risk-neutral investors, on the other hand, judge investments solely on the basis of the expected return, thus eliminating risk considerations from their strategy. Finally, risk-loving investors adjust expected returns upwards when risk is present (Bodie, Kane, and Marcus, 1993).

Sharpe, Treynor, and Jensen Measures

The Sharpe (1966), Treynor (1965), and Jensen (1968) Measures are defined as follows:

$$Sharpe = (R_p - R_f) / \sigma_p \tag{9}$$

$$Treynor = (R_p - R_f) / \beta_p \tag{10}$$

$$Jensen \ (a_p) = R_p - R_f - \beta_p \ (R_m - R_f) - e_t, \tag{11}$$

where R_p is the return on the portfolio, R_f is the riskless rate of return, σ_p is the standard deviation of the portfolio, and β_p is the beta of the portfolio.

Both the Sharpe and the Treynor measures use reward-to-risk ratios. The Sharpe Measure employs standard deviation in its denominator, while the Treynor Measure applies the beta value. The Jensen Measure, which is based on the Capital Asset Pricing Model (CAPM), investigates the investment's performance by calculating the intercept a_p of the regression line: $R_p - R_f = a_p + \beta_p \ (R_m - R_f) + e_t$. If the portfolio fares better than the market, a_p is greater than zero. When it underperforms, a_p is less than zero. If a_p is significantly different than zero and it is positive, the portfolio is considered successful. On the other hand, if a_p is less than zero, the portfolio is a failure. Therefore, the higher the value of a_p, the greater the abnormal rate of return achieved by the portfolio in excess of the market (Jensen, 1968; Levy and Sarnat, 1984). These three measures, however, are not fully accurate since they are statistically biased (Ang and Chua, 1979). The effect of the bias is that each of the measures may rank the performance of a group of portfolios differently from its counterparts.

Reward to Semivariance

The Reward to Semivariance Ratio is defined as follows:

$$Reward \ to \ Semivariance = (R_p - R_f) / SD_p, \tag{12}$$

where SD_p is the semideviation of the portfolio. This ratio is preferred over other alternatives because studies have revealed that the Sharpe, Treynor, and Jensen Measures are statistically biased. Various causes of the biases have been proposed. They include the existence of unequal borrowing and lending rates, the failure to account for higher moments of return distributions, and the elusive "true" holding period (Ang and Chua, 1979). The deficiency of this ratio is that it assumes a fixed utility function by setting $n = 2$. This shortcoming can be overcome by employing the more general Reward-to-LPM Ratio. The degree, n, can then be manipulated in this case to match the utility function of the investor (Klemkosky, 1973).

Stochastic Dominance

Stochastic dominance is an effective evaluation technique for judging the performances of portfolios, because it does not make any assumptions concerning the underlying probability distribution of security returns, and is based on a very general utility function. First Degree Stochastic Dominance (FSD) places no restrictions on utility functions except that they should be nondecreasing. Thus, FSD acts as a preliminary screening that eliminates those options that no rational investor would choose. Second Degree Stochastic Dominance (SSD) applies only to risk-averse investors by assuming a concave utility function. All efficient sets included in SSD are also present in FSD, but not necessarily vice versa. Finally, Third Degree Stochastic Dominance (TSD) further assumes decreasing absolute risk aversion, and hence is applicable to yet a smaller group of investors. Decreasing absolute risk aversion means that the risk premium an investor is willing to pay to be rid of a given risk, declines as his wealth increases. This implies that, at higher levels of wealth, the portfolio owner becomes more risk-neutral (Porter, Wart, and Ferguson, 1973; Francis and Archer, 1979; Francis, 1980; Saunders, 1980; Elton and Gruber, 1984; Levy and Sarnat, 1984).

EMPIRICAL RESULTS

The data cover the period from December 31, 1987, through December 30, 1994. For the purposes of this chapter, an optimal portfolio for the period ranging from July 7, 1994, to December 30, 1994, is used as the basis of the discussion. The average Treasury bill return, which is the assumed risk-free rate for the period, is 3.00%. The performance of the Argentinean, Mexican, Brazilian, Chilean, Venezuelan, Colombian, and Peruvian exchanges are recorded and compared with the S&P 500.[6] The aforementioned time frame has been chosen for several reasons. First, it is more likely to reveal the optimal asset allocation because studies employing this interval have obtained the largest number of optimal portfolios in comparison with any other period. Second, the T-bill rate for the period is the lowest interest rate over the span of the study. Such an environment encourages investors to consider more diversified investment strategies in hopes of securing higher yields.

Table 22.2 indicates that the optimization frontier contains seven different portfolios, each optimizing one or more particular criteria. These criteria are annual return, periodic return, standard deviation, semideviation, utility, probability of loss, and the Reward to Semivariance Ratio (R/SV). The method used is the Markowitz Critical Line Algorithm which computes corner portfolios on the efficiency frontier (Markowitz, 1959). Of the seven optimal portfolios, the one with the highest R/SV is deemed appropriate for the purposes of this study. Portfolio number 4 conforms to this characteristic. Its R/SV ratio of 0.38 surpasses the corresponding R/SV ratios of the six other candidates. Portfolio number 4 yields an annual return of 74.91% on investment. Table 22.3 exhibits the component securities of this optimal portfolio: Colombia 60.38%, Chile 35.10%, Peru 4.35%, and Brazil 0.17%. The standard deviation of the portfolio is 0.96%. The shortfall probability of realizing a return below the risk-free rate is 0.41.

Table 22.2. Markowitz Covariance Analysis

Portfolio	# of Sec	AnnRet	Periodic Return	Std Dev	SemiDev	Utility	ProbLoss	R/SV
EV1	1	91.41	0.26	1.35	0.42	0.19	0.43	0.31
EV2	2	89.69	0.26	1.28	0.42	0.19	0.42	0.32
EV3	3	75.39	0.22	0.96	0.41	0.19	0.41	0.37
EV4	4	74.91	0.22	0.96	0.41	0.19	0.41	0.38
EV5	4	70.57	0.21	0.92	0.41	0.18	0.41	0.37
EV6	4	33.07	0.11	0.61	0.43	0.10	0.43	0.27
EV7	4	9.62	0.04	0.51	0.47	0.03	0.48	0.07

Table 22.3. Characteristics of the Optimal Portfolio Chosen Based Upon Reward/Semivariance (Critical Line Algorithm)

Criteria (R/SV)		Allocation of the Optimal Portfolio	
Annualized Return	74.91	Portfolio #4 EV4	Allocations
Daily Return	0.22		
Standard Deviation	0.96	Colombia	60.38
SemiDeviation	0.41	Peru	4.35
Skewness	-0.12	Brazil	0.17
Beta	0.13	Chile	35.10
Pr (R < 15.00% Annual)	0.43		
Pr (R < 3.00% Annual)	0.41		
Pr (R < .00% Annual)	0.41		
Reward/Variance	0.22		
Reward/Semivariance	0.38		
Portfolio Utility	0.19		

Table 22.4 provides a short summary of individual assets. The annualized return in Argentina is -8.71% and the standard deviation is 2.29%; in Mexico, the return is -33.58% with a standard deviation of 2.14%. In Brazil, the return is 34.33% and the deviation 4.01%; in Chile, the return is 50.35% with a standard deviation of 1.49%. In Venezuela, the return is -32.04% with a deviation of 2.80%; in Colombia, the return is 91.40% with a standard deviation of 1.35%. Finally in Peru, the return is 71.62% with a standard deviation of 2.37%.

It may seem surprising that the Colombian market is not the most volatile, given the high return that it offers. This leads to the conclusion that there must be some additional risk inherent in the Colombian market that is not reflected in the calculated standard deviation. There are two kinds of risk omitted by the numerical observations: foreign exchange and sovereign risks. Foreign exchange risk is defined as the risk that a return denominated in a foreign currency will have a lower value in the domestic currency due to a fluctuation between the

Table 22.4. Individual Assets Summary Report

Country	AnnRet	Periodic Return	Std Dev	SemiDev	ProbLoss	Utility
Argentina	-8.71	-0.04	2.29	1.72	0.51	-0.25
Mexico	-33.58	-0.16	2.14	1.51	0.53	-0.35
Brazil	34.33	0.12	4.01	2.74	0.49	-0.53
Chile	50.35	0.16	1.49	0.99	0.46	0.07
Venezuela	-32.04	-0.15	2.80	0.93	0.52	-0.47
Colombia	91.40	0.26	1.35	0.80	0.42	0.19
Peru	71.62	0.22	2.37	1.60	0.46	-0.01
S&P 500	-3.63	-0.01	0.63	0.47	0.51	-0.03

Table 22.5. Comparison Between the Optimal Portfolio Chosen (EV4), the S&P 500, and an Equally Weighted Portfolio

Portfolio	Periodic Return	Std Dev	Semivar
EV4	0.22	0.96	0.57
Equal	0.06	1.19	0.89
S&P 500	-0.01	0.63	0.47

Portfolio	Terminal Wealth	Utility	R/SV
EV4	1.31	0.19	0.38
Equal	1.08	0.01	0.06
S&P 500	0.98	-0.03	-0.06

Portfolio	Annual Return	Beta	Skewness
EV4	74.91	0.13	-0.12
Equal	16.85	0.70	-1.03*
S&P 500	-3.63	1.00	-0.30

	EV4	Equal	S&P 500
Periodic Return	0.220	0.060	-0.010
Standard Deviation	0.960	1.190	0.630
Sharpe Measure	0.220	0.040	-0.040
Treynor Measure	2.630	0.070	-0.030
Jensen Alpha	0.002	0.000	0.000
Beta	0.130	0.700	1.000
T-Test	0.580	4.260	99.000
R^2	0.000	0.130	1.000
Terminal Wealth	1.310	1.080	0.980
Utility Measure	0.190	0.010	-0.030
Reward/Semivariance	0.380	0.060	-0.060

*Denotes significant skewness at two standard deviations

two currencies. Sovereign risk refers to the danger of a government interfering in its domestic market, in a manner that has an adverse impact on investments (Grabbe, 1991). These risks are present in the Colombian market and, to a lesser extent, in the other South American markets as well. Shortfall probabilities are 0.51 in Argentina, 0.53 in Mexico, 0.49 in Brazil, 0.46 in Chile, 0.52 in Venezuela, 0.42 in Colombia, and 0.46 in Peru.

Table 22.5 shows that the portfolio beta is 0.13, well below the market (S&P 500) beta of 1.00. The Sharpe Measure is 0.22, the Treynor Measure is 2.63, and the Jensen Alpha value is 0.002. In order to provide a complete analysis of the findings, these statistics are compared to the analogous market values. The Sharpe Measure for the S&P 500 is -0.04, the Treynor Measure is -0.03, and the Jensen value is, by definition, 0. The portfolio, therefore, provides substantially more reward per unit of risk, whether variance or beta, than the S&P 500. The results are also compared to statistics derived from a portfolio consisting of equally weighted initial allocations to all securities in the optimal portfolio. Portfolio number 4 outperforms the equally weighted portfolio on all counts. The performance measures considered are Periodic Return, Sharpe Measure, Treynor Measure, Jensen Alpha, Beta, T-test, R-squared, Terminal Wealth, Utility, and the R/SV. Furthermore, portfolio number 4 provides a higher return than that predicted by the CAPM, given its beta and the average market return. Since the Jensen Measure is greater than zero, this means that the portfolio performs better than the market. These results are summarized in Table 22.5.

The optimal portfolio is subject to another test in addition to the variance-covariance analysis. The Lower Partial Moment Algorithm calculates the LPM/CLPM (Lower Partial Moment/Covariance Lower Partial Moment) matrix, given the investor's level of risk aversion. The optimal portfolio derived through the application of this algorithm is listed in Table 22.6. The portfolio yields an annual return of 76.71% and a R/SV ratio of 0.38. These statistics are almost identical to the return and R/SV ratio generated by the Critical Line Algorithm. Table 22.7 presents the allocations within the portfolio. The results generated by the Lower Partial Moment Algorithm (65.53% Colombia, 31.43% Chile, 2.69 % Peru, and 0.35% Brazil) are again similar to those obtained from the Critical Line Algorithm described previously.

Table 22.6. Lower Partial Moment (LPM) Quadratic Programming (QP) Analysis

Portfolio	# of Sec	AnnRet	Periodic Return	SemiDev	ProbLoss	Utility	ProbLoss	R/SV
LPMQ1	1	91.40	0.26	0.80	0.42	0.19	0.43	0.31
LPMQ2	2	90.23	0.26	0.78	0.42	0.19	0.43	0.32
LPMQ3	3	77.86	0.23	0.59	0.41	0.19	0.41	0.37
LPMQ4	4	76.71	0.23	0.58	0.41	0.19	0.41	0.38
LPMQ5	4	68.50	0.21	0.54	0.41	0.18	0.41	0.37
LPMQ6	4	41.72	0.14	0.42	0.42	0.12	0.43	0.31
LPMQ7	4	18.77	0.07	0.36	0.45	0.06	0.46	0.16

Table 22.7. Characteristics of the Optimal Portfolio Chosen Based Upon Reward/Semivariance (Lower Partial Moment Algorithm)

Criteria (R/SV)		Allocation of the Optimal Portfolio	
Annualized Return	76.71	Portfolio #4 EV4	Allocations
Daily Return	0.23		
Standard Deviation	0.98	Colombia	65.53
SemiDeviation	0.58	Peru	2.69
Skewness	-0.16	Brazil	0.35
Beta	0.08	Chile	31.43
Pr (R < 15.00% Annual)	0.41		
Pr (R < .00% Annual)	0.41		
Reward/Variance	0.22		
Reward/Semivariance	0.38		
Portfolio Utility	0.19		

Finally, to complete the analysis, the risk/return performance of the securities in the portfolios is evaluated by using First, Second, and Third Degree Dominance techniques. The assets for each degree of dominance and their corresponding statistical variables are exhibited in Table 22.8. The best risk/return performance is provided by those securities listed under Third Degree Dominance. Under First Degree Dominance all the assets except Peru are included. Peru is exempt because it registers a lower probability of achieving the same level of return as the other markets, given a specific level of risk. Under Second and Third Degree Dominance, only Colombia, Chile, and the S&P 500 are listed. The other securities are excluded from Second Degree Dominance because the cumulative probability of either Colombia, Chile, or the S&P achieving a given return, each taken separately, minus the cumulative probabilities of the other securities achieving the same return, also taken separately, are consistently nonnegative.

CONCLUSION

This chapter studies the daily stock market returns of seven Latin American countries, and the prospect of investment for the purposes of diversification. The period July 7, 1994, to December 30, 1994, is used as the basis of the analysis. An optimal portfolio is generated and evaluated with appropriate performance measures. The optimal portfolio, acquired through the application of the Markowitz Critical Line Algorithm, allocates 60.38% of the funds in the Colombian exchange, 4.35% in the Peruvian market, 0.17% in Brazil, and 35.10% in Chile. It achieves an annualized return of 74.91%, a R/SV ratio of 0.38, a standard deviation of 0.96% and a shortfall probability of 0.41. The portfolio's beta is 0.13, well below the corresponding market beta of 1.00. Hence, it is far less volatile than the market, as represented by the S&P 500. The

Table 22.8. Stochastic Dominance Analysis

Asset	Mean	Variance	Skew	Kurtosis	Min	Max
First Degree Stochastic Dominance						
Brazil	1.00200	0.00160	-0.85500	2.93940	0.89280	1.09660
Argentina	0.99990	0.00052	-0.52760	3.91820	0.92350	1.05370
S&P	0.99990	0.00004	-0.31480	5.03960	0.97730	1.02130
Mexico	0.99860	0.00066	0.63050	5.68500	0.93750	1.08900
Chile	1.00170	0.00022	-0.14250	3.11200	0.96190	1.04010
Venezuela	0.99880	0.00078	0.45744	7.46720	0.89100	1.11380
Columbia	1.00270	0.00018	-0.10080	5.85960	0.94460	1.03920
Second Degree Stochastic Dominance						
Columbia	1.00270	0.00018	-0.10080	5.85960	0.94460	1.03920
Chile	1.00170	0.00022	-0.14250	3.11200	0.96190	1.04010
S&P	0.99990	0.00004	-0.31480	5.03960	0.97730	1.02130
Third Degree Stochastic Dominance						
Columbia	1.00270	0.00018	-0.10080	5.85960	0.94460	1.03920
Chile	1.00170	0.00022	-0.14250	3.11200	0.96190	1.04010
S&P	0.99990	0.00004	-0.31480	5.03960	0.97730	1.02130

Sharpe Measure is 0.22, the Treynor Measure is 2.63, and the Jensen Alpha is 0.002. In addition, the Lower Partial Moment Algorithm is applied to the optimal portfolio. The portfolio allocations obtained though the use of the LPMA are very similar to those generated by the Critical Line Algorithm.

The focus of this analysis is a select group of Latin American markets. While the reward-to-risk ratios, based on stock return volatilities, might be appealing, additional risk factors need to be both examined and accounted for. There are intrinsic dangers in foreign investment. The risk manifests itself in two forms: foreign exchange risk and sovereign risk. The former implies that a foreign-currency-denominated return will have a lower real value following an adverse change between the relative values of two currencies. Sovereign risk refers to the possibility of intervention in foreign markets by the domestic governments, producing an environment that has a negative impact on investments. The optimal portfolio derived above incorporates both of these risks, since it is based on the allocation of funds into foreign securities. Therefore, investors are rewarded for the additional risk they are bearing by higher premiums.

Nevertheless, it is beneficial for contemporary investors to possess well-diversified portfolios, rather than to limit their investments to a single market. The low correlation among stock markets implies that their movements are not perfectly synchronized. Consequently, investing in a portfolio consisting of allocations in several foreign exchanges permits investors to negate the risk that an adverse fluctuation in any given market will have a considerable effect on the return of their portfolios.

NOTES

1. Dollarization refers to holding a large proportion of domestic financial assets in the form of interest-bearing foreign currency deposits. This strategy is undertaken to hedge against high and volatile inflation.

2. While cost and risk are the two principal variables that are considered by most firms, a few firms believe there to be a third factor. This factor, particularly present in emerging markets where the tradition of family ownership is strong, is that of control of the firm. Control can dominate financial decision-making to the extent that management is unwilling to relinquish its monopoly on firm decision-making. Some firms avoid equity issues in apprehension of the loss of control that will inevitably result. Consequently, debt financing is often preferred over equity issues, even when the cost and risk features of such debt are below par, in order to prevent the dilution of control that follows equity issues.

3. These statistics are described in the Appendix.

4. Other algorithms are applied and tested as well. These are Nawrocki's (1991) Lower Partial Moment Heuristic Algorithm, Elton, Gruber, and Padberg's (1976) Beta-Single Index Model and Average Correlation Heuristic Algorithm. The results obtained through the application of these algorithms are similar to those generated by the two algorithms mentioned above and are available from the author upon request.

5. The algorithm used is the Critical Line Algorithm. It begins with the highest return portfolio which, by definition, includes the highest return asset. Each asset is then evaluated using a critical value (pivot conditions) to determine which is the next asset to enter the portfolio. As assets enter into the portfolio, it becomes more diversified and will have lower risk as well as return. Each portfolio derived is called a corner portfolio. A corner portfolio is generated when an asset either enters or exits the portfolio. The result of these corner portfolios is that they map the efficient frontier, where each portfolio represents the lowest risk for a given return or the highest return for a given risk.

6. The S&P 500 is the composite index of 500 U.S. stocks, and is commonly regarded as an accurate representation of the U.S. stock market.

7. Markowitz (1959) was the first to offer the use of semivariance as a substitute for beta and variance to handle both skewed return distributions and investors who have nonquadratic utility functions.

APPENDIX: STATISTICAL MEASURES

The statistical measures used are: geometric mean, variance, beta, and lower partial moment.

Geometric Mean

For the k numbers a, b, c, d, e, and f, the geometric mean is:

$$[a \cdot b \cdot c \cdot d \cdot e \cdot f]^{(1/k)} \tag{A.1}$$

For the purpose of determining rates of return, the method of computing a geometric mean is more accurate than a simple arithmetic mean, since it takes into account the compounding nature of interest over time.

Variance

$$\sigma_i^2 = (1/k) \sum_{t=1}^{k} [R_{it} - E(R_i)]^2,$$ (A.2)

where R_{it} is the return to asset i in period t, and $E(R_i)$ is the expected geometric mean return for asset i. Variance measures the magnitude of deviations from the mean. The greater the deviations, the greater the level of risk. Variance plays an important role in the evaluation of potential investments. For a risk-averse individual choosing between two investments with equal expected returns, the investment with the lower variance is more attractive. Consequently, investments with higher risk (i.e., higher variance) must offer higher expected returns to compensate investors for the additional risk, see Markowitz (1959).

Beta

The beta (β) of an asset measures the variability of an asset relative to the market index. It is a popular risk measure, and has been widely used for the past 25 years. The standard was developed to make the Modern Portfolio Theory (MPT) model operational, which is computationally complex when the variance is used. The β statistic is determined using the following regression:

$$R_{it} = a_i + \beta_i \cdot R_{mt} + e_t$$ (A.3)

$$\sigma_e^2 = (1/k) \sum_{t=1}^{k} e_t^2,$$ (A.4)

where

$$e_t = R_{it} - [a_i + \beta_i \cdot R_{mt}],$$ (A.5)

R_{it} is the return on asset i for period t, a_i is the intercept of the line, β_i represents the slope of the line and is defined as the tendency of the asset's returns to respond to swings in the broad market, R_{mt} is the return to the market index for that same period t, and e_t measures the deviation of R_{it} from the regression line for period t. There are k observations, such that $t = 1, 2, \ldots, k$.

The beta of the market index β_M, is arbitrarily set at 1.0, and serves as a reference value with which to compare individual asset betas. If the beta of an asset is equal to 1.0, then both the asset and the market are equally risky, and will tend to move together. If β_i is greater than 1.0, then the asset is more volatile than the market, and hence, more risky. If β_i is less than 1.0, then the asset is less volatile than the market, and hence, less risky. Furthermore, beta serves to determine the incremental risk an individual asset brings to a well diversified portfolio.

$$\sigma_i^2 = \beta_i^2 \cdot \sigma_m^2 + \sigma_e^2$$ (A.6)

The first component of the variance of an asset ($\beta_i^2 \cdot \sigma_m^2$) is termed the systematic or nondiversifiable risk component, and is the risk inherent in the general market. The second component (σ_e^2) is termed the unsystematic or diversifiable risk component, and can be diversified away as it is due not to the market in general, but rather, only to that particular asset (Sharpe, 1964).

Lower Partial Moment

Both variance analysis and the use of betas to estimate risk levels presuppose a normally distributed set of security returns and investors with quadratic utility functions. In order to address risk levels when these assumptions cannot confidently be made, the Lower Partial Moment was developed.[7] Semivariance is a special case of LPM analysis (Bawa, 1975; Fishburn, 1977). Semivariance is defined as an n-degree LPM with $n = 2$. The variable n refers to the degree that deviations below a target return are raised to. The LPM is defined as follows:

$$LPM_n(h) = (1/k) \sum_{t=1}^{k} Max[0, h - R_t]^n, \qquad (A.7)$$

where n is the degree of the LPM, h is the target return the investor does not wish to go below, k is the number of periods used to calculate the LPM, and R_t is the return for the asset for period t. A problem that often occurs when determining asset riskiness is that security returns have nonnormal distributions. For two distributions, one positively skewed and the other negatively skewed, it is posible that they both have the same mean and variance—that is, the variance measure might not differentiate between the two distributions. However, the LPM measure can handle nonnormal distributions and is able to differentiate between the two. In LPM analysis, $n = 1$ is the boundary between risk-averse and risk-loving investors. If n is greater than 1, the investor is risk-averse and attempts to minimize risk for a given return, while for values of n is less than 1, the investor is risk-loving and prefers higher to lower risk. Furthermore, the use of LPM is less restrictive on assumptions of the investor's behavior than beta and variance analysis. It has been shown that the LPM can match the utility functions of investors who have been described in utility function literature. Decision makers in investment contexts frequently associate risk with failure to attain a target return. Examination of published utility functions which use the maximization of expected utility criterion lends support to the notion of a target return at which the utility undergoes a noticeable change. Depending on the context, the change point may be negative, zero, or positive (Fishburn, 1977).

It is important to note that in equation (A.7), the above-target returns ($R_t > h$) provide negative numbers. Given the choice between a zero or a negative number, the maximization operator will select the zero. Only below-target returns ($R_t < h$) will provide a positive deviation that is raised to the n power and added to the LPM calculation. LPM will, therefore, only provide nonnegative values.

REFERENCES

Ang, J.S. and J.H. Chua, 1979. Composite measures for the evaluation of investment performance, *Journal of Financial and Quantitative Analysis* 14(2), 361-384.

Agmon, T., 1972. The relations among equity markets: a study of share price co-movements in the United States, United Kingdom, Germany, and Japan, *Journal of Finance* September, 839-855.

Alonso, I.T. ed., 1994. *Trade, Industrialization, and Integration in Twentieth Century Central America*. Westport, CT: Praeger Publishers.

Bawa, V.S., 1975. Optimal rules for ordering uncertain prospects, *Journal of Finance* 30(1), 95-121.

Bertoneche, M.L., 1979. Spectral analysis of stock market prices, *Journal of Banking and Finance* 3, 201-208.

Bhagwati, J.N., 1993. Beyond NAFTA: Clinton's trading choices, *Foreign Policy* 91, 155-162.

Birati, A. and Y. Shachmurove, 1992. International stock price movements before and during the Gulf Crisis. In *Atlantic Economic Society: Best Papers Proceedings* Vol. 2(2), 42-47.

Bodie, Z., A. Kane, and A.J. Marcus, 1993. *Investments*. Boston, MA: Irwin.

Chan, C.K., B.E. Gup, and M.-S. Pan, 1992. An empirical analysis of stock prices in major Asian markets and the United States, *The Financial Review* 27(2), 289-307.

Elton, E.J. and M.J. Gruber, 1984. *Modern Portfolio Theory and Investment Analysis*, 2nd ed. New York: John Wiley and Sons.

Elton, E.J., M.J. Gruber, and M.W. Padberg, 1976. Simple criteria for optimal portfolio selection, *Journal of Finance* 31(5), 1341-1357.

Elton, E.J., M.J. Gruber, and T.J. Urich, 1978. Are betas best? *Journal of Finance* 33(5), 1375-1384.

Eun, C.S. and S. Shim, 1989. International transmission of stock market movements, *Journal of Financial and Quantitative Analysis* 24(2), 241-256.

Fishburn, P.C., 1977. Mean-risk analysis with risk associated with below-target returns, *American Economic Review* 67, 116-126.

Francis J., 1979. *Investments: Analysis and Management*, 3rd ed. New York : McGraw Hill.

Francis J. and S. Archer, 1979. *Portfolio Analysis*, 2nd ed. Englewood Cliffs, NJ: Prentice Hall.

Friedman, J. and Y. Shachmurove, 1996. International transmission of innovations among EC stock markets. In J. Doukas and L. Lang, eds., *Research in International Business and Finance*. Greenwich, CT: JAI Press Inc., 35-64.

Friedman, J. and Y. Shachmurove, 1998. Co-movements of major European community stock markets: a vector autoregression analysis, *Global Finance Journal*, forthcoming.

Grabbe, J.O., 1991. *International Financial Markets*. Englewood Cliffs, NJ: Prentice Hall.

Granger, C.W. and O. Morgenstern, 1970. *Predictability of Stock Market Prices*. Lexington, MA: Heath-Lexington Books.

Grubel, H.G., 1968. Internationally diversified portfolios, *American Economic Review* 58, 1299-1314.

Grubel, H. and K. Fadner, 1971. The interdependence of international equity markets, *Journal of Finance* 26, 89-94.

Gwyne, R., 1994. Regional integration in Latin America: the revival of a concept? In R. Gibb and W. Michalak, eds., *Continental Trading Blocs—the Growth of Regionalism in the World Economy*. New York: John Wiley and Sons.

Hamao, Y., W.M. Ronald, and V. Ng, 1990. Correlations in price changes and volatility across international stock markets, *Review of Financial Studies* 3, 281-307.

Haugen, R.A., 1990a. Building a better index: cap-weighted benchmarks are inefficient vehicles, *Pensions & Investments* October 1, 56.

Haugen, R.A., 1990b. New target brings rewards: using EI can lower expenses and raise funding ratios, *Pensions & Investments,* October 15, 50, 52.

Hilliard, J.E., 1979. The relationship between equity indexes on world exchanges, *Journal of Finance* 34, 103-114.

International Finance Corporation, 1996. Emerging markets database. Washington, DC: World Bank.

Jensen, M.C., 1968. The performance of mutual funds in the period 1945-1964, *Journal of Finance*, May.

Klemkosky, R.C., 1973. The bias in composite performance measures, *Journal of Financial and Quantitative Analysis* 8(3), 505-514.

Koch, P.D. and T. Koch, 1991. Evolution in dynamic linkages across daily national stock indexes, *Journal of International Money and Finance* 10(2), 231-251.

Levy, H. and M. Sarnat, 1970. International diversification of investment portfolios, *American Economic Review* 60, September, 668-675.

Levy, H. and M. Sarnat, 1984. *Portfolio and Investment Selection: Theory and Practice*. Englewood Cliffs, NJ: Prentice Hall.

Malliaris, A.G. and J. Urrutia, 1992. The international crash of October 1987: causality tests, *Journal of Financial and Quantitative Analysis* 27(3), 353-364.

Markowitz, H.M., 1959. Portfolio Selection: Efficient Diversification of Investments. New York: John Wiley and Sons.

Meric, I. and G. Meric, 1989. Potential gains from international portfolio diversification and inter-temporal stability and seasonality in international stock market relationships, *Journal of Banking and Finance* 13(4-5), 627-640.

Nawrocki, D.N., 1990. Tailoring asset allocations to the individual investor, *International Review of Economics and Business* 37, 977-990.

Nawrocki, D.N., 1991. Optimal algorithms and lower partial moment: ex post results, *Applied Economics* 23, 465-470.

Porter, R.B., J. Wart, and D. Ferguson, 1973. Efficient algorithms for conducting stochastic dominance tests on large numbers of portfolios, *Journal of Financial and Quantitative Analysis*, January, 71-82.

Reinganuon, M.R., 1983. The anomalous stock market behavior of small firms in January: empirical tests for tax-loss selling effects, *Journal of Financial Economics* 12(1), 89-104.

Roll, R., 1992. Industrial structure and the comparative behavior of international stock market indices, *Journal of Finance* 47(4), 3-41.

Saunders, A., C. Ward, and R. Woodward, 1980. Stochastic dominance and the performance of U.K. unit trusts, *Journal of Financial and Quantitative Analysis* 15(2), 323-330.

Schollhammer, H. and O. Sand, 1985. The interdependence among the stock markets of major European countries and the United States: an empirical investigation of interrelationships among national stock price movements, *Management International Review* 25(1), 17-26.

Shachmurove, Y., 1996. Dynamic linkages among Latin American and other major world stock markets. In J. Doukas and L. Lang, eds., *Research in International Business and Finance*. Greenwich, CT: JAI Press, 3-34.

Sharpe, W.F., 1963. A simplified model for portfolio analysis, *Management Science* 9(2), 277-293.

Sharpe, W.F., 1964. Capital asset prices: a theory of market equilibrium under conditions of risk, *Journal of Finance* 19(3), 425-442.

Sharpe, W.F., 1966. Mutual fund performance, *Journal of Business* 39(1), Part II, 119-138.

Sharpe, W.F. and G. Alexander, 1990. *Investments*, 4th ed. Englewood Cliffs, NJ: Prentice Hall.

Treynor, J.L., 1965. How to rate management investment funds, *Harvard Business Review* 43(1), 63-75.

Von Furstenberg, G.M. and B.N. Jeon, 1989. International stock price movements: links and messages, *Brookings Papers on Economic Activity* 1, 125-179.

23

The Behavior of the Colombian Emerging Capital Market

Harvey Arbelaez
and Jorge L. Urrutia

INTRODUCTION

Currently, the Colombian stock market, with exchanges in Bogota, Medellin, and Cali, is served by about 70 stockbrokers, some of them operating in the three markets. The trading mechanism is the traditional "open outcry," which is gradually being replaced by an electronic system. In fact, fixed-income securities on the Bogota and Medellin Exchanges are now traded electronically, and it is expected that in the near future, stocks will also be traded in the same way.

The purpose of this chapter is to examine the behavior of the Colombian capital market. Using data for the Medellin Stock Exchange, several tests are conducted in order to identify the time series properties and the efficiency of the Colombian stock market. The Medellin Stock Exchange opened its doors on April 3, 1961. By then Medellin had become Colombia's second economic center. The Medellin stock market is used as a proxy of the Colombian stock market for several important reasons. First, the Medellin Stock Exchange is the right place for investors to go, since Medellin's recognition as the industrial capital of Colombia is legendary given the entrepreneurship and creativity of the inhabitants of this part of the country. Second, Medellin has been the most important equity market in Colombia during recent years, with the highest volume of trade and market capitalization. Third, the Medellin Exchange leadership in equity trading; its commitment to provide efficient ways for trading, clearing, and settlement; and its concern for providing timely and relevant information are some of the factors that make Medellin an effective marketplace for investors, issuers and brokers.

METHODOLOGY

In order to investigate the time series properties and the efficiency of the

Colombian stock market, several tests are conducted. The importance of analyzing security return distributions has been recognized in the literature (Singleton and Wingender, 1986; Aggarwal and Aggarwal, 1993). Normality of return distributions of each index is analyzed by using tests of skewness and kurtosis and the Jarque-Bera test. Correlation coefficients between the several indices are also computed. It is expected that the indices will be highly correlated given the small size of the Colombian market and the relatively small number of shares traded. High correlations would indicate some spillover effect between the several indices. The time series properties of the several Colombian indices are also investigated using augmented Dickey-Fuller unit root tests (Dickey and Fuller, 1979). It is expected that prices are not stationary in levels but stationary in their first differences (returns).

Some researchers suggest that government intervention policies may cause stock price changes to be positively correlated (Liu and He, 1991). Spurious positive correlation may also be due to infrequent or nonsynchronous trading that can introduce large trading errors. Stock index returns may show positive auto-correlation if some of the securities in the index trade infrequently (Poterba and Summers, 1988). Also, if returns are not normally distributed, a different test is needed. One test of the weak form of market efficiency that does not require normality is the runs test (Levene, 1952). The runs test is a nonparametric test of randomness in a series. The premise behind the runs test is that too many or too few runs (a run is a change in the sign of the stock return) are unlikely if the series is random. The majority of stocks traded in thin markets have shown deviations from randomness (Jennergren and Korsvold, 1975; Roux and Gilbertson, 1978; Laurence, 1986; Butler and Malaikah, 1992; Urrutia, 1995).

Departures from the efficient market hypothesis, known as anomalies, have been extensively studied. Calendar anomalies, such as the day-of-the-week effect and the month-of-the-year effect, have been reported for the American stock market (Lakonishok and Smidt, 1988; Pettengill, 1989; Ariel, 1990), Japanese market (Jaffe and Westerfield, 1985); and other international markets (Agrawal and Tandon, 1994).

The day-of-the-week effect or weekend effect is a recurrent pattern documented by several researchers (French, 1980; Gibbons and Hess; 1981). It has been reported that the typical Friday-to-Monday return is significantly negative and different from the other weekday returns. The weekend effect is tested with the following regression:

$$R_{i,t} = b_0 + \sum_{t=2}^{5} b_t D_t + \varepsilon_t \qquad (1)$$

where $R_{i,t}$ = index return on day t; D_t = dummy variable equals one for day t, and zero otherwise; and the null hypothesis is that returns in each day are insignificantly different from zero.

The month-of-the-year effect or January effect refers to the empirical finding that returns are higher in January (Klein, 1983; Blume and Stambaugh, 1983).

Some empirical evidence supports the belief that the January effect is connected to tax-loss selling (Ritter, 1988; Reinganum, 1983). The month-of-the-year effect is investigated with the following regression:

$$R_{i,t} = b_0 + \sum_{t=2}^{12} b_t D_t + \varepsilon_t \tag{2}$$

where $R_{i,t}$ = index return on month t; D_t = dummy variable equals one for month t, and zero otherwise; and the null hypothesis is that returns in each month are insignificantly different from zero.

DATA

The data correspond to weekly prices for the following stock indices of the Bolsa de Valores de Medellin, Colombia: general (index Vallejos), industrial, financial, and commerce. The data set covers the time period from December 29, 1987, through August 9, 1994. Daily and monthly prices are also used in testing for market anomalies.

Important economic reforms were introduced in 1990. In order to investigate the impact of these reforms on the stock markets the data have also been divided in two time periods: from December 29, 1987, to December 28, 1990; and from January 2, 1991, to August 9, 1994.

Returns are computed as the natural log difference in prices, $ln(P_{i,t}/P_{i,t-1})$.

ANALYSIS OF EMPIRICAL RESULTS

Basic Statistics

The mean, median, standard deviation, skewness, kurtosis, Jarque-Bera normality test, and Sharpe ratio of weekly returns are computed, but not presented here for the sake of space . In general, the returns and standard deviations are higher than those for industrial and Asian countries. However, the Colombian indices exhibit higher Sharpe ratios than the United States, Europe, and Asia. Thus, the capital market of the country seems to have a better risk-return trade-off than those of developed countries. The skewness and kurtosis measures indicate that the rates of return are not drawn from a normal distribution. The rejection of normality is also strongly confirmed by the Jarque-Bera test of normality. The second time period exhibits higher returns, higher standard deviations, and higher Sharpe ratios than the first time period. That is, the Colombian stock market improved following the economic reforms introduced in the year 1990. Tests of correlation show that the four indices are highly correlated with each other. This result agrees with the American capital market, where the several market indices are also highly correlated with each other. The correlation among the indices are higher for the second time period, suggesting that the indices become more interrelated following the economic reforms introduced in 1990.

Table 23.1. Runs Tests of Weekly Returns

	M	E(M)	σ(M)	Z
Panel A: Whole Time Period (December 29, 1987–August 9, 1994)				
General	110	229.67	7.81	-15.32*
Industrial	128	229.67	7.81	-13.02*
Financial	108	229.67	7.81	-15.79*
Commerce	120	229.67	7.81	-14.04*
Panel B: First Time Period (December 29, 1987–December 28, 1990)				
General	42	103.67	5.24	-11.77*
Industrial	51	103.67	5.24	-10.05*
Financial	46	103.67	5.24	-11.01
Commerce	51	103.67	5.24	-10.05*
Panel C: Second Time Period (January 2, 1991–August 9, 1994)				
General	68	125.67	5.76	-10.01*
Industrial	77	125.67	5.76	-8.45*
Financial	62	125.67	5.76	-11.05
Commerce	69	125.67	5.76	-9.84*

*Significant at the 1% confidence level
M = Actual number of runs
N = Number of observations
Z-statistics: $Z = [M - E(M)] / \sigma(M)$

$E(M)$ = Expected number of runs: $E(M) = (2N-1)/3$
$\sigma(M)$ = Standard error: $\sigma_M = (16N - 29 / 90)^{0.5}$

Tests of Predictability and Market Efficiency

Predictability of returns can be evidence of market inefficiency. Augmented Dickey-Fuller tests, not shown here, indicate that prices follow a random walk and that Colombian stock prices are integrated of order one. These findings confirm results reported elsewhere for prices and returns of national indices of developed and emerging stock markets.

The results of the runs test are presented in Table 23.1. The null hypothesis of randomness or independence is rejected for all cases. That is, results from runs tests suggest that the Colombian equity market is not weak-form efficient. This finding is different from those reported for other emerging markets such Chile (Urrutia, 1995), where stock markets have been found to be efficient in the weak form. The economic implication of the rejection of the weak form of market efficiency for the Colombian stock market is that investors might be able to detect patterns in stock prices and develop trading strategies that would allow them to earn abnormal returns.

Seasonalities

Table 23.2 contains the results for the day-of-the-week effect. A Monday

Table 23.2. Days-of-the-Week Effect

	General	Industrial	Financial	Commerce
Panel A: Whole Time Period (December 29, 1987–August 9, 1994)				
Constant	0.2052*	0.1959*	0.2212*	0.2676**
	(3.31)	(2.74)	(3.20)	(1.84)
D_2	-0.0400	-0.0274	-0.0737	-0.1162
	(-0.480)	(-0.28)	(-0.79)	(-0.59)
D_3	-0.1200	-0.1344	-0.0661	-0.2064
	(-1.44)	(-1.40)	(-0.71)	(-1.06)
D_4	-0.0201	0.0479	-0.0170	-0.0869
	(0.27)	(0.49)	(-0.18)	(-0.44)
D_5	0.0448	0.0685	0.0229	0.0969
	(0.53)	(0.71)	(0.24)	(0.49)
Panel B: Second Time Period (January 2, 1991–August 9, 1994)				
Constant	0.3249*	0.3042*	0.3432*	0.4197
	(3.19)	(2.60)	(2.99)	(1.84)
D_2	-0.1171	-0.0735	-0.1616	-0.2754
	(-0.85)	(-0.46)	(-1.04)	(-0.89)
D_3	-0.2326	-0.2052	-0.1689	-0.2366
	(-1.68)	(-1.61)	(-1.08)	(-0.77)
D_4	0.0117	0.0770	-0.0312	-0.3253
	(0.08)	(0.49)	(-0.20)	(-1.05)
D_5	0.0969	0.1490	-0.0030	0.2656
	(0.70)	(0.94)	(-0.02)	(0.86)

*Significant at the 5% confidence level
**Significant at the 10% confidence level
D_i = Dummy variable for the day of the week, equals one for day i, and zero otherwise

effect is found for the whole period and more strongly for the second time period. No Monday effect is found for the first time period (not reported in Table 23.2). The Friday-to-Monday returns are larger than the returns on the weekdays but, surprisingly enough, they are negative. Even though these results are of the opposite sign of those reported in the literature for developed countries, they clearly represent an anomaly of the efficient market hypothesis.

Another recurrent pattern investigated in this chapter is the month-of-the-year effect. The results are presented in Table 23.3. The January effect is evident with significant positive coefficients in all indices. There is also evidence of significant negative returns in several other months, such as March, April, August, and September. Similar results (not reported here) were found for the two subperiods.

Table 23.3. Months-of-the-Year Effect, Whole Time Period,
December 29, 1987 to August 9, 1994

	General	Industrial	Financial	Commerce
Constant	9.739*	10.292*	9.696*	8.238*
	(3.00)	(3.02)	(3.03)	(1.66)
M_2	-5.715	-6.419	-5.159	-2.443
	(-1.29)	(-1.38)	(-1.18)	(-0.36)
M_3	-9.312*	-9.914*	-9.175*	-8.999
	(-2.10)	(-2.14)	(-2.10)	(-1.33)
M_4	-11.155*	-11.191*	-11.303*	-11.195**
	(-2.52)	(-2.41)	(-2.59)	(-1.65)
M_5	-6.297	-6.313	-7.910**	-3.685
	(-1.42)	(-1.36)	(-1.81)	(-0.54)
M_6	-5.251	-5.360	-6.971	-0.111
	(-1.19)	(-1.16)	(-1.60)	(-0.02)
M_7	-5.951	-7.232	-5.037	-0.702
	(-1.34)	(-1.56)	(-1.15)	(-0.10)
M_8	-7.941	-9.093**	-5.736	-8.819
	(-1.79)	(-1.96)	(-1.31)	(-1.30)
M_9	-8.894**	-9.343**	-8.148**	-10.231
	(-1.94)	(-1.94)	(-1.80)	(-1.45)
M_{10}	-3.949	-4.480	-3.703	-1.494
	(-0.86)	(-0.93)	(-0.82)	(-0.21)
M_{11}	-5.481	-6.892	-4.300	-2.288
	(-1.19)	(-1.43)	(-0.95)	(-0.33)
M_{12}	-0.088	-0.062	0.536	1.922
	(0.02)	(-0.13)	(0.12)	(0.27)

*Significant at the 5% confidence level
**Significant at the 10% confidence level
M_i = Dummy variable for the month of the year, equals one for month i, and zero otherwise

CONCLUSIONS

This chapter examines the behavior of several indices of the Medellin Colombian equity markets: the composite or general index and three sector indices—industrial, financial and commerce. The data cover the time period from December 29, 1987, through August 9, 1994.

The returns are not normally distributed. Skewness and kurtosis are positive and significant. The Jarque-Bera test also rejects normality. The indices are highly correlated with each other, suggesting that they tend to move together and that there is some spillover effect between them. Correlations are higher for the second time period.

The Dickey-Fuller tests suggest the index prices follow a random walk and the returns are stationary. The runs tests also strongly reject the weak form of market efficiency. Finally, the Colombian market presents calendar effects. It is found to have positive weekend and turn-of-the-year effects.

REFERENCES

Aggarwal, R. and R. Aggarwal, 1993. Security return distributions and market structure: evidence from the NYSE/AMEX and the NASDAQ markets, *Journal of Financial Research* 16, 209-220.

Agrawal, A. and K. Tandon, 1994. Anomalies and illusions? evidence from stock markets in eighteen countries, *Journal of International Money and Finance* 13, 83-106.

Ariel, R.A., 1990. High stock returns before holidays: existence and evidence on possible causes, *Journal of Finance* 45, 1611-1626.

Blume, Marshall E. and Robert Stambaugh, 1983. Biases in computed returns: an application to the size effect, *Journal of Financial Economics* 12, 387-404.

Butler, K.C. and S.J. Malaikah, 1992. Efficiency and inefficiency in thinly traded stock markets: Kuwait and Saudi Arabia, *Journal of Banking and Finance* 16, 197-210.

Dickey, D.A. and W.A. Fuller, 1979. Distribution of the estimators for autoregressive time series with a unit root, *Journal of the American Statistical Association* 74, 427-431.

French, Kenneth, 1980. Stock returns and the weekend effect, *Journal of Financial Economics*, 8, 55-69.

Gibbons, Michael and Patrick Hess, 1981. Day of the week effects and asset returns, *Journal of Business* 54, 579-596.

Jaffe, J. and R. Westerfield, 1985. Patterns in japanese common stock returns: day of the week and turn of the year effects, *Journal of Financial and Quantitative Analysis* 20, 261-272.

Jennergren, L. and P. Korsvold, 1975. The non-random character of Norwegian and Swedish market prices. In E. Elton and M. Gruber, eds., *International Capital Markets*. Amsterdam: North Holland, 37-54.

Klein, Donald B., 1983. Size related anomalies and stock return seasonality: further empirical evidence, *Journal of Financial Economics* 12, 13-32.

Lakonishok, J. and S. Smidt, 1988. Are seasonal anomalies real? a ninety-year perspective, *Review of Financial Studies* 1, 403-425.

Laurence, M., 1986. Weak form efficiency in the Kuala Lumpur and Singapore stock markets, *Journal of Banking and Finance* 10, 431-445.

Levene, D., 1952. On the power function of tests of randomness based on runs up and down, *Annals of Mathematical Statistics* 23, 34-56.

Liu, C.Y. and J. He, 1991. a variance-ratio test of random walks in foreign exchange rates, *Journal of Finance* 46, 773-85.

Ljung, G.M. and G. Box, 1978. On a measure of lack of fit in time series models, *Biometrika* 65, 297-303.

Pettengill, G.N., 1989. Holiday closings and security returns, *Journal of Financial Research* 12, 57-67.

Poterba, J.M. and L.H. Summers, 1988. Mean-reversions in stock prices: evidence and implications, *Journal of Financial Economics* 22, 27-59.

Ritter, Jay R., 1988. The buying and selling behavior of individual investors at the turn of the year, *Journal of Finance* 43, 701-719.

Roux, F. and B. Gilbertson, 1978. The behavior of share prices on the Johannesburg Stock Exchange, *Journal of Business Finance and Accounting* 5, 223-232.

Singleton, J.C. and J. Wingender, 1986. Skewness persistence in common stock returns, *Journal of Financial and Quantitative Analysis* 21, 335-341.

Urrutia, Jorge, 1995. Tests of random walk and market efficiency for Latin American emerging equity markets, *The Journal of Financial Research* 18, 299-309.

24

Modeling the Volatility of Share Prices of Stocks Traded on the Athens Stock Exchange

*Michael G. Papaioannou
and George C. Neofotistos*

INTRODUCTION

An assumption commonly used in evaluating the dynamic properties of time series of financial variables is that variances remain constant over time. This assumption is often made by standard models such as the Capital Asset Pricing Model, modern portfolio theory, and the Black-Scholes model in the calculation of option-pricing formulas. However, it has long been recognized that financial quantities exhibit tranquil as well as volatile periods during which conditional variances change with respect to time; Mandelbrot (1963) and Fama (1965) were among the first to observe that large (small) changes in financial variables tend to be followed by further large (small) changes (of either sign), a phenomenon often called volatility clustering.

Time-dependent volatility not only leads to inappropriate inferences, but also invalidates the constant variance assumption which guarantees the efficiency of the ordinary least squares (OLS) methods. In addition, it can lead to mispricing of option contracts. It is not, therefore, surprising that in the last decade several models of conditional volatility have been proposed to cope with these shortcomings (for a comprehensive review see Bollerslev et al., 1992). As Pagan and Schwert (1990) point out, basic to all these models is the notion that volatility can be decomposed into predictable and unpredictable components. Research has thus been focused on modeling the conditional variance, h_t, which constitutes the predictable component of the volatility. This effort has also been motivated by the fact that, in many models, the risk premium often employed in the determination of financial prices is expressed as a function of h_t.

Among the existing models of time-dependent conditional volatility, the most widely used is the family of ARCH (autoregressive conditionally heteroskedastic) models introduced by Engle (1982). ARCH models make the conditional variance of a time series a function of time t, system parameters, exogeneous and lagged (endogeneous) variables, and past errors. ARCH models permit the prediction of changes in the conditional variance (but not changes in the unconditional mean value); for example, they can account for the phenomenon of volatility clustering in which, as described above, large changes in high-frequency financial data tend to be followed by further large changes, thus leading to periods of persistently high or low volatility.

This study investigates the time-dependence of the conditional variances of the share-price indices of the banking, insurance, and industrial sectors for stocks traded on the Athens Stock Exchange (ASE), as well as of the ASE composite index. Monthly data (monthly averages of daily closing values) from January 1988 to April 1995 were used. The autocorrelation structure of these indices was investigated and tests to manifest the existence of heteroskedasticity in the respective time series were performed. Estimation results were obtained by applying a univariate linear ARCH model and a GARCH model to the time series of each index. The ARCH model comprised an autoregressive (AR) process (of order p) coupled with a heteroskedastic dependence (of order q) of the conditional variance on the lagged squares of the residuals of the AR process. The GARCH model, in addition to the lagged squares of the residuals, includes lagged variance values to the heteroskedastic dependence of the conditional variance.

Based on the values of the Schwarz Bayesian Information Criterion (SBIC) test, the AR process for the banking, insurance, industrial, and composite indices has been found to consist of one lagged value ($p=1$) of the dependent variable. It has also been found that the ARCH conditional variances of the banking, industrial, and the composite indices are affected by two lagged residuals ($q=2$), whereas the conditional variance of the insurance index is affected by only one lagged residual ($q=1$). However, only the first-order lagged residuals of the insurance and the composite indices are statistically significant (at the 5% and the 10% level, respectively). In these circumstances, and as already noted, an ARCH (GARCH) model provides a more efficient approach for modeling the banking, insurance, and composite indices than the OLS approach (which seems to retain its efficiency in the case of the industrial index). Investigating for ARCH effects is thus important for characterizing asset prices volatility, pricing option contracts, and for constructing new indices and optimal portfolios of stocks traded at the Athens Stock Exchange.

Specifically, our study on the dynamics of various sectors' indices of the Greek stock market indicates that the banking, insurance, and composite share price indices exhibit ARCH effects, and therefore their respective variances are not constant over time. Then, portfolio allocation decisions and option pricing should not be based on expected prices alone, but rather on expected prices adjusted for possible changes in the variances of the respective prices. Our results are in conformity with those of the work by Koutmos et al. (1993), who have applied similar models to study weekly ASE stock index returns, for the period July 1981 to August 1990, and have also found a time-dependent conditional volatility.

This chapter will present briefly the univariate linear ARCH model employed in this study; describe the data used and results on the autocorrelation structure, heteroskedasticity, model selection, and the distributional properties of the residuals of the AR processes of the time series of the indices; present and discuss results of the ARCH and GARCH estimation on the time series of the banking, insurance, industrial, and composite indices; present estimates of volatility (historical, AR, ARCH, GARCH) and compare their values with the implied volatility of the Hellenic Blue Chip Warrant which can serve as a proxy of the composite index; and will conclude by summarizing the results and discuss the practical implications for the management of assets and pricing of option contracts.

THE ARCH AND GARCH MODELS OF
TIME-DEPENDENT CONDITIONAL VARIANCE

The simplest univariate ARCH model is the first-order, ARCH (1,1), linear model for a financial variable, y_t, which comprises the equations:

$$y_t = \varphi_0 + \varphi_1 y_{t-1} + \varepsilon_t \tag{1}$$

where $E(\varepsilon_t \mid y_{t-1}) = 0$, $Var(\varepsilon_t \mid y_{t-1}) = E(\varepsilon_t^2 \mid y_{t-1}) = h_t$, and $h_t = \alpha_0 + \alpha_1 \varepsilon_{t-1}^2$. Here, φ_1 is assumed to be less than one for the regression to be stable. To further ensure that h_t is positive and that the process is stationary, we must have $\alpha_0 > 0$ and $1 > \alpha_1 > 0$. Intiuitively, α_1 can be interpreted as the heteroskedastic coefficient which shows the correlation between changes in the financial variable and the corresponding volatility of the previous period.

The generalization of the simple ARCH (1,1) model is the ARCH (p,q) model in which the variable y_t depends on earlier $(y_{t-1}, y_{t-2}, ..., y_{t-p})$ p observations, and h_t depends on earlier $(\varepsilon_t^2, \varepsilon_{t-1}^2, ..., \varepsilon_{t-q}^2)$ q squared errors, as follows:

$$y_t = \varphi_0 + \varphi_1 y_{t-1} + \varphi_2 y_{t-2} + \varphi_p y_{t-p} + \varepsilon_t \tag{2}$$

$$h_t = \alpha_0 + \alpha_1 \varepsilon_{t-1}^2 + \alpha_2 \varepsilon_{t-2}^2 + ... + \alpha_q \varepsilon_{t-q}^2 \tag{3}$$

where ε_t follows a white-noise process defined by $E(\varepsilon_t) = 0$ for all t, $E(\varepsilon_t \varepsilon_s) = 0$ for $t \neq s$, and $E(\varepsilon_t^2) = \sigma^2$ for all t. Equations (2) and (3) are estimated by the maximum likelihood (ML) method, and t-statistics of the coefficients are interpreted on the basis of significance levels. If the coefficients α_i, where $i = 1$, ... , q, are statistically significant, then we say there is an ARCH effect.

In order to select the optimum values of the numbers of lags, p and q, in equations (1) and (2), respectively, the Akaike Information Criterion (AIC) and Schwarz Bayesian Information Criterion tests are often employed (Hurvich and Tsai, 1993; Lutkepohl, 1985). In addition, the Bera-Jarque test on the normality of the error terms is performed along with the White test, which is an additional test to investigate the existence of heteroskedasticity and verify the significance of the coefficients attached to equation (3). Significantly large values of the White test indicate an ARCH process of order q.

The ARCH model can be considered a special case of the GARCH model in which equation (3) reads as

$$h_t = \alpha_0 + \alpha_1 \, \varepsilon^2_{t-1} + \alpha_2 \, \varepsilon^2_{t-2} + \dots + \alpha_q \, \varepsilon^2_{t-q} + \beta_1 \, h_{t-1} + \dots + \beta_j \, h_{t-j} \quad\quad (4)$$

AUTOCORRELATION STRUCTURE OF MONTHLY SHARE-PRICE INDEX RETURNS

Data Used

Monthly returns from January 1988 to April 1995 (88 observations) were used to model the autocorrelation structure, distributional properties, and ARCH and GARCH effects of the banking, insurance, industrial, and composite share-price index returns of the respective sectors traded on the Athens Stock Exchange. All monthly index returns were calculated by averaging daily data (closing value prices). Returns are defined as the natural logarithm of value relatives multiplied by 100:

$$R_t = 100 \times log \, (I_t \, / \, I_{t-1}) \quad\quad (5)$$

where I_t is the index return at time t.

Autocorrelation Structure Tests

To investigate the autocorrelation structure of the time series of each index returns, a number of diagnostic tests have been performed (on each index) for AR processes in which the number of lagged variables ranges from one to six. First, the Augmented Dickey-Fuller (ADF) tests were performed to check the existence of nonstationarity in the time series of each index. Then, the Durbin-Watson (DW) and the Durbin h-alternative tests were performed in order to check possible serial autocorrelation effects. Then, the Bera-Jarque (BJ) and White tests were performed in order to check the normality of the residuals of the regressions, and the existence of heteroskedasticity, respectively. Finally, the AIC and SBIC were performed in order to determine the optimum number of lagged autoregressive variables that should be included in the regression sequences of equations (2) and (3).

The results of these tests (on each index), for the regressions $R_t = \varphi_0 + \Sigma \, \varphi_i \, R_{t-i} + \varepsilon_t$, where i, the number of the lagged variables included in the autoregressive sequence, takes the values of 1 up to 6, are shown in Table 24.1, panels A-D.

Table 24.1. Results of Tests

PANEL A

Tests for:	Statistic	Banking Share-Price Index Returns (# of autoregressive lags)					
		1	1-2	1-3	1-4	1-5	1-6
Unit root	Augm. Dickey-Fuller	-9.03**	-9.07**	-9.32**	-8.90**	-9.05**	-8.82**
Serial correlation	Durbin-Watson	1.98	2.00	2.05	1.97	2.02	1.99
	Durbin h-alternative	0.18	-1.65*	-1.37	1.01	-0.75	0.59
Hetero-skedasticity	Bera-Jarque	1.84	1.97	1.86	1.46	0.51	0.38
	White	14.64**	22.01**	26.35**	25.49**	33.80**	37.94*
AR(p)	Akaike Info Criterion	-1.83	-1.79	-1.79	-1.78	-1.76	-1.73
	Schwarz Info Criterion	-4.61	-4.54	-4.51	-4.47	-4.42	-4.36
ARCH	Akaike Info Criterion	-5.88	-6.01	-5.98	-5.95		
(p=1,q)	Schwarz Info Criterion	-8.67	-8.76	-8.70	-8.64		

**Indicates significant *t*-statistics at the 5% level.
*Indicates significant *t*-statistics at the 10% level.

. . . *table continues*

Table 24.1. Continued

PANEL B

Tests for:	Statistic	Insurance Share-Price Index Returns (# of autoregressive lags)					
		1	1-2	1-3	1-4	1-5	1-6
Unit root	Augm. Dickey-Fuller	-9.00**	-9.20**	-9.20**	-9.20**	-9.21**	-9.04**
Serial correlation	Durbin-Watson	1.96	2.01	2.00	2.00	2.01	1.98
	Durbin h-alternative	0.39	-1.67*	-0.15	-0.71	-0.55	1.25
Hetero-skedasticity	Bera-Jarque	59.95**	56.23**	67.93**	64.88**	59.80**	59.12**
	White	9.16**	12.83**	17.26**	35.01**	41.74**	47.24**
AR(p)	Akaike Info Criterion	-1.40	-1.37	-1.37	-1.33	-1.31	-1.27
	Schwarz Info Criterion	-4.18	-4.12	-4.09	-4.02	-3.97	-3.90
ARCH (p=1,q)	Akaike Info Criterion	-4.14	-4.11	-4.13	-4.10		
	Schwarz Info Criterion	-6.93	-6.86	-6.85	-6.79		

PANEL C

Industrial Share-Price Index Returns
(# of autoregressive lags)

Tests for:	Statistic	1	1-2	1-3	1-4	1-5	1-6
Unit root	Augm. Dickey-Fuller	-9.09**	-9.05**	-9.27**	-8.83**	-8.88**	-8.90**
Serial correlation	Durbin-Watson	1.96	1.96	2.03	1.94	1.97	1.98
	Durbin h-alternative	0.34	-0.58	-1.22	1.76*	0.44	-0.27
Hetero-skedasticity	Bera-Jarque	2.02	2.06	1.77	1.47	0.92	0.89
	White	10.98**	13.50**	18.38**	14.47**	16.87**	21.92**
AR(p)	Akaike Info Criterion	-2.40	-2.39	-2.37	-2.35	-2.36	-2.33
	Schwarz Info Criterion	-5.18	-5.14	-5.09	-5.05	-5.02	-4.96
ARCH (p=1,q)	Akaike Info Criterion	-7.49	-7.55	-7.52	-7.54		
	Schwarz Info Criterion	-10.27	-10.30	-10.24	-10.23		

**Indicates significant t-statistics at the 5% level.
*Indicates significant t-statistics at the 10% level.

. . . table continues

331

Table 24.1. Continued

PANEL D

Tests for:	Statistic	Composite Share-Price Index Returns (# of autoregressive lags)					
		1	1-2	1-3	1-4	1-5	1-6
Unit root	Augm. Dickey-Fuller	-9.07**	-9.08**	-9.37**	-8.85**	-8.98**	-8.89
Serial correlation	Durbin-Watson	1.98	2.00	2.06	1.95	2.00	2.00
	Durbin h-alternative	0.15	-1.62	-1.37	1.55	-0.15	0.65
Hetero-skedasticity	Bera-Jarque	0.39	0.53	0.60	0.66	0.09	0.13
	White	17.68**	25.60**	31.94**	31.41**	36.18***	40.62**
AR(p)	Akaike Info Criterion	-2.06	-2.03	-2.03	-2.02	-2.01	-1.97
	Schwarz Info Criterion	-4.84	-4.78	-4.75	-4.71	-4.67	-4.60
ARCH (p=1,q)	Akaike Info Criterion	-6.41	-6.56	-6.53	-6.55		
	Schwarz Info Criterion	-9.19	-9.31	-9.26	-9.24		

**Indicates significant t-statistics at the 5% level.
*Indicates significant t-statistics at the 10% level.

Tests for Stationarity

The first row in Table 24.1 A-D shows the results of the ADF test. ADF is a widely used stationarity test which allows to reject (or fail to reject) the null hypothesis that a time series has a unit root and hence the corresponding variable is a random walk. The ADF test consists of running a regression of the first difference of the series against the series lagged once, lagged difference terms, a constant, and a time trend. If the coefficient of the lagged once series is significantly different from zero, then we reject the hypothesis that the series contains a unit root. That is the case, for example, for $p=1$, where the ADF test gives values of -9.03, -9.00, -9.09, -9.07, for the banking, insurance, industrial, and composite indices, respectively; all values are statistically significant. Therefore, the unit root hypothesis may be rejected and therefore the regression of each index return R_t on its first lagged value, R_{t-1}, may be considered to be stationary. The same result applies to regression sequences which incorporate lagged values of higher order.

Tests for Serial Correlation

The second row in Table 24.1 A-D shows the results obtained by the DW and Durbin h-alternative tests through which we investigate serial correlation effects in the regression sequences. In general, values of the DW test close to 2 indicate the absence of serial correlation effects. As can be seen, the indices show no serial correlation effects for all p values. However, it has been found that when one or more lagged endogenous variables are present, the DW statistic will often be close to 2 *even* when the errors are serially correlated. In this case, another statistic, the Durbin h-alternative, is used. Results obtained by the Durbin h-alternative statistic for the banking index, for example, show values smaller (except for $p=2$) than the critical value of the normal distribution (as indicated by the absence of stars), confirming therefore the results obtained by the Durbin-Watson test. Similar results have been obtained for the other indices.

Tests for Heteroskedasticity

Before we apply the ARCH model on the time series of the index returns, we should test whether the error terms are conditionally heteroskedastic. To diagnose heteroskedasticity in the time series, we have chosen the White test, which does not depend on the assumption of a normal error term. For all orders of the regression, the values obtained are large and statistically significant, indicating the existence of heteroskedasticity in the respective time series. To test the normality of the error term, we have performed the Bera-Jarque test, which is a powerful joint Langrange Multiplier (LM) test of the residuals' skewness and kurtosis. As is shown in Table 24.1 A-D, values of this test are statistically significant in the case of the insurance index, thus indicating a strong departure from normality for almost all orders of regression.

Model Selection

Following the investigation of stationarity, serial correlation, and hetero-skedastic characteristics of the index returns' time series, we now proceed to choose the optimum number of lags that should be included in the autoregresive sequence of equation (2) and the number of squared residual lags in equation (3). We have obtained results from the widely used Akaike Information Criterion and the Schwarz Bayesian Information Criterion. As shown in Table 24.1 A-D, both tests are minimized at $p=1$ for the banking, insurance, industrial, and composite index returns. The AIC and SBIC tests have also been applied to the series of the squared residuals to determine the order in equation (3). For the banking, industrial, and composite indices, both AIC and SBIC are minimized at $q=2$. Their minima depart in the case of the insurance index where AIC and SBIC are minimized at $q=1$.

ARCH (GARCH) EFFECTS OF MONTHLY SHARE-PRICE INDEX RETURNS

The univariate ARCH model described by equations (2) and (3) is esti-mated for $p=1$ and $q=2$ for the time series of the banking, industrial, and composite share price indices. It is estimated for $p=1$ and $q=1$ in the case of the insurance index. Results are presented in Table 24.2.

All estimated coefficients, α_0, α_1, and α_2, are nonnegative, thus ensuring that a positive variance is obtained. However, not all of them are statistically significant, as indicated by the t-statistics (given in parentheses). The presence of first-order ARCH effects ($\alpha_1 \neq 0$) is statistically significant only in the case of the insurance and composite indices. It should be emphasized that the insurance index ARCH effects are statistically significant at the 5% level. Second-order ARCH effects ($\alpha_2 \neq 0$) are present in the case of the banking, industrial, and composite index returns. However, the estimated coefficients suggest statis-tically not significant ARCH effects.

Overall, these results provide statistical evidence that the variances of the indices are not independent over time. We can interpret the coefficients α_1 and α_2, as representing the relative contribution of the respective previous periods' squared error to the conditional variance in the current period. In the case of the composite index, this means that 47% of a month's disturbances is carried over into the following month and 36.3% is carried over into next nearest month. As a final comment, since the principal assumption of constant variance of the error term in an OLS estimation is violated, the OLS methodology should not be used as an estimation procedure for share-price indices. Maximum likelihood estima-tion should instead be used. GARCH results are presented in Table 24.3.

ASPECTS OF VOLATILITY

Volatility estimates play a very important role in making optimal portfolio allocations and in pricing options and other securities. In this section, several

Table 24.2. ARCH Effects (based on 1988-95 data)

Coefficients	Indices			
	Banking	Insurance	Industrial	Composite
φ_0	0.003	0.002	0.005	0.002
φ_1	0.327**	0.397**	0.436**	0.344**
α_0	0.003**	0.009**	0.002**	0.002*
α_1	0.400	0.361**	0.212	0.470*
α_2	0.325	—	0.299	0.363

**Indicates significant t-statistics at the 5% level.
*Indicates significant t-statistics at the 10% level.

Table 24.3. GARCH Effects (based on 1988-95 data)

Coefficients	Indices			
	Banking	Insurance	Industrial	Composite
φ_0	0.005	-0.106	0.005	0.003
φ_1	0.339**	0.370**	0.400**	0.332**
α_0	0.0008	0.0006	0.001	0.0007
α_1	0.283*	0.310**	0.233	0.389
β_1	0.639**	0.709**	0.547	0.526*

**Indicates significant t-statistics at the 5% level.
*Indicates significant t-statistics at the 10% level.

forecasts of return variances are calculated—namely, the historical volatility, the AR volatility, and the ARCH and GARCH volatility—and their accuracies are compared. A further comparison with the implied volatility of the Hellenic Blue Chip Warrant is presented.

Historical volatility is estimated by calculating the standard deviation of percentage price changes. The steps of this calculation are the following: First, the percentage price change from one period to the next is subtracted from the average price change over the total historical period. Second, each difference in the first step is squared. Third, the averages of the squared differences are calculated. The historical volatility for the measurement period is calculated by taking the square root of the average of the squared deviations in step three. Historical volatility represents a historical average and it is the best forecast if the time series of returns were strict white noise.

Implied volatility is that implied by an option price observed in the market. Knowing the option price, the remaining unknown in the Black-Scholes pricing formula is the volatility; iterative numerical schemes are employed to invert the Black-Scholes formula and obtain a solution for the volatility (to a required degree of accuracy). The implied volatility approach has been found to give better results than the historical volatility approach.

The AR volatility is calculated by taking into account the first lag autocorrelation in the returns:

$$AR\text{-}volatility = \sum_{i-1} (R_i - R_{ave})^2 \times (1 + (2/N) \sum_j (N - j) \, \varphi^j) \qquad (6)$$

where R_{ave} is the mean, φ is the first lag autocorrelation coefficient, and N denotes the time horizon (future time return); i runs from 1 to N, and j runs from 0 to N-1. This equation provides a more realistic measure of volatility (Akgiray, 1989).

The ARCH-volatility takes into account existing ARCH effects and is calculated as (Akgiray, 1989)

$$ARCH\text{-}volatility = \sum_i (1 - \varphi^i / 1 - \varphi)^2 \times (A^{N-i} g + \sum_j \alpha_0 A^j) \qquad (7)$$

where φ is the first lag autocorrelation coefficient, $A = \alpha_1 + ... + \alpha_p$ and $g = \alpha_0 + \sum_k \alpha_k e^2{}_{1-k}$ (e represents the error term,) αs are the ARCH coefficients; and k runs from 1 to p, i runs from 1 to N, and j runs from 0 to N-1-i. Tables 24.4 and 24.5 present results on the above-mentioned volatility expressions.

The implied volatility presented in Tables 24.4 and 24.5 is the one quoted by Reuters on the Morgan Stanley Warrant (Hellenic Blue Chip Warrant). Since the Warrant comprises banking and industrial sector stocks, its volatility can be well approximated by the composite index volatility. Its numerical value falls between the AR volatility estimate and the ARCH volatility estimate. Its value is definitely far away from the numerical value of the historical volatility. This Result indicates that the inclusion of autocorrelation (AR) effects as well as heteroskedastic effects (ARCH) clearly improves the volatility estimates

Table 23.4. May 1995 Forecasts of the Composite Index Volatilities Based on April 1994–April 1995 Monthly Data

Volatilities (%, per annum)

Index	Historical	AR	ARCH	Implied
Composite	14.3	19.8	31.2	25.5

Table 24.5. July 1994 Forecasts of The Composite Index Volatilities Based on June 1994–June 1995 Monthly Data

Volatilities (%, per annum)

Index	Historical	AR	ARCH	Implied
Composite	30.6	40.25	31.9	42.6

obtained. Note that Table 24.5 presents volatility estimates of the same warrant when it was first introduced (on July 1994). Furthermore, the AR volatility estimate gives a better approximation to the warrant's volatility, with ARCH volatility giving a better result than the historical volatility. Again, the AR and the ARCH volatility are superior to the simple historical volatility estimates when compared to the implied volatility values.

CONCLUSION

The study of the autocorrelation structure and the existence of ARCH effects in the index returns' time series provide evidence that would enable investors to make more accurate calculations of (1) optimal strategies in managing their portfolios, and (2) volatility estimates for option pricing. The gains in accuracy depend directly on how asset price variances (or risk measures) change over time. To test whether the variability of various sectoral share-price indices of stocks traded on the ASE is constant and to provide estimates of their variation, we employ the ARCH model. On the basis of monthly returns data for the banking, insurance, and composite indices traded on the Athens Stock Exchange from 1988 to 1995, the results presented in this chapter generally suggest that an ARCH model, which takes into account the time-dependence of each index variability, provides more accurate estimates of the sectoral share price index variability than ordinary OLS and historical volatility models.

A significant ARCH effect in a particular share price index implies that its variance is directly affected by changes in the uncertainty concerning that index. That is, an increasing disturbance term in a sectoral share price index will lead to increases in the conditional variance of that index. Such analysis may assist investment managers, designers of new indices, or policymakers, in their decisions to isolate sectors that exhibit the smallest price volatility and thus provide the highest insulation in unexpected shocks.

REFERENCES

Akgiray, V., 1989. Conditional heteroskedasticity in time series of stock returns: evidence and forecasts, *Journal of Business* 62, 55-80.

Bollerslev, T., 1992. ARCH modeling in finance: a review of the theory and empirical evidence, *Journal of Econometrics* 52, 5-59.

Engle, R.F., 1982. Autoregressive conditional heteroskedasticity with estimates of the variance of United Kingdom inflation, *Econometrica* 50, 987-1007.

Fama, E., 1965. The behavior of stock market prices, *Journal of Business* 38, 34-105.

Hurvich, C.M. and C. Tsai, 1993. A corrected akaike information criterion for vector autoregressive model selection, *Journal of Time Series Analysis* 14, 271-279.

Koutmos, G., C. Negakis, and P. Theodossiou, 1993. Stochastic behaviour of the athens stock exchange, *Applied Financial Economics* 3, 119-126.

Lutkepohl, H., 1985. Comparison of criteria for estimating the order of a vector autoregressive process, *Journal of Time Series Analysis* 6, 35-52.

Mandelbrot, B., 1963. The variation of certain speculative prices, *Journal of Business* 36, 394-419.

Pagan, A.R. and G.W. Schwert, 1990. Alternative models for conditional stock volatility, *Journal of Econometrics* 45, 267-290.

Index

About the Editors and Contributors

J. (JONGMOO) JAY CHOI is Professor of Finance and International Business at Temple University, where he teaches corporate and international finance. He taught at Columbia University, was an international treasury economist at Chase Manhattan Bank, and visited numerous universities around the world. He has written over 50 books and papers in major academic journals, is an editor of *Journal of Economics and Business*, and is on editorial boards of four other journals. He is President of Korea-America Finance Association.

JOHN A. DOUKAS is Professor of Finance and International Finance at Old Dominion University. He has published over 40 articles in numerous major journals, is the founding editor of the *European Financial Management* journal, is the founder of the European Financial Management Association, and co-editor of the JAI Press Annual Research Series in International Business and Finance.

HARVEY ARBELAEZ is Associate Professor of International Finance, Fisher Graduate School of International Business, at the Monterey Institute of International Studies.

OLEG BONDAR is an independent financial analyst in Toronto, Canada.

ROSITA P. CHANG is Director of the Sandra Ann Morsilli Pacific-Basin Capital Market Research Center and Professor of Finance at the University of Rhode Island.

PAUL W.K. CHEN is Professor of Banking and Finance at National Chengchi University in Taiwan.

MING-CHONG CHIANG is a senior clerk at the United World Chinese Commercial Bank.

THOMAS C. CHIANG is Professor of Finance at Drexel University.

EDWARD H. CHOW is Professor of Banking and Finance at National Chengchi University in Taiwan.

PAUL M. DICKIE is Director of Infrastructure, Energy, and Financial Sector Development for the Asian Development Bank.

JUNE DILEVSKY is Professor of Finance at the Hebrew University of Jerusalem.

ERLINDA S. ECHANIS is Senior Lecturer at the University of Philippines.

PHILIP FANARA, JR. is Professor of Finance at Howard University.

DILIP K. GHOSH is Editor of the *International Journal of Finance* and Professor of Finance at St. John's University.

SHMUEL HAUSER is Chief Economist of the Israel Securities Authority and Associate Professor of Finance at Ben-Gurion University.

GEORGE HONDROYIANNIS is an economist with the Bank of Greece.

VINCE J. HOOPER is Senior Lecturer of Finance at the Australian National University.

QAIZAR HUSSAIN is an economist with the International Monetary Fund.

MANSOR MD. ISA is Dean and Associate Professor of Finance at the University of Malaysia.

ARVIND K. JAIN is Professor of Finance at Concordia University in Canada.

BANG NAM JEON is Associate Professor of Economics and International Business at Drexel University.

GEORGE W. KESTER is the William H. Dunkak Professor of Finance at Bucknell University.

YONG H. KIM is Professor of Finance at the University of Cincinnati.

YU-KYUNG KIM is Director of Securities Research for the Korea Stock Exchange.

WEIPING LIU is Assistant Professor of Finance at Montana State University.

SARANTIS LOLOS is Assistant Professor of Finance at Panteio University in Greece.

SANDIP MUKHERJI is Associate Professor of Finance at Howard University.

GEORGE C. NEOFOTISTOS is a researcher at the Lambrakis Research Foundation in Greece.

EDGAR ORTIZ is Professor of Finance at the Universidad Nacional Autónoma de México.

MICHAEL G. PAPAIOANNOU is a senior economist for the Treasury Department of the International Monetary Fund.

EVANGELIA PAPAPETROU is an economist for the Bank of Greece.

SUNIL POSHAKWALE is Lecturer of Finance at the Canterbury Business School, University of Kent in the U.K.

VAL SAMONIS is Editor of the *Journal of East-West Business* and President of the Samonis Emerging Markets Institute at the University of Toronto.

YOCHANAN SHACHMUROVE is Professor of Economics at the City College of New York and Visiting Professor at the University of Pennsylvania.

CAN SIMGA-MUGAN is Associate Professor of Accounting at Bilent University in Turkey.

MICHAEL T. SKULLY is Chair of Banking at Monash University in Australia.

SUSATIO SOEDIGNO is Director of PT Wartaartha in Indonesia.

SUSAN F. STONE is International Economist at the Joint Warfare Analysis Center in Washington, DC.

DONGWEI SU is Assistant Professor of Finance at the University of Akron.

GORDON Y.N. TANG is Professor of Finance and Decision Sciences at Hong Kong Baptist University.

KAI-CHONG TSUI is Senior Lecturer of Finance and Banking at the National University of Singapore.

JORGE L. URRUTIA is Professor of Finance at Loyola University in Chicago.

DOUGLAS WOOD is the Natwest Bank Professor of Banking and Finance at the Manchester Business School in the U.K.

HAI-CHIN YU is Associate Professor of International Trade at Chung Yuang Christian University, Taiwan, and Visiting Scholar at the University of Chicago.

AYCE YUCE is Associate Professor of Finance at Bilent University in Turkey.

ISBN 1-56720-177-6

EAN

9 781567 201772

HARDCOVER BAR CODE